APHORISMS
AND
Reflections
ON
MEN, MORALS AND THINGS.

TRANSLATED FROM MSS. OF

J. G. ZIMMERMAN.

WITH

NOTES CRITICAL AND EXPLANATORY.

Nemo sese tentat descendere.
·PERSIUS.

WIPF & STOCK · Eugene, Oregon

Wipf and Stock Publishers
199 W 8th Ave, Suite 3
Eugene, OR 97401

Aphorisms and Reflections on Men, Morals and Things
By Zimmerman, J. G.
ISBN 13: 978-1-5326-1871-0
Publication date 3/9/2017
Previously published by Thomas Maiden, 1800

TO THE

RIGHT HONOURABLE

HENRY, LORD HOLLAND,

THIS VOLUME IS INSCRIBED AS

A MARK OF RESPECT AND

ADMIRATION.

APROPOS.

THE *Reflections* contained in this *Volume* were written in German by the Hand of the celebrated Author whose Name they bear, and were entrusted to an Officer of the *Mortimar* Regiment for his Opinion. ZIMMERMAN's *Death,* the Distance of his Friend, and the Impossibility of Conveyance, were the Cause of their being retained. It cannot appear illiberal to publish them; for the Family of the Author cannot possibly be injured by their being translated into *English.* Besides, TISSOT is said to possess a Copy of them, which can doubtless be obtained, if 'tis necessary they should appear in their vernacular Tongue. The Editor returned the Original, from which these were taken, to the Gentleman whose Kindness obliged him, and whose Permission warranted the Licence of publishing. There is yet another Volume; its Appearance will be determined on by the Reception this meets with. To give the Public more of what they do not relish would be impertinent Obtrusion; as to withhold what is suited to their Taste, would be Cruelty.

The Officer alluded to has frequently expressed his warm Approbation of the Sentiments and Maxims of his deceased Friend; and this honourable Testimony of their Merit, from a Soldier of enlarged Understanding, will prove, 'tis to be hoped, an unerring Prognostic of the favourable Verdict of those Judges to whom they are now submitted.

REFLECTIONS

OF

ZIMMERMAN.

REFLECTION THE FIRST.

TO* grow good, or ceafe to be bad, fhould be our fole employ, from the time the refolution is made, 'till that awful period when we are to become neither.

WOMEN with women are, in private, either noviciates, or adepts; with men, they are either prudes, or fenfualifts.

---

* " An entirely honeft man, in the fevere fenfe of the word, exifts no more than an entirely difhoneft knave: the beft and the worft are only approximations to thofe qualities. Who are thofe that never contradict themfelves? yet honefty never contradicts itfelf. Who are thofe that always contradict themfelves? yet knavery is mere felf-contradiction. Thus the knowledge of man determines not the things themfelves, but their proportions, the quantum of congruities and incongruities."

LAVATER's *Aphorifms*.

The priest* is certainly a good character in his pulpit; the residue of the sacerdotal reputation is accidental. Who then would wish him to risk his fame by quitting his province?

Gain a friend by a quarrel, if 'tis possible: never lose one, however this is possible; for there is a peculiar mode of conduct even when dissention reigns, that commands veneration, and generates esteem.

There must be a specific object to pursue; or life, like a disease-smote beauty, has no attraction.

Gambling-

---

* J. C. Doderlin published at Jena, in 1787, a Thesis, in which he asserts, " That Christ gave no civil laws." *Christum alienum fuisse a legibus civilibus ferendis.*

It has been lately said by some, that Jesus affected empire in the garb of humility; and by others, that a city in which the Christian law should be truly observed, would come to nought; so that Christ has made either vain attempts, or foolish laws. To refute these, M. Doderlin shews, that the laws of Christ tend much to the public good, but that he has ordained nothing relative to temporal government: that he did not fulfil the expectation of the Jews, who looked for a new King in their Messiah; the founder of a new city, and of a new law: and that those precepts which relate to civil government (as the prohibition of swearing, resisting of injuries, and divorcing a wife) are to be understood only as private precepts.

Annales Literati, Helmstadt.

Gambling-houses are temples where the most sordid and turbulent passions contend; there no spectator can be indifferent: a card, or a small square of ivory, interests more than the loss of an empire, or the ruin of an unoffending groupe of infants, and their nearest relatives.

'Tis torture to the envious to return their injuries with complacency and kindness.

Be * not so bigotted to any custom, as to worship it at the expence of truth. All is custom that goes on in continuity: all customs are not alike beneficial to us.

Fools take ingenious abuse for kindness, and often make one in the laugh that is carrying on at their own expence.

The fatalist stands a good chance of being contented with his lot, unless 'tis ordained to the contrary.

---

* When the King of Poland had recovered Livonia from the Czar John Bazllowitz, he wished to abolish the custom of whipping the peasants for their faults; but they, insensible of the favour, threw themselves at his feet, and begged that he would alter nothing in their ancient customs.

Subaltern tyrants* are ever the most intolerant, and intolerable.

An † ardent pursuit of wealth or sensuality ossifies the heart: in the very moment of gain, or enjoyment, their denial is most peremptory.

The more you speak of yourself, the more you are likely to lie: say but little, 'twill scarcely gain belief; so strong are partiality and envy.

Those beings only are fit for Solitude ‡, who like nobody, are like nobody, and are lik'd by nobody.

We

---

* "Power is what all covet, but few are fit to be trusted with; and there is no appendix to it so petty, but a man may find room enough to play the tyrant in it."

† "As the wily subtilty of him who is intent on gain, so the abrupt brutality of him who has gained enough."

Lavater's *Aphorisms.*

‡ Zimmerman's definition of the word Solitude does not appear to be correct. Solitude he calls that intellectual state in which the "mind voluntarily surrenders itself to its own reflections." The philosopher, therefore, who withdraws his attention from every external object to the contemplation of his own ideas, is not less solitary than he who abandons society, and resigns himself entirely to the calm enjoyment of lonely life.

By

We sometimes measure the favours we grant by the necessities of those who solicit; not from the intrinsic value of what is granted. Pitiful advantage!

The burthen increases with the value. Those we love, anxiously do we watch; and we merit their esteem by our disquietude.

Open your mouth and purse cautiously; and your stock of wealth and reputation shall, at least in repute, be great.

If 'tis fortunate for the living, that the dead cannot revisit the earth, 'twou'd likewise be fortunate for them, if many of them had never existed. The Athenians were counsell'd to be sure that King Philip was dead before they expressed their joy at the report of it, lest they should find him alive to avenge their hasty triumph.

Beware* of profession; 'tis often put to severe proofs. Beware, likewise, of those who profess;

By solitude I understand a local separation from society; by meditation I understand the mind reflecting on its own contents.

* " I have had occasion a thousand times, since I saw you, to wish myself in the land where all things are forgotten; at least,

profefs; 'tis the trick of the frivolous, and the hypocritical.

GREAT fpirits there are many; but many of them want judgment and wealth.

ALWAYS to fpeak what you think, is the way to acquire the habit of thinking and acting with propriety.

VIOLENT

leaft, that I did not live in the memory of certain reftlefs mor‑
tals who are *vifitors by profeffion*. The misfortune is, no retire‑
ment is fo remote, nor fanctuary facred, as to afford a protec‑
tion from their impertinence; and though we were to fly to the
defart, and take refuge in the cells of faints and hermits, we
fhould be alarmed with their unmeaning voice, *crying even in the
wildernefs*. They fpread themfelves, in truth, over the whole face
of the land, and they wafte the faireft hours of converfation. For
my part, I look upon them not as paying vifits, but *vifitations*; and
am never obliged to give audience to one of this fpecies, that I
do not confider myfelf as under a judgment for thofe numberlefs
hours which I have fpent in vain. If thefe fons and daughters
of idlenefs and folly would be perfuaded to enter into an exclu‑
five fociety, the reft of the world might poffefs their moments
unmolefted; but nothing lefs will fatisfy them, than opening
a general commerce, and failing into every port where choice
or chance may drive them. Were we to live, indeed, in the
years of the Antediluvians, one might afford to refign fome
part of one's time in charitable relief of the infufferable weight
of theirs; but fince the days of man are fhrunk into a few
hafty revolutions of the fun, whole afternoons are much too
confiderable a facrifice to be offered to tame civility. What
heightens the contempt of this character is, that they who

have

Violent asseveration, or affected bluntness, look not more suspicious than strained sanctity, or over-offended modesty.

Which is most dangerous, thinking too well, or too ill, of mankind? Which are we warranted to do, to think well or ill of mankind? Perhaps this does not admit of a question!

'Tis possible to look without staring; though the guilty, and those who endeavour to conceal an affectation they are not conscious of possessing, think otherwise.

A graceful compliance, or a courageous rejection, are the alternatives of the great.

When ill news* comes too late to be serviceable to your neighbour, keep it to yourself.

---

have so much of the force have always the least of the power of friendship; and though they will " craze their chariot-wheels," as Milton expresses it, to destroy your repose, they would not drive half the length of a street *to assist your distress*."
Fitzosborne's *Letters*.

* " If thou hast heard a word, let it die with thee; and be bold, it will not hurt thee."

" A fool travaileth with a word, as a woman in labour of a child." *Ecclesiasticus*.

"He who can at all times sacrifice pleasure to duty, approaches sublimity," 'tis said. How much closer is the approximation when our duty is itself a pleasure! Besides, what chance is there of having that well and constantly performed, which is considered as a sacrifice ordained by necessity?

Those * alone may be vouched for who are good alone. Those who are not good alone, may be bettered by association; good company cannot pejorate.

Though you highly respect, or bitterly execrate, any opinion you may hear delivered, do not assimilate the character of the utterer to it. Out of a clean vessel muddy water may proceed; and the contrary.

Pride causes us to admire those most, who in love or war make the best defence.

One

---

* " Whenever a man undergoes a considerable change in consequence of being observed by others, whenever he assumes another gait, another language, than what he had before he thought himself observed, be advised to guard yourself against him."

Again:

" Distinguish exactly what one is when he stands alone, and acts for himself, and when he is led by others. I know many who

One act of immortality, or extensive utility, is a fair acquittance! Those capacitated to perform more, may never find the opportunity; and many opportunities are thrown away on the supine and imbecile.

Certain failings,* it is not only generous, but convenient, to overlook: kindred nature has kindred faults.

> Virtue, for ever frail as fair below,
> Her tender nature suffers in the crowd,
> Nor touches on the world without a stain.
> The world's infectious; few bring back at eve,
> Immaculate, the manners of the morn.
> Something we thought, is blotted; we resolv'd,
> Is shaken; we renounc'd, return'd again.
> Each salutation may let in a sin
> Unthought before, or fix a former flaw.
> Nor is it strange; light, motion, concourse, noise,
> All scatter us abroad.

who act always honestly, often with delicacy, when left to themselves; and like knaves when influenced by some overbearing characters whom they once slavishly submitted to follow." Lavater's *Aphorisms*.

* " He who loses the sun in his spots, a beautiful face in a few freckles, and a grand character in a few harmless singularities, may choose, of two appellations, one --- *wrong-head*, or *knave*."

Again:

To communicate his knowledge* is a duty with the wife man; to learn from others, is his highest gratification.

If women fix their eyes on a rose they will have it, though in the plucking they prick their fingers.

Green girls often delay their happiness 'till they have destroyed their health, or feed their pride to a plethora, whilst their love is absolutely starving.

New landlords are over-civil; good ones have civility enough: rich landlords shew little civility to any customer; to a poor one, none: but the obsequious give the beggar his offals with a bow.

Correction

Again:

"There is none so bad as to do the twentieth part of the evil he might; nor any so good, as to do the tenth part of the good it is in his power to do. Judge of yourself by the good you might do, and neglect; and of others, by the evil they might do, and omit: and your judgment will be poised between too much indulgence for yourself, and too much severity on others." Lavater's *Aphorisms.*

* "Wisdom that is hid, and treasure that is hoarded up, what profit is in them both? Better is he that hideth his folly, than a man that hideth his wisdom." *Ecclesiasticus.*

Correction * resembles an amiable act of courtesy when it proceeds from those we justly venerate.

What is eccentricity morally considered? Place yourself at your neighbour's point, enter into his view of things, then describe your circle: nothing then appears extraordinary. Beholders seldom consider how extravagant their manners appear in their turn.

Advertise your abilities if you would give publicity to them: if you have none, still it may be necessary to advertise.

Be sure to entrust no person with more power over your heart than can be recalled. 'Tis disgusting to those who love the species, to hear any of them declare, " I am entirely guided by my friend." We act well but when we are most responsible.

When mistresses have notoriously an ascendancy, every act of the keeper is supposed to be planned behind the curtains.

" * He who is loved, and commands love, when he corrects, or is the cause of uneasiness, must be loveliness itself; and, he who can love him in the moment of correction, is the most amiable of mortals." Lavater's *Aphorisms*.

With the vulgar, and the learned, names have great weight: the wife use a writ of enquiry into their legitimacy when they are advanced as authorities.

Who would be the slave of insignificance*, and live in subservience to an hour, or a fashion?

A serious look well tim'd, will often check the obstreperous mirth of a fool, or disconcert the florid attempts of the insects who slander with a smile, and cover cruelty with the warmest expressions of concern.

Can those have any character to lose who have no reputation to gain?

The best born, and the first born, are oft-times the worst, and the last to be borne.

The

---

* "There is such a plague every morning with buckling shoes, gartering, combing and powdering. Pshaw! cease thy impertinence, I'll dress no more to-day. Were I an honest brute, that rises from his litter, shakes himself, and so is drest, I could bear it.

Prythee, what have we to do with time? Can't we let it alone as Nature made it? Can't a man eat when he's hungry, go to bed when he's sleepy, rise when he wakes, dress when he pleases, without the confinement of hours to enslave him?"

Twin Rivals.

The strongest instance of friendship, or of disinterestedness,* shall be the least regarded, if it thwarts our wishes, or crosses our inclinations.

One of the safest methods of criminating is, to represent a supposed impossibility of your having been able to commit the crime.

Virtue,† when sensuality grows strong, is in a precarious state; and the more we are pleased by it, the greater is our danger.

Idlers ‡ cannot even find time to be idle, or the industrious to be at leisure. We must be always doing, or suffering.

Lovers presume more upon the strength of their passion, purse, or their personal charms, than their integrity, or understanding. 'Tis but

---

* " Let me repeat it; if you cannot bear to be told by your bosom friend that you have a strong breath, you deserve not to have a friend."   Lavater's *Aphorisms*.

† *Count de Buckebourg* declared, " that the greatest danger, and no danger, were the same thing."

‡ *Cato the Censor* tells us, that *Publius Scipio* made this declaration: " Nunquam se minus otiosum esse, quam cum otiosus, nec minus solum, quam cum solus esset."

but a cold courtſhip now-a-days where the virtues preſide.

We deck trifles * with the drapery of importance when they are requeſted of us. There is too much of the ſpirit of traffic in all our reciprocities.

The adultreſs expoſes her offspring to ſcorn and danger; a privilege motherhood alone cannot warrant her in, though ſhe aſſumes a right to diſpoſe of her own perſon.

Hell is an inexhauſtible mine, whence cheating prieſts draw their revenues; the miniſtry † of the true religion diſclaim any proprietory in the infernal demeſnes.

Seldom compute a man's wealth by his mode of living, dreſs, or the company he keeps.

Though the male is early indulged in habits of inconſtancy, 'twill not damp the fiery fury

---

* " Who, in receiving a benefit, eſtimates its value more cloſely than in conferring one, ſhall be a citizen of a better world."   Lavater's *Aphoriſms*.

† " And in caſe he believes more of the prevalency of an ill-deſigning principle than a good one, he is rather a demoniſt."
     Lord Shaftsbury.

fury of a wife to tell her, that cuftom prevails over reafon; nor, when the female becomes the defaulter, does the hufband make allowance for the contagion of example.

I ONCE* heard it afferted, *that the executioner did more towards the confervation of good order than the prieft.* Yes, I replied, but he neither has, nor does he deferve, fo much refpect. The prieft only frightens you. *But the hangman puts you out of fear*, the fellow replied.

PITY fools ever; never truft to them. Well has Lord Chefterfield declared, that "we may fafely judge of a man's truth by his underftanding." Doubtlefs, the ftrength of virtue depends upon the vigour of intellect.

FOR† here, or hereafter, for things of magnitude or trifles, our hopes or fears, patience is all: the great hour of determination will arrive.

'TIS

---

* VOLTAIRE is of opinion that hanging is an advantage only to the executioner, who is paid for putting men openly to death: if punifhments are invented for the benefit of fociety, they fhould be ufeful to fociety; but a man is not good for any thing after he is hanged.

† "Las d'efperer, & de me plaindre
De la cour, des grands, & du fort,
C'eft ici que j'attends la mort
Sans la defirer, ni la craindre." MAYNARD.

'TIS a contradiction in physics * to affirm, that something, which once was not, has since been brought into existence. Matter was, is, and must be equal perpetually, though its forms are perpetually varying. Dissolution of form every part of matter is subject to: all is in motion.

THE weak may be jok'd out of any thing but their weakness.

A GOOD name will wear out; a bad one may be turn'd; a nick-name lasts for ever.

PETRARCH was of opinion that pleasure, by occasional interruption, became more lively. Does this account for the capriciousness and bickerings of the married state?

NEGATIVE

" * The actual existence of a thing must either be concluded upon observation, or sufficient testimony, or else reasoned out from the necessary connection it has with something the existence whereof we are well assured of.

" Nil posse creari
De nihilo, neque item genita, ad nihilum revocari."
LUCRETIUS.

" C'est un cercle roulant, ou les mêmes chosese font que reculer, & s'approcher."
CHAMM.

NEGATIVE virtue * is a positive vice, if the means exist of improving it.

WIVES who often make free with the characters of their husbands, will not be overscrupulous in making free with their sheets.

AFTER revenge has been taken, or atonement has been made, most injuries are WILLINGLY forgiven.

BUT that the recollection of my own insignificance holds me back, I fear I should be seduced by the hyper-critics, cavillers, and carpers, who surround me. So much are they admired, so happy do they seem in their own opinions. Right or wrong † is at their command.

VIRTUOUS sufferance ‡ lays up a store of rich sensibility, which is afterwards expended

---

* " Withhold not good from them to whom it is due, when it is in the power of thy hand to do it." *Proverbs of Solomon.*

" La plus sublime virtu est negative; elle nous instruit de ne jamais faire du mal a personnne." ROUSSEAU.

† " Who rapidly decides without examining proofs, will persist obstinately." LAVATER's *Aphorisms.*

‡ " La fermete d'un homme qui soufre avec constance les persecutions qu'on lui fait, le met infiniment au dessus de ceux qui le persecutent." *L'Abbé de Bellegarde*

pended in acts of compaſſion in behalf of the
diſtreſt.

There is no great riſk or expence in a great
preſent, * if the perſon, time, and manner, have
been judiciouſly choſen.

Every impediment, morally ſpeaking, is prejudice, that prevents mankind from enjoying the
fulleſt portion of felicity.

If we are not reprehenſible for thoſe qualities which do not depend on our will, but appear to be the effect of ſurrounding objects acting on our temperament, for which are we cul-
pable?

Such is the cecity of man, † ſuch is the cruel
delicacy of his choſen companions, he remains
ignorant of his greateſt loſſes 'till 'tis too late to
replace them.

Past help is not always paſt hope; paſt hope
is not always paſt cure.

WHAT

---

* " Preſents and gifts blind the eyes of the wiſe, and ſtop up
his mouth that he cannot reprove. *Eccleſiaſticus.*

† " You are not very good, if you are not better than your
beſt friends imagine you to be."

Lavater's *Aphoriſms.*

What is so hard as the heart of a creditor? Thousands repeat the question. They compare it to stone,* iron; nay, they want a proper term to come up to their opinion of its insensibility. And what can have indurated his feelings? Who sits in judgment on the provocation he has received, the inconveniences he has undergone, the petty evasions, and cruel insults he has passed? 'Till these have been made known, who is warranted to oppugn his proceedings, or arraign his humanity? We cannot endure for war; nay, we shou'd not do it! This may be declared without becoming an advocate for persecution.

Speak plainly; act decisively; out of doubt, out of controversy.

The best advice is not always that which is, or can, but which ought to be, abided by.

If those who depend on casualties for their amusement, have seen much of the world, they must be often baulk'd.

Many will anxiously endeavour to learn the opinion of the critic, who never think of forming

---

* The Chinese are said to have a stone, called *Yu*, harder and heavier than marble, capable of a fine polish; and so sonorous, as to be used as a musical instrument.

forming one for themselves. The oracles of the literary world, whose decisions regulate the ideas of the public, and govern their sentiments, owe their consequence to the cowardice of those who dare not think for themselves.

The reign of incredulity* is as fatal to the temporal interest of religion, as that of superstition is: 'twill be best understood in an age when good sense conducts dispassionate enquiry.

Prodigals may stop when they please in their career; they must stop in the end: but 'tis easier to convert the ruffian in the very act of murderous perpetration, than arrest by reason the son of pleasure in his course.

A hero's goal is mark'd out by impossibility.

Never exhaust your stores, if you wish the admiration of the circle you frequent to be of long continuance. Indeed, to abound in any particular,† frugality must be observ'd.

Our

---

* We must destroy the press, or the press will destroy us, said *Cardinal Wolsey*.

† " Genius always gives its best at first, prudence at last.
Lavater's *Aphorisms.*

Our worst relations are good to us; they wish us in heaven: sometimes, to secure us this blessing, they consign themselves to a worse place.

Few tables where convivial talents will not pass in payment, especially where the host wants brains, or the guest has money.

The fashionable require very little from those they associate with, besides their purse, praise, time, and chastity.

An angry man * should neither be believ'd or oppos'd; his intellect is derang'd. Mark well how his passion subsides; on that determine for or against the duration of your intimacy. But let me intreat that you never trust the sulky wretch; malice is in his heart; revenge, hatred, and more passions than there is names for. He is a spider who spins delicate filaments on all sides, to enmesh his unwary victim.

The credulity † of the bigot ever keeps pace with his ignorance, and the fear his ghostly director has inspired. Wine,

* " Anger is like
" A full hot horse, who, being allow'd his way,
" Self mettle tires him.   Shakespeare.

† Mrs. Bendysh, grand-daughter of *Cromwell*, gravely insisted, in conversation, that Oliver was one day seeking the
Lord

WINE, and love, though they may be the best at home, are thought to have the best relish when enjoyed abroad.

LUCKY men are frequently thought to be dishonest ones. The envious and narrow-minded invariably fabricate disgraceful causes for sudden or great prosperity.

KEEP an eye of rigid scrutiny over your own thoughts and actions; then the lenity shewn to the peccable will be highly honourable.

THERE will be little virtue extant when good intentions cannot obtain credit. Those deserve to suffer by vice who bruise the seed before it is earth'd.

REFORMERS

Lord with such fervor of devotion, and striving for a gracious answer with such vehemence of spirit, that the tears were forced from him in such abundance, as to run under the closet door into the next room. This, to be sure, was snivelling to some purpose! A gentleman, to whom this information was particuly addressed, observed, in reply, " that it was difficult to say precisely what abundant fountains of tears might fill up and run over the Lord's chosen vessels; yet he could not help suspecting that the flood under the closet door, occasioned by the Protector's struggles, was derived from some other source than his eyes."

Reformers* begin generally at the wrong end: they should not destroy; they should perfect.

---

* " In a certain part of the world, where ingenious men are wont to retail their speculations, I remember to have seen a valetudinarian in a long wig, and a cloak, at the upper end of a table, with half a dozen of disciples about him. After he had talked about religion in a manner which would make one think atheism established by law, and religion only tolerated, he entered upon civil government, and observed, that the natural world was in perpetual circulation. Animals, said he, who draw their sustenance from the earth, mix with the same earth, and in their turn become food for vegetables, which again nourish the animal kind. The vapours that ascend from this globe, descend back upon it in showers; the elements alternately prey upon each other. That which one part of nature loseth, another gains; the sum total remaining always the same, being neither bigger nor lesser, better nor worse, for all these intestine changes. Even so, said this learned professor, the revolutions in the civil world are no detriment to human kind; one part whereof rises as the other falls, and wins by another's loss. A man, therefore, who thinks deeply, and hath an eye on the whole system, is no more a bigot to government than religion. He knows how to suit himself to occasions, and make the best of every event; for the rest, he looks on all translations of power and property, from one hand to another, with philosophic indifference." Our lecturer concluded his discourse with a most ingenious analysis of all political and moral virtues into their first principles and causes, shewing them to be mere fashions, and illusions of the vulgar. As philosophers of this stamp lay it down for a maxim, that there is nothing sacred of any kind, nothing but what may be made a jest of, exploded, and changed like the fashion of their cloaths; so nothing is more frequent than perfect. It cannot be suppofed fo many ages have paffed away, without leaving us in poffeffion of fomething that is intrinfically valuable, fomething that may ferve for improvement to build on.

The fafeft gallant is the hufband's beft friend. So thinks the wife. The anathemas of all who can feel purfue the traitrefs who can folicit, or fubmit, in fuch a cafe, to be folicited!

If thofe who are united folely by affection are not the beft, they are certainly the happieft, portion of fociety.

Are the crimes that neceffity occafions neceffarily objects of punifhment?

"The world's a fchool
"Of wrong; and what proficients fwarm around!
"We muft or imitate, or difapprove;
"Muft lift as their accomplices or foes:
"*That* ftains our innocence, *this* wounds our peace."

Eloquence

than for them to utter their fchemes and principles not only in feleft companies, but even in public. There are many fpontaneous lecturers, in every corner of the ftreets, ready to open mens' eyes, and rub off all their prejudices about religion, loyalty, and public fpirit." Bishop Berkely.

Eloquence is admired, though wisdom is no where to be heard.

Can any means be devised to keep a fool in awe that are so efficacious as a greater fool?

'Tis as promising a task to attempt recovering the life as the reputation of one who has been hanged.

What * is there that hope, fear, or avarice, will not induce the necessitous, the ambitious, or adventurous, to undertake?

The change we personally experience from time to time we obstinately deny to our principles.

---

* "The extremity we endured was more terrible than befel any ship in the eighteen years war: for, laying aside the continual expectation of death by shipwreck, and the daily mortality of our men, I will speak of our famine. For fixteen days together we never tasted a drop of drink, either beer, wine, or water; and though we had plenty of beef and pork, of a year's salting, yet did we forbear eating of it, it making us drier. Many drank salt water, and those that did died suddenly; and the last words they usually spake were, 'Drink! drink! drink!' And I dare boldly say, that of five hundred men that were in that ship seven years before, at this day there is not a man alive but myself, and one more." —

Vide Tracts by Sir William Monson.

Let your lot be bad, good, or indifferent, convince the world that you merit a better: 'twill cause even your remains to be respected.

To struggle in misery and with misery at the same time, appears to be the acme of human sufferance. Who, acquainted with the number of propitious circumstances required to make a vigorous effort * of the mind, can read the advertisement of the great British lexicographer emotionless? " It may gratify curiosity to in-
" form it, that the English Dictionary was writ-
" ten with very little assistance from the learn-
" ed, and without any patronage of the great;
" not in the soft obscurities of retirement, nor
" under the shelter of academic bowers, but
" amidst inconvenience, and distraction; in sick-
" ness, and sorrow."

All who presume to judge in their own cause, presume that reason is on their side.

Though † words are 'uncertain evidences, they decide the most momentous concerns.

RIGID

---

* " But 'tis not thought, for still the soul's employ'd:
" 'Tis painful thinking that corrodes our clay."

ARMSTRONG.

† " Oral discourse (whose transient faults dying with the sound that gives them life, and so not subject to a strict review) more easily escapes observation." LOCKE *on Education.*

Rigid authority makes rebellious wives, children, and subjects. 'Tis this bastard power that prevents men in certain situations from being adored; so over-thankful is the human heart for gentle treatment.

If falsehood dwells on the lip, so does temptation.

Vivid imaginations prevent, and occasion a thousand inconveniences that dull souls are liable to, or insensible of.

Rich garments * have no privileges, though the wearers may.

Charity is the expletive of justice; mercy, the abuse of it. These vices are spoken of as pompously, and as ostentatiously, as if they changed their nature for the occasion.

Impudence † requires more than it merits; Greediness, more than it can use; Penury,

---

* " A man's attire, and excessive laughter, and gait, shew what he is."

Ecclesiasticus.

† " He who goes round-about in his request, wants, com-
" monly, more than he chuses to appear to want."

Lavater's *Aphorisms.*

less than it can obtain: but the Modest and the Haughty perish, and the list of their wants with them.

Ornaments are adscititious: the beauty of the thing is in itself, (if there is any,) or in our opinion of it.

When we meet with better fare than was expected, the disappointment is overlooked even by the scrupulous. When we meet with worse than was expected, philosophers alone know how to make it better.

Those who hesitate to publish their thoughts* must certainly be ashamed or afraid of uttering them. The English proverb, contained in the following distich, says,

"He that wou'd live at peace, and rest,
"Must hear, and see, and say the best."

Such dehortations deserve our contempt: they stifle that manliness and sincerity which all legislators should cherish.

Suicides

---

* Sinesius said to those employed to consecrate him, "I must acquaint you that I will neither deceive nor force the conscience of any man. I will allow every man peaceably to retain

his

Suicides pay the world a bad compliment. Indeed, it may so happen, that the world has been beforehand with them in incivility. Granted. Even then the retaliation is at their own expence.

'Tis enough to rive a sensible heart to injure the generous poor: there are critical situations, that make it inevitable: a momentous crisis it is, when self-preservation can only be obtained by acts of cruelty.

A foreign legislation is one of the monstrous substitutes that weak politicians devise to remedy errors that fall within their own province to rectify.

'Tis no uncommon thing to meet with persons who carry the rewards and trappings of prostitution as proudly as if the profession was an honourable one.

Mutual * accommodation is the object and essence of politeness and morality.

Never

his opinion, and I will adhere to mine. I will not teach any thing I do not believe. If you will confecrate me on these conditions, I consent; if not, I renounce the bishoprick."

* " There is often a magnificent pride and ill-nature in men of a great deal of wit and learning, which almost overthrows all
their

Never look for your ancestors, or your titles, in the imperfect records of antiquity; look into your own virtues, and the history of those who liv'd to be benefactors to society.

When females disclaim admiration, 'tis a feint to prevent your discovering that they are on the look-out for it.

The past may be a very proper counsellor for the present, or the future but a very improper director for either.

There is no way to surmount the virulence of dangerous prejudices, like a patient and unbiassed examination of opposite doctrines.

" He * who is master of the fittest moment to
" crush his enemy, and magnanimously neglects
" it, is born to be a conqueror." To these words of the citizen of Zurich let there be added : " Those who are compelled to yield, can feel no disgrace; those who submit, are cowards."

---

their merit; or at least makes one angry to find things so valuable in such ill hands."

* " As the lust of an eunuch to deflower a virgin, so is he that executeth judgment with violence.

Ecclesiasticus.

No citizen can look for impunity who expects refponfibility from his fellow-citizens.

* When the malign are compelled to utter truth, the tone in which it is delivered frequently operates to the difadvantage of thofe it fhould ferve.

† Benevolence is kept in motion by its own acts. When 'tis genuine, nothing impedes its progrefs; and a trifle preferves the fpirit of its action: nay, the very acknowledgments of the relieved are frefh and irrefiftible motives to exertion.

How many muft ftrip if every one could claim his own!

‡ There is, in the circles of traffic, nothing more common, than to hear one tradef-
man

---

* " There is a wicked man that hangeth down his head fadly; but inwardly he is full of deceit; cafting down his countenance as if he heard not: where he is not known, he will do thee a mifchief before thou art aware." *Ecclefiafticus.*

† " Call him faint who can forget his own fufferings in " the minute griefs of others." Lavater's *Aphorifms.*

‡ When a couple of broom-men had chatted one day
   On a number of things in a fociable way,

A new

man wonder how another thrives: the more the spirit of trade is within them, the greater the astonishment!

Caution is perpetual care. The cautious are are often timid, or affected. With the wisest of them, enjoyment must be incomplete: whilst the sun shines, they foresee storms.

* The *earnest* of the present is with some less enticing than the *promise* of futurity.

Confident

A new subject they started: says Jack, "My friend Joe,
"I have long been most plaguily puzzled to know
"How you manage to sell your brooms cheaper than mine,
"As I *steal* the materials."——"I like your design,"
Replied Jack; "but improvement's the soul of a trade:
"All the brooms I dispose of, I *steal ready made.*"

Anonymous.

* "The Saxons were undoubtedly a stout and hardy people, delighting chiefly in war; holding it all times far more honourable to take the necessaries of life from others by force, than by their own industry to provide for themselves. War was, indeed, part of their religion; for they not only held it dishonourable for a man to die of a disease, or in his bed, but supposed that he would be entirely excluded from the joys of a happy state hereafter, which was a place in *Woden*'s hall, where, in an endless round of quiet and contentment, they would sit, and quaff full cups of ale in the skulls of their enemies. This was their heaven: and their place of punishment plainly proves their detestation of sloth and indolence; for they supposed the torments to be a continual succession of laziness, sickness, and the most miserable infirmities." Strutt.

Confident ignorance frequently bears away the reward from the timid, fcrupulous, and deferving. The moſt deferving muſt put themfelves in the way of preferment.

The eſſence of rectitude and error, does not depend on words and clauſes inſerted in a ſtatute; it depends on reaſon, and the urgency of circumſtances; and theſe were antecedent to all laws.

Always flatter women; ſometimes flatter men. Such is the advice of one worldly ſycophant to another. Follow it, if you think proper. Remember, by the bye, never to flatter yourſelf. If, in the firſt caſe, 'tis dangerous to omit it; or if, in the ſecond, the hazard is in not knowing when, or how, to apply the doſe; remember, that in the third, both danger and hazard muſt be your own.

* The blandiſhments of art may engage our attention the quickeſt, but ſimple nature will have the longeſt claim to it.

---

* " Pray, Madam," ſaid a celebrated painter, to a certain toaſt upon *le plus haut ton,* whilſt ſhe was ſitting for her picture, " does your ladyſhip mean to be painted twice over?" The lady, ſomewhat diſconcerted, ſaid, " Sir, I do not underſtand you." " View the glaſs, and that painting, and determine
whether

WE are prepared to love those we hear praised. With what advantage that being enters a company whose fame has been founded!

* WHILE *there is any thing to do, there is nothing done :* thus runs one phrase. Another says, *Much is done by making a beginning.* In truth, things are often completed before they are finished.

† GENUINE love is no respecter of circumstances: there is a species of it that commences, though it seldom thrives, where they are unequal.

DOMESTIC veneration we may safely aspire to; the honours that are paid at home are not *exacted*, and they excite no murmurs.

WHEN

whether your rouge is not apparently more artificial than my carmine?" Her ladyship flew down stairs; and, in the violence of perspiration at the discovery, left a whole ruby cheek, and three blue veins.

* Lucan.

† " La beauté, les attraits, lésprit, la bonne mine,
" Echauffent bien le cour, mais non pas la cuisine."
P. CORNEILLE.

Senza Cerere, & Bacco, Venere e di ghiaccio.
Italian Proverb.

When women rifk their reputation, the chances are that they lofe it. One comfort is, the rifk is not difcovered 'till the danger is over.

The neceffities that exift are in general created by the fuperfluities that are enjoyed.

If contradiction unfettles the temper, prejudice predominates. Neverthelefs, if you cannot diffent from your friend fafely, change the converfation. The enmity of a human being no man will call forth who knows the value of his amity, or the infignificance of a verbal triumph over his failings.

* Torture is neither a juftifiable or ready means of obtaining the truth; yet 'tis ftill a maxim with deteftable ftatefmen, to deftroy where they cannot intimidate or perfuade.

---

* Though it had been for ages afcertained, that coercion produced no beneficial change of fentiment, yet all the prelates of France, confulted by Louis the Fourteenth, anfwered this queftion in the affirmative: "Is it right to force a peo- "ple of heretics to believe?"

An ordinance paffed in France, July, 1652, permitting the killing of *Huguenots* wherever they were to be found; and it was to be read every Sunday from all pulpits!

It strains the body to ascend; it shakes it to descend: the first effort is attended with difficulty; the second, with danger.

If the serpent had not cheated Eve, she might have been an overmatch for the serpent; and 'tis not improbable but there are some women who will at last escape the devil's claws.

'Tis iniquitous to form an opinion of the messenger from the tendency of his news. The man who brought intelligence to *Tigranes* of the approach of *Lucullus*, was instantly beheaded.

By the lover or the scholar, the defaulter or the dealer, the advantages of concealment are generally over-rated.

Servants often wear the livery whilst their employers do the work: indeed, the kitchen sometimes appears to be the place adapted to the meridian of their understandings.* We are not all cloathed as we deserve to be.

---

* " Who comes from the kitchen, smells of its smoke; who adheres to a sect, has something of its cant: the college air frames the student; and dry inhumanity, him who herds with literary pedants.

Lavater's *Aphorisms*.

The singularities and oddities to be observed in individuals, do not always proceed from good sense: where they are very remarkable, we must be prepared to meet with extremes.

Who can murmur at not succeeding, when the best have been refused?

* Purchasers conceive themselves to be possest of the power, as well as the right, of judging.

Such as have been fleeced by worldly duplicity, are accused of acerbity in their animadversions.

---

* " When his last comedy of the Wedding Day was in rehearsal, an actor said, he was apprehensive that the audience would make free with a particular passage; therefore begged it might be omitted. " No, damn it," replied the bard, " if the scene is not good, let them find that out." The play was brought out without alteration, and the disapprobation of the house was provoked at the passage before objected to. The performer retired into the green room, where the author was indulging his genius, and solacing himself with a bottle of champain. He had by this time drank plentifully, and cocking his eye at the actor, whilst streams of tobacco trickled down his mouth, " What's the matter, Garrick?" says he: " What are they hissing now?" " Why, the scene that I begg'd you to retrench." " Oh, damn 'em," replied the author; " they have found it out, have they?"

Murphy's Essay on the Life and Genius of Henry Fielding.

38 REFLECTIONS OF

ſions. Thoſe who bring this charge are incompetent to the taſk of maintaining it, if they have eſcaped the ſhears.

Family pride entertains many unſocial opinions.

The proſpect of pleaſure, or of pain, is ſufficient apology for preferring or quitting any road.

There is a local as well as a perſonal attachment; and 'tis not uncommon to entertain a partiality for certain places, in conſequence of a partiality to certain perſons.

Who is it that advocates for ſlavery? Thoſe who are neſcious what an immenſe benefit a ſingle freeman is of to the general family of mankind.

Better to be in a ſtate of inſipience, than to be guilty, and be conſcious of it. There is no criminality, unleſs there is a conſciouſneſs, a ſenſe of it.

The eye is an expreſſive organ, and lays the mind under heavy penalties; it alſo contributes moſt to its riches.

Neglect the first opportunity of liquidating your debts, and another may never occur. Pride hurries many a man to get out of debt; fear prevents as many from getting into it.

From fools, knaves, or wits, there is little prospect of obtaining a direct answer to a simple question. To their simple questions they always expect one, though they do not deserve it: nor is there any existing obligation to give it.

The bustle of the insignificant is the finest lesson for those who wish to become humble in their demeanour.

* Taste is perpetually varying, yet is it the standard of excellence.

Inmates of courts and cottages differ less in principle than in the way of demonstrating them. The vulgar of the city exclaim against the chicanery and servility of the former, as loudly as they apostrophize the innocence and honesty of the latter.

---

* Horace, in his Ninth Ode, says,
"This is the time to be possest;
"The best is but in season best."

The rich have juft as much as they can ufe: thofe who poffefs more, have in their cuftody what would make others rich.

In all cafes 'tis the weak who fuffer, and the weakeft who acknowledge the *juftice* of the punifhment awarded to them.

* Whores, even in their profperity, are unhappy. Gold cannot filence the apprehenfions of confcience. The fate they have been told they merit, they are in continual expectation of.

The fureft criterion of a man's difpofition, is the inftantaneous effect that cheerfulnefs or joy produces on his fpirits. The countenance in this cafe is the mirror of ineffable fatisfaction.

Solitude muft render the heart callous. What has it whilft alone to pity, or to cherifh? It makes no provifion but for itfelf; there its care begins, there it terminates. Humanity is unknown to the Solitaire. Without it, and all

the

---

* " There is a finner that hath good fuccefs in evil things, " and there is a gain that turneth to lofs."

Ecclefiafticus.

the dear cares that it includes, of what worth is exiftence?

A want of conjugal happinefs is the pretence of every married gallant; and the fubtle hypocrite into whofe arms he falls is glad of the complaint: under the veil of pity, fhe gives loofe reins to her inordinate defires.

Dissipation is abfolutely a labour when the round of Vanity Fair has been once made; but fafhion makes us think light of the toil, and we defcribe the circle as mechanically as a horfe in a mill.

* To know how fweet friendfhip is, we muft be houfelefs, and deftitute. One who has never loft fight of a throne is in a ftate of infcience. The Second Charles, or his father, might have felt the extatic thrill of being thought worth the care of a brother.

The wife regret, the fool fears, to die.

'Tis

---

* " To fhare a heavy burden merely to eafe another, is noble; to do it chearfully, fublime.

Lavater's *Aphorifms.*

* 'Tis certain that a violent affection can take place but once during life; for it, in some shape, occupies the whole attention during our existence: we *may* renounce the object of it; the passion will perpetually recur.

Though your mirth displeases, do not precipitately conclude that the heart is badly organized. There is a season for joy.

If adversity does not teach a man how far he can depend on himself, at least it instructs him what

---

* On Mrs. Vanbruggen (ci-devant Mrs Montford) Gay made his Black-ey'd Susan. She fell in love with Booth; but the desire of retaining an annuity left her by Lord Berkeley, on condition that she never married, prevented their union. Booth afterwards married Miss Santloe. No sooner did the perfidy of her lover, and the ingratitude of her friend, come to her knowledge, than she gave way to a desperation that deprived her of her senses. During a lucid interval, she asked her attendant what play was to be performed that evening, and was told that it was Hamlet. In this piece she had with great applause performed Ophelia. The recollection struck her; and, with that cunning usually allied to insanity, she found means to elude the care of her servants, and got to the theatre: there she concealed herself 'till the scene in which Ophelia was to make her appearance in her insane state. She pushed on the stage before her rival, who was the appointed representative for the night, and exhibited Ophelia herself to the amazement of the performers and the audience. Nature in this last effort was exhausted. On her exit, she exclaimed, " *It's all over;* " and the prediction was soon verified! *Vide* G. A. Bellamy's *Apology*.

what portion of reliance is to be placed on his coadjutors.

Continuance is the foul of peace, love, pleafure, and amity.

In politics, or ethics, the right moft univerfally eftablifhed, appears to be the right of doing wrong.

* Poverty, the raillery of women, or the fneers of opulent relatives, operate more violently on fome difpofitions than the dread of pain or death.

† Error is never fo fatal as when 'tis cloath'd in the garb of confiftence.

Children have no appeal, but in extreme cafes: the tyranny within doors frequently needs a check. ‡

When

---

* " You ridicule me becaufe you know what I do; did I know your actions, I could return it."
Eaftern Sentence.

† " Who by kindnefs, and fmooth attention, can infinuate a hearty welcome to an unwelcome gueft, is a hypocrite fuperior to a thoufand plain dealers." Lavater's *Aphorifms.*

‡ The Spartans could not fuggeft an idea that parricide could be committed, and had therefore fuggefted no punifhment for it.

When we extol or defend the characters of absent intimates, we are as often actuated by motives of pride as of justice. Of absentees we always speak in extremes.

Let such as wish to familiarize with the inseparable insignificance of their state, look into the sepulchres of the most illustrious; around are visible the mementos of mortality. Where can be found a solitary grain of the original, to identify of what earth it was compounded? Yet the marble informs us that it once received the body of some mighty warrior; one who had dispatched thousands to a premature and blood-damp grave, that his glory might outlive his consciousness of it.

* Want of respect for ourselves is a tacit licence for the neglect of all the world: the meanspirited alone avail themselves of the oversight.

Those who are very scrupulous, and tender of their own honour, will notwithstanding make very free with the honour of a friend, or his wife. "Honour," said the philosophic prelate, " is
but

---

* 'Twas well replied of a French Peasant to a young Nobleman, who wished her to leave her rustic state, and accompany him to Paris, " Ah! my Lord, the farther we remove from " *ourselves*, the greater is our distance from happiness."

but a fictitious kind of honesty; a mean, but necessary, substitute for it in societies who have none. It is a sort of paper credit, with which men are obliged to trade, who are deficient in the sterling cash of true morality and religion."

THE pity of benevolence is a delightful kind of melancholy, where it cannot relieve. Pity, 'tis to be feared, is an ephemeran,* even with the best, whether it comes in the shape of a kindness, an insult, or an injury.

THERE exists no stimulus to activity when every thing is within our reach, or when the value of life is brought too low by the galling conditions on which 'tis enjoy'd: then the soul becomes listless; or, if it has a desire, 'tis for the advent of death.

'TIS easier to undertake than to retract, especially in momentous affairs. Good, excellent is the advice of the poet Shenstone: " Whatever
" situation in life you ever wish or propose for
" yourself, acquire a clear and lucid idea of the
" inconveniences attending it."

THE

---

* επι, *upon*, and ημερα, a day.

Ephemera, in physic, is a continual fever, that lasts but a day.

The first act of innovation, though the most dangerous, is the last which is detected.

When paupers evince any consciousness of neglect, they are instantly spurn'd; if they complain this time of a scanty dole, the next they will have none. Though our donations are made to please ourselves, we insist upon those who receive our alms being pleased with them.

Great gaiety may exist without impurity; 'tis a question if great gravity can. Hilarity is consentaneous to a guileless heart: deep and dis-coloured are the motives for reserve.

* How can you convince, or be convinced, if you irritate, or are irritated?

† When government tolerate no opinions but their own, what opinion can we form of them?
How

---

* "We can do all by speech and silence. He who understands the double art of speaking opportunely at the moment, and of saying not a syllable more or less than is demanded, and he who can wrap himself up in silence when any word would be in vain, will understand to connect energy with patience."
Lavater's *Aphorisms*.

† "Let us seek truth, but seek it *quietly* as well as freely. Let us not imagine, like some who are called *free-thinkers*, that every man who can think and judge for himself, as he has
a right

How shall it be published? It appears like an act of madness to attempt it! Yet, when the general sentiment is ripen'd, it may be done with safety, and under the unanimous protection of the community.

'Tis not possible to hear the genuine sentiments of some women, 'till their love, or your purse, is exhausted.

Those who scatter their promises unmeaningly, are liberal of cruelty.

Frequently it happens that we have no more idea of the significations of the words we utter, than of the value of the gold that passes through our hands.

* Wit, to be well defin'd, must be defin'd by wit itself: then 'twill be worth listening to.

Many a right to do, has therefore a right of speaking, any more than than of acting, according to the full freedom of his thoughts. The freedom belongs to him as a rational creature, but he lies under restraint as a member of society. We may communicate our thoughts only so as it may be done without offending the laws of our country, and disturbing the public peace."

Lord Bolingbroke.

* " Wit is fine language to advantage dress'd;
" Been often thought, but ne'er so well express'd"

Dryden.

* Many of the modern systems of religion have more relationship to absurdity than to virtue. This remark is not thrown out against the church of Rome. "It forbids private judgment, and the exercise of reason in matters of religion. Now nothing is more evidently absurd than to reason against the use of reason; for if the argument itself is good, reason must be a good thing; and if the argument be bad, it only proves the folly of him who used it."

A HERO stands for nothing by itself, nor does a fool; but they both count for something amongst numbers.

† 'Tis good to have enemies, if 'tis only to hear of our faults.

ANGER is extraneous: we must desert the subject, when we give way to expressions of ill-nature.

MANY

---

* Justice for an hour is better than devotion for a year.
Eastern Sentence.

† " There is a reproof which is not comely; again, some man holdeth his tongue, and is wise. It is much better to reprove, than to be angry secretly; and he that confesseth his fault, shall be preserved from hurt. How good is it when thou art reproved to shew repentance! for so shalt thou escape wilful sin. *Ecclesiasticus.*

Many species of wit are quite mechanical: these are the favourites of witlings, whose fame in words scarce outlive the remembrance of their funeral ceremonies.

Attention to dull details, is a way to fortune by the road of patience. Listen, and the hearts of half the world are gained.

Under the vizors of prudence and sentiment, lurk artifice and lust.

The inexperienc'd only consider the present: remote advantages determine the wise man's actions. *You cannot draw a line, but it must have a beginning, and an end. A wise man knows, first, the principle and origin of all things; and, secondly, is not ignorant of their end.*

Civility and good breeding, are as much matters of interest as virtue is.

Every human agent should be his own historian: 'tis for the credit of the individual, and the advantage of the community, that all the contingencies of their transactions should be brought to light.

"Three* things characterise man; person,
"fate, merit: the harmony of these constitutes
"real grandeur."† How accidental is the greatness of which the vain mortal boasts! Two of the three constituents are independent of him: and the poor wretch whose merit is his all, what is his fate? Let us not think of Bossuet, Chatterton, and the long train of letter'd victims!

Pay the greatest attention to your enemy; from him you have the most to dread.

‡ There are a sort of friends, who in your poverty do nothing but torment and taunt you with

---

* "Search carefully into the unisons and discords of a man's person, fate, and merit, and you may analyse his character so clearly, that you may almost certainly foretel what he will be." *Again:*

"As the present character of a man, so his past, so his future. Who recollects distinctly his past adventures, know his destiny to come." Lavater's *Aphorisms*.

† Before thou callest a man hero, or genius, investigate whether his exertion has features of indelibility; for all that is celestial, all genius, is the offspring of immortality.

Lavater's *Aphorisms*.

‡ "The study of man is the doctrine of unisons and discords between ourselves and others.

"He who has but one way of seeing every thing, is as important for him who studies man as fatal to friendship."

Lavater's *Aphorisms*.

with accounts of what you *might* have been had you followed their advice: and this privilege comes from the comparative state of their finances and yours.

Who would be instrumental in raising a mob, whilst the march of the Poissardes from Paris to Versailles is before their eyes? Who would precipitate political changes, who considers that the very hurry of the measure prevents any benefit it may produce to be of a long continuance? Besides, all the advantages that revolutions by force bring, cannot restore one of the many lives that have been destroyed to produce it.

Men and their avocations should be carefully separated.

Despotism is the will of the most powerful carried into effect by force.

* Urgent must be the occasion, when we can submit to be serv'd by the lukewarm, or those who enumerate their services.

---

* " The gift of a fool shall do thee no good when thou hast it: neither yet of the envious for his necessity: for he looketh to recive many things for one. He giveth little, and upbraideth much; he openeth his mouth like a cryer; to-day he lendeth, and to-morrow he will ask it again: such a one is to be hated of God, and man. *Ecclesiasticus.*

* Every necessity is a trial of patience and ingenuity.

† Better to be conjoin'd with the dead than the dull. Mezentius had no punishment equal to a lifeless, yawning, dissatisfied female companion.

'Tis not possible to avoid dealing with fools; but 'tis mortifying to be out-fool'd by them.

‡ Who shall arraign my singularities, if they neither incommode him, or debase me? Follow thine own customs, slave: if they are right, persevere in them: for thy credit, have a better authority than custom for so doing.

No man can judge for, tho' he may of, another.

---

* " Then talk of patience, when you have borne him who has none without repining."
Lavater's *Aphorisms.*

† Mezentius, by way of punishment, fastened a dead corpse to a living body, that hunger, putrefaction, and noisome smells, might by small approaches destroy the victim of his rage.

‡ " He alone is a man, who can resist the genius of the age,
" the tone of fashion, with rigorous simplicity, and modest cou-
" rage."
Lavater's *Aphorisms.*

Those who expose their persons to the assaults of danger for fame, or for the defence of improper conduct, certainly have more blood than brains to spare.

When beauty is not supported by fortune, it generally is by presumption.

* Laws made after the commission of crimes, with an intent to punish, are cruel; before them, ridiculous.

An open confession of a single crime, or imperfection, will do more towards consoling the dissatisfied than an example of ten common virtues. When persons are represented as more than mortal, we are apt to think ourselves less than human. What an interesting detail has Rousseau set forth! What original plainness has Charlotte Elizabeth de Baviere in her account of herself! Daughters of frailty! listen. " In all " the world, I believe, there are no hands uglier " than

---

* In 1776, thirteen of the principal bankers funded 25,000,000 livres for the establishment of a bank at Paris, to discount bills of exchange, part in cash, and part in notes, for the purpose of facilitating trade, and of supporting the occasional wants of government. On the 25th of September, 1783, an unexpected and extraordinary run put the directors to the necessity of stopping payment. This event occasioned universal alarm; the ministry

" than mine. The late king * often told it me
" laughing, and made me laugh at it too; for as
" I am totally free from all perfonal beauty, I
" am always the firſt to laugh at my own home-
" lineſs; and if laughing adds to the fum of
" happineſs, I have my ſhare of it."

To pleaſe ourſelves, or friends, is too eaſily
effected: to pleaſe thoſe who have antipathies
againſt us, is almoſt impoſſible.

'Tis not that the courſe of things changes,
but peeviſhneſs paralyzes our ſenſes: every thing
is wrong when the temper is off its poiſe.

CONVICTION

niſtry made uſe of every means to prevent bad conſequences: four edicts appeared from the king, which they had the precaution of antedating five days. The firſt forbad all notaries to proteſt notes iſſued by the Caiſſe d'Eſcompte, under penalty of a mulct, beſides corporeal puniſhment; the ſecond ſtopping all future demands till January 1, 1784; the third enjoining perſons to receive the above notes in payment; the fourth laying duties on all ſpecie exported.

Theſe particular words are in the firſt arret: " His majeſty, " reſerving to himſelf, and his council, the hearing of all diſ- " putes and proſecutions concerning this arret, withdraws it " from his courts, and other judges."

* Louis the Fourteenth.

Conviction should regulate our conduct, we are told. Where are the exalted souls who will take the pains to convince us?

It hurts both the feeling, and unfeeling, to solicit for their assistance.

'Tis acknowledg'd that the motives for our own actions are difficult to discover; those that guide his neighbour, every simpleton knows.

* Is a "sympathy in years, manners, and "beauties," essentially necessary to the nuptial copartnership? Will not a coincidence of sentiment as firmly attach refin'd souls, as corporeal charms do the sensual?

† Retailers of anecdotes are dangerous newsmongers: what they have to relate is seldom correct; and if it is the *status rei*, 'tis generally so tim'd, that it becomes mischievous.

---

* Othello.

† "A wise man will hold his tongue 'till he see opportu-
"nity: but a babbler and a fool will regard no time."

"An unseasonable tale will always be in the mouth of the
"unwise. A wise sentence shall be rejected when it cometh
"out of a fool's mouth; for he will not speak it in due
"season." *Ecclesiasticus.*

'Tis for story-telling, that is " the lottery of
" genius, which no one should venture to play
" deep in, without possessing a considerable stock
" of sterling wit, and brilliant humour."

The establishments of royalty and priesthood, are the most stupendous monuments of human ambition.

Amidst the diversity of religious systems, and the numerous and contradictory explanations of the tenets belonging to each, the judgment is perplex'd, and confidence destroy'd. How can the ministers of God expect concording sentiments from the laity, when they themselves cannot settle what is, or is not, the true gospel, or the true construction of its principles?

When we know the poverty of the parent, the affluence of the offspring astonishes us. Sylla, after boasting of his exploits in Libya, was ask'd, " How can'st thou be an honest man,
" who, tho' thou hadst not a groat left thee by
" thy father, art now master of such large pos-
" sessions?"

Rich fancy and matur'd judgment conjoin'd, produce works that can never be exceeded.

* WHAT will correct the vanity of man, if familiarity with his own infignificance and infirmities cannot?

SINCERITY requires more fortitude, and acquires more reputation, than war. 'Tis alfo more honourable, and full as dangerous.

TAMENESS under unjuft perfecution often increafes it, and can never increafe the fear of offending.

Is there any impropriety in difpoffeffing the holder of affets, that he has neither a right to, or can enjoy? The *law* declares that there is.

CURES are often protracted, if not loft, by fearching for the nature of the evil.

---

* " I myfelf am alfo a mortal man, like to all, and the offspring of him that was firft made of the earth.

And in my mother's womb was I fafhion'd to be flefh in the time of ten months, being compacted in blood, of the feed of man, and the pleafure that came with fleep.

And when I was born, I drew in the common air, and fell upon the earth, which is of like nature, and the firft voice which I utter'd, was crying as all others do.

I was nurfed in fwaddling clothes, and that with cares.

For there is no king that had any other beginning of birth.

For all men have one entrance into life, and the like going out. *Wifdom of Solomon.*

ENEMIES, as well as friends, follow the victor's heels: their rejoicing, or anguish, is ever in proportion to his succefs.

* PARTIALITY is a bofom traitor, born and nourish'd within us. "The Gods forbid (faid Themiftocles) that I fhould fit upon a bench of juftice, where my friends found no more favour than ftrangers."

WOMEN poffefs in their own hands the fureft means of repelling the folicitations of amorous coxcombs. If they prate of thefe fort of addreffes, they may be fufpected of aiming at faintfhip; if they do not mention them, they may be fufpected of fomething worfe.

GAMBLERS may be pitied; Gamefters muft be defpis'd: one plays to live; the other only lives to play.

LADIES are not fo much incenfed at a rape as at neglect: they have no objection to enjoy pleafure without fin; but they had rather fin than not be pleas'd.

DEATH

---

* "Abfolute impartiality is not, perhaps, the lot of man; but where, open or hid, bitter partiality dwells, there too dwells inward anarchy and infanability of mind.

LAVATER's *Aphorifms*.

Death sometimes comes in at such a critical juncture, that it compleats, destroys, or saves a great man's reputation.

Happy follies, and prudent intemperance, make up the charms of adolescence. Age, necessarily temperate, may have pleasing emotions; transports of joy it can never have.

There appears to be more zeal in causing laws to be obey'd, than in rendering them worthy of obedience.

Make a woman independent of you, and she is in a fair way to become dependent on some other person.

* The depravity or virtue of a court is generally reflected by the people.

---

* "A wise judge will instruct his people, and the government of a prudent man is well order'd. As the judge of the people is himself, so are his officers; and what manner of men the rulers of the city is, such are all they that dwell therein."
Ecclesiasticus.

"Kings have no reason to condemn the people when they
"change sometimes for their interest, since in that they do but
"imitate them as the great examples of unfaithfulness and
"treachery; holding him the bravest that makes the least ac-
"count of being an honest man." Plutarch.

Any inconvenience will be submitted to for the sake of fashion, none for that of propriety; yet amidst the absurdities of fashion some accommodation may be found.

'Tis not possible for a man to be his own enemy; tho' he may, through ignorance, injure himself.

To the atmosphere our humours and tempers may be ascrib'd, not to our will.

Amongst the numerous enemies that kings have, very few wise men are to be found! And, with Fenelon, I believe, that he, who to-day unmercifully censures kings, wou'd govern worse than they to-morrow, and commit the same faults, with others infinitely greater, if he were invested with the same power.

Insinuation works in an unguarded moment; 'tis a tremendous and invisible weapon in the hands of the subtle; its wounds are incurable; and the villain who makes them cannot be punished beyond contempt.

Delicacy and prejudice think it indecent to call men and things by their proper names! I knew a girl of fortune who refus'd to learn the

pedal

pedal harp, becaufe it put her in an indelicate pofture; and fhe afterwards elop'd with her father's negro!

The pen wants oiling as well as the hinges.

Often is there more given up to obtain wealth, than can be obtain'd by it; and much oftener is the abufe of wealth to be found than the want of it.

* The means whereby greatnefs and laudable diftinction is acquir'd, are more impartially diftributed than is generally apprehended; but the immenfe refources of human intellect feem to be either undifcover'd, or, if difcover'd, are wrongly directed. "We yield fupinely to the fuperior me-
"rit of our predeceffors, becaufe we are accuf-
"tom'd to indulge the inactivity of our own
"faculties. All formal repetition of other mens'
"ideas feems to be a fcheme for imprifoning for
"a long time the operations of our own mind."

Immoderate forrow is a fpecies of tardy fuicide.

---

* Marius afked the people "if they did not think that their anceftors had not much rather have left a pofterity like him, fince they themfelves grew famous not by their nobility, but by their valour and great actions." Plutarch.

* The rich are cool with their equals, abject to their superiors, intolerant to their inferiors.

We have fellows who sneak into company † as if they bore all the sins of their family on their shoulders. And before whom is it that they thus crouch and bend? Arrogance in holiday cloathing, and female foppery!

Those who jump into your proposals immediately, are not so safe to deal with as those who wait to weigh them.

Justice

---

* " If thou be invited of a mighty man, withdraw thyself, and so much the more he will invite thee. Press thou not upon him, lest thou be put back: stand not far off, lest thou be forgotten. Affect not to be made equal unto him in talk, and believe not his many words; for with much communication will he tempt thee, and, smiling upon thee, will get out thy secrets. But cruelly will he lay up thy words, and will not spare to do thee hurt, and put thee in prison.

What agreement is there between the hyena and a dog? and what peace between the rich and poor? As the wild ass is the lion's prey in the wilderness, so the rich eat up the poor. As the proud hate humility, so do the rich hate the poor."

Ecclesiasticus.

† A Frenchman wants nothing else to recommend him in company, but his own address and manners. An Englishman is nobody without his estate, his parliamentary interest, his fine hunter in the stable, or some relative adventitious advantage, which he thinks gives him consequence in the eyes of the world. The Frenchman's maxim is, " *Quod petis in me est.*"

Anonymous.

Justice fhou'd never be adminifter'd by a felf-appointed authority; yet I fhou'd be glad that men were capable of being judges in their own caufe: none can underftand the extent of the trefpafs fo well, or the neceffity of retribution.

On fpeculative fubjects there is the greateft chance for originality of thought. Of the common occurrences of life we muft entertain nearly the fame ideas as thofe who liv'd four thoufand years fince.

The more perfect, the more vicious friendfhip is: 'tis drawing the rays of the fun to a point, when to diffufe an equal heat they fhould be fpread.

In large fchools every paffion but love rages violently: there may be found urchin mifers, defpots, cowards, hypocrites: in ftilts you fee the orator, artift, warrior, and the ftatefman!

We feldom expect to find a feducer in print; therefore, by reading without precaution, we are often mifled.

There wou'd be lefs envy extant, if we fixt on feparate ways to obtain fame.

Out-talk

Out-talk the loquacious, or they will stun you.

If 'tis your wish to become sensible of the gradations of vice, bring a thief into the company of a gambler, or a girl of the town into the presence of a woman of gallantry.

Egotism is more like an offence than a crime; tho' tis allowable to speak of yourself, provided nothing is advanced in favour: but I cannot help suspecting that those who abuse themselves, are, in reality, angling for approbation.

Speak in behalf of human-kind; praise their exalted sentiments and benevolence, their bravery and urbanity; 'tis a sure trap for the vain; instantly they claim their part, as belonging to the species: but they will shut their door on you when the storm is at its height notwithstanding.

Do not think that your learning and genius, your wit or sprightliness, are welcome every where. I was once told that my company was disagreeable because I appear'd so uncommonly happy; and many good housewives declare they do not like *your learned, bookish husbands*.

How

How artlefsly females fcreen their firft peccadilloes under inexperience!

We fhall never act completely, 'till the whole train of advantages, and difadvantages, are before us at the period of determination.

How far in delicacy is the fpinfter who has had many fuitors, or the widow who has had many hufbands, above the condition of thofe who have once partaken of illicit love?

Those who are fatisfied with compliments, may, with the camelion, live on air.

Never recal the periods of infignificance; we can always difpenfe with fuch recollection.

Nothing is fo defpicable as the buffoon, who, by aukward endeavours to raife a laugh againft others, becomes himfelf the object of it.

Women always execrate the man who has broke his marriage fetters, tho' their own poor partners wou'd lay down half their days to enjoy the others in peace.

The affemblies of women are too frequently mark'd by malice to each other, and flander of
the

the abfent: the meetings of men by noife, inebrity, and wrangling.

Where there is cruel cunning, 'tis fortunate if there is turbulence of temper.

If a man cannot pick up knowledge enough of the world in a year to fatisfy him, he may in an hour difcover enough to ficken him.

There is more in the choice of an object than is generally acknowledged: exertion on all occafions, and in all perfons, is near upon a par.

Those who have ftudied the nature of man, have but to read a page more, and they will difcover what men are.

What repentance there is in a jail cannot be carried beyond its walls; for thofe who are difcharg'd from its ftrongly fecur'd doors, are forc'd immediately to have recourfe to the fame practices for a livelihood as configned them to its dungeons.

We do not always like thofe we vifit, or invite thofe we like. Where hofpitality alone fhou'd be found, there is frequently envy, felfifhnefs, deceit, or oftentation.

Of what significance is the ridicule, if it cannot destroy the utility of the thing?

Economy is an excellent lure to betray people into expence.

Passion is too often complimented with the name of spirit, and weakness as often passes for tenderness.

When the discussion of certain characters is brought forth with solemnity, 'tis not unfrequently a trap for the inconsiderate.

For the little most hosts have to give we pay dear enough.

A book or bottle needs not the courting that a woman requires, 'tis true; and if there is no pleasure in wooing, it must be drudgery indeed.

A traveller thinks light of his journey, if the reward is at the end of it.

* Men in high situations are not great men; by courtesy 'tis suppos'd they are.

---

* Louis the Fourteenth asked the Duke de Vivonne, "Of what use it was to read?" And, after the death of *Fenelon*, with his own hands, he burnt all the manuscripts that the Duke of Burgundy had preserved of his preceptor.

Many think, or affect to think, more of the distress than those who undergo it.

'Tis possible to judge of the impudence of a man by the effect female modesty has on him; but the modesty of the male appears to encourage the woman in her boldness.

The order of justice is inverted, when women are punished for that generous attachment which, in other situations, would raise her fame as high as her merit.

Oppression disagrees as well with the oppressor as his drugs do with the physician.

* Has scepticism or presumptuous confidence been carried to the greatest extreme of folly? The followers of Pyrrho are few, and their errors less dangerous than those of the opposite opinion.

---

* *Pyrrho*, the painter, was born at Elis, and flourished in the time of *Alexander*, about the 110th Olympiad. He died at ninety years of age. The perusal of *Democritus* caused *Pyrrho* to apply to philosophy. He left nothing in writing; but a summary of his principles is transmitted to us by *Sextus Empericus*, an acute and learned author of his sect: and the Pyrrhonic hypothesis, or ten books of sceptic philosophy, are to be found in *Stanley's* Lives and Opinions of the Philosophers.

We receive the jokes of our superiors with constrain'd pleasantry; those of our inferiors, with smother'd indignation; yet our own we pass with glee and satisfaction.

Men of lively parts, and generous dispositions, should be born to fortunes; gain them they never will.

* In the eagerness to be serviceable, we sometimes forget how little we can perform. This is a sweet earnest of benevolence, that wants only the means to be compleat.

General exclamations are to be heard against the vast change that public opinion has undergone: there is, indeed, a revolution, and old opinions have revolv'd with the wheel.

How pleas'd a female fool is with a bargain! So she is at first with her husband: her vanity feeds on his wit and personal charms: the instant she meets a friend who has made a better purchase, the rage for bargains is reviv'd, and her spirits are in a flutter when she thinks of it.

If

---

* " There is that for bashfulness promiseth to his friend, and maketh him his enemy for nothing.

Ecclesiasticus.

If there was no pride in witneſſing the ſucceſs of a family, I know not what other reward there wou'd be at all proportionate to what is renounced to ſecure it.

'Tis an axiom in logic, that by endeavouring to prove too much, you prove nothing; this is the error that untaught reaſoners ofteneſt fall into.

Those upon the *qui vive* have a pleaſant and profitable mode of laughing at the world.

In the ſallies of badinage a polite fool ſhines; but in gravity is as aukward as an elephant diſporting.

I cannot agree with Lavater, when he ſays, " The freer you feel yourſelf in the preſence " of another, the more free is he: who is free, " makes free." Many affect to be diſembarraſs'd purpoſely to throw others off their guard, when they themſelves are labouring with conſtraint.

Both mind and body acquire a habit of bearing calamity; but the mind has a method of beſpeaking it.

Perhaps, in the abundance of poſſeſſions, the felicity of the lordly owner is fixt upon the moſt inſignificant parts of it.

A student's

A student's temper is seldom even; so is it with those who labour with envy, malice, or pride: but hope gives it a cheerful turn.

Women who delight in obscene language, are either the deepest in, or the farthest from, practical sensuality.

The rich delight in the burlesque.

* 'Tis not often that we can bear our prosperity so well as our griefs; and seldom with our friends we often become tormenters in their prosperity, and comforters in their adversity.

Very few public men but look upon the public as their debtors, and their prey: so much for their pride and honesty.

Sorrow is arbitrary and fictitious.

Which happens soonest, which is most to be lamented; that we know the world, or that we are known by it?

Men

---

* " Who partakes in another's joys, is a more humane character than he who partakes in his griefs.

Again:

Who can conceal his joys, is greater than he who can hide his griefs." Lavater's *Aphorisms*.

Men of brilliant capacities are more miserable in the drudgery of mean employs, than those who are conscious of their inability are in the higher employs of life.

* The virtuoso takes more pains to discover the curious of inanimate than breathing nature; and meets with the reward of his insensibility in the contempt of all men capable of distinguishing frivolous from useful pursuits.

There are periods in the lives of most adventurers when their affairs must take a retrograde course, if they are scrupulous or cowardly.

If a man made the world his conclave, the variety of opinions would dissuade him from undertaking the most trivial matter, unless his mind was made up before he convoked the council. How then is it made out, that in the multitude of counsellors there is wisdom?

Tho'

---

* The connoisseur in painting discovers an original by some great line, though covered with dust, and disguised by daubing; so he who studies man, discovers a valuable character by some original trait, though unnoticed, disguised, or debased: ravished at the discovery, he feels it his duty to restore it to its genuine splendor. Him who, in spite of contemptuous pretenders, has the boldness to do this, choose for your friend."

Lavater's *Aphorisms*.

Tho' a favour does, or does not, deserve to be return'd, the manner in which it was granted deserves to be remember'd.

Those who admire the sex, care but little for the woman: those who are wrapt up in the woman, are inattentive, if not rude, to the rest of the sex.

Women have more and more diversified modes of praising than men have.

Frequently we hear one opinion in society; but society are seldom of one opinion.

When girls hear a man violently censur'd for his spirit of intrigue, their curiosity to see him, propitiously indulg'd, generally terminates in his favour.

Excuses are more studied for what is really becoming the dignity of our nature, than what disgraces our understanding.

Frequently to laugh, is the surest way of being laugh'd at.

Plain men make a poor figure in courtship; they must have every thing nuncupative. Now, the

the greatest puzzle a woman can have, is to express what she means in love.

* THERE would be a great advantage resulting from the separation of morality and religion: then the difference of theological principles would be perfectly insignificant.

A COLDNESS may be thrown upon talents that will destroy their effect; therefore 'tis necessary to prepossess those we associate with in favour of them.

SHEWING a woman that she is a slave at home, is a ready way to make both fool and slave of her abroad.

THOSE who insist upon having what is agreeable, will often want what is necessary.

BUTTS are to be the prey of the supercilious, the vain, and over-bearing: emmets who have little wit, but make great and frequent attempts at it:

a butt

---

* " I know Deists whose religiousness I venerate; and Atheists, whose honesty and nobleness of mind I wish for; but I have not yet seen the man who could have tempted me to think him honest, who publickly acted the Christian, whilst privately he was a positive Deist."

LAVATER's *Aphorisms.*

a butt is sure to put his company in good temper, especially if he loses his own.

Those who stay at home to watch, find no relief.

* Spinsters seem to be considered as a common property: when they alter their state, they do not get rid of the spurious claims that are upon them.

The first blow a child receives is the worst: if from the hands of a parent, the evil is augmented: those who can see the consecution of such acts, check their ire before it becomes too hot.

A youth introduc'd suddenly into life, feels as aukwardly as one immers'd for the first time in water; and the chances are that he sinks as soon.

Those who care not for the loss of their liberty, will never defend it.

---

* "An easy, good-natured man is like one of the *feræ naturæ*; every body hunts him as their prey; and, instead of being cherish'd by every one, he is claim'd as their property: if he is caress'd, it is only to draw him into a snare."
Anonymous.

* I have long debated, whether more agreeable are the sensations of discovering faults that you are in a capacity to amend, or finding out excellencies that please as well as amend you.

If coquettes or prudes ever marry, their calumniators are in the same proportion as their coquettry and prudery have been.

Good economists are the most ornamental members of society.

† Deaf men must have singular ideas: they see the transactions of life without discovering whence they spring.

I wou'd pardon a liar before a man of rude manners, if they are assum'd: for his mendacity there may be a thousand exculpations: what can apologize for voluntary rudeness?

---

* " Just as you are pleased at finding faults, you are displeased at finding perfections. He gives me the most perfect idea of a fiend, who suffers at the perfections of others, and enjoys their errors."   Lavater's *Aphorisms*.

† Blind people are generally observed to be more cheerful than those who are deaf: the sight only furnishes us with our own reflections; the hearing, with those of different persons of different characters.

Anonymous.

When an upstart salutes you, or a coxcomb, 'tis that you may notice him.

Sailors are the last people who pity; for being able to laugh at their own misfortunes, they despise it.

The first question on extraordinary occasions is, " Who is he?" This appears as necessary to be known as the crime that has been committed.

Those who are all innocence there is a combination to ridicule; whilst those who are all vice, are scarcely despised.

Always consider yourself in danger when you object: the more objections you make, the more will be made.

If you appear to be pleased with every thing, you will have a number of blind admirers.

There is an hour propitious for every offering; to find it out is the difficulty.

Lower your pride, and you may defy disrespect; but rudeness is a wound; and 'tis impossible

possible to smart and be insensible at the same time.

Men are apt to conceit themselves wise, after having made their observations on a particular circle, forgetting how many may be described within the great circle.

* In company with the poor, the greatest only think themselves accidentally rich.

Those who revenge the sins of the world, shou'd be careful that the innocent do not suffer.

'Tis possible for a man to know how to make a fortune without having much knowledge.†

Hunger is the mother of impatience and anger: and the quarter of an hour before dinner is the worst suitors can chuse. The Latins have said, *Venter non habet aures.*

Silence

---

* " Could you but hear how one speaks to the poor and despised, when he thinks himself unobserv'd, you might form a judgment of his character."

Lavater's *Aphorisms.*

" † Good animal spirits, and activity, are more necessary to a man's success in the world, than genius and knowledge."

Anonymous.

Silence is the safest responfe for all the contradiction that arises from impertinence, vulgarity, or envy.

Look attentively how a man governs his own affairs, or retrieves them if derang'd, before he is entrusted with the regulation of yours.

Who asks the prostrate why he fell, merely to eke out his crude materials for accusation, deserves not a categorical answer.

Right and wrong often change places when faith is searching for its catachrestical reasons for faith.

Great minds may, by repeated ill treatment, be brought to a state of indifference; but even the extensive powers of insolence, or wickedness, cannot excite personal animosity in them.

Even the comparative frivolity of their pursuits cannot wean some artists from their application, tho' their health is imminently endanger'd by it.

The ignorance of the people is less fatal than the ignorance of their governors, unless they undertake to correct the blunders of the former.

Choice words are not intended for the ear alone.

* 'Tis difficult to walk your own pace amidst observers.

A modest youth may become a confident man, but never an impudent one. Indeed, modesty appears to be the minority of confidence,† and confidence the maturity of reason.

‡ Distrust has two causes; the certainty or the apprehension of guilt.

---

* " He who, in questions of right, virtue, or duty, sets himself above all possible ridicule, is truly great, and shall laugh in the end with truer mirth than ever he was laugh'd at. Lavater's *Aphorisms*.

† " There are but three classes of men; the retrograde, the stationary, the progressive." Lavater's *Aphorisms*.

‡ Sixtus the Vth. saw the gates of the convent of the Holy Apostles open. Quitting his chariot, he went into the porter's lodge. The porter, a lay brother, was eating beans and oil. Sixtus took a spoon, and emptied two platters. He thanked the man for his entertainment; and turning to his courtiers, said, " We shall live two years longer for this: for we have eat with an appetite, and without fear. The Lord be prais'd for letting a Pope once in his life make a meal in peace."

No man will ever believe that you are not to be flatter'd. If you take good care to prevent their endeavours, there will be no infecurity in flattering them with the poffibility of what they have afferted.

The danger is in heating or cooling too fuddenly.

Trifles are often neglected becaufe their connection is not apparent: they often turn the beam in matters of the laft importance.

'Tis to be fear'd that our greateft exertions have no other end in view, than to avail ourfelves of the weak, or fubdue the ftrong. "What," faid father Arduin, "do I rife every "morning two hours before day to think like "the reft of mankind?"

Treat every ftranger as a friend; every friend as a ftranger; and treat them both as they deferve, without reference to any other claim.

Unsuccessful merit will never have many followers, tho' admirers may be found.

Flattery is fometimes more profitably directed to a fecond perfon, efpecially with overfond parents.

Beauty gains little, and homeliness and deformity lose much, by gaudy attire. Lysander knew this was in part true, and refus'd the rich garments that the tyrant Dionysius proffer'd to his daughters, saying, "That they were fit only to make unhappy faces more remarkable."

If our word is pledg'd for a villain, 'tis cruel that we shou'd suffer if he becomes a defaulter: the trust is not in this case granted to the person suspected, but the bondsman.

What business has humility or meekness in this bustling scene of passions? 'Twill not even recommend you to the notice of the meek or humble.

* The pertness of the last age is superseded by indifference: we have few fops, but many conceited apathists.

† Great men cannot forgive: 'tis an affectation of omnipotence that satirizes terrestrial ambition. Indolence

---

* "He knows little of man, who trusts him with much that cares for no one." Lavater's *Aphorisms*.

† "There is a manner of forgiving so divine, that you are ready to embrace the offender for having call'd it forth."

Lavater's *Aphorisms*.

Indolence merits more punishment than the activity of the thief: indolence is a perennial; crime an ephemera; 'tis the nurse of all civil offences.

Justly you cannot deal with any being unless you know him: this justice likewise includes your own interest.

Ask a man for protection or assistance, that instant you make out his indictment, unless 'twas impossible for him to have discovered that you stood in need of either.

Those who remember this adage, *Virtue is its own reward*, will not be surpriz'd at their poverty. This is prohibitory, instead of an encouraging sentence.

'Tis rarely the case, that those who are accustom'd to public notice, are at all solicitous about private opinion; or, indeed, do they often acquire it. The talents that distinguish them from the throng in a house of legislation, the bar, or theatre, are not call'd for in domestic life.* Besides,

---

* " No man can make a figure in public, without possessing what in private renders him disagreeable---audacity and arrogance."
Anonymous.

sides, the loftiness that follows the world's idolatry, accompanies them in every petty act; and having acquitted themselves well in particulars, they conceit that their merit is general.

Do not think you can secure the regard of a good man by heaping your favours on him.

* Give me the man who has been tried in the crucible, who has been purified by the fire of misfortune, and comes forth purg'd from vanity and its train of demands.

The gay by day are sad by night. Those who toil all day rest well at night.

Whilst there are many women, there will be many desires.

Our own errors we cannot so well discover, because we contemplate them through the medium of inclination.

Impure love is said to be a vice. How severe is the man's sentence! He has to bear the woman's fault, and his own. Women seem

to

---

* Darius, in all his misery, wore adversity gracefully. Alexander was conquer'd by success.

to think they are clear'd of the trespass, because they are not the party who solicit.

Let us commiserate the being who is satisfied that he ought to be dissatisfied.

* We are too fond of giving permanence to opinion. In this particular the inhabitants of all countries, and all the inhabitants of each country, are consentient. *My mind is made up*, says one. *Is not my word past?* cries another. *On that subject my sentiments will never change*, adds a third. It is our pride to deal in the irrevocable; though 'tis often to our advantage to revoke.

† In the fulness of the heart impossibilities are utter'd; hence the protestations of love, the rantings of anger, and the plans of ambition.

Good

---

* " The prospect of affairs looking now very dismally, the Confederates sent an embassy to Sparta, to desire that Lysander might be chosen admiral. Cyrus too dispatched letters thither to the same effect. Now there was a law among the Lacedemonians, that obliged them never to confer that command twice upon the same person; yet they were desirous to gratify their allies; so they gave one Acacus the title, but Lysander the power." Plutarch.

† " Love sees what no eye sees; love hears what no ear hears; and what never rose in the heart of man, love prepares for its object. Hatred sees what no eye sees; enmity hears
what

Good laws muſt proceed from good ſenſe, which neither bluſhes at amendment, or abolition; though laws have been eſtabliſhed in defiance of law, juſtice, or reaſon.

* The warmeſt praiſe of the riotous rabble is not worth a minute's purchaſe. Look at the fate of their idols! look at the heroes of a revolution! Often has it happened that, betwixt their riſe and fall, they have been denied time to make their will: ſo unſtable is their faith.

Nature's child liſtens to no inhibition againſt her laws. The child of art is often puniſh'd for his rebellion: though art ſhould modify, it ſhould not deſtroy.

Caprice is a ſeed plot whence enmities ſpring.

Gold turns bitter into ſweet: thus artful phyſicians diſguiſe all nauſeous drugs.

Extremes

what no ear hears: and what never roſe in the murderer's breaſt, envy prepares for him that is fortunate and noble."

Lavater's *Aphoriſms*

* " In the tremendous breaking forth of a whole people, in which all degrees, tempers, and characters are confounded, and delivering themſelves by a miracle of exertion from the deſtruction meditated againſt them, is it to be expected that nothing will happen?" Paine's *Rights of Man*.

* Extremes in dress often create a personal dislike: this folly is censurable only, not criminal.

Disguise reproof in a question, let it not follow the offence too rapidly, and utter it in a mild tone.

† The patient can oftener do without the doctor, than the doctor without the patient.

Never suffer your refusal to dissolve the esteem of the solicitor: you can, or cannot, grant. "I am your friend as far as the altar," said Pericles.

The fate of books resembles the fate of men. Some are as often over-read as they are read over: others are condemn'd ‡ wholly for a part, or for a part

---

* " All finery is a sign of littleness.

Lavater's *Aphorisms*.

† Louis Cornaro, the Venetian, was perplexed with infirmities till the age of forty; but, by his own endeavours, in one year he freed himself from all diseases. He continued sound, and cheerful, and vegete to his eightieth year; and in 1631 expired in his chair with very little pain, and all his senses entire.

‡ Voltaire declared he never found a book that did not contain something good.

Utile per inutile non vitiatur.

a part the whole is fav'd. Some are cenſur'd before, and all are by ſome cenſur'd after, they have been examin'd.

Purchase a bleſſing,* a woman, a ſmile, or a character, and they are dear at a farthing.

When the parent's choice is the ſame as his child's, then may the parent chooſe.

Counterfeits, of all deſcriptions, are confin'd to time and place.

Courts of fraud, and force, can never do more than ſet up a ſpecious imitation of diſtributive juſtice.

Is † wit any thing more than delicate and refined humour? or humour more than a lively or whimſical repreſentation of things and opinions?

Fortune

---

* The reply of the Lambeth apple-woman to an Archbiſhop of Canterbury has often pleas'd when it has been narrated.

"Take off your bonnet, good woman, and you ſhall receive my bleſſing."

"Nay, your Grace, if the bleſſing will not go through bonnet and all, I can't think it is worth much."

† "A ſtriking analogous repreſentation of latent ideas, and a whimſical heterogeneous aſſociation of familiar ones, ſeem to be the brief general diſtinction between *wit* and *humour*. Oppoſition

FORTUNE seldom stands still, even amongst the poor; their affairs grow worse; and the treasures of the Mammonist still increase.

MILDNESS is often the disguise of weakness, and complaisance of cowardice or servility.

THOSE who view mankind through the medium of an exalted philosophy, take flights* beyond the ken of plodding; drudging mortals, who trade through life, indulging no emotions, except such as arise from sordid self-interest.

WHOEVER wins, the apostate suffers.

In-

sition also of ideas belongs to both: when remote, to the former; when homely, to the latter. These are their outlines, from which it appears that many thoughts must intermediately have a share in both." *Anonymous.*

* "What stubbing, plowing, digging, and harrowing, is to land, that thinking, reflecting, examining, is to the mind. Each has its proper culture; and as the land that is suffered to lie waste and wild for a long time, will be overspread with brushwood, brambles, thorns, and such vegetables, which have neither use nor beauty, so there will not fail to sprout up in a neglected, uncultivated mind, a great number of prejudices, and absurd opinions, which owe their origin partly to the soil itself, the passions, and imperfections of the mind of man, and partly to those seeds which chance to be scattered in it, by every wind of doctrine which the cunning of statesmen, the singularity of pedants, and the superstition of fools shall raise."

BISHOP BERKELEY.

In this particular all women are alike: speak lightly of their sex, and they are offended. Do they imagine that resentment makes them better than they are?

Contempt is frequently regulated by fashion.

Fruitless is the critic's endeavours, if the actor is belov'd.

The purse of the patient frequently protracts his cure.

Cheering approbation comes coldly from the envious or conceited; deliberately from the exalted; quickly from the fool, or parasite: those of *petit gout* know not what it means.

Louis the Fourteenth was titularly great;* Denis the Critic thought himself great: from ourselves, or others, comes all title to greatness.

Every citizen is debtor to the general stock of all that he possesses; though there is no written law to make the debit good.

* "He who gives himself airs of importance, exhibits the credentials of impotence."

Lavater's *Aphorisms*

Laws act after crimes have been committed; prevention goes before them both.

Mild answers encourage cowards, and torment the irascible.

Is this a maxim to be depended upon? The qualities or affections that we generate we possess?

Calmness under contradiction, is demonstrative of great stupidity, or strong intellect.

We dare not say all, yet all will out. This instant have I expung'd a declaration of my principles: whether from motives of fear, or delicacy, 'tis not necessary to affirm.

Remember, that if you act from reason, you are to be judg'd by law: and what the law allows, reason often condemns.

* If you cannot read or hear the opinion of your judges without being depress'd or exalted, never offer yourself as a candidate for fame.

---

* " The richer you are, the more calmly you bear the approach of poverty: the more genius you have, the more easily you bear the imputation of mediocrity."

Lavater's *Aphorisms.*

You are not at peace with yourself, if you cannot see the diurnal routine of luxury, hear the brouhahas of the enraptured throng, or witness the extravagant freaks of joy, without repining.

Hereditary sin is not more extraordinary than hereditary jurisdiction.

This question I would willingly have satisfactorily answered, but cannot: *Why should laws exist to controul what does not, what never may, or what never can exist?*

Pious pride is the burlesque of sanctity, as military pomposity is of valour.

Be well assur'd that the issue will be secure and advantageous, then there will be no crime in breaking the chains that gall you.

Humane enemies, after a defeat, are found to be safe friends.

The path is clos'd where it should be widen'd, and widen'd where it should be clos'd. There is no room for those who would amend, but plenty for those who would grow worse.

Virtue

* Virtue has nothing fortuitous about it; tho' 'tis generally discover'd by chance.

† If the presence, or absence, of any creature, whether 'tis the tenant of the thatch'd building or stone mansion, can flutter your spirits, or divert the free course of your sentiments, you lack manhood.

Ignorance, poverty, and vanity, make many soldiers.

Eloquence and beauty are great impostors: they are both good advocates, and better than a good cause in any court.

Many pictures please us; our own ravishes and intoxicates us.

Toleration divides power, which to those in power is as intolerable, as the idea of immunities is to those who enjoy extensive privileges.

The

---

* " Pendant que la paresse, & la timidité nous retiennent dans notre devoir, notre vertue en a souvent tout l'honneur."
Rochefoucauld.

† " Who, in the presence of a great man, treats you as if you were not present, is equally proud and little."
Lavater's *Aphorisms.*

The amorist praises her lover through vanity as much as ignorance.

Before good sense, or a good dress, is a good address.

As readily as you offend those who stand in requisition of your favours, so readily will you crouch to those who have offended you whose assistance you require.

Polite assemblies are all of them masquerades: the masque is not worn on the visage, 'tis on the heart.

Independent characters (as some are call'd) are generally as offensive as the insipid is fearful of giving offence.

What can make us so ambitious of fashionable acquaintance? They never can respect interlopers, for they do not regard even their intimates.

* When your pecuniary want sours the temper of an intimate, depend on this, that he thinks money is the best of your qualities.

---

* A bad man, according to a Scotch philosopher's opinion, is wholly the creature of the world: to a virtuous man, success in worldly matters is but a secondary object.

* Never suffer the prejudice of the eye to determine the heart.

The deference paid to wealth by beauty and ability, and the neglect shewn to virtuous poverty, are conjointly, or separately, potent enough to drive Patience from her anchorage, and shipwreck Content.

Few, very few, are familiar with the luxury of indulging their feelings: policy prohibits them; hence the genuine disposition of man is not visible.

To subdue the passions of creatures who are all passion, is absurd, impossible; to regulate them appears to be absolutely necessary: and what are those passions that make such havoc, causing striking differences, exalting and depressing the spirits, leading to extatic enjoyment, or plunging us in the severest afflictions; what are they more than the developement of our sensibility?

To preserve her reputation, or part with her chastity, is the most perplexing in the female's catalogue of concerns.

---

* "Nature bids thee not to love deformity; be content to discover, and do justice to its better part."

Lavater's *Aphorisms.*

The ore is not visible on the face of the earth: intrinsic worth is deeply earth'd.

Personal care does ever include a strong desire to please; at least one's self.

For one action, sometimes, many motives may be discovered: few commit the same action from the same motive, or with the same view.

* If this is an age of licence, or licentiousness, the succeeding may profit by it: one indulgence naturally includes another; and the liberty that was granted from capricious or libertine principles, may ultimately conduce to general good.

Henry the Eighth allowed no male servants to read the scriptures; nor any females, except ladies who had leisure, and might ask somebody the meaning. Edward the Sixth repealed this law.

Tho' it is questioned if any thing be new, it cannot be denied that the mind delights in novel combinations, without respecting the age of

---

* The limits of civil liberty are best ascertained after excessive freedom; 'tis grafting policy on experience.

of the materials. The chief aim of criticifm feems to be to give dates inftead of qualities.

Surmise is the goffamour that malice blows on fair reputations; the corroding dew that deftroys the choice bloffom. Surmife is primarily the fquint of fufpicion, and fufpicion is eftablifhed before it is confirmed.

Personal injuries have been frequently productive of national good: when fatisfactory redrefs is to be obtained no other way, injured greatnefs makes a public caufe of a private quarrel or affront. The welfare of the community is the fanctuary to which difappointment, or perfecuted villainy, flies for protection.

When inebriety appears lefs to be apprehended than its oppofite, liquor is fwallowed to an excefs. Remedies may be great evils, yet fome drunkards are empowered to excufe their practice. Sorrow lifts up the goblet, and ignorance of good remedies fills and replenifhes it.

Mortality is the refult of the laws of motion, and age is death's friendly preparative. All die who have lived; all have not lived who die.

We frequently dread what we see, yet cannot abstain from the sight: this is a species of self-inflicted torment, that cannot be easily accounted for. *

Each censures or praises, according to his particular aversion, suffering, or interest. †

When the atonement is not to be in kind, why should it be in blood? Such laws make us sanguinary! When the atonement is to be advantageous, it may make the accuser mercenary. ‡

Those who carry on the machinery of the puppets, think but little of the shew: nor would the Spanish peasant worship the *new image* of St. Nicholas, when he knew it was made from one of his plum trees, tho' he did the old one.

The contempt of danger may be equal in the assassin or the warrior, but their reputation can never be on a par. Reputation depends on the sphere you act in, and on circumstances.

---

* Anxiety goes far—for those that cannot be relieved.

† The neglect of the great is always excused as long as we continue to think them great.

‡ A robber is one who forcibly contracts a debt, at the forfeit of life or liberty.

An affaffin affumes, in his own perfon, the privilege of judging, and executing; yet the fuppofed or real injury has not been always done to himfelf alone; and what he complains of, he has frequently provok'd.

Many old monuments fhew the perfeverance and prejudice of the ancients more than their wifdom.

When people of warm temperament, and fhallow underftandings, are convinced, they will not cool before they attempt the conviction of thofe who know lefs than themfelves.

Silence is a fpecies of artificial fpeech; it negates, it affirms.

Silence is a trick when it impofes. Pedants and fcholars, churchmen and phyficians, abound in filent pride.

Youth are apt to think too much, and not enough, of women.

Sloth is a fallacious love of eafe; fluggards are moft uneafy: activity is neceffary to enjoyment; and moderate enjoyment is a ftate of eafe.

SLOTH is the torpidity of the mental faculties: the sluggard is a living insensible.

SOCIAL insufficiency characterizes sloth.

SLOTH reflects its own odiousness, for it detects and derides the sloth of others.

YOU may dress* a beautiful woman; you cannot ornament her.

SOLDIERS are not more like machines than the nymphs appropriated for *concupiscence*; pleasure or love it cannot be call'd.

SCHOLARS whose liberality exceeds not their understanding, are such niggards that they would conceal even the names of the authors they have read, if vanity, and poverty of information, did not cause them to repeat their sentiments.

PERFECTION is a chimera; a thousand causes arise to declare it. The difference of the materials, the workman, the end, motive, &c. But tho' perfection is not attainable, it should be ever before

---

* Aristonetus has the honour of first publishing what every man agrees to! " *When a fine woman is drest, she is beautiful; when she is undressed, she is beautiful:* or, as Mercerus has emphatically latinized it, *Induitur formosa est, exuitur ipsa forma est.*

before us, that the mind may be ftimulated to reach *poffible* excellence

More plagiarifts in fpeech than in writing. Our language is always like our manners.

Virtue unlocks no gates but thofe of heaven; and for this privilege fhe paid dearly whilft on earth.

Wives who build their confequence on the character of their hufbands, are in themfelves, generally, very infignificant creatures. Even culprits refufe not to divide in fame with their colleagues!

The favour refufed is the identical favour that we are moft folicitous for. There is a tyrannic monopoly in expectation: befides, what we do poffefs bears no comparifon in value with what we are defirous to poffefs. Though we have enough, the moft material part is wanting, if we are not confcious of having it.

Genius ftagnates in folitude: where merit fhines, merit is kindled.

Replies are not always anfwers.

In most concerns 'tis much more difficult to get the opportunity than to succeed; especially in courtship.

The sage laments his ignorance even before a a fool, and the most robust his inability before a woman!

Man *may* make a fine melody; woman is necessary to make up harmony. Solitaires are socially immusical.

Inexperience is ever most violent and enterprising

Concise replies, or answers, purposely include or exclude much information.

Woman has seldom more to grant than she has to receive; but the imaginary difference of her favours is immense.

Let a woman solicit, the favours of the *solicited* are then special: but man knows not how to market them.

Accept from appearance; continue or relinquish from experience. Welcome comes best after trial!

It

It destroys all relish to hear it pronounced, *Now you must eat.* Not an appointment is made without affixing to a minute the time of your hunger.

Youth has more obstacles to encounter in the practice of virtue, than senescence has to avoid pleasures that are incommensurate with virtue.

Money is oftentimes the only patent of nobility, besides lofty pretensions!

After a reputation or character for courage is once established, your word or prowess is seldom disputed.

* Objects of aversion or fear frequently become the idols that we adore; disgust is removed by attention, and timidity dispelled by frequent intercourse.

Maids who have received large presents, had rather be ungrateful than unchaste, if their assertions are to be credited: great donations are successful saps to the virgin fort.

---

* What is said of prejudice, may frequently apply to personal disgust:

"Les prejuges font les raisons des sots." *Voltaire.*

Indeed, disgust is often a personal prejudice.

When we see no joys superior to our own, the coarsest pleasures are enjoyed rapturously.

Deceit is only solicitous to accomplish its end.

Meditation is to the mind what a perspective glass is to the eye.

Women act more from love and duty, than from reason or prudence.

Society is indebted to every citizen who suffers patiently; tho' the poor sufferers have, alas! no benefit from their debtors.

When respect originates in sincerity,* it must be gratifying; 'tis a flight that the haughtiest mind dares not take to refuse its homage: yet modesty affects to withdraw from it.

To anticipate personal animadversion, is the surest way to defeat the petty assaults of snarling illiberality.

Defective

---

* Cardinal de Retz informs us, that Emire, the superintendant of the finances, dared to say in full council, *that sincerity was only made for merchants; and that the Maitre des Requêtes, who urged it as a reason in the king's affairs, deserved punishment.*

Defective knowledge should be amended, not punished; as personal liberty should be restrained, not annihilated.

Separate systems are as fatal to the commonwealth of happiness, as factions are inconsistent with patriotism, or sects with religion.

Practical integrity is the citizen's badge of distinction; his nobility is known by its effects. There is so much difference between a cunning man, and a wise man, in point of ability, as well as honesty, that craft often perishes for want of craft, whilst wisdom flourishes by its own strength.

The body, and its early prepossessions, generally have the same grave.

Those who are old in error, are old enough; the wisdom of youth is priority of intellect.

There is a particular disgrace that each of us dreads. The Indian archer represents the universe. Tho' a captive, and commanded by *Alexander* to shoot, he refused; for as he had neglected to practise for some days, he preferred death to the hazard of disgrace.

Liberty is necessarily bounded; licentiousness is naturally without bounds.

Man has many enemies besides himself. The Spanish adage exclaims, Guarda me dios, de mi! and the Italian, Dagli amici mi guardi dio, & de nemici mi guardero Io.

A conquest over error is of more importance than all the importations of Eastern monopolizers, or the victories of belliferous madmen.

If there exists one man of probity, more may be brought into existence by the same means that produced the first. A truism that all legislators are deaf to.

Crimes that cannot be prevented, should lose the name and character of *crimes*.

Events produce no change in certain dispositions; such may be safe friends, tho' they can never be pleasing companions. Some dispositions are easily offended, and pleased with difficulty; others pleased easily, and offended with difficulty. The first class are generally quarrelsome; the second, weak brained.

The multiplicity of inclosures open the door to trespasses.

Virtue insures virtue, and benevolence is a selfish sympathy.

Justice bridles sensuality, or we should be woman mad, and expence would have no tournequet on desire.

Repudiation is not often a punishment: adulterers can have lost all regard before they offend. To be attached to what they hate, would indeed be a punishment that the nation of Batta* could not exceed.

Philacity (self-love†) looks beyond the grave! Agesilaus was so sensible of his personal defects, that he would not suffer any picture or statue of him to be made during his life, or after his demise.

---

* In the north-west part of the island of Sumatra there is a nation known by the name of Batta; it is customary with these people to eat criminals convicted of treason or adultery.

† Curtius lived in a superstitious age, and devoted himself to an ignominious death, under the pretence of serving his country; but, in reality, to obtain a place among the gods, which, according to Plutarch, was the supposed honour to be obtained by those who devoted themselves to its service.

Our inclinations have no fixity; therefore the law should make no agreement perdurable that is formed for its gratification. Mezentius the tyrant joined the living to the dead by way of punishment; such is the state of the party whose prepossession is extinct.

To live for another is to alienate self from self, which is impossible.

If man* be naturally vicious, those who detest vice must detest man; a deduction that leads to antisocial principles.

Any thing rather than own a fault, tho' every thing depends on owning it. Seneca's wife, to conceal her own blindness, asserted, that the world was in darkness.

We are equal as to rights when we are equal as to faculty, and moral observance.

Forbearance will sometimes disarm a ferocious assailant; tho' 'tis a dangerous experiment to be resorted to where the powers of competition are incalculably unequal.

When

* " Homines natura fraudulenti sunt ut pisces spinosi."
 Architas apud Ælian.

WHEN nations can subdue their enemies by their manners, the instruments of war may be destroyed: this is possible; for the lowest ruffian pays a sort of respect to principle, character, forbearance, and non-resistance.

HANG the sword over the head, the body will be sufficiently suppliant: convince the world of superior merit, and the mind will be suppliant enough.

SERMONS have a negative perfection; they do not enforce obedience to what they contain.

THE extravagance of protestation as often discovers the kindness as the villainy of the human disposition; it evinces how much we wish to do, and what a weight morality is upon passion.

ADVERSITY, tho' it minifies the world's respect, magnifies the vanity of the poor wretches that it castigates. Unfortunately, this presumption that the afflicted entertain in their own behalf, retards their redemption, tho' it considerably abates the severity of their lot.

PUBLIC trial frequently overwhelms the unconfirmed sinner: after he has been launched into the full ocean of shame, the firmness of his
sensibility

sensibility is numbed; he has little farther to dread; he becomes a culprit *professionally*; and public punishment being the ultimatum of his career, 'tis encountered as a consequence constantly expected, therefore preparation has been made to encounter it with insensibility.

During the feudal times, there were many governors; now they are consolidated, and kings are, in appearance, the sole feudalists: but opinion, opinion reigns paramount over the universe!

'Tis the pride of the political reformer, or some stimulus of a more sordid nature, that makes him so precipitate. He should remember that truth envelopes the principles of its own increase, as error does the seeds of its own destruction; and that time is required to ripen what impatience would put forth in a crude state.

Many of those who *flourish* in the trappings of office, or display the insignia of distinction, even glory in debasement, and are vain of vanity. Read the English preacher *. " But it is thy own dexterity, and strength, which have gained thee this eminence! Allow it. But art thou proud that thou standest in a place where thou art

* Sterne.

art the mark of one man's envy, another man's malice, or a third man's revenge; where good men may be ready to suspect thee, and whence bad men will be ready to pull thee down? I would be proud of nothing that is uncertain."

Quietism is the extreme of forbearance. This modern species of pusillanimity results from frigid indifference, apathy, profound ignorance, or idleness.

Old monuments often lend a character to error that they want for themselves. Age is as often taken for the test of excellence, as youth is for demerit, exclusively, and fatally.

Sanguine dispositions require such advice as leads to the end, tho' destructive; and will receive it more thankfully than any salutary exhortations against the object; for in these cases the objects of consultation is always ardently desired.

'Tis, at times, impracticable to get credit either for the possession of virtues, or vices, if they are specified. Notwithstanding every man is occasionally what he ought to be perpetually.

Errors are good examples.

Craft

CRAFT works haftily and fecretly, not fe‑
curely or honourably; whilft *the graceful pride* *
*of truth knows no extremes, and preferves in every
latitude of life the right-angled character of man.*

WHEN obftinacy is avowed, when an intent
to perfift in it is declared, then madnefs contri‑
butes to the invigoration of error. Opiniatrety
and contradiction have not inaptly been compared
to paper kites; they only keep up whilft you
pull againft them.

'TIS an awful crifis † when the populace, fol‑
lowing the heels of an ambitious demagogue, or
artful incendiary, inflamed with a defire of re‑
venge for fancied wrongs, affume the adminiftra‑
tion of executive juftice.

AN old Englifh prieft has declared, that *a
fkilful manager of the rabble, fo long as they have
but*

* Paine's Rights of Man.

† The national affembly, immediately on the new miniftry
coming into office, paffed a decree, which they communicated
to the king and cabinet, that they would hold the miniftry (of
which Foulon was on,) refponfible for the meafures they were
advifing and purfuing; but the *mob*; incenfed at the appearance
of Foulon, and Berthier, his fon-in-law, tore them from their
conductors before they were carried to the Hotel de Ville, and
executed them *on the fpot*. A barbarian tore out the heart of
Berthier, and fixed it on his hanger; and the head was borne
aloft with that of his father.

but ears, needs never enquire whether they have any underſtanding.

INDIFFERENT poets write their own epitaphs* without leaving the materials for a ſtone to inſcribe it on: their ſtupidity is recorded *gratis.*

IF riches eſcape pity, they hardly ever eſcape cenſure: if they gain corporeal reſpect, they ſeldom have mental adoration.

FATALISTS may find apologies for their bad actions; but fatality once admitted, robs them of all merit for thoſe that are good: the pride of man ſtops the progreſs of truth when it derogates from his conſequence!

SYMPATHY of taſte, or ſimilarity of purſuit, forms more durable connexions than when a likeneſs of principle exiſts.

MENDICANTS have great comforts; they require a good addreſs †, tho' they can diſpenſe with

---

* Facile eſt epigrammata belle ſcribere.
May not as much be ſaid of epitaphs?

† "Beggars, by their daily obſervations of peoples' faces, make a ſhrewd gueſs at the tender and compaſſionate, and therefore lift up their tone, and purſue thoſe they eſteem merciful, with the greateſt paſſion and concern."

with a good dress; this dispensation is exclusively theirs: they have little to care for, and their expectations are great: of them nothing is required; and what forms their calamity, forms likewise a fund for its own emergencies.

Law *is* the wrong man's faint; he cannot approach the legal shrine without an offering.

In the grave the sprinkling of the fount scarcely dries.

When we reflect honour on our parents, our birth may be considered as a blessing to the great brotherhood.

On the agents of our will our remorse is often vented in furious chastisement: the second in villainy is the foremost in peril.

Pry not into the mysteries of Venus, if *desire* is all you have; her votaries must be effective; will alone is not sufficient to perform her rites: then leave them to *wishing girls and growing boys:*[*] youth wants only opportunity and an object.

Adversity exasperates fools, and dejects cowards; it draws out the faculties of the wise and

[*] Congreve.

and courageous; emboldens the timid, and puts the modest to the necessity of trying their skill: it awes the opulent, and makes the fallen industrious! Much may be advanced in favour of adversity: the worst of it is, it has no friends.

If peace is not to be found at home, is it not natural to expect that we should look for it abroad? The parents, and husbands, who know not this, may be brought to repent of their ignorance.

Even the great conceit of the little is not sufficient to reduce the little conceit of the great. 'Tis easier to despise a failing than to remove it.

The sole moral difference between co-citizens is this, *Each acts for the whole, or each acts for himself.* In this case civil war is declared by the unit, and, instead of the protection, he incurs the resentment of the aggregate body.

* So great is the concern we have for the fate of the beautiful, and the well-informed, the

brave,

---

* " A lady whom I have seen, a young lady, and one of the handsomest in the island, gave a grand dinner: furious at seeing a dish of pastry brought to the table overdone, she ordered her negro cook to be seized, and thrown into the oven,

yet

brave, or the great, that we hear of their vices with emotion; whilst those of the deformed, or the cowardly, the ignorant, or the poor, scarcely appear to exceed what we expected. To be distinguished is every thing.

When less labour is required from necessity, or compulsion, there will be more done, if quantity may be allowed to stand for quality. We are with difficulty persuaded of the advantages or beauties of any pursuit that is forced upon us.

A child may apprehend this proposition in an instant; the greatest disappointment must exist where there has been no disappointment.

In thought kings may be more, in act less, than men; they are heroes in history, gods amongst their courtiers, and idols set up by prejudice; useful as executive members of civil police, and deriders of the law when they are above it.

---

yet glowing with heat! And this horrible Megæra, (whose name I suppress out of respect to her family,) this infernal fiend, whom public execration ought to drive with every mark of abhorrence from society; this worthy rival of the too famous Chaperon, is followed, and admired; for she is rich and powerful."
Baron de Wimpfenn.

The lust of dominion innovates so impercep-
tibly, that we become complete despots before
our wanton abuse of power is perceived: the
tyranny first exercised in the nursery, is exhibited
in various shapes and degrees in every stage of
our existence.

* THOSE who make the idol, will fashion
and clothe it after their own conceit; and after
supplying it with attributes, produce testimonies
of them. What surprises those who are not
fully apprized of sacerdotal villainy is, that
these *god-makers* should afterwards fear the idol
they have set up.

QUALITIES of a contrary nature are not supposed to belong to the same individual, tho' we
hourly

---

* The Puelches, a tribe of Patagonians, who defeated the Spaniard Baldivia, have a notion of a future state, and imagine that after death they are to be transported to a country where the fruits of inebriety are eternal: there to live in immortal drunkenness, and the perpetual chase of the ostrich.

In respect to religion, they allow two principles, a good, and a bad one: the good they call the Creator of all Things, but consider him as one that never solicits himself about them: he is styled by some Soucha, or Chief in the Land of Strong Drink; by others, Guayara-cunnee, or, Lord of the Dead.

Extracts from a Pamphlet, written by Pennant, printed, but not published.

hourly affect to be surprized at the inconstant conduct of our intimates.

WRITERS who meditate, publish slowly; there is but little thought of, or in, hasty productions.

How averse we are to attend to all that Reason asserts, when she speaks against established errors!

AFFECTED ignorance, or wilful cecity, are a species of finesse practised in many eases besides conjugal infidelity. Livia, by Caligula called the Ulysses in woman's dress, when asked by what means she attained so much influence over Augustus, replied, *My secret it very simple: I have always behaved prudently; and I have never been indiscreetly curious neither about his affairs, nor even his gallantries, of which I was contented to appear ignorant.* This sort of toleration exhibits excessive love, or weakness; great senility, or duplicity!

OVID writes thus: Nos duo turba sumus: but a wise man is equal to a multitude.

WHERE the unity of counsel promises to be greatest, the diversity of knowledge must be least.

Those who are converted are convinced. Religion and politics have many converts; yet intereſt will apoſtatize them. Many bear the croſs who are not Chriſtians.

Flint emits ſparks of fire by a colliſion with ſteel, which could not be effected by the moſt violent ſtroke from wood.

Learning requires learning to bring it into play.

Motives are always complicated, frequently inſcrutable: they are often as little known to the agent as the beholder who comments on the action; yet the firſt will aſſume a conſequence for what does not depend on himſelf, and the ſecond a merit for imperfect reaſoning.

Well may ſages aver they know nothing, if mortals are compelled to act by inviſible and impervious direction.

Shallow reaſoners are always puzzled if they digreſs from their theme; yet if they have the *cacoethes loquendi*, they are ſure to do it.

Talking fools are ſocial peſts; buſy abſurdities.

Age is not often suspected, tho' it generally is suspicious.

Authoritative exemptions are frequently set up, that in the progress of time create a false reverence.

The exact degree of rational wisdom or prosperity is not to be ascertained by the probity, sagacity, imbecility or villainy of its rulers; nor from the obedience or refractory disposition of the people.

The political is as precarious as the physical atmosphere: the causes too are as occult.

How *conveniently* women can offend! how *conveniently* they can pardon offences! No animal temporizes like a woman!

Strained sensibility causes the actions of the rest of the world to appear, on many occasions, brutal.

Comparison is the mirror of beauty, or deformity.

Corporeal indulgence does not, as a matter of course, exclude mental purity; for the mind
and

and the body are not connected in their refponfibility; tho' the former, in many cafes, directs the latter: therefore, if an honeft woman may be a whore, a whore may be an honeft woman.

Repeating the fame act with one or with different men, makes an immenfe difference in the value of a male or female: the difference of gallantry and crime.

When the effects of crimes or favours ceafe, punifhment and obligation fhould alfo ceafe. It may be fafer to perpetuate the latter than the former.

If philofophers and phyficians could effect what they propofe, we fhould be immortal indeed!

The immenfe views of theory produce good effects in practice.

If there is fometimes an advantage in delay, there is alfo a fecurity in difpatch. Lucullus conquered two of the moft potent of all the kings by two very different expedients, celerity and delay: he broke the flourifhing power of Mithridates by fpinning out the time; and that of Tigranes by pushing on without allowing him leisure to look about him.

Greatness possesses to the power to act, and the wisdom to adopt, its energies to the occasion.

For want of opportunity and power, there is much forbearance practised.

Negative virtue conceals the most hideous portion of moral deformity.

There is much difficulty in getting women or wine to suit the palate; there is more difficulty in enjoying them with moderation.

The danger that is remote is generally considered as precarious; and when the earnest of pain is pleasure, it will frequently be accepted.

Many are discontented with the name of idler, who are nevertheless content to do worse than nothing.

A certain indication of error is wincing at an appellation.

When women know a single partiality a man has, they decide instantly upon the whole of his character.

'Tis from a particular virtue, or vice, all are appreciated, except the rich.

Reason is not a private property, tho' the use of it is a particular privilege: those who usurp it pay dearly for their boldness.

Our greatest wants arise from the part of our possessions that is unemployed.

Great occurrences can occur but seldom, therefore they astonish.

To the inertness of our energies we are indebted for the major portion of surprize.

The vicious may be, the virtuous must be friends: those whose views are alike may co-operate, but their views must be alike good for this co-operation to be attended with sincerity.

The friend's * friend is our friend, for we naturally suppose the intimate alliance of the virtuous.

* A Swifs proverb.

Tho' *gifts* may be acceptable, dependence is hateful to the woman who adds to it the surrender of her person.

Tout amant* qui donne n'eſt jamais bien aimé.

Where the merit of the atchievement conſiſts only in the difficulty which attends it, no beneficial conſequences are produced by it. Many are the idle efforts of petty ambition!

Two drops of foul water are not more alike than the pair who, by mutual crimination, think to gloſs over their conjugal infidelity.

More pains is taken to appear good, or make vice paſs for its oppoſite, than is required to be really virtuous.

We are puniſhed, not governed, by the laws. Count Stolberg has, with much acuteneſs, diſcovered, that in politics there is frequently a dead letter, but a living ſpirit. Manners make laws uſeleſs. The ſpirit of wiſdom, benevolence, and moderation, deſcending from father to ſon, will better ſecure the freedom of a people, than all the ſplit-hair theories of any conſtitution. In

† *Le Grand.*

In good families good citizens are formed.

Our enemies increase with our conquests, and our poverty with our possessions.

It may be doubted whether we profit by change of circumstances, tho' we can by change of opinion.

When reason and passion are in equal proportion, energy may be expected, and such effects as excite our rapturous wonder.

Rapture is the extatic state of admiration.

Travellers who eat with an appetite, never cast their eyes towards the kitchen.

Care to feed includes something beastly, or over-delicate.

Guard against assumed folly. Tarquin despised Junius Brutus, yet he unthroned him.

Great characters are seldom known; great merit is as seldom understood. Greatness is, in fact, only a term of comparison, tho' 'tis not always allowed to see what is greater than itself.

'Tis the inferior mind that cries out that is great.

The distinctions of a court are now of most value within its precincts; tho' they are still coveted most by those dwarf minds that wish to be most respected out of a court.

Most of our follies have a reference to the opinion of others.

Truth lies in a small compass! *The Aristotelians say, all truth is contained in Aristotle in one place or another. Galileo makes Simplicius say so, but shews the absurdity of that speech by answering, All truth is contained in a lesser compass, viz. in the alphabet.*

Truth is the history of facts!

Good companions are seldom good writers; 'tis seldom that good writers are good companions.

Different situations require different faculties. An observation so trite, that 'tis only repeated, that the surprise of those who have nothing to be surprised at may cease.

There is a confiderable portion of fociety fet apart and diftinguifhed by the appellation of the vulgar. Yet thofe who caufe this diftinction, this degradation of their fellows, are the moft familiar with the epithet, and ufe it with moft acerbity.

Pride is not always difgraceful; tho' what we pride ourfelves on is very frequently.

Act from advice that you cannot comprehend, or act contrary to your judgment, how can you be perfuaded that you act properly or juftly?

A man at the fummit of his glorious career, has frequently no more felf-direction than the hands of his watch.

The art of living upon good terms with the world, appears to confift, chiefly, in the indulgence and affumption of falfe feelings.

One of the greateft inftances of cruelty is to require what you condemn.

Conceit and confidence are both of them cheats; the firft always impofes on itfelf, the fecond frequently deceives others too.

Is there more ingenuity exercised to deceive others or ourselves?

Affliction is continually courted, and nourished; seldom is it merited, or conquered.

Sufference is sometimes a species of consent; covetousness often embraces what is inimical to our peace. Oppression falls indiscriminately, and idleness gives quarter to our enemies.

Ugly and handsome women are alike in this respect; both are elated when their flatterers commend them for qualities which they do not possess.

Vanity must be gratified, tho' the means differ.

In the history of every creature's life may be discovered a gradation of passions, humours, virtues, and vices, strengthening and declining with age, unfolding themselves with opportunity, or concealed from the dominacy of their superior.

We are all alike in the branches, but not in their proportions.

Age and cunning find immenfe and frequent advantages in the tractability of youth.

Age is a great ufurper.

* Laconism is the expreffive felicity of wifdom and affection.

Those who know how to fay much alone, can fpeak much in a little.

Grief, gravity, and humilty, tho' they are hacknied difguifes, will continue to impofe as long as they are accompanied with grace or virtue.

Manner and character are great impoftors.

That we are affured may, or muft be, we ftruggle moft to fupport.

---

* What fafhionable lover has ever painted his paffion for a lovely miftrefs with fuch brief tendernefs and effect as the village chorifter of Hanover did on the death of a young and beautiful country girl, with whom he was enamoured? After erecting in the cemetry of the cathedral a fepulchral ftone to her memory, he carved, in an artlefs manner, the figure of a blooming rofe on its front, and infcribed beneath thefe words: *C'eft ainfi qu'elle fut.*

A Pagan made this reflection when he saw a girl cry as if she had been torturing on the rack over a broken pitcher; and a woman with her hair loose, her hands lifted up to heaven, her eyes swoln with crying, and her discourse nothing but despair for the loss of a little infant. *Well, after all these Christians talk of heaven, and their hopes of eternal life, 'tis certain there can be no philosophy in their religion, or else they are very ignorant of it: they must be very silly people, that hav'nt taught their children to know that pitchers would break; and their women, that little children will die.*

In the streets of every metropolis wanton mercenaries gain a sustenance by unhallowed prostitution, that is denied afterwards to their actual misery.

The senses are the best pay-masters.

Zealous partizans are ready to destroy their zeal by excessive jealousy or envy, unless interest chains down their passions.

Service is the step to elevation, amongst those of superior intellect, or violent ambition.

Some

Some are too wife, or too difficult, to be pleased.

If diffatisfaction arifes from any caufe but fuperior difcrimination, it is a vice.

The higher the weak are elevated, the more they are enfeebled: the more courage is depreffed, the more it accumulates.

There is an allotted fphere for every defcription of ability!

Always give a bawd her price, yet you may be ill ferved; if you bate her, you are fure to be tricked.

No good bargain can be made with the wicked.

* Our enemies deferve our greateft attention always, fometimes our extreme refpect; from them comes amendment and correction.

---

* On mere indifferent objects, common bounty will fhew relief; but when our bittereft foe
    Lies funk, difarm'd, and defolate, then, then
    To feel the mercies of a pitying God,
    To raife him from the duft, and that beft way
    To triumph over him, is heroic goodnefs.
                      Thomfon's Sophonifba.

Amendment is the advance of improvement; correction the check of error.

Great characters are their own heralds, tho' they have thousands to announce them.

Doubt, and you damn a reputation; but virtue once admitted, is speedily in a state of exaltation.

The surprize resulting from disappointment of promised excellence is great; and for this there are many reasons to be assigned, besides that the rapidity of praise is only to be equalled by that of abuse when once an object is fixed upon.

A beggar's garments seldom fit, nor are they often fitting. Our cloathing comes from a capricious purveyor.

Many hymeneal couples do not separate because they cannot: so much for the perpetuity of the bond, and so much for the cruelty of the institution! Affections fluctuate; but the law fixes hypocrisy.

Silence is sometimes a noble way of passing over wrongs; but in a pusillanimous sufferance insensibility is exhibited.

A fool

A fool struck Cato in the bath; when he expressed some sorrow for the action, Cato had forgot it. Seneca says, *Melius putavit non agnoscere quam ignoscere.*

Those who cannot retort, will assuredly remember the offence.

Make no injuries for thyself; in this respect the world will become thy factors.

Scorn not the advice of an inferior; the underling of fortune may be, in merit, thy superior. Situation never determines ability.

Women had rather that men should guess in the gross, than that they should be reduced to detail the explanation of their meaning. Those who mean fairly need not object to scrutiny.

Enjoyment comes before possession, then with possession generally comes disgust: so that we have before we have, and have not when we have. This is probably one of the rifest paradoxes to be met with.

A paradox is self-evident to those who can see without prejudice.

'Tis

'Tis not always the strongest mind that delights in the strongest emotions.

Sailors, gamesters, and soldiers, languish, generally speaking, if they are in a tranquil state; yet this tranquillity is the very state that the sage endeavours to arrive at.

Avarice and brutal valour prefer throwing for great stakes.

We are taxed heavily for what we possess, whether 'tis fame, wisdom, or fortune; and for what we do not possess we pay heavily.

What is worth having, is worth retaining at some expence and hazard: what is worth obtaining, is necessarily obtained with difficulty.

Miracles are more extraordinary and remarkable for the miraculous effects they have produced in the intellectual than in the natural kingdom.—Miracles that can be explained lose their essence.

All we have to do on this terrene stage, is to learn our allotted part; repeat it before the immense auditory of society; correct the errors of the performance, give place to the succession of younger actors, and then quit the scene.

As nothing is to be remembered, we may felicitate ourselves on the conceit that leads us to believe there is something to *appear to be* worth remembering: this conceit is the earthly actor's support.

* GENERALLY there is an excellent part in the character of our neighbour, and as well an infamous one in our own disposition, that we know not of.

'Tis safe to have a good opinion of others †. Of ourselves the excess is sometimes attended with danger.

'Tis not easily possible to be reconciled with those who corrected us rudely.—What we endeavour to amend in others is always for our own advantage:

---

* Every writer issues fresh directions for the study of man; it cannot be otherwise, whilst a marked and essential difference exists in the species. All agree with Abbé de Bellegarde, that we are interested to know ourselves and others; yet the impossibility of knowing either seems to be unknown to all.

† Though you do not find men so perfect as they might be, take them for what they are, or their amendment is rendered impossible.

advantage: when the humour of the party is confulted, 'tis to facilitate the progrefs of reproof.

In order to form a tolerable opinion of certainty of certain ladies charms, we fhould be tolerable connoiffeurs in the art of painting.—Whilft fictitious ornaments are admired, natural embellifhments will be neglected.

We often fee without crediting, and credit without feeing.—Prejudice throws many impediments in the way of belief; and many lures to caufe it. *

Men of probity are always the moft hurt at their own defalcation, tho' not the moft furprized if they are wife.—The pride of integrity wifhes to make moral rigour fuperior to circumftances.

Be deaf to the quarrelfome, blind to the fcorner, and dumb to thofe who are mifchievoufly inquifitive.—Urbanity or wifdom only demand attention.

Those who are conftrained to folicit for affiftance are really to be pitied; thofe who receive

* Which caufes the greateft portion of evil, bad propenfities, or hoftility to fuch as are good?

ceive it without, are to be envied; but those who bestow it unasked, are to be admired.

Goodness is not the patron, but the associate of merit: when merit is relieved, none, save the meritorious, are found to rejoice.

Nations must be strongly afflicted who fly to war for the remedy.—The diseased seldom chuse a good cure.

* To your neighbour's mode of living 'tis necessary to conform in part.

The relish for existence is lessened if our habits are destroyed.

The affection of our servants repays the expence of keeping them.—A good servant is the being of all others we ought most to serve.

The best are deceived by the worst, and the best will sometimes deceive the worst.

Ingenuity is an over-match for morality, and the most moral must yield to necessity.

When

---

* " He who would be useful to mankind must accommodate himself to their manners." *Schiller.*

When greatnefs provides its meal without pillaging the tables of their inferiors, no eye will fcowl at their profufion.

* O Rois, fi la pompe a pour vous tant de grandes charmes, qu'elle ne coûte, point nos foupirs, & nos larmes."

We have two claffes of proficients; the clever, and the too clever.

Nick-names often apprize us of what men are not.

Poor wine at the table of a rich hoft is an infult without an apology. Urbanity ufhers in water that needs no apology, and gives a zeft to the worft vintage.

There is a mode of prefenting that gives value to any thing.

The welfare of ftates will always depend more on thofe who govern, than on the laws that are laid down to govern by.

Between pity and deteftation the man of fentiment is divided.

Those

* C. Da Baar.

Those who lose nothing when they lose all, are the most deplorable of mortals: and those who gain nothing when they gain the most, deserve the greatest portion of pity.

Necessity frequently causes us to do what reason cannot; yet reason makes us do that which necessity alone without it could effect.

* What the Count de Tessin said of a prince, is a document for every man. Il n'y a pas de science à faire ce qu'on veut mais c'est le caractere d'un grand prince, de ne vouloir, & de ne faire que ce qu'il doit.

The courser appears to go from inclination; the sorry jade from the sting of the whip; but *the man* acts from conviction.

Robust people are apt to mistake their strength for valour, and the debility of their antagonists for proofs of pusillanimity.—The effect it is that confirms opinion.

Excessive

† Malheureux alui qui s'imagine que rien n'est plus aisé que de gouverner en un état; mais plus malheureux encore est le pays, dont le souverain font l'importance de ses devoirs sans avoir la volonté de les remplir.

Moser.

Excessive prudence, or zeal, have often destroyed the best planned enterprizes. In bold undertakings, more will be gained than lost by rashness than timidity.

That kingdom is accursed where a hero presides *.—The exploits of Charles are to this day remembered in Sweden, so is the peaceable reign of their Frederic.

Many will proudly refuse to wear their neighbour's cast-off cloaths, who meanly take up with their bad habits.—Prejudice is blind to all difference.

Decided villains are less, much less dangerous than amphibious moralists; creatures of doubtful probity.

With the thief we are never at a loss how to act, tho' we do not act properly.

What is violently applauded, or condemned, may have merit; but what is both violently applauded, *and* condemned, must possess intrinsic value.

* Alexander despised comedians; nay, he asserted that they were born only to deprave the morals of mankind! Could the vices of all the comedians that ever existed contribute as much as his single example did to perjorate the manners of the world?

value.—Between the extremes of opinion lies true excellence.

How much the juſtice of antiquity is diſgraced by their depreciation of female faculties,* and their tyranny in depriving of equal civil rights!—Moral equality is the fair adminiſtration to each of whatever is due to each.

Tho' the injury done to a worthy citizen is ſingle and perſonal, he is not called upon to reſent; but many are called up to obtain a redreſſal.—Reſentment is the fiery humour of a wounded mind.

Cowards love not peace ſo much as the brave.—Principle often attaches ſtronger than conſtitution.

Want of uniformity and independence bankrupts pride.

Learning

Generoſity is different from humanity: thoſe two qualities, which, at firſt ſight, ſeem ſo nearly allied, do not always belong to the ſame perſon. Humanity is the virtue of a woman, generoſity of a man. The fair ſex, who have commonly much more tenderneſs than men, have ſeldom ſo much generoſity. That women rarely make conſiderable donations, is an obſervation of the civil law. Raro mulieres donare ſolent.

Smith's Theory of Moral Sentiments.

Learning without wealth, is the jeſt and ſcorn of ignorance: before the rich ſcholar ignorance crouches, and affects aſtoniſhment.

Many good qualities are not ſufficient to balance a ſingle want—the want of money.

Consistency cauſes even vice and folly to be tolerated; ſomething to be reſpected.

Those whom the wicked commend *may* be good; and wickedneſſes may be converted by commendation. When praiſe* is an involuntary tribute, it may come indiſcriminately from all deſcriptions.

Morality is ſupported by demonſtration, as well as any of the mathematical ſciences.

What is neceſſary and poſſible to do for the welfare of others, or ourſelves, that morality requires ſhould be done.

Personal devotion ſeldom fails to obtain its object.

Antisthenes

---

* Antiſthenes, upon hearing that he was commended by certain wicked perſons, exclaimed, *Good Gods! what evil have I done?*

Antisthenes* rudely rejected Diogenes: after his surprise he bowed his head, and said, *Strike*, if you please: while you discourse in public, you will find no stick that is hard enough to keep me from you." The philosopher, overcome by this declaration, received him for a disciple.

The road to greatness is servility; and to servility, idleness.—Activity performs prodigies, and prosperous servility includes much of it.

Fair pretensions are expensive, and will chain you down to an eternal poverty.

A painter spent the whole of his fortune in a court of law, without bringing his cause to issue: he afterwards drew a picture of justice supported by hunger and thirst!

Strength and art are the columns that support the social fabric.

Pascal asserted, that it was easier to find monks than reasons—What convention makes reason its regent?

Where

* This Athenian was a scholar of Socrates, and the chief of the Cynics.

WHERE you please, there you may enjoy the highest esteem; perhaps, even be beloved.—Insure your own pleasure by pleasing others.

THOSE who conceal their age do not hide their folly.

MORE blush for a silver-coloured hair, than for an act of folly.

MANY fall who conceit that virtue dwells on high: many more overshoot the mark, yet their false flights are not sufficient to destroy the romantic.

MUCH conceit in virtue: more in the mode and means of obtaining it.

* THAT insect thou hast crushed beneath thy feet, was more curiously composed than thyself! Alas! like many others, his claims could not postpone his destruction.

THERE is very little philopanousiasm on earth.

FAST

---

* " Tous les miracles de l'intelligence reposant sous la mousse, nous les foulons aux pieds, & ils nous auroient été inconnu sans le microscope."

Mercier.

Fast for a day, and you may feast for years.

One act of self-denial often determines the fortune of those who have sacrificed.

The severity of confinement makes the captive ingenious; restraint has many active prisoners in its cell.

Socrates has affirmed, that women in mischief are wiser than men.

Should huntsmen once conceive that the human species are proper objects to gratify their venatorial passion, they may *as easily* find reasons to justify the practice, as they can for the sportive destruction of those animals that inhabit the woods.

What certain people will, they will have is right.

When the hero disdains to speak, his actions are in a full blaze of eulogy.

" Let me repeat it : * He only is great who has the habits of greatness; who, after performing what none in ten thousand could accomplish,

* Lavater's *Aphorisms*.

passes on like Samson, and tells neither father or mother of it."

Slight is the value affixed to labours we do not relish, or ingenuity that is not understood, unless interest, or the controuling voice of fashion, command approbation; then it is great indeed, and in full proportion to our ignorance and servility.

Every active citizen is a laborious adventurer.

There is a fitness of disposition admirably calculated for the state of friendship; it is fashioned with mechanical exactitude, and tallies as the screw to its socket.

Friends are pillows on which we repose, or cordials that inspirit the system without injuring it.

Activity is liable to commit some injuries; but indolence is sure to do no good.

What we cannot avoid is venial; what we leave undone, criminal.

Wisdom, and rigid honesty, cannot be united in equal portions. Those who unite wisdom to honesty, will, alas! always have more wisdom than honesty.

NOTHING makes depravity more hideous than modesty of any kind. Erroneous is the maxim that declares, *False modesty is the most decent of all impositions.*

WHEN we declare that we are convinced, we are frequently not more than half persuaded; now women are fully persuaded frequently before they are half convinced.

APPARENT conviction is used as a finesse to retard the current of impertinence, or trifling chat.

CROAKERS are living repositories of evil, composed of materials that are physically and morally combined in error.

FREQUENTLY we quarrel with what we have on account of those things we have not; and feeling the present to be inconvenient, set down that the future must assuredly be worse.

COMEDIANS are not actors; they are only imitators of actors.

GREAT atchievements are leaders; the hero feebly follows their steps.

Ships to sail must yield to the wind.

'Tis easy to oblige a fool; and, in return, his silence becomes an obligation: 'twill act as a drawback on merit, when 'tis commended by insignificance, and the shallow boast of its favour.

The difficulty is frequently less in obliging than in obliging conveniently.

It would often puzzle us to account for our fits of anger or pleasure; tho' 'tis expected others should be brought to account for theirs.

The mastery we arrogate is disgraceful, even if we have mastered ourselves.

Many have been ruined *by* their fortunes; many have escaped ruin by the want of fortune. To obtain it, the great have become little, and the little, great.

Supineness and activity terminate where the other sets out from.

Indigence exists by the vanity of opulence: the vanity of poverty is gratifying; but its pride is death to the grandees of the earth.

We despise aukward imitations; but to be excelled is intolerable.

The deaf are not so unhappy as those whose organs are more imperfect suppose them to be.

Those who are forced to hear all, either wince or whine.

Tiberius Gracchus* had unquestionably ascended to Reputation's summit: his virtues were greater than his honours, and his honours were as great as they could be.

The act brings the honour, though it is not always stampt with public acknowledgment.

The strength of the mind may be seen, imperfectly, in speech; deeds affix the portion of intellect.

Those who think with energy † may speak with energy: those who think and speak, may act with energy.

---

* See Plutarch.

† "Ceux qui pensent fortement parlent fortement."
Voltaire.

The husband's honour is in his own keeping; that of his wife is in her own poſſeſſion too, but the huſband poſſeſſes the key that ſecures it.

* " Thou mayſt hold an elephant with a
       thread, eat fire
And not be burnt, or catch birds with deſire;
Quench flame with oil, cut diamonds with glaſs,
Pierce ſteel with feathers;—this thou mayſt bring
       to paſs
Sooner than hope to ſteal the huſband's right,
Whoſe wife is honeſt, and no hypocrite."

Vanity ſtrengthens diſſenſion more than diſlike does; and pride cements friendſhips cloſer than merit can.

Choose your intimate in any ſeaſon, except when the ſun ſhines: during the ſtorm, zeal and hatred, ſocial or anti-ſocial principles, are put into the crucible.

Those who value time know how little there is to enjoy, and that alone is enjoyable whilſt in ſeaſon.

" You

---

* The City Night-Cap, *a Comedy,* by Davenport.

"You never saw a vulgar character difinterestedly fensible of the value of time*."

CERTAINLY there are periods in the lives of the moft deformed and aged, when they refolve to ape the gallant.

THOSE who are not womens' fools, are in danger of reverencing extravagantly fomething lefs rational; yet to be at once obfequious and incapacitated followers of thefe regents of the heart is the acme of folly.

YOUTH is full of pretenfions; and age pretends to youth.

RESTLESS as his defire is the being who labours to be thought any thing, or every thing, but what he is.

IF you have no principles, you can have no character; acting in conformity to certain well-digefted rules, proves principle; the exercife of principle conftitutes character.

THERE is no fafer principle than is—Embrace the firft that appears fafer than the laft.

* Lavater.

He is not the most known who receives the most salutations, loved, or admired.

Multitudes hear of a name; few can investigate the nature * of the man!

Assassins seldom know the use of arms; those who frequently assassinate.

The soldier of reason is invincible whilst he is mortal.

Virtue, in its extremes, excludes many companions; Vice, in its extremes, includes many friends—amongst the rich.

Extreme vice, and equal poverty, is always extreme in its sufferance and persecution.

Religion is local!—" What care I † to see a man run after a sermon, if he cozens and cheats as soon as he comes home?"

The

---

* The irritability of his nerves has sometimes caused him to do wrong; it has perhaps led him to be guilty of extravagancies that may have made them who did not perfectly know judge hardly of him. His first wife said, when she was dying, " *My poor Zimmerman, who will comprehend you?*"

Tissot's Life of Zimmerman.

Seldon.

The difgust is greater againſt hereditary honours than againſt hereditary wealth.—What cecity!

'Tis fafer to drain the ſtream of honour dry, than prevent the free and equal circulation of wealth.

Less fatisfaction arifes from the arrival of what was ardently hoped for, than from thofe things that arrive unexpectedly.—Good, and unthought-of, is always fure of great welcome.

Foreign commerce leads to war, and war to commerce: one terminates in luxury, the other in blood.—'Tis impoffible to *gain* by what it is our greater intereſt to fupprefs! Domeſtic trade is neceſſary.

Many facrifices are proffered at the altar of religion, that would difgrace the altar of folly.—The external fymbols of all religions fhew the childifh ſtate of man, and his puny ideas of an Omnipotent!

We *regard* fometimes what we cannot eſteem: and look with apparent calmnefs on what we violently deteſt.

INFANT attachment or prejudice is frequently too powerful for its grown reason.

WHEN certain folks volunteer to explain—a puzzle * is the consequence!

IN mobs all are desirous to speak; tho' none know how or when to begin.—Henry IV. passing by a small town, was met by several deputies, who presented themselves before him in order to compliment him. One of them was proceeding according to his design, when an ass began to bray loudly—"Gentlemen," said the king, "one "at a time, if you please; or I shall be able to "understand nothing."

NATIONAL power depends on the strength of its neighbours: its welfare on itself.

POLITICAL importance is the vanity of states!

SINGULARITY commonly disdains to account for it, for want of reason, or through a conviction, that its defence would make few proselytes.

HOTTENTOTS

---

* "Examine closely whether he who talks of illustration means to clear up, or only to glitter, dazzle, and confuse."
LAVATER's *Aphorisms.*

Hottentots answer thus to all interrogatories that concern their strange manners; " 'Tis the custom of the Hottentots; they never act differently."

Those who will not *condescend*, as they term it, should be extremely careful not to assume any sort of deportment indicative of superiority.

Our exactions exceed our tribute.

In infancy most habits of iniquity are fitted to the pliable body.

'Tis cruel to punish maturity for consequences it has had no concern in: the man is not, tho' he *was*, the infant.

Folly, hope, and obstinacy, appear in the amount of the wager, and the eagerness with which it is staked.

We place a large seal on the bond of our own absurdities!

The ass who cannot exonerate himself is to be pitied: if he could, but will not, he is contemptible: if he knows his oppression, and his incapacity,

incapacity, he calls for a sympathy that would embrace the first opportunity to relieve him.

Passive endurance is exemplary; it has many causes besides indolence.

Superfluity creates necessity; and necessity superfluity. Take care to be an economist in prosperity: there is no fear of your being one in adversity.

Man neither divides well, or fairly, either for himself, or the brotherhood.

Characters of contrary pursuits stagnate for want of a theme for conversation; they become reciprocally dull and dissatisfied, till the topics of the day are adopted by tacit consent.

Wrapt up in the importance of our particular pursuits, all others appear insignificant: politics, and the weather, are common concerns, and commonly acceptable.

Fashionable folks think every pleasure of life is included within their circle, and that the residue of mankind are miserable; yet the greatest portion of the community pass this identical circle

circle without dreaming of its exclufive advantages.

Fancy works up fuperiority to nothing beyond commiferation.

Many are content if they can but attract the eyes of the populace, tho' it be only as they afcend the boards of the fcaffold.

Even in the modes of death, diftinctions are eminent, and numerous, and coveted.

The accufation of being romantic, comes either from a cold heart, or a correct judgment.

Romantic difpofitions carry fingularity to an excefs, from principles of generofity, or extent of paffion.

The public entertain not more bad opinions than are entertained of it.

Virtue begs from talents the pen to write the anathema of falfe paffions.

One great atchievement is the harbinger of many; and the firft ill deed that is accomplifhed is the parent of many.

Success

Success in vice, or virtue, is an encouragement to perfift: and example is prolific.

Good companions are neither mere fcholars, or detailers of anecdote: nor will over-ftrained courtefy make one. Thofe whofe fociety is always refrefhing to the fpirits, have the art to take objects as they rife, and make of them themes for converfation.

To difcufs a metaphyfical point, and to the exclufion of all others, and to perfift whilft the eye is gloating on a beautiful paffage, is ill-timed, and dry abftraction. Lavater writes, *The fool feparates his object from all furrounding ones; all abftraction is temporary folly.*

General fatire * appears to the culprit an open blow at his private villainy: and raillery cannot be fo delicate, as not to appear grofs in the eyes of the little.

---

* Phædrus was a native of Thrace, and was brought to Rome as a flave: whilft in the fervice of Auguftus, he procured his favour, and was made a free man. In the reign of Tiberius he tranflated into Iambic verfe the Fables of Efop, and was perfecuted by Sejanus, who, confcious of his own delinquency, fufpected that he was obliquely fatirized in the commendations beftowed on virtue by the poet.

Who does well to call the cap his own, when it has been thrown out merely to make a scramble?

Never can prudence be allowed to stand as a proof of genius, tho' it may of caution, learned from precept or experience.—Genius is always associated with a fearless disposition.

The rich are full of distress; and their visionary wants are more afflicting, and more perplexing to gratify, than the substantial wants of the poor.

Poverty admits of this definition; a state where money alone is wanting.

'Tis unfair to require mortals to be satisfied with their condition because they were born to it: for their own peace they should be satisfied when they cannot amend it.—Content is the sweetest state of opinion.

Those women who wed for money, are in the likeness of hypocrites; they live in a long prostitution, and have not always the plea of necessity.

Rewards are proportioned to success, not to merit.—Success is itself a reward.

A PROSTITUTE

A PROSTITUTE is a female who yields up her perfon to the temporary gratification of one who complies with certain conditions.

UNTRIED fpirits are lefs daftardly or courageous, than they really fuppofe themfelves to be.—Imagination is corrected by trial.

WHEN nature revolts, cuftom is at ftrife with propriety.—Follow Nature's impulfes the inftant they are perceptible; fhe never antedates.

THOSE who affect to be fuperior to obligations, take infinite pains to deceive, mortify, and expofe themfelves.—The commerce of civil life depends on reciprocal kindnefs.

ILL-DIRECTED activity of mind has produced all thofe great national diforders that fociety fo feelingly deplore! Indolence lives fupinely content within its mud-walled cabin; the inftructed fearch, orderly, for a more comfortable habitation; but ftrong animal fpirits, without the guidance of reafon, fet forth tumultuoufly to raife a palace they can never give permanence to.

DISCRETION is leaft where capability is ftrongeft.

WHEN

When a man obliges you to talk about a beaſt, is it not natural to ſuppoſe, after his example, that you are in company with one?—Many delight to conceit that they are poſitively addreſſing the identical character that they are ſpeaking of.

Fools with bookiſh knowledge, are children with edged weapons; they hurt themſelves, and put others in pain.—*Un demi ſçavant eſt plus ſot qu'un ignorant.*

We wonder at the automata of the mechanic, without noticing the ſpeaking ſtatues that ſtand in the way of ſociety.—What is perpetually before us is not ripeſt in our memory, or the common ſubject of our reflection.

If fortune is all, to be a fool is to be fortunate.—Fools are the envy of thoſe who are but a degree beyond them on the ſcale of rationality.

We cannot raiſe the opiniative value of life too high. This declaration is an expreſs contradiction to the author * who thinks that the moral fault of tragedians is giving too much importance to life and death.

Those

---

* Chamfort.

Those who dread death as a relief, will assuredly possess the art of making life valuable.

There is a turn for all!—Fools give so much voluntarily, that they have nothing left to answer the instant of requisition.

Interruption is nothing from a superior; from inferiors 'tis insupportable.

Those who can bear interruption patiently, are defective in the head or heart.

Challengers, who make the first advance, are shallow wits, if they lay themselves open; and if they are incapable of defence, they deserve to be beat.

The scholars who met the old woman that was driving her asses is apposite. " Good morrow, good mother of asses," said one of them. " Good morrow, good children," quoth the woman.

Certain members of the forlorn sisterhood, vulgularly hight *old maids*, deserve commiseration more than contempt, (especially from such as are conjugally happy;) for their eyes are not only mortified with the aspect of felicity they

cannot

cannot attain, and their ears with scornful insinuations, but all their whole system is likewise disturbed *with the agonies of unaccomplished love!

Sneerers are all copyists; the subject, and the object, are both pointed out by prejudice.

In some cases a faint refusal is a positive consent; in others, a faint consent is a positive refusal. Worldly adepts † easily decypher the mysteries of negation and affirmation.

We appear to yield when we defy; and submit when we subdue.

News-hunters have great leisure, with little thought; much petty ambition to be thought intelligent, without any other pretension than being able to communicate what they have just learnt. The instruction and intelligence of fools is but a minute old when 'tis delivered.

In

---

* Dryden.

† As there is a *no* which the man of gallantry perfectly understands to mean *yes*, so there is a *yes* which the man of delicacy perfectly understands to mean *no*. In the first instance you will discover, if you have any discernment, that, while the lips refuse, the heart concedes; and you will therefore be little mortified by the refusal: in the last instance, if you have any feeling, you will discern, that while the lips grant, the heart denies; and you will be as little flattered by the concession.

Mrs. Pruilla.

In England news is the manna of the day.

Those who have too much, have little to enjoy; those who have too little, have much to suffer.

A prince having asked his physician, *How much daily food was required to support the body, and keep up its strength?* The physician replied, *That one pound was enough; such a measure being very well capable of supporting him; and should he take more, he must support it.*

What is only a physical abundance is imaginary poverty; what is a physical poverty, no imagination can convert into an abundance.

The male children of affluence are beset by avaricious harpies: the hypocrite affects a personal attachment; the prude strikes at their judgment; the coquette plays with their feelings; and the harlot lays out her man-traps to rouse their passions.

Money has more female adorers than beauty, worth, or merit.

Opiniatrety, pride, and envy, are permanent and universal in mortals: avarice, jealoufy,

fy, and revenge, are only temporary, and accidental.

Body and mind have each their chronic and acute difeafes.

Civility is often miftaken for homage; and the refpect that is paid to the office, is frequently placed to the fcore of perfonal merit.

Only flatter—you need not be folicitous about a caufe.

Great projects are oftener ruined by precipitation, delay, or the neglect of trifles, than by want of capacity.

Minuteness is not the province of ability.

Many literary characters find their tongues in their pen: women generally fpeak better than they write; their happieft efforts are called forth by the moment.—Genius makes but little previous arrangement.

Plato hearing it afferted, that he was an infamous perfon, faid, *I fhall take care to live fo that no body will believe the reporter.*—Our deportment

ment falls not under the ocular, tho' it may reach the auricular cognizance of every citizen.

* PUNISHING the flanderer does not get rid of the flander; nor does there appear to be any method of obliterating it.

SIMPLICITY and fincerity appear to be the grand arcana of civil life.—As we ftray from truth, we are involved in complexity.

WHEN the author is no more, his work *may* ftand on the bafis of its merit; tho' revenge wars even with the demifed.

'TIS feldom that the opinion or judgment of an author is biaffed againft his own writings; tho' 'tis eafy to change or direct thofe of the public refpecting them.

GENIUS has acute feelings; and they are often, tho' aukwardly, imitated.

INDOLENCE

---

* " I am fatisfied the perfon difobliging is of kin to me; and tho' we are not juft of the fame flefh and blood, yet our minds are nearly related, being both extracted from the Deity. I am likewife convinced that no man can do me a real injury, becaufe no man can force me to mifbehave myfelf. For thofe reafons I can't find it in my heart to hate or be angry with one of my own family. We are all made for mutual affiftance, no lefs than the parts of the body are for the fervice of the whole." *Marcus Antoninus.*

* INDOLENCE appears to be the principal support of evil report.

EXCLAMATION follows exclamation; in vain they denounce the world; credulity is never at the pains to examine!

MORE priests are found disputing on the road to heaven than ever enter its portal.

LADY-LIKE sensibility mimics the mode in which expressive sorrow shews itself.

WHERE there are many opinions, the error lies perhaps in the supposed object. There is a certain and early intelligence where the sun is; from parhelions no beams issue.

FEW who complain of life's brevity are apprised of its value; those who are, have the greatest cause for complaint.

† *Hours have wings, and fly up to the Author of time, and carry news of our usage: all our prayers cannot intreat one of them to return, or slacken his pace: the mispence of every minute is a new record against us in heaven.*

---

* He that is hasty to give credit is light minded.
Ecclesiasticus.

† Milton.

There appears to exist a greater defire to live long than to live well! Meafure by man's defires, he cannot live long enough; meafure by his good deeds, and he *has not* lived long enough; meafure by his evil deeds, and he has lived too long.

'Tis difficult to affail vice, without making an enemy of thofe who are implicated, or fuppofe that they are; yet we do not even under the fevere operation of the furgeon's knife curfe the hand that is lacerating our flefh.

What is intended for our amendment, fhould not excite animofity, tho' it pains.

Secondary confiderations are frequently primary ones in value, tho' not in order: we difplay our abilities to promote our intereft; we parade our principles to recommend ourfelves.

No man can bear to fee what no man can bear to reveal—his naked intent.

What you know, even that fhould be made known.

Reserved knowledge is the ftock of mental avarice; they give not, but lend out for ufance.

A LIBERTINE'S

A LIBERTINE's devotion is the harbinger of his demise.

THE closer to the grave, the nearer to repentance.

STRUMPETS, when detected, deny or confess their infamy with as much effrontery as they committed the acts that constituted it.—Every offence has its justification and punishment.

HARVESTS cannot be expected from a single grain: but in the hands of skilful husbandmen, great will be the produce, tho' the means are scanty.—LEAN skill is before fat plenty.

IF the human capacity for pleasure, and the power things have to contribute towards it, was once ascertained, the pursuit after it would cease to be dangerous: we sure grow grey, and become enfeebled in the research.

EXQUISITE pleasure is that which communicates as much as it receives.

BY fools, knaves fatten; by bigots, priests are cloathed.—Every knave finds a gull.

Make no vows of enmity whilſt you are ſmarting with a ſenſe of neglect or cruelty.—Pain ſpeaks with little propriety.

The man of opulence is always the principal figure on the canvas: the great artiſt does not always make him the *beſt*.

In the back ground are characters that are too great to obtrude.

Indifference is the forerunner of mental decay, or the barometer of idleneſs.

To be ſatisfied, we muſt examine, and have reaſons ever ready.

Our *word* is a ready and convenient pledge: when 'tis forfeited, 'tis but a word.—The greateſt ties are the moſt inſignificant.

Remote poſſeſſions, inſtead of being diſtant bleſſings, are curſes that knock at our very doors.—* The enormous and unwieldy dimenſions of an overgrown empire, form not ſtrength, but extended weakneſs.

* Rutherford's View of Ancient Hiſtory.

Four characters are pre-eminently detestable amongst the herd of insignificants: the sneerer and the supercilious; he who disdains to open or to shut his mouth.

Caution should specify its objects. " The frigid smiler †, crawling, indiscreet, obtrusive, brazen-faced, is a scorpion-whip of destiny—avoid him!"

" Fly him who affects silence."

" Volitility of words is carelessness in act; words are the wings of actions."

Obedience is tolerable to those who perceive the necessity of it.

Submission is the identical thing that pride dreads.

" As I have dealt with others, so deal with me," is a modest demand, and a bad rule.

Prudence must affix some measure for what is to be received, and disbursed, because it keeps the mind just by the conjoint operation of well-founded hope, and fear of default.

† Lavater's *Aphorisms.*

Trusts may have been imperfectly discharged; yet compared with what preceded, it may be positively meritorious. *

The first who introduces practical reform in official situations, has an extra claim to deference.

Force constitutes no right; nor can it be safely used to recover lost privileges.

Oaths are a species of coercion, originating in perfidy, and continued by suspicion. Protestations of the most solemn kind cannot make truth more evident, or smother the intent to deceive. When an oath is imposed, an unjust accusation is instantly established.

Deceit is tolerated with as much kindness, as there is ingenuity exercised in the practice of it.

Losers often rail, and railers often lose: to act with temper under loss, or gain, requires a discretion

---

* When St. Evremond went to thank Mazarine for having released him from the Bastile, the Cardinal said, *That he was persuaded of his innocence; but, in the post he occupied, he was obliged to listen to so many things, it was very difficult to distinguish the true from the false.*

discretion untainted with avarice, and a fortitude that can brave poverty.

We see, are pleased, and adore: we are smote, sicken, and die: such are the revolutions of a moment!

Rapture terminates in languor; sometimes in death; or, what is more to be apprehended—incurable melancholy.

The outrageous have their calms; they are the consequence of exhausted spirits: the mildest disposition * may become outrageous, but it soon re-assumes its former placidity.

Those instances of adversity against which we have uttered so many execrations, do nevertheless form, in age, the comforts of its chimney corner; and its boast is in proportion to their magnitude.

The inquisition could not rack me into a belief that 'tis possible to be privately vicious, and publicly good; unless they could at the same time

* A baited cat may grow as fierce as a lion.

English Proverb.

time convince me, that a line ceafes to be a line, becaufe it is extended beyond another to which it is compared. Sir Charles Morel* appears to have been of the fame opinion. "He who, in his private life, doth combat every duty, and lives at variance with every domeftic virtue, fhall vainly ape the generous figure of his country's patriot: for what are the bleffings of fociety, but thofe which in a leffer fcale we meet at home, as peace, honour, and love? Will he then, who gives up thefe within his own houfe, cherifh and extend their influence abroad?" Yet it is poffible for thofe who are virtuous in the private to act corruptly in the public walk of life; for there is a portion only of temptation that we can refift; and the fortitude that will bear us through a petty trial, is infufficient when we are tried by objects of magnitude.

WILL is the idol of ambition, the fcourge of humility, the plaything of woman, a puzzle to wifdom, and a torment to all who have long defpotized.

WHEN laws do not alike coerce all offenders, they are either infignificant, evaded, or completely adminiftered. The neceffity of lenity, pardon,

* Vide Tales of the Genii.

pardon, or mercy*, should be attended to before the verdict is pronounced, or they burlesque it.

WHAT we do voluntarily, we are always prepared to do; inclination calls forth all the energies.

THE resistance has, and will, produce more dangerous consequences than the adoption of reason. Reason is the only code that is congenial with human nature.

OUR faults are sometimes so flagrant, that as a blind, we arraign the conduct, and bring to light the peccability, of our neighbours. 'Tis a paltry, insidious, inefficacious, skulking trick; and tho' it cannot deraign the guilty, it will have a sort of vogue with the depraved, as long as an excuse or apology can be extracted from comparison.

---

* " Equity in law is the same thing that the spirit is in religion—what every one pleases to make it. Sometimes they go according to conscience; sometimes according to law; sometimes according to the rule of court.

Equity is a roguish thing. For law we have a measure, know what to trust to: equity is according to the conscience of him that is chancellor; and as that is larger or narrower, so is equity: 'tis all one as if they should make his foot the standard for the measure." *Selden.*

When we hold a poifoned chalice to a friend, yet are ignorant of the nature of its contents, we may have the merit of a good intention, tho' the claim is withdrawn during the reign of the calamity, in which juftification from intended injury is more earneftly defired than the honour of rendering a fervice.

When women yield, intereft or fenfuality triumphs over policy or pride.

Before the gueft is preffed to fatisfy his appetite, the table fhould be covered: we know not *when*, *whether*, or *what*, we can eat till the viands are before us. Both hoft and gueft are frequently backward.

We too often tolerate folly out of complaifance; and play the fool from the fame difgraceful motive.

When folicited to comply with what is difagreeable, 'tis oftentimes more difficult to refufe than to comply: when courted to accept of, or participate in, what is agreeable, 'tis fometimes more eafy to refufe than to comply.

When the ceremonies of a religion are fcoffed at, or its minifters defpifed, 'twill not be long before

before its principles will be detefted: what is raifed by impofition muft be continued with increafing art.

* VERBAL delicacy is referved for feftivals; when there is no holiday, perfons and things have their common names.

ATTEND to contradiction, there is fomething to be learned by it: the habit of attending patiently and mutely to it, has filled many a purfe. Thofe who ferve the petulant cannot be too well rewarded!

BE perfuaded of this, (that you may be neither obfequious or affuming,) 'tis vice that degrades, virtue

* After the acceffion of George I. the Whigs fplit into two parties. Walpole had thought of a meafure to diftrefs his opponents, which he communicated to the heads of his party; they approved it, and thought the Prince fhould be let into it. Walpole would not agree to this: He faid, "That the Prince would communicate it to his wife, and that fat a---'d bitch would divulge the fecret." The Princefs was informed of this. When fhe came to the throne, her fettlement, in cafe fhe fhould furvive the king, came on the carpet: 100,000l. a year was propofed. Sir Spencer Compton thought 60,000l. an ample provifion; but Walpole found means to acquaint the Queen, that if he were minifter, her expectations fhould be gratified. She fent him this anfwer: "Go tell Sir Robert, that the fat a---'d bitch has forgiven him" He was foon after declared minifter; and Sir Spencer Compton removed to the Upper Houfe with the title of Earl of Wilmington.

virtue that elevates, mankind: beauty and fortune are independent and fortuitous.

Cover the steed with gaudy trappings, and the unskilful think not of his faults: defects may be concealed that cannot be amended; and such are venial.

Severe wounds, and exquisite entertainments, are those we least expected; great pleasures * those we are least capable of bearing.

There would be few appointments, or invitations, if each citizen was of an urbane disposition.

To give or take there is a shyness, a reluctance, an avarice, an unsocial apathy, that satyrizes mankind.

Where the distinctions of virtue and vice are shifting, an arbitrary injustice presides: and the petty culprit is judged by unequal laws.

'Tis neither the quantity or quality that determines—'tis the use. The pale student is not
wiser

---

* A French philosopher is of opinion, that pleasure is not so coincidental with human nature as pain is, and that we are too weak to support it long; whilst, on the contrary, we are capable of enduring pain for a length of time.

wifer for his bibliomania: the brain oppreffed with words cannot fhew its ftrength. That preaching moralift is not a jot more virtuous than his neighbour; he is fo anxious to ftore up rules, he overlooks the occafion of practifing them.

THE weather is not a fafe topic of difcourfe; your company may be hippifh: nor is health; your affociate may be a *maladé imaginaire*: nor is money; you may be fufpected as a borrower.

* PRONENESS to intoxication is a very precarious rule to judge of the principle or intellect by. 'Tis a ftrong brain that can repeatedly facrifice to Bacchus, tho' only weak minds will confent to become daily facrificers. Drunkennefs is fometimes the grave of immoderate forrow : Would it be fair to conclude *fuch* people to be villains? Know the drunkard's motive before you condemn him.

---

* How late drunkennefs became a practice in this ifland may be difcovered in Camden's Annals. Under the year 1581 he has this obfervation: "The Englifh, who hitherto had, of all the Northern nations, fhewn themfelves the leaft addicted to immoderate drinking, firft learned in their wars in the Netherlands to fwallow a large quantity of intoxicating liquor, and to deftroy their own health by drinking that of others."

Such as depend moſt on themſelves for entertainment, will not always be the beſt able to entertain others. Who is ſo well pleaſed with himſelf as a fool? Who can be ſo irkſome to fools as the wiſe?

* When contempt, pride, or ſelfiſhneſs, feed the miſanthrope, and ſolitaire, no ſacrifice can abate their unreaſonable expectations.

There are a thouſand cauſes why a woman accepts of your hand, each of which had more weight in her determination than your merit.

To barren prudence, the offals of genius prove a fortune; 'tis ſtrange that little minds can turn things to a good account.

Opposites are ſometimes good cures, if they can be digeſted. The fear of the trial will ſometimes cauſe the complaint to be forgotten.

Nice men are reported to have naſty ideas; certainly very delicate women have very filthy practices: probably delicacy, like genius, is only to be exerciſed on certain objects.

Oppression

---

* " Le materialiſme eſt l'antidote de la miſanthropie."
De la Mettrie.

OPPRESSION insists upon respect from its immediate victims; and this appears to be its last and most extravagant act.

WE complain of neglect 'till we really are what we deserve to be—neglected: the time that is lost in regret, and the lamentations that dependence utters, might be so employed as to raise the complainant above it.

THE blow that can be returned *may* be forgotten; to lack the power of revenge, and forgive an injury likewise, seems to be a great effort even for the greatest to make.

THOSE who have expelled all sordid thoughts, compute how little has been lost, not how much the robber has gained. Let the amount be what it may, 'tis probable, that the loser can better sustain the loss, than the thief put up with the want of it.*

DEBTS are pardoned oftener than robberies; yet a debt is no other than a robbery, if return is not intended; and being contracted on the presumption of faith, aggravates the offence.

---

* " Helas, aux cœurs heureux les virtus font faciles.
M. de Bellay.

When there is no pleasure in retirement, there can be no profit.

The sluggard, like the Bonasus, finds a defence in his filth.

Sloth is too lazy to undertake its own defence if it could; and it could not, if it would.

Sloth travels the snail's pace, and all its motions are retrograde.

When we cease to care, we begin to enjoy; where we no longer care, we no longer value.

Timidity * and courage reign temporaly in the same person, and in particular transactions they are mean and generous.

There is an expensive and an ungenerous silence; a silence that flatters, and that offends: wisdom and cunning have also a *silence* that they alone know how to time.

After we have liberty to chuse, we want prudence to measure.

Suspense

---

* Fear magnifies and minifies; it increases the danger, and decreases the means of escaping from it.

Suspense is the balance of expectations.

Enthusiasm is the wine that gives spirit to eloquence: and money the cordial that gives voice to the advocate!

When the good assemble, they are in a fair way to grow better.

The wife of duty always behaves as if she really did love.

Philosophers are disposed to turn all events to beneficial ends.

Bodies may be tied together; minds meet.

Husbands must see no women wiser, younger, more beautiful, or juster, than their partners. So, according to Marmontel, in order to be virtuous, we must have neither ears nor eyes. Conjugal virtue is singular in its nature!

Reforming profligates redeem their credit at the expence of the fools in succession.

The lover's triumph is amidst his unfortunate rivals: 'tis a cruel mistress who decrees it.

No difguife is neceffary where there is neither villainy or affectation. What we *are* can never be fo difgraceful as the practice of impofing makes us.

A SAMEIST makes a woman yawn—Variety of characters they muft have, and they expect to find it in the fame character.

THE youth who can play alternately the coxcomb and the hero, will be agreeable even to his great grandmother.

ACTIVITY without anxiety is not pleafing, but muft be beneficial immediately, and remotely.*

SUSPENSE decreafes as confidence augments.

LIFE is a continued ftate of fufpenfe interrupted by this certainty, that fimilar caufes will produce fimilar effects.

HABITUAL fufpicion arifes from a fixed opinion, that all mankind are virtually in a ftate of apoftacy.

SUSPICION

---

* Perfeverance, which is continued activity, is patience, ability, and power, conjoined.

Suspicion is, in many cafes, as legal a branch of wisdom, as caution is, which precedes it.

Suspicion sometimes is the offspring of exceffive timidity.

Women who avoid what are called *delicate situations*, generally miftruft themfelves.

Women confirmed in their virtue, fpeak, and act, more boldly than the fceptical, or untried part of the fex.

When fufpicion refults immediately from the complexion of exifting circumftances, its admonitions fhould be attended to in the fame proportion as abftract or extraneous fufpicion fhould be difcountenanced.

'Tis infamous to allow pre-entertained opinion to fway more than facts.

Suspense includes more hope than doubt does; doubt has confequently moft apprehenfion.

Independence fears leaft of all.

Scholars declare that perfection is the *end* of improvement; if 'tis so, happy ought we to be, congratulate, not complain to, each other, because perfection is not attainable.

When improvement ceases, enjoyment stagnates.

If legislators mean that there should be but few culprits, let them take away all advantage from crime.

* The hopes of profit lead more astray than those who suffer by the law.

The favour refused, is generally the identical favour that makes us anxious.

People do not always want what they have, tho' they are *sure* to *want* what they have not.

What we do possess, cannot, in opinion, stand in any degree of comparison with what we want to possess.

Scruples lessen our means in all undertakings; hence arises the advantage that villains have

---

* When the advantage of the state collectively is provided for by the laws, citizens will be well disposed to obedience.

have in their progress towards Fortune's favours.

DANTON cried, *General Dumourier wants energy; his mind has never risen to the true revolutionary pitch.* This opinion arose from the latter's refusing to act in concert with the former when he had laid down a plan for his conduct in Belgium of a disgraceful nature.

FOLLIES are sacred where pride and authority are extensive.—Pride holds both its crimes and absurdities in supreme reverence.

THOSE who examine the state of their circumstances, and dive into the expensive cause of their derangement, may be surprized to find that the monosyllable *no* has been the principal cause of their ruin.—*No* * is a response that is proudly impolitic.

EVERY

---

* Le roi de Navarre ayant reconnu Décour, garçon très plaisant, & très vaillant, lui demanda, d'où il venoit ? à quoi il repondit *Oui* ; & comme il continuoit toujours de repondre *oui* hors de propos à toutes les questions qu'on lui faisoit, il dit enfin---" Sire, je des toujours *oui*, parce que ce qui fait chaper les " gens de bien d'auprès les rois, c'est pour ne pas proferen ce " mot d'*oui* à toutes les demandes qu'ils leur font."

Memoires d'Agrippa d'Aubigny.

Every fool may torment a proud man beyond the power of retaliation.

The lowest are frequently beyond the reach of the highest.

When self-approbation is set greater store by than fame, (which is no more than the approbation of the community, or a major part of them,) then may the injustice of the world be derided.

Our fame is of our own coining, tho' it may not pass current.

What accident gave, accident may take away.

Change is the only thing not changeable: yet the rich * act as presumptuously as if their station was beyond mutability.—Riches can make no creature worthy, tho' they may develope his excellent qualities, if he has such.

Industry cannot be wholly unfruitful.— *There is a kind of good angel waiting upon diligence,*

---

* To be rich is to be three parts of the way onward to perfection: to be poor, is to be made a pavement for the tread of the full-minded man.

gence, that ever carries a laurel in his hand to crown her.

Those generous souls who care least for wealth, as far as it relates to themselves, care least for the want of it.

Beneficence, the second species of self-love, is a propension to act morally towards others; and in all its acts duty seconds inclination.

'Tis bad to be vicious; 'tis worse to conceal a vice.

Those who conceal, in some degree, tolerate error: yet 'tis needless to reveal it, unless some good can arise from the discovery.

We all merit reproof, tho' few can bear it, and fewer still know how to reprove.

Remember that where approbation is insignificant, censure is not harmless.

Let praise be voiced to the spreading air,
But chidings whisper'd in the kissed ear. *

Knowledge

* Resolves by Ow. Felltham, Ed. 5th, 1634.

Knowledge is the treasure of the mind; discretion is the key which makes all confident who know their treasure is so secured.—Discretion is the completion of wisdom.

Intended benefits are often received as insults, owing to the aukwardness of the tender, or the opinion the receiver has of the giver.*

Sweet manners gloss over the cruellest injuries.

By turns we are actors and spectators.

Vicissitude is not only the lot of the world, but its support.

Better to be lapidated than pitied by those who rise at your expence, and conceal both inhumanity and duplicity under affected sympathy.

Girls and boys are ideally, if not actually, men and women, before they reach the age of muliebrity and virility.

Tho'

---

* The favour that must be returned is a debt.

Tho' fools are great *make bates*,* they know a safer way to escape from quarrels than their superiors in understanding.

There is a species of contradiction that every being loves to enjoy; sometimes he applies it to others; sometimes he delights to have it applied to himself; our conceit augments as we bear or offer it.

Few expectants come to great fortunes. Can it happen otherwise? The capital prizes are few, compared with the multitudes who adventure in the great lottery of life.

Hope grows stronger the nearer we approach the wihning post.—Desire is extravagant, if it excludes hope.

True courage is no more than a prosecution, according to ability, of those measures that reason prescribes according to the exigencies of the case before her.

Ambition does not confine her ravages to domal visits; she frequently disturbs the peaceful neighbourhood of nations.—Le premier † de biens est la paix de nos cœurs.

Never

---

* Voltaire.   † i. e. *make debates.*

Never tell even your grandmother that she is an angel: not that there is any danger of being discredited, but she will lay you under some sort of contribution for having made it.

Where is no constriction, there the tongue, and the press, will have freedom, and the government *can* have nothing to fear.

Never imagine that you deserve what you was born to, if you lack abilities to hold up the dignity.

What is done without passion, is generally done coldly; what is done from passion alone, you may have reason to repent of.

Words have no more connection with sensations, than painting has with natural objects: always suppose that descriptions fall short or exceed reality. Pleasure, or pain, to be known, must be felt.

The most important and awful precept of the day is its departure.

There seems to be something brotherly in compulsative religion: to force the wayward to ascend

ascend the ladder of heaven *nolens volens*, certainly implies a solicitude for the welfare of his *soul*, whatever inconvenience it may produce to his mind or body.

Of what immense importance is a word! A monosyllable more or less, drives us to the extremes of endurance. Many copies of the old English translation of the Bible sent this text forth: " Thou shalt commit adultery."

Possession is a good claim; but not always a rational one, or a proof of right.

What is vehemence good for? It can neither recommend, or be recommended; neither obtain an impartial hearing, or an impartial arbitration.

'Tis never safe, or prudent, to give way to first emotions, whatever causes they may proceed from, tho' it appears necessary to make records of them.

These were original thoughts on this subject. I afterwards (obeying the maxim) started these simple questions.

Must we deliberate when time admits of no interim 'twixt declarations of threats and their execution?

execution? Should we demur and parley about the *propriety* of relief, whilst death's shadow is playing on the mendicant's face? Ought we, in justice to ourselves, to postpone a proffer'd pleasure, that never may return, in compliment to cold caution, when it has no substitute for lost and innocent fruition?

If violence is the promptest mode of deciding altercations, 'tis also the worst: amongst the numerous and potent arguments that brawny arms possess, not one can strike conviction.

* Policy stands centinel over the lips of the worldly: its vigilance suffers no expression to escape that could wound their interest. From Nature's

---

* " Chirac, a physician, being called to a lady, heard, as
" he entered her house, that the stocks were falling: he had
" bought to a considerable amount, and was so deeply affected
" by the news, that, whilst feeling his patient's pulse, he
" could not help repeating perpetually, *Good God! it falls! it*
" *sinks! it sinks!* The lady, alarmed, rang the bell, and cried
" out to her maids ' *Oh! my God, I am dying! M. Chirac*
" *says my pulse sinks! it sinks!*' *Not at all, Madam,* replied the
" physician, recovering: *Your pulse beats admirably; you are*
" *out of all danger: it is the stocks I mean; by which I am a con-*
" *siderable loser.*"

 Fragments of original Letters, deposited in the House of B⸺ W⸺ley, Madame Char. El. de Baviere, the widow of Monsieur, brother to Louis the Fourteenth.

Nature's unsophisticated children, what is uppermost will out, whether good or bad, for or against. Oft is this genuine trait of sincerity treated as a vice, oft is it punish'd, scoff'd, and rated by stung pride.

Retort is a good friend to the insulted; it should be sure to act promptly, and pertinently; give proofs of spirit, without exhibiting any disposition to enter the field.

Apply to *little* people in the season of distress, they instantly become great: they are surprized at their own importance.

Why are we excluded from praising a wife? Is it her vanity, or your friend's concupiscence, that prevents it? Wives, indeed, never praise their husbands face to face; tho', in that situation, they often flatter and cajole them.

Of the political rights, *consent* stands foremost: it implies both personal consequence, and responsibility.

In Fame's temple there is always a niche to be found for rich dunces, importunate scoundrels, or succesful butchers of the human race.

* When circumstances change suddenly, the difference between entering and retiring is wonderful. Opinion in this case is only the reflected state of your circumstances.

† Let hosts allow their guests to *drink what they like*, and there is a probability that they may *like what they drink*.

How are children to ascertain the period when truth becomes necessary, if they are not under the necessity of speaking it always? The first lessons of a Persian were, to manage a horse, to use the bow dextrously, and to adhere to truth! In our seminaries youth is taught fiction in a foreign language!

‡ What address or prepossession bespeaks, knowledge secures. Lord Bacon has declared, " that

---

* " The presence of him is oppressive, whose going away " makes those he leaves easy; and he whose presence was op- " pressive, was either *good* in *bad*, or *bad* in *good* company."
Lavater's *Aphorisms*.

† " You enjoy with wisdom, or with folly, as the gratifi- " cation of your appetites capacitates or unnerves your pow- " ers." Lavater's *Aphorisms*.

‡ According to Aristotle, the Ethiopians and Indians suffered the beauty and stature of their kings, and magistrates, to determine their choice of them.

" that a pleasing figure is a perpetual letter of
" recommendation." Many are content to see,
not weigh objects.

If industry *is* no more than habit, 'tis at least
an excellent one. " If you ask me which is the
" real hereditary sin of human nature, do you
" imagine I shall answer pride, or luxury, or am-
" bition, or egotism? No; I shall say, indolence.
" Who conquers indolence will conquer all the
" rest." * Indeed, all good principles must
stagnate without mental activity.

With handsome legs many harlots and beggars jump into good stockings; 'tis seldom that
they fit well.

† A frothy jest sinks to the bottom of a
weak heart: a naked truth cannot get half as
far.

Delicacy increases or decreases, in a direct
ratio with affluence, or poverty, squeamish affectation, or rough hardihood.

* Lavater.

† Caius Cæsar Caligula burnt alive, in the middle of the
amphitheatre, the writer of a farce, because it contained a
short, jocular sentence with a double meaning.

* After having studied yourself accurately, you have a diagram to account for the tortuitous hypocrify, and capricious humours, of all you meet.

The badness of the times (as the vulgar phrase expresses a scene of distress) frequently depends more on those who govern the ship than on the weather.

When the spirit of intellect purifies the grossness of sensuality, the table furnishes a cheering recruit for nature, and the feast is exquisitely gratifying, and fit for a rationalist.

Our

---

* "Each heart is a world of nations, classes, and individuals; full of friendships, enmities, indifferences; full of being and decay, of life and death: the past, the present, and the future; the springs of health, and engines of disease: here joy and grief, hope and fear, love and hate, fluctuate, and toss the sullen and the gay, the hero and the coward, the giant and the dwarf, deformity and beauty, on ever-restless waves. You find all *within* yourself that you find *without*: the number and character of your friends within bears an exact resemblance to your external ones; and your internal enemies are just as many, as inveterate, as irreconcileable as those without: the world that surrounds you is the magic glass of the world, and of its forms within you; the brighter you are yourself, so much brighter are your friends; so much more polluted your enemies. Be assured then, that to know yourself perfectly, you have only to set down a true statement of those who ever loved or hated you."

Lavater's *Aphorisms*.

Our fojourn on this globe is like unto a long infancy: we are moſt of us *en liſiere*: we cannot go alone.

What cruelty there is in accuſing the ſoft ſex of loquacity! 'tis but little they ſay; nor ſhould this little be objected to: much more is oftentimes comprehended in their little than is apprehended.

Political ſyſtems, of every denomination, will ſtand as long as they poſſeſs the excluſive power of puniſhing: puniſhment is the key-ſtone that keeps the fabric together.

We have many medicines, and few cures, and many cures without medicines.

Coquettes are creatures who unite pride with cruelty, and apparent artleſſneſs with the profoundeſt cunning. Not one of their admirers will give teſtimony to this character of them.

Those who have long claimed your attention, ultimately claim your confidence. Thus has Solomon written: " There is that ſpeaketh like the piercings of a ſword, but the tongue of the wife is health."

* Prosperity reconciles the moſt obdurate; ſo does the merit we cannot ſubdue.

The habit of controuling is the firſt we aſpire to; the laſt we renounce. Dominion is the univerſal paſſion.

Hospitals and priſons reſemble manſions of cruelty and diſeaſe, more than edifices appropriated to the amendment of health or morals.

† On as ſlight a pivot as opinion, the political and the moral univerſe move round. Yet, what is this opinion? ‡

Influenced

---

* The once-rebellious Americans are now our very good friends; we court their alliance; we applaud the very principles we conteſted.

† "La plupart des coutumes, & des opinions ſont telles, que ſi l'on ceſſoit de les inſinuer dens les cervaux encores tendres des enfants juſqua ce que la generation, qui vit aujourdhui ſur la terre, fut entierement éteinte (en ſort que la ſit de prevention ſe trouvat coupé, & interrompu) ces mêmes opinions qui ſont ſi fortement appuiées ſur les prejuges; ces coutumes qui ſont ſi puiſſamment etablies ſur la prevention, perdroient couts les avantages qui leur font donner le preference."

Traité de l'Opinion.

‡ "Opinion is, when the aſſent of the underſtanding is ſo far gained by evidence of probability, that it rather inclines to one perſuaſion than to another, yet not altogether without a mixture of uncertainty and doubting."

INFLUENCED by inscrutable motives, we appear to act contrary to reason, or our own advantage; many are the feints made to conceal from observers the secresy of intent.

NEVER believe that rank necessarily includes superiority, whilst there is a single scoundrel near the throne; or that the multitude are without dignity, whilst a solitary individual is to be found who proudly worships at Reason's shrine.

THOSE who like home best, have good reasons for the preference; and a curse to the mischief-maker whose practice it is to destroy domal compacts. Where Hymen is propitious, happy in reality must be his votaries.

THE most venomous conceal their poison; and never, till occasion calls, is the sage discovered, or the sinews of the strong man bar'd to view: so deep is good or evil.

A COMPLETE hypocrite is a good resemblance of complete honesty.*

THERE is (and instances of the fact are not uncommon) as essential a difference 'twixt the

---

* " Who writes as he speaks, speaks as he writes, looks as he speaks and writes, is honest." LAVATER's *Aphorisms.*

works of the same author, and the actions of the same person, as 'twixt those of distinct characters and distinct writers.

Patriotism, and the love of our country, appear to be as essentially various as selfishness and generosity.

The vulgar tumult of manual applause, the shouts of furious mobs, are instances of approbation that gratify vulgar minds: like beggars with their pouch, any hand is welcome that contributes.

* Simplicity of appearance does not exclude profoundness of intellect, or great experience; or does age always include them.

That man who disclaims pride, proclaims it aloud: the wise do as much, and glory in it: aye, even the humble are proud of their humility, and the proud of being humble.

Suffer without repining, or repine without suffering. " He will do great things who can avert his words and thoughts from past irremediable evils."

Much

---

* " Copiousness and simplicity, variety and unity, constitute real greatness of character." Lavater's *Aphorisms*.

* Much conceit and cunning lurk under a question, an answer, a sneer, or advice.

When possession changes the tenor of opinion, there is something wrong on one side: and when many opinions are entertained of one thing, the thing, or the opinions, are of little value.

Better to be a coward before than after a deed: better still to be no coward either before or after.

† 'Till that period arrives when justice changes its nature, atonement for injuries cannot be disgraceful, but honourable.

Who is there that sees the thoughts of the most religious of mortals, the bravest or chast-
eft?

---

* A timid Cockney enquires about the disposition of the horse he is prepared to mount. "Oh, Sir," replies the ostler, "the beast has a *rare* temper." "Does he go well?" "Aye, he's a nice one for going; tho' 'tis not very easy to say which way he'll go." "What faults has he?" "None—worth speaking of."

† "He who has genius and eloquence sufficient either to cover or to excuse his errors, yet extenuates not, but rather accuses himself, and unequivocally confesses guilt, approaches the circle of immortals, whom human language has dignified with the appellation of Gods and Saints."

Lavater's *Aphorisms*.

eſt? There wants a window for the mind, not the heart, good philoſopher.

If women have light heads (which may be doubted) they have lighter heels; of this many are aſſured.

* Ye guardians of the poor, ye protectors of the fatherleſs, are not *regard* and *preſervation* hacknied, ſpecious pretexts for their ruin? A veil you muſt have for iniquity, and this is it.

The neceſſitous often give gold for their braſs, and receive braſs for their gold.

Optimism ariſes either from a ſtagnation of intellect, or inſuperable indolence. Who, ſaving the Optimiſt, will indiſcriminately approve of the good and the evil, pain and pleaſure, life or death?

That identical crevice which deſpotiſm leaves open is the portal of liberty.

Knaves are forced to pawn their honour— the honourable can live on their credit.

ADVISE

* Like to that Spaniard who, ſtrangling Don Carlos by order of his father, ſaid to him, " Calla, calla, Senor Dom Carlos, todo loque ſe haze, es per ſu ben." i. e. Comfort yourſelf, Don Carlos; all this is for your good.

* Advise with friends, confult with phyficians, but be your own doctor and advifer. Well has king Charles expreffed himfelf on this fubject: " I am not fo confident of my own fufficiency, as not willingly to admit the counfel of others: but yet I am not fo diffident of myfelf, as brutifhly to fubmit to any man's dictates."

† There is as much vulgarity and inconfiftence in the *mufk'd* as in the *greafy* mob, and much more infolence.

‡ Novels do not *force* their fair readers to fin, they only inftruct them *how* to fin; the confequences

---

* " Advice is feldom well received, well intended, or productive of any good. It is feldom well received, becaufe it implies a fuperiority of judgment in the giver; and it is feldom intended for any other end than to fhew it: it is feldom of any fervice to the giver, becaufe it more frequently makes him an enemy than a friend; and as feldom to the receiver, becaufe, if he is not wife enough to act properly without it, he will fcarcely be wife enough to diftinguifh that which is good."

† " But hear their raptures o'er fome fpecious rhime,
Dubb'd by the mufk'd and greafy mob, fublime."

Armstrong's *Tafte.*

‡ " 'Tis probable that, of all the caufes which have injured the health of women, the principal has been the prodigious multiplication of romances within the laft century. From the cradle to the moft advanced age, they read them with an eagernefs

quences of which are fully detailed, and not in a way calculated to seduce any but weak minds; few of their heroines are *happily* disposed of.

When wagers exclude brutal animosity, and promote investigation, they terminate differences advantageously for both parties.

* 'Tis possible to grow so familiar with our failings, that their fabrication is entirely forgot; then the liar believes his own fiction; the parasite his own praise.

Good

ness which keeps them almost without motion and without sleep. A young girl, instead of running about and playing, reads, perpetually reads, and at twenty becomes full of vapours, instead of being qualified for the duties of a good wife or nurse. These causes, which influence the physical equally influence the moral man. I have known persons of both sexes, whose constitutions would have been robust, weakened gradually by the too strong impressions of impassioned writings. The most tender romances hinder marriages, instead of promoting them. A woman, while her heart is warm'd by the languor of love, does not seek a husband; a hero must lay his laurels at her feet. The fire of love does not warm her heart, it only inflames her imagination."

Tissot.

* Epitaphe d'un Hypocrite.

" Ci gît dont le zele feint
" Lui tenant lieu de merite,
" Cru être devenu Saint
" A force d'être Hypocrite."

Good flatterers have few outstanding debts: neither will those who are praised take up the praise on credit.

* Genius has seldom much constancy, or have shewy abilities much profundity; the plodder has the greatest constancy.

He who acts uniformly virtuous, and without deductions, for the treachery of mankind, as morality now stands, should be brought in guilty—of an honourable error.

Take care to give all the relief or information that is required of you: do as much as this for your own sake; and bestow to the full of what is *wanted*, for the sake of those who deserve it.

Here is a paradox. Human beings are subject to justice, they are not the subjects of its executors: man is not justice, yet man has the power of controuling.

'Tis

---

* " One science only will one genius fit;
" So vast is art, so narrow human wit."

Pope.

" Who in the same given time can produce more than many others, has *vigour*; who can produce more and better, has *talents*; who can produce what none else can, has *genius*."

Lavater's *Aphorisms*.

* 'Tis as daftardly to triumph over the uninformed, or the wicked, as over the weak or defenceless.

Shoot home, then your praife or cenfure will reach the ears of its object; and you may depend upon being complimented for your difcernment, or denounced for your ftupidity.

We injure without hatred when exceptions are taken up on credit, which is frequently done to the difadvantage of enemies, foreigners, neutrals, and inferiors.

Who has done certain things *once*, may be expected to repeat them a thoufand times. I fay, who has done certain things *once*, has done them a thoufand times.

Our intereft, it appears, muft not at all times be infifted upon, if we wifh to fecure or augment it. Fenelon afferts, "The true way to gain much, is never to defire to gain too much, and to know when and how to lofe."

Excessive

" * Ignorantia juris non excufat."

" Who, without call or office, induftrioufly recalls the remembrance of paft errors, to confound him who has repented of them, is a villain."

Lavater's *Aphorifms.*

* EXCESSIVE sensibility is the foppery of modern refinement: the punishment accompanies the folly, and the error its excuse.

ALL the merit is in playing the game; the chances are all settled before the dice are thrown.

† IN spight of the injunction, " Et neminem oportet esse sapientiorem legibus," and the various checks that truth may receive, yet it will advance.

‡ WHERE there is wisdom, there will be good temper, calmness, and cheerfulness.

MANY

---

* Somewhere I have seen an Ode to Sensibility that begins thus:

> " Offspring of the manly mind,
> " And female tenderness combin'd;
> " If e'er I bow'd beneath thy sway,
> " Or felt thy animating ray,
> " Still thy true votary let me be,
> " Angelic Sensibility!"

† Galileo was condemned by the inquisition for having asserted, that the earth moved round the sun. " Però si muove," said the Philosopher.

‡ " Where true wisdom is, there surely is repose of mind, " patience, dignity, delicacy. Wisdom without these is dark " light, heavy ease, sonorous silence."

MANY fortunes are made *by* the poor; and the poor make many fortunes by the rich: the difference is in the manner of making them.

* SUCH as yield to circumstances, appear, to superficial observers, to want dignity, consistency, and integrity.

THOSE who weep after guilty conduct, send forth their showers at the conclusion of a dry harvest.

THE pleasures of sin, with the reputation of saintship, is the prude's motto.

BEAR the yoke as long as you are forc'd, and you will have borne it long enough.

THE

The mode of wording the last part of this aphorism, Lavater appears to have borrowed from Shakespeare.

" Love heavy lightness, serious vanity, &c."
Romeo and Juliet.

Indeed, who reads the Avonian without borrrowing from him?

* " What is a man? a congregation
" Of disagreeing things; his place of birth
" A confus'd crowd of fighting elements,
" To nothing fix'd, but to eternal change:
" They would lose all their natures should they fix."
Old Play by CROWNE.

" He

* The puerile ambition of doing things quickly, is the parent of impropriety and error; nothing is then well done, and many things are neglected.

To exist, 'tis necessary to subsist. A truism not much attended to. Our exertions are required by society; as for the means of supporting life, for that you must depend on the bounty of chance.

† Every thing may be bought, where there is nothing so good but it may be sold.

If this observation has experience for its ground-work, *that the public seldom forgive twice,*

" He who acts most consequentially, is the most friendly, and the most worthy of friendship; the more inconsequential, the less fit for any of its duties. In this I know I have said something common; but it will be very uncommon if I have made you attentive to it."   Lavater's *Aphorisms.*

* " Who seizes too rapidly, drops as hastily."

Again:

" Who grasps firmly, can hold safely, and keep long."
Lavater's *Aphorisms.*

† " Him whom opposition and adversity have left little, fortune and applause will not make great. Enquire after the sufferings of great men, and you will know why they are great."   Lavater's *Aphorisms.*

twice, how well prepared should that vessel be, which puts to sea on so merciless, so unrelenting an ocean!

* Every wither'd crone pretends to prescience: their prognostications, however, are seldom mumbled out before the event has taken place.

A man that is rich, may be any thing besides, without decreasing his reputation: a man that is poor, may be every thing besides, without increasing his reputation.

† There is nothing so apodictical that the vanity of scholarship, opiniatrety, or ignorance, will not contradict: but " the wrangler, the puzzler, the word-hunter, are incapable of great thoughts or actions."

Craft

---

* M. Dacier observes, that nothing is more natural, or usual, than for people, in their imagination, to make what they see bear some resemblance to their own personal circumstances.

† " Examine carefully whether a man is fonder of exceptions than of rules: as he makes use of exceptions, he is sagacious; as he applies them against the rule, he is wrong-headed. I heard, in one day, a man, who thought himself wise, produce thrice, as rules, the strangest, half-prov'd exceptions against millions of demonstrated contrary examples, and thus obtained the most intuitive idea of the sophist's character.

Craft cannot prevent adultery; confidence encourages it. What security, then, is there for the wedded? None; unless they have contrived to generate a mutuality of affection that defies rivalship.

This *shall* be your creed, says the Catholic church, therefore investigation is useless. Of late, it has become a maxim, to suspect all judgments that are not open to revision.

It concerns us materially, that our neighbours should be as wise as ourselves.

When the sacred necessity there is existing, to perform for our own advantage social duties, is made fully apparent, the word *favour* will soon become obsolete.

" Of all human forms and characters, none is less improveable, none more intolerable, and oppressive, than the race of sophists. They are intolerable against all nature, against all that is called general, demonstrated truth; they attempt to demolish the most solid and magnificent fabric with a grain of sand, picked from off its stones. Such knaves, whom to tolerate exceeds almost the bounds of human toleration, avoid like serpents. If you once engage with them, there is no end of wrangling.

" A sneer, and the helpless misery of better hearts, are their only aim, and their highest enjoyments."

Lavater's *Aphorisms.*

THINK not of *doing as you like*: the expression characterizes the headstrong, the unjust. Do as you ought to do. 'Tis a golden precept. Pythagoras has not a richer.

WHEN *certain* persons are resolved to praise, or censure, they will make occasions rather than forego their intent; truth, or personal reputation, cannot impede them.

TURN your back on prudence, in order to face danger, and the most powerful enemy you have is left behind.

INSTANTLY that the conscientious perceive their errors, they amend them: when the crimes of the less-informed are detected, *they* should be amended.

* PICTURES for the mind should be found in every volume; nay, in almost every page: the present age is satisfied to please the eye alone.

---

* Cawthorne, the bookseller, would not treat with *Henry* for the purchase of a History of the Islands of Guernsey and Jersey, *because* he had no views to accompany it. " Nay, Sir," said he, " I have recently refused, from a Scotch author, as well " written a book as ever I read, and for the same reason. The " public *prefer* books with pictures in them!!!"

Let those who can't prove to the contrary, confess that the vices of such who are contemn'd, and set apart from the mass of society, appear like instances of justifiable revenge; and the devices of the necessitous, like lawful retaliation on their peculators.

The son of traffic may be richer for the past; the child of science is better for it.

Violent ambition admits of no co-partnership; or avarice of friendship.

Reason is the best leader for all sects: it would, ultimately, lead to the closest union, and sects would be no more.

* To die, or to live, requires little courage: the inhabitant of the forest can do both. To die, or to live becomingly, requires much fortitude. *Great*† *let me call* the human being who can do either! Let it be remember'd, that the one is a consequence of the other.

In morals, or the arts, if persons, or things, are not distinct in their individualities, if they have

---

* The poorest gladiator, says Cicero, dies before us without a groan, or exhibiting the slightest proofs of weakness.

† Vide The Revenge, by Dr. Young.

have no character, they come to us with worfe than no recommendation.

* If an artift fends the refult of his ftudies modeftly forth, pity, do not infult him, if they fall fhort of your unconfcionable expectations: 'tis impoffible to be judge, and be an artift too!

† Of two difputants, he is unqueftionably in the wrong whofe choler rifes; at leaft, for giving way to paffion.

Within the circle of deception, no creature is fo completely and frequently gull'd as a hufband—unlefs it is a wife.

Drunkards, of all the candidates that fafhion makes mad, are the moft infipid, taftelefs; they do not tafte even their wine, and who can relifh their company?

Age,

---

* " Who (to fpeak with Shakefpeare) lets flip the dogs of war on modeft, defencelefs merit, and burfts out into a loud infulting laugh, when pale, timid, innocence trembles, him avoid —avoid his fpecious calmnefs, the harbinger of ftorms; avoid his flattery; it will foon turn to the lion's roar, and the howl of wolves." Lavater's *Aphorifms*.

† " The ftrong or weak fide of a man can never be known fo foon as when you fee him engag'd in difpute with a weak or malicious wrangler." Lavater's *Aphorifms*.

* Age, from affectation, refuses to continue, or countenance, those habits in which youth delights, and reason sanctifies. Gravity, by the senescent, may be carried to extremes, as well as levity by the juvenile.

† Those who are similarly, or dissimilarly, situated, cannot disagree, or agree, in their thoughts. Could we be assimilated to each other in all respects, would it contribute to our felicity?

Be careful to set, or follow, good examples; both of these are in your power: Indeed, by doing one of the two, the second is included.

Tho' you have acted with integrity, and circumspection, yet be solicitous about the consequences: care keeps the moralist continually awake.

---

* " All affectation is the vain and ridiculous attempt of poverty to appear rich." Lavater's *Aphorisms*.

† " Two men view a picture; they never see it from the same point of view, and therefore, strictly speaking, never see the same picture.

" If they sit down to hear a lecture, they never sit down with the same degree of attention, seriousness, or good humour: the previous state of the mind is different, and therefore the impression received cannot be the same."

Political Justice.

Put only this restriction on your pleasures; be cautious that they hurt no creature that has life.

We are all of us deceived at times; and those who do not know as much, are the most deceived.

Very modest folks will lie very confidently, and unblushingly; tho' they tremble and blush to declare the truth.

When silence is the trick of villainy, it operates as fatally as slander or reproach.

Agreeable faults are more frequently tolerated, and more profitable, than austere virtues.

Inasmuch as there is no safety, it behoves us to be vigilant, and take daily lessons from fortitude, that we may be provided against the fierce darts of fortune. The Arabians are of opinion, " that the habitation of danger is on the borders of security; and that a man never runs greater hazards than when he least fears them."

If between conscience and guilt there are many compromises, 'twixt crime and punishment there are also many chances.

* 'Tis difficult to praise or censure without the semblance of flattery or malice: yet respect for merit is the converse of adulation, and 'tis possible that blame may be unting'd by acrimony.

† Is not the insolvent debtor full as unfortunate as the creditor who cannot obtain payment? Severe frequently is the fate of them both.

Of the established injustices under which women labour, the severest is their treatment after criminal love. Antoninus, the emperor, said, " 'Tis unjust that the man should demand that chastity from his wife which he himself will not observe towards her: it is as if a man should persuade his wife to fight against enemies that conquered him."

---

* " He is a great and self-pois'd character whom praise unnerves not: he is a greater one who supports unjust censure: the greater is he, who, with acknowledged powers, represses his own, and even turns to use undeserved censure."

Lavater's Aphorisms.

† " The creditor, whose appearance gladdens the heart of a debtor, may hold his head in sun-beams, and his foot on storms."

Lavater's Aphorisms.

" If you mean to escape your creditor, or enemy, avoid him not."

Lavater's Aphorisms.

A formal demeanour stands between pride and ignorance, as a fulsome compliment does 'twixt nonsense and insult.*

Where there is too much anxiety required to keep a treasure, *there* is possession a curse.

A wise fool will undertake any thing you desire: when called upon to act, he is bewilder'd, and puzzled how to set about every thing that is necessary to be executed.

† Those who can be happy by themselves, indubitably possess the *wherewith* to felicitate others to a certain degree; if it be not so, the Solitaire should remember that virtue is only practical excellence.

---

* " Receive no satisfaction for premeditated impertinence; forget it, forgive it; but keep him inexorably at a distance who offer'd it." Lavater's *Aphorisms.*

† " That the temper, the sentiments, the morality of men, influenced by the example and disposition of those they converse with, is a reflection which has long since passed into proverbs, has been rank'd among the standing maxims of human wisdom."
Rogers's *Sermons.*

" Think not, Sultan, that in the sequester'd vale alone dwells Virtue, and her sweet companion, with attentive eye, mild, affable Benevolence! No; the first great gift we can bestow on others, is a good example."
Tales of the Genii, by Sir Charles Morell.

The midnight pillow is the fcite where the wretch caftigates, and where the difciple of probity confoles himfelf.

Even the lacquey of your patron may determine your fortune; when your fortunes are fubject to one, they are fubject to all.

Tho' perfonal decoration is not neceffary for exiftence, 'tis eminently requifite for our fubfiftence: drefs, if you wou'd give your talents fair play.

When a namelefs perfon is the avowed hero of a tale, 'tis fair to conclude that the narrator alludes to himfelf, if there is any fpecific object in view that he means to compliment.

Pride dreads familiarity, becaufe familiarity enables us to appreciate objects.—Familiarity is abfolutely neceffary to regulate acts of benevolence, and point out the neceffity of them; whilft contempt, which it is vulgarly accufed of producing, withers the effufions of philanthropy.

* Silence hatches the moft fatal brood.

---

* " The moft ftormy ebullitions of paffion, from blafphemy to murder, are lefs terrific than one fingle act of cool villainy: a ftill

MUTUALITY of duty, and of right, makes up the whole civil code.

LESS shame accrues from praising our own actions, than in omitting to perform such as are praise-worthy. Why should we not speak well of what we have done well?

WHO scrutinizes the value of the man after having look'd into his rent-roll?

TWO descriptions of people laugh at the practice of taking oaths; those who do not, and those who do know that 'tis their duty to be just.

BEAUTY is worse than liquor; it intoxicates both the holder and the beholder.

THOUSANDS complain of lacking fortune, whose merit keeps no pace with their advancement, or early expectations. Reward a citizen till he cries, *hold*; *enough*: that is the man who knows himself, and deserves to be rewarded.

RESERVE appears to be either the effect of cunning, diffidence, or cowardice.

LET

---

a still *rabies* is more dangerous than the paroxysms of a fever. Fear the boisterous savage of passion less than the sedatory grinning villain.   LAVATER's *Aphorisms.*

Let the captious know, that the best way to get rid of a quarrel, is not always the quickest way of getting out of it.

The husband's civilities lessen at home as they increase abroad: perhaps in either case he is the only person not aware of it.

* What cou'd induce mad Peregrinus, at the Olympic games, to jump into a fiery furnace? Vanity! Vanity, the first, the strongest, the last of our follies.

All the world look *favourably* on youth. Alas! its inexperience knows not how to take advantage of it! There are many tho' who know how to take up this neglected advantage; and, alas! on all such youth looks favourably.

Certainly there *is* an advantage in getting married; 'tis not long after the ceremony has been perform'd, but we become wiser.

* " A woman whose ruling passion is not vanity, is superior to any man of equal faculties." Lavater's *Aphorisms*.

The same night that Olympias was delivered of Alexander, the Ephesian temple of Diana, one of the seven wonders of the world, was destroyed by fire. The incendiary Eroftratus was apprehended, and, after being tortured, confess'd that the only inducement he had to commit the act was to become memorable.

Many avoid speaking much, who, nevertheless, think much, of themselves. One who knew mankind well, recommends this as a rule: "Let the degree of egotism be the measure of confidence." The artful do not lay themselves open to detection by laxity of speech.

* Besides the fatigue and sameness of his office, how much the preceptor has to encounter on the score of incapacity and inattention! When the scholar has a brilliant capacity, genius is nurtur'd at the expence of genius; the augmentation of this part of nature is from the waste of that.

Contests are acts of insanity, where all the chances are in favour of an adversary.

Little things form the first rounds of a ladder, by which laudable ambition ascends to greatness.

> "* ⸻⸻ It hurts me to the soul
> "To brook confinement or controul;
> "Still to be pinion'd down to teach
> "The syntax, and the parts of speech;
> "Or what, perhaps, is drudging worse,
> "The links, and joints, and rules of verse:
> "To deal out authors by retail,
> "Like penny-pots of Oxford ale:
> "⸻ Oh, 'tis a service irksome more
> "Than tugging at the slavish oar."
>
> Lloyd.

nefs. Lavater tells us to " imitate him whofe obfervation paffes not even the moft minute, whilft it follows only the higheft objects; the feeds of grandeur lie already in himfelf; he gives his own turn to every thing, and *borrows* lefs than he *feizes* with one immediate glance. Such a one never ftops; his flight is that of an eagle, who, like an arrow, wings the mid air, whilft his pinions appear motionlefs.*

By trufting continually and implicitly to others, is it not poffible that we acquire the abfurd and difgraceful habit of miftrufting ourfelves? †

Abate from the works of fuperogation, officious meddler! Look into fociety; count the many acts of *kindnefs* which have been perform'd that nobody requir'd, that nobody appears thankful for. In thy duty alone fhalt thou find fufficient to perform.

'Tis

---

* Cardinal Retz marked out Cardinal Chigi for a man of a little mind from the moment that he told him " he had wrote three years with the fame pen, and that it was an excellent good one ftill."

Rochefoucauld fays, " Ceux qui s'appliquent trop aux petites chofes, deviennent ordinairement incapables des grandes." In truth, *les petites chofes* are great in their fituation."

† " The more independent of accidents, the more felf-fubfiftent, the more fraught with internal refources, the greater the character." Lavater's *Aphorifms.*

'Tis more charitable to kill than scorn, or call one knave instead of fool.

Poverty and senescence talk much of what they have been, or deserve to be. The sanguine of what they are to be, and seldom of what they are.

Compassion, if carried to an excess, is an infirmity: if the Stoics spoke of it in its extremes, they were wise to condemn it. Whether compassion is ingenite, or factitious, may, I think, be questioned.

* " Treasures of wickedness profit nothing." These words are taken from the Proverbs of Solomon; and to them may be added, As rain to a parched soil, so is the death of an usurer beneficial to society.

Munching

---

* *M. Jabineau*, a counsellor at law, published, in the year 1787, at Paris, a work bearing this title: " L'usure considerée relativement au droit naturel, &c." And the writers of the Journal Encyclopedique think he has fully established this position, *That usury is agreeable to the law of nature.*

Cumberland, in his comedy of the Jew, has introduced a character that stands forth as an apologist for the Miser. These words are employed on the occasion: " Misers are not unuseful
" members of the community; they are like banks to rivers,
" hold up the stream that would else run to waste, and make
" deep waters where there wou'd be shallows."

Munching is the deluded bigot's faſt. All unnatural laws are imperfectly obſerv'd.

If girls will not kiſs, they may do worſe: if they will kiſs, to a certainty, they will do worſe, unleſs they ſtop immediately.

Minds accuſtomed to activity are more impatient under inertion than fatigue.

Joy is the medicine of life—the rational panacea; and, by forcing the finer machinery of the organs into play, relieves the ever-toiling heart.

Confidence, if it is an act of flattery, partakes very much of the nature of ſincerity.—How can we doubt the being who confides in us? 'Tis not poſſible! We may whether he does confide tho'.

* Nations are often vilified for the delinquency of a few outcaſts and marauders: indeed, inſtances are not unfrequent of multitudes becoming ſufferers for the treſpaſſes of a few.

* " He is a poor local creature, who judges of men and things merely from the prejudices of his nation and time: but he is a knave who, in poſſeſſion of general principles, deals wanton condemnation on the ſame narrow ſcale."

Lavater's *Aphoriſms*.

Prosperity is complimented with every excellence.—'Tis a compliment to suppose that indigence is free from vice. Opulence may always have the credit of as many good qualities as it can pay for.

* Parties, separate connections, particular interests, are all of them fatal to the commonwealth of happiness.

Imagination makes us pay dear for its meanders: whilst we hand in hand wander in airy regions of false hope, and unsubstantial promise, we are either diverted from useful realities, or, by making a false step, are immerged in futurity's dismal gloom, where phantoms continue to appal, till recurring truth delivers us from these ideal drama of the mind.

† 'Tis not unfair to conclude, that those who expose their own affairs, unask'd, will pry officiously

---

* " He knows nothing of man, who expects to convince a determin'd party-man: and he nothing of the world, who despairs of the final impartiality of the public."

Lavater's *Aphorisms*.

† " Trust them with little who, without proofs, trust you with every thing; or when he has prov'd you with nothing."

Lavater's *Aphorisms*.

ciously into the concerns of their neighbours: something they must have to prate about.

'Tis easier to *seem* than to *be*, but 'tis not so honourable.

* Be fit to live; be ready to die! Never can I peruse these words without the strongest agitation. What has been undergone, what has been suffered, what struggles have been made, before we are fit to live! and, the point once attain'd, we are to be *ready* to enter into a state totally unconnected with life! Oh, 'tis a melancholy reflection, that those creatures who *are* fit to live shou'd ever die. What do the present and the future lose by one such death?

Regulated violence is the most that can be advanc'd in favour of many existing governments. " 'Tis incredible how easily the people are

---

* " Emori nolo, sed me esse mortuum nihil æstimo," said *Epicharmis*.

An Arabian poet and philosopher says, in an epigram, " that since his entrance into the world was mark'd by tears, tho' all the friends of his house were rejoicing, he thought it best to die laughing, that his friends might cry in their turn, if they thought proper."

Charles the Fifth was so indifferent about dying, that he assisted at his own obsequies, and, laying in his coffin, look'd at the preparation for his funeral.

are govern'd." This infulting fentence comes from Count Oxenftiern. Perhaps this queftion never occurred to the writer: In fuch cafes *how* are the people govern'd?

* WITH the mean, what merit can atone for a mean appearance?

AT

---

* Philopæmen had invited fome friends to meet him at an inn. He arrived firft. The hoftefs did not know him, but, encouraged by the meannefs of his appearance, employed him to draw water, and affift the maids in preparing a fire for Philopæmen. The gentlemen of his train arrived prefently after, and expreffed their furprize at feeing him fo employed. When they afked him what he was doing, he replied, " I am paying the penalty of my uglinefs."

We have a recent anecdote of the fame tendency. General Lee was remarkably negligent of his drefs. Attending Wafhington to a place diftant from the camp where they were to dine, he arrived firft, and proceeding directly to the kitchen, demanded fomething to eat. The cook anfwered, fhe would give him victuals in a moment, but that he muft firft help her off with the pot. He complied, and in a few minutes was ordered to put it on again ; and afterwards requefted to take a bucket, and go with her to the well. In the interim, Wafhington arrived, and an aid de camp was difpatched in fearch of Lee, whom, to his great furprize, he found engaged at the well. Guefs at the girl's confufion when fhe heard her affiftant called " His Excellency." Lee, ever ready to fee the impropriety of his conduct, but never willing to change it, gave the girl a crown ; and turning to the aid de camp, faid, " You fee, young man, the advantage of a fine coat ! The man of confequence is indebted

AT the well-provided banquet our care ends and begins.

WHEN flanderers, gamefters, and drunkards, affociate with their chofen friends, they are in the greateft danger.

WHEN a petition is prefented for relief, add no advice thereto, (it decreafes your dole full half,) unlefs the neceffitous afk for more than alms! 'Tis not fair to conclude, that thofe who are not pecuniarly on a par with you, fall fhort of it in every other qualification.

So callous are fome, 'tis no matter what they fee; others, who may be brought to feel, can get no further: avarice is too powerful for nature.

A NOBLE-MINDED being defcending from the throne of unnatural elevation to meet his brethren on the floor of equity, would do more to excite an enthufiafm in the caufe of Majefty, than all the pageantry of birth-days, or fhewy infignificance of ftate.

THE

debted to it for refpect; and neither virtue, or abilities, without it, will make him look like a gentleman!!!"

" As you treat your body, fo your houfe, your domeftics, your enemies, your friends: drefs is a table of your contents."
LAVATER's *Aphorifms.*

The nearer to truth, the worfe the epitaph muft be, unlefs we could be contented with the truth alone.

A certain plainnefs contained in the following lines have impreffed them on my memory.

Epitaph on an Englifhman.
Ci-gît Jean Rofbif Ecuyer,
Qui fe pendit peres fe defennuyer.

Colas eft mort de maladie,
Tu veux que j'en pleure le fort;
Que diable veux tu que j'en dis?
Colas vivoit, Colas eft mort.

We are ready with our money on two occafions; when it is not wanted, or when there is a certainty of great intereft *of fome kind* accruing from the loan of it.

* Tis a punifhment too fevere for the moft ftrong-nerv'd and patient of our enemies, to be confined

---

* " Frequent laughing has long been called a fign of a little mind, whilft the fcarcer fmile of harmlefs quiet has long been complimented as the proof of a noble heart: but to abftain from laughing, and exciting laughter, merely not to offend, or to rifk giving offence, or not to debafe the inward dignity of character, is a power unknown to many a vigorous mind."

Lavater's *Aphorifms.*

confined to the company of a long and violent laugher. To laugh at him is too much; to laugh with him is intolerable.

Ecclesiastes affirm, "That those who serve the altar should live by it."—It appears unjust tho', that those who built the altar should make others pay for it.

'Tis to contend with the authority of Custom; 'tis mortifying to comply with it. Pindar calls Custom, the King of all Men.

Never pronounce your opinion to a writer freely respecting the excellence of his writings, without recollecting the archbishop of Grenada* and his secretary.

† When the English meet, and part, how joyous they appear! How cold and indifferent they are whilst in company! yet friendship is not an exotic, it grows naturally, and thrives vigorously, in Britain.

---

* Vide Gil Blas.

† " As a man's salutation, so the total of his character: in nothing do we lay ourselves so open, as in our manner of meeting and saluting."

Lavater's *Aphorisms.*

Listen cautiously to those who make strong professions of attachment on a slight acquaintance, or those who court your suffrage eagerly on any occasion. The Italians have a good watch-word:

" Chi ti fa carezze più che non vuole
" O' c'ha ingannato, ò ingannar ti vuole."

* *Where* there is no fix'd character, *there* may be found the greatest aptitude for imitation. This observation is fully justified by the servile tribe of artists, writers, composers, who give duplicates of a duplicate, *ad infinitum*. No sooner does a genius arise (singular and admirable) than the petty manufacturers commence their aukward mutilations. *Peace to thy manes, O Sterne; but since thou suffer'd thy feelings to overflow on all occasions, what a deluge of sentiment has flow'd in on us, and carried away sense and nature!*

† Those who look for nothing more than sexual gratification, and provide no more for those

---

* " He who is always in want of something cannot be very rich. 'Tis a poor wight who lives by borrowing the words, decisions, mien, inventions, and notions of others.

Lavater's *Aphorisms*.

† " A languid, leaden iteration reigns,
And ever must, o'er those whose joys are joys

Of

thofe who do, foon weary of each other; hence the frequent and mutual difguft of the wedded; whilft the children of fcience, and thofe whom principle attach, return with increafed appetite to *the feaft of reafon*, and the flow of foul.

Vicious means cannot produce virtuous confequences. Whatever is employed to effect a good purpofe, is of itfelf good.

'Tis a common practice to reprobate vices in which we have no concern, and praife the virtue we moft excel in. Be affured, none who are habituated to this paltry, left-handed policy, (tho' you, Sir, are included in the number) have morality enough to cover the fins of a neighbour.

As vermin fallen, the generous animal decays.

Whatever

> Of fight, fmell, tafte:—The cuckow-feafons fing
> The fame dull note to fuch as nothing prize
> But what thofe feafons, from the teeming earth,
> To doating fenfe indulge. But nobler minds,
> Which relifh fruits unripen'd by the fun,
> Make their days various; various as the dyes
> On the dove's neck, which wanton in his rays.
> On minds of dove-like innocence poffeft,
> On lighten'd minds, that bafk in virtue's beams,
> Nothing hangs tedious."
>
> Young

* Whatever is by convention agreed upon as the token of distinction, will be ardently sought after. The Roman reward for saving the life of a citizen was a few oak leaves! The person who received this *corona civica* wore it at public spectacles, and sat next the senators: when he entered, the audience rose up as a mark of respect.

If you feel any inclination, or have any occasion, to flatter a fool, ask for his advice: if you wish to put yourself upon a par with him, follow it after it is obtain'd.

Cupidity, brutality, and superstition, are prominent features in the chronicles of most civilized nations.

How

---

* " Distinguish with exactness (if you mean to know yourself, and others) what is so often mistaken; the *singular*, the *original*, the *extraordinary*, the *great*, and the *sublime* man.

" The *sublime* alone unites the singular, original, extraordinary, and great, with his own uniformity and simplicity: the *great*, with many powers, and uniformity of ends, is destitute of that superior calmness, and inward harmony, which soar above the atmosphere of praise: the *extraordinary* is distinguished by copiousness, and a wide range of energy: the *original* need not to be very rich; only that which he produces is unique, and has the exclusive stamp of individuality: the *singular*, as such, is placed between originality and whim, and often makes a trifle the medium of fame." Lavater's *Aphorisms*.

* How do or can philofophers, or adjufters of contrarities, reconcile this? Man is the only animal that appears to defpife himfelf; yet is man the vaineft and proudeft creature on the earth.

The refpect that is paid folely to wealth, is often placed to the account of age or talents.

Those who connive at an injury, may be eafily induced to commit one: to the fcaffold there are only few fteps.

Bad

---

* "No two qualities in the human mind are more effentially different, tho' often confounded, than pride and vanity: the proud man entertains the higheft opinion of himfelf; the vain mind only ftrives to infufe fuch an opinion into the minds of others: the proud man thinks admiration his due; the vain man is fatisfied if he can but obtain it: pride, by ftatelinefs, demands refpect; vanity, by little artifices, folicits applaufe: pride, therefore, makes men difagreeable, and vanity, ridiculous.

Admiration is a common, unalienable privilege; and when this fenfation is once excited, cherifhed, and approved by judgment, 'tis manifeftly an injuftice to the object that occafioned it, not to give this admiration all the publicity we can. "Thofe who act becomingly are confcious of doing fo." 'Tis certainly true that they are, or they have only done good by chance, which does not conftitute virtue; but this confcioufnefs fhould be echoed by thofe who are immediately benefitted by them. To be *told* that our duties have been perform'd, is part of the reward for having perform'd them.

BAD children may make bad parents; bad parents are sure to make worse children.

* LYING may originate in cowardice, idleness, malice, vanity, meanness, treachery, and equivocation from fear or cunning.

DWARFS, who are asham'd of being what nature was not asham'd to make them, conceit themselves to have become actually taller by getting into stilts.

FROM

---

* "The additory fiction gives to a great man a larger share of reputation than belongs to him, to enable him to serve some good end or purpose."

ARBUTHNOT's *Art of Political Lying.*

"Who', without pressing temptation, tells a lie, will, without pressing temptation, act ignobly and meanly."

Again:

"Who, under pressing temptations to lie, adheres to truth, nor to the profane betrays aught of a sacred trust, is near the summit of wisdom and virtue."

Again:

"Between passion and lying there is not a finger's breadth."

Again:

"I know no friends more faithful, more inseparable, than hard-heartedness and pride, humility and love, lies and impudence." LAVATER's *Aphorisms.*

From certain perfons only, and at certain times, can relief be fafely preferred or required. 'Tis incredible that in a brotherhood as much difficulty fhould exift in obtaining, as in conferring, affiftance; tho' our neceffities make one common fund.

* The ear of a friend is the fanctuary of evil reports; there alone they are fafely conferved.

Compacts for the toleration of reciprocal duplicity are the monftrous devices of falfe delicacy, or of confirmed villainy.

Ancient philofophers have been loft in the immenfity of mechanical, and modern philofophers in the omnipotence of intellectual power.

† Had we a place to ftand on, we might raife the world, cries one. Another exclaims, The day will arrive when mind fhall triumph over matter.‡

Rancour

---

* "Admonifh a friend; it may be he hath not done it; and if he have done it, that he do it no more. Admonifh thy friend; it may be he hath not faid it; and if he have, that he fpeak it not again. Admonifh a friend; for many times it is a flander; and believe not every tale." *Ecclefiafticus.*

† Archimedes.

‡ Shakefpeare fpeaks of a man who had fuch a conceit in his brain; and the late Dr. B. Franklin gives fome weight to this hypothetic poffibility.

Rancour triumphs over fallen merit; whilſt it contemplates even the fall of rancour with wiſhful lamentations for its converſion.

Much adverſity is requiſite to make us hate life: a beckon from proſperity will recall this hatred inſtantly.

When we pardon, we only renounce the power of puniſhing; a power that muſt be proved legitimate, before any merit can reſult from the exerciſe of it.

'Tis a queſtion whether the major part of our ſuppoſed virtue does not ariſe from withholding from the exerciſe of poſitive vice.

We ſhould go bareheaded till honour crown us: but we can ſhameleſsly wear a uſurped ornament, rather than endure the ſhame of being ſuppoſed to deſerve one that is real.

Dotards, like over-hunted dogs, take a ſcent they cannot follow.

What we were bound to do, and have done, indubitably, we have a right to expect; nay, *enforce*, if 'tis withheld.—Juſt expectation is founded on actual performance.

FEW secrets that can be are worth knowing: the grave inurns many of value.

OUR best companions are *multis curis*, and without the obstinate pride of opinion.

UNIVERSAL knowledge is less presumptive, and more agreeable, than particular excellence of any sort.

LONGANIMITY is the art of steering free from the Scylla and Charybdis of troublesome society.

FLATTERY or interest has always a lullaby for the conscience of grown children.

THOSE who are lurkish, are open to the attacks of every ingenious scoundrel whose art will not alarm their indolence.

LIP-WISDOM is *ne plus ultra* of many moralists: and critics themselves are apparently more interested for their logomachy than for the cause of truth.

WHAT is done under the auspices of inclination, and a sense of duty, never occupies time enough in the performance of it.

PRODIGALS unite folly to imprudence, and injuftice to profufion; they are always on the other fide of enough, as paupers are of nothing.

LIBERTINES, fools, and runaways, are joyful acceffaries to their own ruin.

INFAMY has been the doom of thofe who have provided the cuckold with antlers; it may therefore belong to thofe who wear them.

GOOD breeding often conceals the deadlieft averfion. Vulgar hatred generally goes bare-faced; but the dubious arrangement of features that wait for opportunity to fawn, or curfe, is the moft to be apprehended.

NEITHER quantity, or quality, determines; fo there may be enough in a little.—The mind has a pleafing mode of judging independent of things.

A SMILE from affability is a beam from the fun of the mind; a tear of fympathy, a facred drop iffuing from the well of life: both are fweet to behold; and 'tis an enviable ftate to be the object of either.

PRECAUTION is, from its nature, precarious.

RUDENESS

Rudeness dictates; amity admonishes; confidence gives its advice, in which there is always too much of self.—'Tis the nature of the dilemma, and the means of extrication, or redemption, that wants to be explained, not the personal feelings of the by-stander.

Wet cheeks may easily win, or be won; they are either signals for solicitation, or the crocodile traps for stray affections.

* Grief certainly softens the heart; and that is the widow's apology.

We are both mortal and immortal when we are no more.

'Tis easier to act with integrity in poverty than in affluence, but it is more honourable to do so in prosperity.

When the people are good, the government is good for nothing.

Know the past; attend to the present.

---

* Amongst the Patagonians 'tis customary for the wives of the deceased to black their faces for one year.

Those who expect a repetition of events, and build upon their advent as upon a certainty, will be egregiously deceived in their calculations.

The power of the pen is great. Aristophanes overwhelmed Socrates by the force of his ridicule. States have fallen by ink; and more revolutions may be expected from the same cause. There is not at present a government that a philosophic citizen would contribute to the speedy destruction of.

Truth has always the support of reason, tho' it is in secret; error has often the support of force! The armies of every monarch on the earth are composed of men who enforce robbery, and discipline citizens by that social curse—the sword.

Opposition to truth is opposition to the welfare of mankind: in any shape it appears to be censurable; in most it deserves to be punish'd.

Affected bluntness, obsolete words pompously deliver'd, austere looks, slovenly dress, and contempt of customary forms, bring many half-bred scholars into notice—with the vulgar.

WHAT a security, what a serenity, there is in the bosom of the upright man! He is above surprize; a stranger to fear. When the memoir was offer'd to Caius Cæsar Caligula relative to his own security, he would not receive it. " I have nothing to render me odious, and have no ears for informers."

NEITHER despise yourself for being poor or ignorant; tho', left the world should despise you for being so, seize the first opportunity of becoming wise, and the best mode of becoming rich.

A FOOL's enmity is less fatal than his friendship; they are both to be apprehended: by kindness, or inadvertence, they are both occasioned.

CONTRADICTION frequently rivets a partiality that the weight of a hair would weigh down.

* LET your company either please, instruct, or transport, if you would have it sought for.

IN morality all citizens may be equal. Xenocrates was a man of such truth and fidelity, that the Athenians

---

* Who of mans' race is immortal?—He that fixes moments, and gives perennity to transitory things.

LAVATER's *Aphorisms.*

Athenians gave him this privilege, that his evidence should be lawful without swearing.

There is a trite error which youth always falls into; they suppose that Reason presides over the transactions of the world: their disappointment strongly induces them to believe that it ought.

The niggard, tho' he has drank to excess, will not direct the thirsty to the same stream.

Never judge of the preacher's piety by his professional zeal; the semblance of righteousness may be put on as mechanically as a surplice.

If the mazes of the heart are inscrutable even to its possessor, is it so astonishing that we frequently form false opinions of others?

Coxcombs may be very acceptable visitors to those who are fond of seeing new cloaths, hearing the jests of the last century, the slander of the day, and egotistical narrations.

Abstract ideas are most beneficial to the classes of society who live by them.

Mixt

Mixt company, and mixt wine, are both voidable, and unavoidable.

Anarchy is the feafon of toleration for every bafe paffion.

General courtfhips, like general invitations, invite many, without feafting any.

Poets, fiddlers, and beggars, are always dull in dull weather.

* Do not childifhly lament over your wants and defires; devife adequate means to obtain and gratify them.

Tumultuous are the rejoicings of ignorance and villainy; that of cowardice is brutal: the triumphs of virtue and wifdom are peaceful, but of a long duration.

---

* " Diftinguifh with exactnefs in thyfelf and others, between wifhes and will, in the ftricteft fenfe. Who has many wifhes, has generally but little will. Who has energy of will, has few diverging wifhes. Whofe will is bent with energy on one, muft renounce the wifhes for many things. Who cannot do this, is not ftored with the majefty of human nature. The energy of choice, the unifon of various powers for one, is only will, born under the agonies of felf-denial, and renounced defires.

Lavater's *Aphorifms.*

Frequent violations of right frequently apprize citizens of their rights.

When the excellence of your fare invites, think lightly of your own consequence, whatever opinion you may entertain of the understandings of your guests.

Tho' thrones are rear'd on the ignorance of mankind, they *may* be fill'd by virtuous kings.

Ignorance often exclaims, and declaims; it seldom reclaims.

If a jester will jest even with his own reputation, he is in a fair way to become a very dangerous member of the social community.

To anticipate felicity, is as infallible a proof of unadulterated affection, as ante-dating misery is of despondence.

* 'Tis not every head that will fit a crown, tho' every upstart thinks himself fit to wear one.

---

* While Franklin resided in France, he had numerous applications made to him by projectors of every kind, and of every country: amongst the rest, there was one who offered himself

The Arabians have said, that the greater the head is, the more it is expofed to danger.

Error's long dominion is almoſt fufficient to make us doubt the power of Truth.

Wits feldom are profperous; and profperity has brought many a man to the end of his wits.

Is there not a price too great to be paid for any thing woman or man have to beſtow?

When Jews poffefs the learning of Scotchmen, and the firmnefs of Englifhmen, they will be an overmatch for the reft of the world.

---

to be King. He introduced his propofal to the Doctor by letter, ſtating firſt, that, as the Americans had difmiffed, or fent away, their king, that they would want another. Secondly, that himfelf was a Norman. Thirdly, that he was of a more ancient family than the Dukes of Normandy, and of a more honourable defcent, his line having never been baſtardized. Fourthly, that there was already a precedent in England, of kings coming out of Normandy. And on thefe grounds he refted his offer, enjoining, that the minifter would forward it to America: but as the Doctor neither did this, or yet fent him an anfwer, the projector wrote a fecond letter, in which he did not, it is true, threaten to go over, and conquer America, but only, with great dignity, propofed, that, if his offer was not accepted, an acknowledgment of about 30,000l. might be made to him for his generofity!!!"

Why should we look lightly, or suspiciously, on those services that are voluntarily tender'd? Is it impossible for one brother to act uprightly, or disinterestedly, towards another?

* We are amiable, we are happy, as long as we are enthusiasts in the cause of love or philanthropy.

The superfluities of life are the most superfluous things in it.

Neglect of merit shou'd neither abash its spirit, or suspend its efforts, for it cannot diminish its value.

Envy, indulgence, and admiration, separately, or collectively, have stinted the growth of many early plants of promise.

† Instantly that the mind becomes inactive, or that the eyes wander indeterminately, evil thoughts obtrude.

Multiplied and complex laws, what are they less than enregistered proofs of a vicious community,

---

* La sensibilité fait tout notre genie.

† " The gazer in the streets wants a plan for his head, and an object for his heart." Lavater's *Aphorisms*.

community, or an ignorant, oppreffive legiflation? Even thefe evils may be decreafed by equity—Equity, the *modern* cenfor of Juftice!

It behoves the great to be vigilant and circumfpect; not one, even of their moft infignificant actions, can pafs unobferv'd, or terminate in neutrality.

Women feldom hear tales of youthful diftrefs, or plaufible villainy, in a beautiful fhape, without pitying;* or pity, without loving; or love, without adoring. Lord Corke fays, " *Great* endowments of the mind are apt to charm us into compaffion, where, perhaps, we ought to fhew abhorrence, or, at leaft, contempt. We forget the villain; we adore the man: but, in truth, no abilities can make amends for treachery; nor can the beft head atone for a bad heart."

The richeft flower may be placed too near the nofe, or continued there too long: there is a diftance, as well as a time, for all things.

The credit is always on the fide of the debtor, and the difcredit frequently on the fide of the creditor.

---

* " Things do not plague mankind; 'tis the opinions and prejudices that are entertained of them." Epictetus.

* Denial is the laconism of injustice, as consent is of prodigality.

'Tis fruitless to chide if you smile, or threaten, if you do not enforce: children will discover and take advantage of this weakness, so obvious and resistible is it.

Pedants are more easily to be endur'd than triflers: their errors are at least tinctur'd with learning.

† The smallest injury is a great favour from a tyrant; their greatest kindness is only abstinence from cruelty.

Depravity is at its highest, when the frequency of prostitution has obliterated all sense of shame, and the riches it has accumulated enables it to treat virtue with indignity.

Interest should go hand in hand with duty; but they are as seldom to be found together as law and justice.

---

* Er hat einen beutel mit geld, so grofz evie ein affenschwanz. *i. e.* He is as well provided with money as a monkey is with tale.

† " A tyrant may imprison, but he cannot prevent us from despising and hating him: from speaking of his cruelty, and traversing his projects." Epictetus.

* THE meritorious are all brethren; and compaffion allies us to thofe who are deftitute.

IN certain cafes 'tis as criminal to withhold as to purloin.

BRIBE rogues with millions, 'twill not ftop their detraction; give fycophants your fhirt, they will crave your fkin.

† IF you have an averfion to the water, and muft fwim, fwim with the tide, or you will be exhaufted.

‡ THE flatterer's practices do not difgrace or deftroy himfelf alone.

IT has been faid, that making property the ftandard of fuffrage is an unjuft way of meafuring

---

* " The poor man who envies not the rich, who pities his companions of poverty, and can fpare fomething for him that is ftill poorer, is, in the realms of humanity, a king of kings."
LAVATER's *Aphorijms*.

† No advantage is fo complete, but 'tis attended with fome difadvantage.   *French Proverb.*

‡ Der knittel liegt allemal beynt hunde.
German Proverb.

ing the value of citizenship; 'tis, at leaft, a ridiculous one: money and man have no affinity.

Take away the citizen's pride in being rigidly virtuous, and how little confolation there is under the curb that fo feverely galls him!

* Give caufe for jealoufy, (no matter if it be real or fictitious,) and 'twill revive what dormant paffion there is remaining, whether in a lover or a truant hufband. By the bye, this experiment is a dangerous one. If the heart is valuable that you wifh to recover, 'tis worth fome rifk.

Satiety, difguft, or thwarted expectations, make many apathifts and mifanthropes.

The fuperficial affect to defpife what they do not immediately comprehend; the inquifitive are delighted with it.

In popular commotions, the great mind feems in its proper fphere. A trifle calms or inflames: judicioufly to propofe, or contradict, requires wifdom, and a noble contempt of perfonal danger: the whole foul muft be engag'd.

Immortal

* " A whifper can difpel the flumbers of hatred and of love." Lavater's *Aphorifms*.

Immortal be the memory of the French prefident Mounier! He declar'd, in the hour of extreme peril, " that 'twas unlawful to tear people in pieces for wearing cockades of a wrong colour."—Such are the difpofitions calculated to check the ferocity of civil tumult, and, by drawing the mind from infignificant diftinctions, (that have too often caufed the fpoliation of human blood,) direct it to its proper object—reform without animofity.

Probity is tenable; fame is not: the former depends on ourfelves alone; the latter exclufively on others. In many cafes I fhou'd no more fubmit to be told what deferv'd to be call'd probity, than for what I merited to become famous.

Scholars are frequently to be met with, who are ignorant of nothing—faving their own ignorance.

Timidity is no more natural to woman than courage is to man. It has been too long the illiberal practice of the world to faddle the fex with the faults of their education.

How can abftinence be a virtue, unlefs enjoyment is a vice? It may be practifed out of policy;

cy; then our return to pleasure has more piquancy.

* ADVERSITY and prosperity are often suppos'd, but falsly, to include wretchedness and felicity.

† SILENCE has occasionally the semblance and effect of authority; never of virtue; tho' Zeno preferr'd it to all the others.

ADVICE is sure to be relish'd, if you can contrive to echo the sentiments of those who seek it.

'TIS not because we depreciate that we do not covet; or blame, that we do not wish to praise. A thousand mean motives hang over the balance at the hour of valuation.

THE instant our successor is fix'd, we look upon him with secret, in-felt detestation.

OF

---

* " Desunt inopiæ multa, avaritiæ omnia."
SENECA.

† " He knows not how to speak who cannot be silent; still less how to act with vigour and decision. Who hastens to the end is silent: loudness is impotence."
LAVATER's *Aphorisms*.

* OF external devotion, and speculative knowledge, there is still plenty in the world; but they produce very little practical wisdom or piety.

Those will not be bankrupts within a century who trade with the vices or follies of their cotemporaries.

Laugh as loud as you please at your companion's wit: do not even smile at his folly.

The envious had rather take an asp to their bosom than admit the deserving to their friendship.

No creature resembles a harlot so much as a hypocrite by profession; he smiles on all he meets, and prostitutes his integrity for profit.

The trite expression runs thus: He is nobody's enemy but his own." Is it not possible to add, If he is any body's enemy, he must be his own; and if he is his own enemy, the same must he be to all others?

Errors,

---

* " Formerly, Sir," said a bookseller, " very comfortable livelihoods were to be picked up by the sale of bibles and testaments: now those sacred volumes are but seldom call'd for ! ! !"

Errors, like girls of a certain defcription, are not only expenfive in the outfet, but ruin us by their maintenance.

Restraint and indulgence have, in fome cafes, fimilar effects.

Coquettes frequently lofe all their admirers. Is it furprifing? Which of them can be affur'd of their fincerity?

Hearts that are eafily won, are eafily deferted: difficulty of obtaining feems to enhance their value: yet the gueft may be, to the utmoft, as deferving of our efteem, as the one who, from affected coynefs, requires much folicitation.

*'Twixt the difagreeing hufband and wife, thofe who attempt to interfere, muft be, at leaft, able to cope with them both.

---

* Madame Mara received at Berlin marks of Royal favour. Frederick often converfed with her at his concerts, and feveral times accompanied her finging with his German flute. At one of thefe concerts the entertainment was obftructed by the abfence of Madame. Her abfence was occafioned by the corporeal caftigation fhe had received from her hufband. The king, as ftrong a difciplinarian in his concert-room as in the field, no fooner heard of this, than he decreed a retribution in kind; and obferving that the hufband of Mara was thus fond of *beating*, ordered

Those who are alive to the calls of honour, hold their lives on an ideal tenure.

Policy is sometimes a subtle refinement; at other times an ornamented cheat.

What is dislik'd, or despis'd, what is beyond our purse, or has been lost by our imprudence, is too frequently painted in odious colours.

Compliments fill up the hiatus, when intellect, sincerity, or affection, are mute.

Such adulation as we pay is afterwards usuriously exacted.

* Seek for no man's invitation; qualify yourself to fit at any man's table; and always prefer that

---

dered him to a drill some distance from Potzdam, where he should beat a drum for three years. When he had been some time at this new musical employ, his wife, unusually successful in her singing, drew from the king more than ordinary marks of applause. Thinking this a favourable hour, she threw herself at the monarch's feet, and supplicated for her husband's return. 'Twas, after some ludicrous remarks, granted: But the king said, If ever she was beaten again, 'twou'd be in vain to look to him for redress.

* " He who chooses to consider the ambiguous action of an enemy in its fairest light, has some acquaintance with the heart of man, and is a friend to virtue. Lavater's *Aphorisms.*

that of your adverfary or enemy: your generous attendance on his hofpitality may convert him.

* Those who have exalted fentiments, thofe who are animated with the fpirit of philanthropy, will divide your anguifh rather than your joy. No mother's child has more felicity than he can find heart-room for; but the chalice of affliction often overflows.

† Inconveniencies of all defcriptions are tolerated with more temper out of doors than within; tho' with lefs patience abroad than in our own country.

If

---

* A young prince, on a hunting party, faid to his preceptor, " 'tis cold; give me my mantle." The gentleman replied, " My lord, your highnefs ought to know, that great princes, fpeaking of their perfons, always exprefs themfelves in the plural number; you fhould therefore have faid, give us our mantle." The prince did not fail afterwards to obferve this leffon exactly; and one day faid to his preceptor, " Our teeth ach." " Mine, I am fure," replied he, with a fmile, " do not ach " in the leaft, my lord." Then," anfwered the prince, a little chagrined at the remark, " I plainly fee, that the mantle muft be *ours*, but the tooth-ach muft be *mine* alone."

† " Him who inceffantly laughs in the ftreets, you may conftantly hear grumbling in his clofet."

Lavater's *Aphorifms*.

If monarchs take all power from the people, the more they take the lefs they poffefs.

The infolence of fudden profperity is moft afflicting to thofe who have beheld the change without being included in it.

To affume with propriety the auguft office of an hiftorian, befides fuch qualities as in themfelves would be well worth a record, requires co-exiftence with the facts defcrib'd.

Evasions are the feints of villains or cowards.

No correfpondent ever did, or can, write as he wou'd fpeak. The prefence of a fecond perfon deranges the formality of previous arrangements, and gives a different turn to thought.

Moderation in maintaining our pretenfions, or fentiments, is as ftrong an earneft of good fenfe, as renunciation of error is of manlinefs, or forbearance of magnanimity.

Those Sectarians who contend for a freedom of will, are nefcious how much more capricious and arbitrary it wou'd make the leaft wilful of us appear.

* To conquer trifles is an irksome, not an impossible, task to a lofty mind: the difficulty must be equal to its faculties; when 'tis superior, the trifle neglected subdues the greatest.

When a king appears in his peaceful territories guarded, either the laws or his person are not overmuch regarded.

* Impromptu by Bishop Atterbury.

The words of the wife man, thus preach'd to us all,
Despise not the worth of those things that are small.

The quill of a goose is a very slight thing,
Yet it feathers the arrow that flies from the string,
Makes the bird it belongs to soar high in it's flight,
And the jack it has oil'd, against dinner go right:
It brightens the floor, when turn'd to a broom;
And brushes down cobwebs at top of a room:
Its plumage by art into figures is wrought,
As soft as the hand, and as quick as the thought!
It warms in a muff, and it cools in a screen;
It is good to be felt, and as good to be seen.
When wantonly waving, it makes a fine show
On the crest of the warrior, or hat of the beau.
The quill of the goose (I shall never have done,
If thro' all its perfections and praises I run)
Makes the harpsichord vocal, which else wou'd be mute,
And enlivens the sounds, the sweet sounds of the flute;
Records what is written in verse or in prose,
By Ramsay or Cambray, by Bayle or Despreaux:
Therefore well did the wife man thus preach to us all,
Despise not the worth of those things that are small.

At the feast of the Great Biram, the Grand Signior, with his grandees, go to the mosque of Sultan Ahmed. On his appearance, a deep silence is observ'd. The janisaries line the streets; they stand with their hands across, and bow as the Grand Signior and his Viziers pass: they return the salute. I ask'd a captain of the janisaries why they had no arms? "Arms," said he, "you infidel! they are for our enemies: we govern our subjects with the law."

Obedience does not always include approval or attachment.

Chastity cannot, in all cases, be reckon'd a part of female duty, tho' a breach of it sometimes may.

How many censors had the Romans for the whole city? How many have European cities in every street? And for the state of ethics, do we exceed or fall short of the Romans in moral perfection?

Great men are allow'd, by an over-stretch'd licence, to say any thing; but those who take advantage of the indulgence, say nothing.

The dilatory muſt wait till a bridge is built before they can paſs the river: thoſe who are expeditious, like Julius, will ſwim acroſs the ſtream.

Those who are fully appriz'd that they ſacrifice the rights of mankind to the maintenance of their ſplendor, deſerve more than the contempt of thoſe they injure.

Under the pretended ſanction of the Divinity, the moſt ſolemn farces, and cruel tragedies, have been perform'd. The actors call themſelves his ſervants; and the words they uſe, they affect to have receiv'd from heaven.

* Select a lofty object for your abuſe, if 'tis your fix'd intent to ingratiate yourſelf with the vulgar: they know not how to complete their wiſhes, and are glad of any deputy to level ingenuity with ignorance, and poliſh'd manners with brutality.

When woman is inveſted with all that juſtly belongs to her, then ſhall we ſee how far conſtancy

---

* " There is always ſomething great in that man againſt whom the world exclaims, at whom every one throws a ſtone, and on whoſe character all attempt to fix a thouſand crimes without being able to prove one." *Vide Zimmerman on Solitude.*

stancy to a hated or cruel object is consistent with free agency.

* A LEGISLATIVE adept will cause shame and pride to supersede gibbets and criminal statutes.

† WHAT danger is there in avowing that virtue is no more than a code of laws for the accommodation of society? Is there any thing more dear to us than our comfort? Is there a single being (so inimical to himself) who will not make this comfort secure where he can, or cannot from his own necessities see what his neighbour requires?

THOSE who are restless under obligations, are either very slow themselves to oblige, very proud, or they have accepted favours from necessity.

KEEP all disappointments to yourself; trust him who has deceived you no oftener than you can

---

* " In the death of a man there is no remedy: neither was there any man ever known to have returned from the grave."
The Wisdom of Solomon.

† Speaking of the laws, Sophocles, in his Œdipus Tyrannus, asserts, that they were not the invention of men, but that they descended from heaven; that they were the daughters of Jove, and by nature were exempt from the ravages of time.

can help: tho' he has been in the habits of strict‑ est intimacy; nay, tho' he was lodged in the same womb with you, or is a *sworn brother* *, keep steady to the determination; but do not let him see the cause: those who repeatedly offend this way, are past amendment: find employ for such where there is no trust.

The best of those professional hypocrites, call'd courtiers, have most of the *versitale ingenium*; this recommends them to the notice of their su‑ periors; and the habit of bearing despotism grace‑ fully continues them in favour.

Sincerity is indicative of an exalted mind; it has a peculiar tone; once heard, it cannot be forgotten: it throws the challenge to imitation; so the mind cannot suffer by the mis‑judgment of the ear.

A HAIR

---

* The Sclavonian ritual contains a particular benediction for the solemn union of two male or two female friends in the presence of the congregation. The male friends thus united are called *Pobratimi*; and the females, *Pofestreme*; which means half brothers, and half sisters. Friendships between those of differ‑ ent sexes are not at this day bound with so much solemnity. From these confecrated unions among the Morlacchi, and other nations of the same origin, it should seem that *the sworn brothers* arose; a denomination frequent enough among our common people, and in many parts of Europe. The sole creed of this brotherhood is reciprocal service and advantage.

Travels into Dalmatia by the Abbé Fortis.

* A HAIR may often divide wit and folly, vice and virtue, wisdom and absurdity, industry and idleness.

THE greatest courtezan in the city, is the individual against whom every base passion is directed: She is abused, envied, cheated, contemned, lov'd, and lusted after.

OLD favours, tho' previously liquidated, are, by the niggardly, always reviv'd when their solicitations are rejected: with them no reason can justify refusal.

HONOURS, as rewards, shou'd never be permanent or hereditary: why wealth shou'd be descendible I know not.

---

* Cardinal Richelieu, notwithstanding his wit, was subject to violent fits of insanity, during which he sometimes imagined himself a horse, and pranced along round a billiard table, striking his heels against his servants, then neighing and making a dreadful noise for the space of an hour. When his fit had subsided, his domestics put him to bed, where he was well covered with cloaths, and slept, and perspired hastily: on waking, he never remembered one circumstance that had passed.

"The east and west,
Upon the globe, a mathematic point
Only divides: thus happiness and misery,
And all extremes, are still contiguous."

Denham's Sophy.

Amongst the nobility we often fee avarice fubordinate to oftentation: it generally is paramount to all other paffions.

* Death itfelf is lefs terrible to fome than the preparation for it. When Paul Scarron's bed was furrounded by weeping attendants, "Ah," faid the wit, "my good friends, you'll never cry for me fo much as I have made you laugh."

* Rabelais, juft before his death, ordered a domino to be put on him: "Then," faid he, "I fhall be fafe; for the fcripture affirms, Beati qui in domino moriuntur."

"The Marquis de Villette, with whom Voltaire refided in Paris, when he perceived his vifitor's death approaching, fent for Monfieur Bonnet, curé of St. Sulpice, to perfuade him, if poffible, to comply with the ufual cuftoms of their religion, in order that the proper honours might be paid to his remains. The curé began by queftioning Voltaire if he believed in the divinity of Chrift, but was haftily ftopped by the wit's faying, "Ah, Monfieur le Curé, if I pafs that article to you, you will demand, if I do not alfo believe in the Holy Ghoft, and fo on, till you finifh by the bull Unigenitus."

"The curé departed; but, in a few hours after, a great change appearing, he came a fecond time, and began with putting his hand on the dying man's head as he lay in bed; upon which Voltaire raifed his own hand to the curate's head, and pufhed him away, faying, "I came into the world without a Bonnet, and will go out without one; therefore let me die in peace." He turned his back, and died without fpeaking! 30th of May."

The Morlacchi put fugar in the mouths of thofe who are departing, that they may pafs into the next world with lefs bitternefs.

CAREFULLY diftinguifh 'twixt the player and the part which he plays: he is *forc'd* to affume a character; however defpicable or amiable that may be, do not blend it with his unaffum'd character.

SYMPATHY makes a copartnerfhip with forrow, and adminifters confolation with exquifite delicacy: its compenfation is in the mind!

To know a man thoroughly, is to know him perpetually. Turn your eyes for an inftant to the right, or left, and not lefs than a hundred determining principles will have efcap'd. Lavater infifts that we fhou'd not fay we know another entirely, till we have divided an inheritance with him.

THE moft fuccefsful juggler keeps his fpectators the moft in the dark.

WE feem *ourfelves* to be the propereft perfons to raife the barriers betwixt moderation and excefs in all fenfual gratifications. We can meafure our draught to our thirft, and which of us will drink to a furfeit becaufe the Thames is acceffible?

What you have been is immaterial; what you may be is now inscrutable; what you are—aye, that is the point for consideration! And how shall we make out the valuation? Oh, it must be a sordid wretch, who will not, in this fluctuating scene, suffer a retrospect of what is past to prevail a little at the present.

* Anger continued terminates in revenge; and, by calling up the anger of the opposite party, converts a temporary disagreement into an everlasting hatred. Hear the great philanthropist: " Know that the great art to love your enemy, consists in never losing sight of man in him: humanity has power over all that is human: the most inhuman man still remains man, and never can throw off *all* taste for what becomes a man:—But you must learn to wait."

Insolence is always contemptible: without authority 'tis dangerous; with it, cruel: how is it to be apologized for, without committing an act of fresh insolence?

The acme of philosophy is to behave consistently on extraordinary occasions.

When

---

* " The wrath that, on conviction, subsides into mildness, is the wrath of a generous mind." Lavater's *Aphorisms.*

When our faults do not keep pace with our abilities, then we ſtand ſingularly eminent.

* Examine what mental information has been gain'd, before you enter a ſecond time the ſame company of males. Get into the ſociety of the other ſex at any rate; if you are not inſtructed, 'tis your own fault if you are not pleas'd.

When we conceit that we are acting the hero, we are frequently playing the brute.

Few are to be found who do not amuſe themſelves with a toy of ſome kind in every ſtage of their lives.

Great qualities as naturally beſpeak the partiality of the ingenious, as beauty does the adoration of the ſenſual.

Dull ſouls are content to admire; great ſouls are ſedulous to rival or excel.

Those who are not corrupted, are corruptible, if they are mercenary.

---

* Stratonicus, an excellent muſician, left a houſe where he had been well entertain'd, becauſe he found every fool and rogue were there made welcome.

Women never need be taught how to indulge their inclination; the liberty of doing is all they require.

Armies often expose themselves for an opinion:—they will fight for fame; through fear, or necessity; for a commander, or for money. When do they engage for justice?

* To-morrow is a new day: To-morrow I shall be a new man.

The atheist's only hope ceases where the Christian's strongest hope begins: He leaves life without being reduced to the necessity of repentance, for he thinks his race is run: The latter takes the last opportunity of preparing himself for a state where every thing worth enjoying is to be placed before him.

'Tis cruel to conceal love, tho' sometimes it augments by it. Nothing encourages love like brooding over it.

Women

---

* " There was a Grecian proverb, " To-morrow is a new day " It arose from Archias, the tyrant of Thebes, who, the night before Pelopidas put his plot into execution for killing him, in order to restore his country to liberty, had an account of the whole conspiracy delivered to him at supper; but he deferred the opening of it, saying, " To-morrow is a new day."

* Women who have holy men continually at their elbow, frequently, in their fits of devotion, allow them to approach nearer.

The situation of the priesthood in an age of free discussion is critical: if the citizens will become priests, priests must become citizens.

Servants sometimes profit by the vices of their employers, and sometimes are ruin'd by them.

† Neither accept an opinion, or except against it, merely on the score of its novelty: all that is new is not true, but much that is old is false.

Pride lives at its own expence, it cannot be denied: 'tis also very expensive to all its associates; no man keeps company with the proud without paying dearly for it.

The strongest wish a miser has to accumulate is always the last.

---

* " The more honesty a man has, the less he affects the air of a saint: the affectation of sanctity is a blotch on the face of piety. Lavater's *Aphorisms*.

† " All is not, cannot, be new; but all ought to be true, useful, important." Lavater.

* If the severity of their castigation was taken into account, 'twou'd not be extraordinary if a superficial observer shou'd mistake virtues for vices, levities for crimes.

'Tis in the extremes of condition that the extremes of licentiousness are to be found: the great art of the politician appears to be bringing mankind nearly on a level with regard to pecuniary circumstances.

† A LUCKY thought, or look, has made many a fortune.

WOMEN are more open in their flatteries than in their injuries.

THRICE

---

* The Stoics esteem'd all sins equal.

† Notwithstanding that 'tis very improbable that St. Peter ever officiated as bishop of Rome, yet 'twas commonly believed that the identical chair used by him in his sacerdotal character was in the possession of the Romans, and the 18th of January was always set apart as the festival of the said chair. In 1662, whilst it was cleaning, in order to be placed in some conspicuous part of the Vatican, the twelve labours of Hercules were discovered engraved on it: this would have certainly diminished its value, but Luchesini explained the labours of the Grecian hero into a mystical representation of the future exploits of the Popes, and Clement X. rewarded the writer's ingenuity!!!

Thrice happy is the creature who has reason to thank his parents for his birth; much happier are those who, by the energy of their own endeavours, have rais'd themselves superior to adventitious circumstances, and have obtained the esteem of their co-citizens.

After we have weigh'd ourselves with scrupulous caution, 'tis probable that we attain something valuable.

There appears to be three chances in shewing civility to a rival, or competitor. It may abate, or prevent, animosity; it may put him off his guard, by the unexpected appearance of security; and, by such complaisance, a party before indifferent, prejudiced, or partial, may be brought over to your interest.

* On paper there are many philanthropists, yet there is very little active benevolence to be found; therefore 'tis to be fear'd that their words and actions, capacity and intentions, are not pertingent.

---

* " The moral enthusiast, who, in the maze of this refinement, loses, or despises, the plain paths of honesty and duty, is on the brink of error." LAVATER's *Aphorisms*.

Many contingencies, besides the excellence of the verse, must concur in order to procure for the poet either wealth or reputation.

Authority may exist without power; that is the awful moment of political revolution.

Strange designs lurk under a gift!—"Give the horse to his holiness," said the cardinal: "I cannot serve you."

Often does it happen that we starve our best friends to pamper our greatest oppressors.

Mysticism is the grand arcanum of duplicity, as obscurity is of superstition.

Whilst we are in a precarious state of uncertainty and danger, whilst we are dependent for all the comforts we enjoy, why should we affect to exalt ourselves above human considerations?

* Joy is not always communicable; seldom in the same degree that it is felt.

---

* "The glad gladdens: who gladdens not is not glad. Who is fatal to others, is so to himself; to him, heaven, earth, wisdom, folly, virtue, vice, are equal: to such a one tell neither good nor bad of yourself."

Lavater's *Aphorisms*.

Is it the fault of women that we sicken before we grow tir'd of them?

* Curiosity and intrusion are alike, when the former is carried to an extreme. Curiosity is a good servant when under the controul of discretion.

Students who cannot grace their brows with laurels, may avoid disgracing them with a fool's cap: industry alone will place them above contempt.

Occasionally declare your principles, least what you are, and wish to be, shou'd be liable to dubiety, or misinterpretation. For want of opportunity we cannot completely manifest the purity of our intentions.

What is original is in its kind perfect. An original may be imitated; it cannot be exceeded.

Wives authorize, or prohibit, the truantry of their husbands too early or too late; too often, or not at all.

---

* "Who forces himself on others, Is to himself a load. Impetuous curiosity is empty and inconstant. Prying intrusion may be suspected of whatever is little."

Lavater's *Aphorisms*.

* Knaves speak of themselves as they think proper; good men are content to speak properly of themselves.

Many even of the skilful, or scientific, blame or praise to proclaim their ingenuity. On caprice frequently depends the rise or fall of the poor noviciate.

† Those who are deeply in love, generally suffer by and for the passion.

‡ Servants are not unfrequently reduced copies or miniatures of their masters—if either of them are worthless.

Neither the sensual or opulent know how much they want, tho' they may know how much they have.

A LITTLE

---

* " Let the degree of egotism be the measure of confidence." Lavater's *Aphorisms*.

† " Spare the lover without flattering his passion; to make the pangs of love the butt of ridicule is unwise and harsh; soothing meekness and wisdom subdue, in else, unconquerable things." Lavater's *Aphorisms*.

‡ " This Aristion was a compound of lewdness and cruelty; the very *sink* of all the vicious humours and ill qualities of his master Mithridates." Plutarch.

A little ingenuity will convert a peevish charge into a compliment: thus may the machinations of the morose be defeated.

Tho' you're close to the altar, you are not a gry the nearer to heaven; tho' the nearer you get to the throne, the further you are from the gallows.

Where we are confident of approbation, or can command despotically, we are apt to be indifferent about pleasing.

* From his desires the being is to be appreciated, when lack of opportunity prevents us from ascertaining the mode and extent to which they are gratified.

Wives are all devotion; they would sacrifice health, wealth, or life, to compleat the felicity of their idol; but 'tis at his peril to be happy by any other means than those she prescribes.

---

* " The less you can enjoy, the poorer, the scantier yourself: the more you can enjoy, the richer, the more vigorous."

Again:

" He scatters enjoyment who can enjoy much."

Lavater's *Aphorisms.*

There is nothing so good, or bad, that does not lead to something better or worse than itself.

The romantic are under the influence of artificial feelings; and whilst they are congratulating themselves on the refinement of their hearts, they are, in reality, plunging deeper into depravity.

* Fear is as much the consequence of experience as of ignorance, self-love, or nervous relaxation: 'tis not a vice, but a misfortune.

People who are over difficult to please, often choose the worst at last; and those who will have nothing but the best, must either submit to frequent mortification, or stay 'till none but the worst is left.

The warmth of a new convert makes many proselytes among his associates.

Troops of furies march in the drunkard's triumph.

---

* Frowns will be totally indifferent to a child who has never found them associated with the effects of anger. Fear itself is a species of foresight, and never exists till introduced by experience
Political Justice.

'Twou'd be a confiderable confolation to the poor and difcontented, cou'd they but fee the means whereby the wealth they covet has been acquir'd, or the mifery that it entails.

* Men have the fame fort of faculties, 'tis true, tho' they are not of the fame quality: this variation is not adventitious; it arifes out of the nature and ordain'd conftitution of things. To attempt to reduce us to a common ftandard, is a political abfurdity; 'tis impoffible; and, if poffible, 'twou'd be unjuft. The great ftimulus to exertion wou'd be at an end, if rewards were alike; there wou'd then, indeed, be a ftupid equality, and we fhou'd crawl through life with as much indifference as the very animals that 'tis now our pride to excel in every thing ornamental, ufeful, and ingenious.

To

---

* " All men are born equal; but a burgefs of Maroc does not fufpect that this truth exifts. This equality is not the annihilation of fubordination; we are all equally men, but not all equal members of fociety. All natural rights belong equally to the Sultan and the Boftangi: both the one and the other ought to difpofe, with the fame power, of their perfons, their families, and their fortunes. Men are therefore effentially equal, altho' they play on the theatre of life different parts." *Voltaire.*

" Know, in the firft place, that mankind agree in effence as they do in their limbs and fenfes. Mankind differ as much in effence as they do in form, limbs, and fenfes, and only fo, and not more." Lavater's *Aphorifms.*

To acquire or support any sort of character, great sacrifices are required, great mortification must be supported.

* " He who, to obtain much, will suffer little, or nothing, can never be called great; and none ever little, who, to obtain one great object, will suffer much."

Enthusiasm surmounts all the difficulties that untoward circumstances can bring to bear against it.

† Prudence is essentially its own check, but passion grows madder for its chain.

Youth and dotards take women at any price; wisdom and experience never offer beyond their value. When women are capable of appreciating themselves, or the contrary sex, every thing on their part will be gratuitous; no payment can come from man but merit.

Cunning is the offspring of necessity or selfishness; violence is the issue of ignorance or brutal

---

* Lavater's *Aphorisms.*

† " He submits to be seen through a microscope who suffers himself to be caught in a fit of passion.

Lavater's *Aphorisms.*

brutal precipitance; fear is the child of religion, infipience, or nerval relaxation.

Besides the immediate gratification of vanity, much is infinuated by a peculiar mode of drefs. What a woman wifhes to be her garments always proclaim.

The largeft edifices are dedicated to dangerous folly, or difgraceful fuperftition.

It does not follow that evil is the parent of good, becaufe it fometimes arifes from it; nor that it is the effect of good, becaufe by doing good evil fometimes follows.

Be above envy, if poffible; never confent to be below it.—Better to be looked up to than fpurned.

Beware! if there is any gall in the joke, it flows from yourfelf.

Insignificance is often a very ftrong protection; tho' the moft infignificant hefitate to acknowledge their obligations to it.

The countenance plays off as many tricks as the tongue; its duplicity is not fo well known.

On the map, the earth appears as the theatre of injury. Despotism has mutilated what elementary conflicts have spared. The whole is cantoned out by usurped authority, and each subdivision is unnecessarily inhabited by slaves.

Those who repent unseen, have transgressed reluctantly; but " the worst of all knaves are those who can mimic their former honesty."

How happens it that those legal codes which are compos'd of abstract or general propositions, are, nevertheless, applied to particular and positive facts? Should the law be made for the offence, or the offence for the law?

If the parents' reputation cannot atone for their childrens' deficiency, shou'd their infamy be allow'd to attach? Should their calamities be perpetuated? Multitudes fatten on the credit of their forefathers. Numerous are the descendants who suffer from their principles or profligacy.

* Under the banners of patriotism, most revolutionists, or reformers, have enlisted for their

own

---

* Luther, an Augustin monk, exclaimed against the Romish church, because the exclusive privilege of selling indulgences was not confined to his Order. Had the Dominicans enjoyed no

share.

own advancement; yet thefe very reformers, in their cry for reformation, always *forget* themfelves.

Lend unfparingly to virtue; 'tis for the benefit of yourfelf, of the virtuous, of all mankind: ultimately the loan muft turn to good account.

Whilst under the neceffity of enduring either, which is the fharpeft curfe, to be hated by thofe we love, or to be lov'd by thofe we hate?

Shou'd you efcape cenfure, attribute the exemption to chance, not to merit; or you will expofe yourfelf to the very ftigma you have providentially and fingularly efcaped.

Even content does not exclude hope. Content is only a comparative ftate of reft from defire; a ftate oftener fpoke of than felt: yet content is the dulleft part of happinefs.

Injuries

---

hare of this fpiritual licence to fwindle, 'tis more than probable hat the reformation in religion would not have taken place fo oon.

" He who reforms himfelf, has done more to reform the ublic, than a crowd of noify, impotent patriots."

Lavater's *Aphorifms.*

Injuries from strangers are frequently forgiven; from friends they are seldom even forgot. It appears, then, * that where we profess the greatest regard, there we exercise the greatest cruelty.

A living coxcomb, a pageant, or a new dress, will put the most morose of her sex into tolerable humour, if not into high spirits.

They say wit is scarce; 'tis oftener met with than honesty; yet 'tis difficult to pick up a companion, high or low, who does not pretend to both. Gentlemen think honesty and wit are part of their birthright.

† Pay extreme attention to the favourites, and even the parasites, of those you expect to be serv'd by; no matter whether they are dogs, monkies, or female dolls. There is a routine for all who solicit. If you find your spirit revolt,

* "He who forgives a trespass of sentiment to a friend, is as unworthy of friendship as that friend."

Lavater's *Aphorisms.*

† Vide Quintus Curtius for the conduct of the eunuch Bagoas.

"Say what you please of your humanity, no wise man will ever believe a syllable, while *I* and *mine* are the two only gates at which you sally forth and enter, and through which alone all must pass who seek admittance." Lavater's *Aphorisms.*

volt, or flag, retire with the dignified air of one who knows his value, and will not tarnish it.

* " As reason and speech are sufficient to regulate the jarring interests of the world," all coercion must be unnecessary. Oh, Roman, how few are there who join in thy creed!

† We often sport and wanton with the feelings of our brethren, on the vile presumption that their integrity, sensibility, or intellect, is base, like their appearance. 'Tis natural for those who are aware that their own exterior is more valuable than their interior, to judge, that the heart of the poor must be of still less worth than his ragged covering.

The proud and the wise are restless under the bann of censure—if 'tis just or degrading.

Comparison

---

* These words are taken from Cicero.

† Upon the assumption of Sixtus the Fifth, the king of Spain sent the high constable of Castile to congratulate his holiness. The pope took him gently by the chin, and asked, if the dominions of his master were so thin of subjects, that he could not find an ambassador with a beard somewhat longer than his? The constable answered, If the king had been aware that merit consisted in a great beard, he would have sent a ram goat for his ambassador.

Comparison often confoles, flatters, and debafes. In the firft and fecond cafe we are the comparers; in the third our *good friends* make the comparifon.

When the firft opportunity is irretrievable, contrive to take double advantage of the fecond.

* Suffer no mortal to think worfe of you than you do of yourfelf. Or, if you choofe, let this be your rule: allow no creature to think better of you than you have reafon to think of yourfelf.

Tho' tears and fmiles are often falfe figns, they often move and pleafe: but " thofe whom fmiles and tears make equally lovely, all hearts may court."

Misanthropists draw their chief confolation from the very qualities that difgrace them.

The afpirations of ambition never ceafe. After Alexander had monarchis'd the globe, he afpir'd to celeftial honours.

Plentiful

---

* " Who makes too much, or too little, of himfelf, has a falfe meafure for every thing."

Lavater's *Aphorifms*.

PLENTIFUL tables make even knaves popular; their credit, indeed, evaporates with that of the wines and viands.

* MORALITY and Religion are as diftinct as fky and earth: yet the Chriftian code appears to be principally fupported by the excellent fyftem of ethics it contains.

REPORT is a quick traveller, but an unfafe guide.

WARRIORS ftride over fields of defolation, and ftalk amidft ruins, when they wifh to collect their honorary trophies.

† THE failings of the beautiful obtain more indulgence than the unmerited afflictions of the poor or deferving.

---

* Alexander Severus allowed Chriftianity out of love to this precept—"Do not that to another which thou wouldft not have done to thyfelf."

Suetonius informs us, that, in the reign of Nero, "The Chriftians were feverely punifhed: a fort of people who maintained a new and mifchievous ufurpation."

† "It is treafon to fay the fame of beauty, whatever we do of the ornaments and arts with which pride is wont to fet it off: the weakeft minds are moft caught with both, being ever glad to win attention and credit from fmall and flender accidents, through difability of purchafing them by better means: in truth, beauty has fo many charms, one knows not how to fpeak againft it." STERNE'S *Sermons*.

To little minds thofe productions are highly agreeable, that entertain without reducing them to the neceffity of thinking.

There are few mortals fo infenfible that their affections cannot be gain'd by mildnefs; their confidence by fincerity; their hatred by fcorn or neglect.

Similar acts, committed by different people, are not only attended with different confequences; they are likewife defignated by different names.

* If 'tis your plan to thrive at any rate, if honefty is an inferior confideration, you muft frequently fhut your eyes, or look without fpeculation.

Those fcrupulous men who queftion the privileges of their condition, or the honefty of their profeffions, are, at leaft, entitled to an attentive hearing.

Fashion has power over more than we apprehend; not only our garments, it controls our

---

* " To know man, borrow the ear of the blind, and the eye of the deaf." Lavater's *Aphorifms.*

our taftes, prejudices the cradle that receives the royal infant, and the coffin that enclofes the earl.

* 'T is as eafy to weigh up a fhip from the bottom of the deep, as merit that has funk through misfortune: fhould the attempt even fucceed, it will not bear its priftine reputation.

Those who are attack'd, may fight, or reply; the caufe is good, as all defenfive caufes muft be.

Few speak truth; that may be true: fewer dare to hear it fpoken. Which is the trueft?

If you cannot take the lead, take good care to be follow'd. " Not to be the *laft* ftands in fome rank of praife."

---

* " A rich man beginning to fall, is held up of his friends; but a poor man being down, is thruft away by his friends. When a rich man hath fallen, he hath many helpers; he fpeaketh things not to be fpoken, and yet men juftify him: the poor man flipt, and yet they rebuked him too: he fpake wifely, and could have no place.

" When a rich man fpeaketh, every man holdeth his tongue, and look what he faith, they extol it to the clouds: but if the poor man fpeak, they fay, What fellow is this? And if he ftumble, they will help to overthrow him."

Ecclefiafticus.

If adversity did not periodically diminish the vanity of those mushrooms which spring up under the cover of darkness, the earth wou'd be over-run with their insolence.

Fear and knavery never sunder till they have destroy'd each other.

When a proud man forbids you his presence, he aukwardly confers a favour upon you.

* *Too much*, or *too little*, leads us into as many perplexities as *mine* and *thine*.

Tho'

---

* Bernard's Trop et Rien.

"J'aime à trouver quand il fait froid,
Grand feu dans un petit endroit;
Les délicats font grand chére,
Quand on leur sert dans un repas
De grands vins dans de petits verres,
De grands mots dans de petits plats."

"Il resulte de ce langage
"Qu'il ne faut rien de trop;
"Que de sens renferme ce mot!
"Qu'il est judicieux, & sage!
"Trop de repos nous engourdit,
"Trop de fracas nous étourdit,
"Trop de froideur est indolence,
"Trop d'activité turbulence,
"Trop d'amour trouble la raison,
"Trop de remede est un poison,

"Trop

Tho' it may be unsafe, and unprofitable, to be a jot more scrupulous than your neighbours, yet it may sometimes be more honourable.

The necessity of virtue once clearly understood, remorse, and the consequences of deceit, evidently demonstrate the evil resulting from a want of it: virtue is never follow'd by repentance.

Tho' the parent's folly is the child's curse, yet it descends to the next succession; the standing prejudice awaits their birth.

"Trop de finesse est artifice,
"Trop de rigueur est dureté,
"Trop d'economie avarice,
"Trop d'audace témerité,
"Trop de bien devient un fardeau,
"Trop d'honneur est un esclavage;
"Trop de plaisir nous mene au tombe,
"Trop d'esprit nous porte dommage.
"Trop de confiance nous perd,
"Trop de franchise nous dessert,
"Trop de bonté devient foiblesse,
"Trop de fierté devient hauteur,
"Trop de complaisance bassesse,
"Trop de politesse fadeur.
"Ce trop pourroit à la bien prendre
"Aisement de changer en bien;
"Cela vient faute de s'entendre
"Le tout souvent dépend d'un Rien."

* Courtesy is the agreeable adminiſtration of juſtice.

Truth, like medicine, muſt be qualified for the weak and infantine.

Compute how much others want, if you would aſcertain how much you poſſeſs.

Speak of the abſent as if they were preſent; then if you do not ſay all that you think, think all that you ſay.

† Some merit is requir'd to rail; more to bear raillery; but moſt to forbear it.

Vast is the difference 'twixt pleaſure and ſatisfaction. Revenge is criminal; yet ſatisfaction only ariſes from its indulgence, not pleaſure.‡

Obstinacy and docility characterizes the oppoſite extremes of intellect.

If

---

* La douceur de la ſociété ſubſiſte par les petits plaiſirs que l'on ſe fait mutuellement.

† La raillerie eſt ſouvent une marque de la ſterilité de l'éſprit; elle vient au ſecours quand on manque de bonnes raiſons.

‡ On ne goûte point impunement le plaiſir de la vengeance, c'eſt ce punir ſoi même que de hair.

IF you would deftroy your own repofe, break the reft of your neighbour.

MERIT, like gold, muft be ftampt to pafs current: merit often wants nothing but a name.

IDLE citizens deferve more punifhment than thofe whofe tranfgreffions are temporal.

PRODIGALS are rich for a moment; economifts, for ever.

THOSE who laugh at the gallante fhew, forget that they are puppets for another exhibition.

FOOLS love no fools like themfelves.*

BE firft to praife, and firft to deferve it.

SOCIABILITY comprehends all the minor duties of citizenfhip.

POSSESS one vice, you do not therefore exclude all virtue; nor wanting one virtue, do include all the vices.

FORCE is neceffary where reafon fails.

* Ce font nos paffions qui nous irritent contre celles des autres.

Neither build happiness or fame at the expence of others.

* Those who boast of their birth, have little to boast of; nay, 'tis building pride on accident. †

Be belov'd,‡ esteem'd, or admir'd. The first is the safest state; the second evinces most perfection; and the third is the most dangerous.

Impertinents have neither the wisdom to refrain, or judgment to support, conversation.§

The most inveterate dissentions arise from mutual obstinacy and folly: *quarrels would soon terminate, if only one side was in an error.*

Confessing

---

* Vanter sa race, c'est louer le merite d'autrui.

Quand on n'a rien de grand que la naissance, on est, & l'on paroit d'autant plus petit que cette naissance est plus grande.

† L'eclat de la gloire de nos ancêtres ne rejaillit sur nous, que pour mieux eclairer nos vices, & nos vertus.

‡ On craint trop d'être meprisé, & l'on ne craint point assez d'être hai.—Il nous importe beaucoup plus d'être aimés que d'être estimés: ce n'est pas à ceux qu'on estime qu'on se plait à faire du bien, c'est à ceux qu'on aime: l'estime toute seule n'est point bienfaisante.

§ Le plaisir le plus délicat est de faire celui d'autrui.

CONFESSING a folly is an act of judgment; a compliment we often refuse to pass on ourselves.

'TIS as easy to discover the vanity of pleasures past, as 'tis difficult to accredit the insufficiency of those to come.*

THOSE who receive, know best how the thing should be given.

LESS is requir'd to gain love than hatred.

THE superficial are more tiresome than the ignorant to the wise; but to the ignorant they are supremely acceptable.

INCIVILITY is the extreme of pride: 'tis built on the contempt of mankind.

THINGS, books, and persons, are taken at their suppos'd, not their real value; opinion is the sorry arbiter.

THOSE who refuse to risk an encounter with ingratitude, will never become *extensively* benevolent.

---

* Qui n'étudie pas l'art d'être heureux à peu de frais, sera toujours malheureux.

'Tis poffible to afcertain the riches of a man by the temper with which he fupports a lofs.

Never offer advice to profperity; to adverfity offer relief.

Peremptory deciders are always credulous.

* Bad examples produce more good than good ones, yet they are more rife: this paradox wants a refolution.

We remember our creditors better than our debtors.

Advisers are fo much like lawgivers that they incur deteftation.

'Tis fafer to maim your neighbour, than to deftroy the good opinion he entertains of himfelf; therefore never mock him; mockery is exaggerated reflection of his worft, as praife is of his beft qualities.

Politeness is hard driven when it endures impolitenefs placidly.

---

* The example of fome men is worfe than the evil they commit, as the evil they commit is more venial than the example they fet is laudable.

When a man will do only what ought to be done, he should certainly be allow'd to do what he likes: his duty is then his pleasure.

Never confide that to your friend that is beyond his capacity to support, or that may, if declar'd, endanger his safety.

In the fashionable mode of pleasing there is too much art; benevolence is lost in much servility of mind, and ceremonious distortion of limbs.

Do we not forget to weep for our own misfortunes when we sympathize with those of others?

When the learned hunt after impossibilities, they frequently find impossibilities on the road. The ultimatum * of all science is an impossible attainment.

Contradiction is an arrogant, a rude asserter of pre-eminence, that humiliates to triumph,

---

* Toutes les sciences ont leur chimere. La chimie a sa pierre philosophale; la geometrie sa quadrature du cercle; l'astronomie ses longitudes; le mecanique son mouvement perpetuel; la morale a aussi sa chimere, c'est le disinteressement, la parfaite amitie.

umph, and is, thro' jealoufy and pride, an object of deteftation.

Sceptics are often more dogmatic than they ought to be; and the dogmatic more fceptical than they pretend to be.

Virtue is the warfare of nature againft moral inftitution.

The rich are puzzled to account for the independent fpirit of the poor, affured that, with all advantages, they are enflav'd.

* The greateft reward of having well done, is the confcioufnefs of having fo done.

Heed not the nature or extent of your crimes, if they are pecuniarily productive; money qualifies all denunciation; befides, cenfure falls on misfortune, not on guilt: indeed, misfortune is fynonymous with guilt when there is a vacuum in the purfe.

Disgrace, unmerited, is incidental to greatnefs; 'tis likewife the effect of mortified and
difappointed

---

* On ne'ft plus généreux des qu'on recherche la réputation de générofité.

disappointed *littleness:* when frustrated, it vapours into contempt.

Reproof is useless to the good; the evil and conceited despise it; whilst there is a species of admonition that each will *listen* to at least.

The answer that is postpon'd is seldom reveal'd: policy does any thing but contradict, and uses any stratagem to secure its interest, which answers that include truths are frequently calculated to destroy.

Excellence depends absolutely on the taste of the times.

The love-lorn are laugh'd at for the insignificance of their pursuit; or render themselves insignificant by acting to its idol as if the worth of the whole sex was united in an individual.

Plutus' wand calms the leonine disposition of the warrior, tho' it cannot cool the lover's heat.

If the liquefcency of the female was at all times perceptible, a virgin would scarcely be found in a state of muliebrity.

Never take the child of a poet or an artist.

Schoolmens' subtlety make them conceitedly unintelligible; their speculations have done more mischief to the world than their best discoveries have done good.

* Longanimity is the art of steering thro' troublesome society: the offence that we know how to tolerate, we can either convert to our own advantage, or the disadvantage of its offerer.

Vanity has many silly tricks; despotism many cruel devices; love, many strange ways; but folly is constant.

There is little sensibility in the being who passes through his ordain'd course without being disgusted, or without pitying his fellows, their pursuits, sufferings, and destructive prejudices.

Good imitations are at least equal to those originals that are of no value.

There is more solicitude to keep than to gain. Better would it be that the excellence
we

---

* What can meliorate the malicious effects of our enemies like the temper that recoils to their exposition?

we are familiar to fhould expire, than ftifle the efforts of new-born genius.

When the reward goes not with the labour, the workman has no vigour, unlefs he has taught himfelf denial and hope.

* We calculate diftances, and are calculated for them.

If the thiftle grows the better after the afs has brows'd upon it, the dullnefs of criticifm may enlighten the fubject it has attempted to deftroy.

When 'tis impoffible to appear what you wifh to be, 'tis poffible that you may be taken for what you really are.

Perseverance accomplifhes more than genius—for itfelf: a genius is a rich bleffing for fociety; to itfelf—a curfe.

What fcholars and artifts borrow, they fhould make their own.

Without pride and folly, what mifery and want there would be in this life!

---

* Titian's colouring admits of clofe infpection; Rembrandt's will not.

Every extreme is the destruction of its cause.

Before the merit of pardoning is proclaim'd, the right to punish should be ascertain'd.

Many of our pleasures are purely ideal; and both our pleasures and afflictions are measur'd by opinion.

Extorted promises may be kept; voluntary promises seldom are: indeed, until we can foresee what is to happen, 'tis rash to confine our agency.

* Truth deceives as often as it surprises.

The ambitious man is the idolater of opinion; the miser evinces the inhumanity of society, and the prodigal the inequality of its distributors.

Refuse praise, and he who tenders it accuses you of pride to conceal his flattery.

† In proportion as we value ourselves, we diminish our estimation of others.

---

* Les hommes sont si ridiculement soupçonneux qu'on reussit souvent mieux à les tromper par la verité même que par le mensonge, & le deguisement. *Count Oxenstirn.*

† Quand on trouve son bonheur en soi même, on fait peu d'estime de celui qui peut venir d'ailleurs. *Count Oxenstirn.*

Why expect extraordinary virtues should be in one person united, when one virtue makes a man extraordinary? Alexander is eminent for his courage; Ptolemy for his wisdom; Scipio for his continence; Trajan for his love of truth; Constantius for his temperance.

Freedom is no more, when love, avarice, or ambition, or the desire of distinction, get into the brain. Count Oxenstirn has said, that liberty is, of all the world's vanities, the most precious.

Fools have great privileges; they may speak truths without being accountable for them. A buffoon in the Spanish court ask'd Philip the Second what he would be, if his subjects took it into their heads to say *no*, as often as he said *yes*?

Where virtue thrives most, it is most a matter of interest. Small rewards for virtue are more efficacious than great punishments for vice.

Age changes our taste, and this is held as an argument against marriage: it should be recollected, that 'tis possible, even after change, that the taste of the parties should agree in favour of each other.

Never contradict, and you will seldom be contradicted: those who tolerate error, are more graciously receiv'd than those who offer to amend.

Those who flout at distress, become parties in their ill treatment.

Without money, without care: without money—a man may hope for every thing. The Italians say, *Il danaro e un compendio del poter humano.*

One enemy is too much; as much may be said of a thousand friends.

In proportion to hope and pride, is the pain that refusal gives.

Those who are placed under disappointment, will be the last to disappoint, if their calmness is the effect of their philosophy.

If God is every where worshipp'd, he is honour'd in no place.

Climate may be a great cause of superstition.

Religions of all descriptions are the companions of fear, villainy, and mistaken gratitude.

The Indians assert that Brama was a son of God: the Christians maintain that Christ was the only begotten son of God!

'Tis an artful way of hiding your own sense of injury, by inducing any person equally implicated to consider their wrongs as the greatest, and rouzing them to vigorous revenge.

Facts that are nearly alike, observ'd by creatures who are nearly in the same state of intellectual improvement or debasement, must give birth to sentiments * that are nearly alike. Morality is compos'd of the same principles or elements all over the world—for the wants of man are nearly alike.

All sins are of the mind, tho' the body is not always employ'd in their commission.

The body is the seat of punishment; the mind, of transgression.

Major part of evil is conceited.

---

* La chute de l'homme dégénéré est le fondement de la theologie de presque toutes les anciennes nations. *Voltaire.*

Our anceſtors could neither conceive why their diſtreſſes were ſo numerous, or from what cauſe they proceeded. Conſcious of not meriting them, they fancied ſome culpability of their predeceſſors occaſion'd their fall from a pre-exiſting ſtate of perfection.

* Want, ambition, and avarice, make conquerors.

Disputes do not ſo often originate about things of conſequence, or eſſential to our well being, as to maintain the ſuperior of ſuppos'd conſequence.

Fear is a ready believer in matters of religion: what it rejects is of little magnitude.

By valuing life, life will be reſpected. The Indians, who credited the doctrine of the Metempſychoſis, fear'd to become murderers; the horrors of becoming parricides taught them to reſpect even animals: the ſame diſpoſition might be produc'd from moral cauſes.

Without intereſt or ambition, few would undergo the fatigue of thinking.

Pride's

---

* Le beſoin fit les premiers brigands. *Voltaire.*

*Pride's highest step is its boasted alliance with the Divinity.

Who governs so safely and so completely as those who instruct?

Those who presume to revenge their own injuries, should also possess the power of remuneration for services perform'd.

† The immense follies of a whole nation are frequently destroy'd by an individual.

Affirmations are strongest where knowledge is weakest. The Chinese say nothing about future rewards and punishments; and Voltaire assigns this as the reason, *ils n'ent pas voulu affirmir ce qu'ils ne savoient pas.*

The fallen have their source of consolation either in what they merit, or what they formerly possess'd.

In matters of religion, believing as much as you can is not satisfactory, nor as much as you ought. "Believe as much as I do," vociferates
the

---

* See the *Vedam*, under the article *Matricha Machom.*

† They have frequently been established by one.

the persecuting bigot, " or the stake shall be prepared for your incredulity."

Such respect as physicians pay to the strength of the patient's constitution, ought to fill the moralist's pen when he is about to infirm the poison of prejudice: a violent expulsion might destroy—his object is only to amend.

In time is not always at the time appointed.

Allegorical writing is the resource of mystery or fear, ingenuity or ignorance.

The merit often lies in finding merit out.

Destroy despotism without hostility to persons.

Those who make you wait, weaken their merit in proportion as they raise expectation.

The greatest are the oldest absurdities.

Women must be gain'd by degrees, if they are wooed; when they love, there is no more requir'd than a capacity to receive, and a disposition to bear.

We boast of national antiquity, tho' we affiduoufly mifreprefent and veil our own.

Priests keep their lay-brethren as far from themfelves, and each other, as they themfelves are from God.

No one nation is of greater antiquity than another: temporal priority is afcertain'd by their knowledge of facts, not by the facts themfelves.

The immutability of laws is no compliment to a legiflator; if they are bad, fo they muft remain; if good, this fixity prevents them from becoming better.

Pride boafts of family antiquity; duration is made to ftand for merit.

Fortify the empire, and its towns are well fecur'd.

'Tis with man as with his money; his weight and title fixes his value.

Multiplying credit, fometimes deftroys inftead of augmenting wealth. Refources are beft untouch'd: credit is a refource. He that takes credit, confeffes to poverty.

Gold

* GOLD buys man, and his opinion, when they are worth nothing.

NAVIGATION is an art of neceffity. The Chinefe, who have no wants at home, do not, becaufe they need not, voyage.

EVERY nation imitates, more or lefs, the Chinefe, and every individual too. Old habits, tho' inconvenient, are worfhipp'd; whilft new, tho' convenient, are fcorn'd.

PATIENCE, fortitude, and ingenuity, are requir'd from the navigator; then his eftate is honourable. What fhall he be call'd when his faculties are employ'd to affail the fhores of unoffending ftrangers, and rob them of their patrimony, to indulge falfe wants, or gratify avarice?

NATIONAL wants create as many felonies as the neceffities of individuals: but what great bodies do, none but greater bodies can punifh.

No place is too public for the acknowledgment of injuries; no atonement too great, unlefs it exceeds the inconvenience it has produc'd.

---

* In the time of Juftinian filk was worth its weight in gold: here opinion makes two things of equal value.

'Tis not the ceremony, but the motive, that characterizes the slave.

If we pardon those who have offended us, what should we do for those we have offended?

Mankind must all of them have had one and the same origin, tho' they came not originally from one.

Hereditary sin is not more extraordinary than hereditary dominion or honour.

Right and wrong differ not more than reason and law frequently do. In this case law stands as the wrong, reason as the right; yet those who act rationally are to be judg'd legally.

'Tis difficult to walk your own pace amidst observers who have authority. Amongst inferiors 'tis yet more difficult to assume the port that becomes us.

What prejudices imagination gives birth to, even those will reason attempt to legitimate.

If reflection cannot give courage, no citizen can discharge his duties who is not constitutionally brave.

What we affect to possess, points directly to what we want.

Those things that we have been without half our lives, we deplore if they are lost for a day.

Great robbers never expose themselves to the eye of justice, therefore their secret support is great.

Most people affect to have discovered the insipidity, or frivolity, of that pursuit or enjoyment they are no longer capacitated to pursue.

* Atheists have all in this life; *néantisme*, that alarms religionists, is theirs by expectation; their disappointment, therefore, will be less, should their speculations be unfounded, than the Diccolists, if their opinions are false.

Widowers on the point of re-marrying, pay the sex a higher compliment than petulant mysogynists can destroy.

Credulity, liberality, and mendacity, are destroy'd by their own fecundity.

---

* Il n'est rien qui fasse mieux connoitre la fureur brutale de l'ateé que de lui voir faire parade de néantisme qui fait l'objet de l'horreur de toutes les autres creatures. *Le Comte Oxenstirn.*

Choice words are intended more for the heart than the head; to take advantage of weakness, or leffen the advantage of power; to draw from the poffeffions of others, or fave our own.

The errors of the eyes require moft fkill to correct.

Great truths are only known to great people.

Misfortune is as convenient a fhelter when the effect of our folly or ignorance overtakes us, as cruelty is for the criminal.

'Tis wrong to vociferate againft mankind; we do not hear how much they are wrong'd by us.

Fools are always in the majority.

Opinion feldom rifes, if it was originally founded on the love of novelty or fafhion.

Good men, as morality is now practifed, are victims of duty.

Which of us has great enemies without poffeffing great faults, and being under great obligations?

No moralist can answer for the correctness of his calculations, tho' he certainly proposes to be correct.

Why scruple to use or attend to the sentiments of another, if they are superior to your own?

* Personal interest sets us all in motion.

When the prejudices of the upper portion of society are abolish'd, there will be no necessity to establish any for the lower classes.

It requires much consideration to determine on the dissipation of agreeable or consoling illusions.

When a notion of a divine existence has once established itself in the mind, it becomes a central point that every thought is referr'd to; it explains every physical effect by general declarations †, or theologic dogmas, and teaches perfecution

* Craindre, & desirer sont les deux grands ressorts des actions humaines. Toute crainte suppose un mal: tout desir suppose un bien.

† Newton fut aussi foible dans ses raisonnemens métaphysiques, que profond dans ses calculs; il n'osa rien conjecturer sur le premier mobile de cette attraction dont il fixoit les loix:

il

cution for immorality, tho' religion and morality are as widely sundered as the poles: in short, religion is the cause of more misery than morality can alleviate: and priests are the severest scourges to the mind, body, and circumstances, that earth ever was affected by.

Light cannot lose its nature, tho' it will not suit every organ of vision.

Books have more influence on the happiness of mankind than all the governments on earth.

Though there is no crime in opinion, yet there is nothing criminal but in opinion.

The gallows is a fine conclusion of legal wisdom!

There is a beautiful contempt apparent, when a wise man yields to the force of folly, or the coercion of cruelty.

The nursery or fire-side is an improper school for the young moralist: all our principles are obtain'd by chance.

---

il partit d'une cause obscure, dont les effets connus expliquoent peu, & replongea la physique dans les qualités occultes du péripatétisme, d'on ses predicésseurs sétirent afforcés de la tirer.

Major Weiss.

WHAT you declaim againſt, even that you are. The ſage* ſmiles at his ſuppos'd wiſdom, and the fool enters a ſtrong proteſt againſt his own folly.

PARTIAL or particular kindneſs is frequently impartial or general cruelty.

IGNORANCE is the great ſectator; Mahomet has thouſands of followers! Where, Socrates, are thy adherents?

WOMEN make their admirers pay a heavy tax for indulging their imagination.

TRUTH is vulgar prejudice with the vulgar.

USEFUL prejudices are pronounc'd more rational than the truth that would deſtroy them. What prejudices are uſeful? If there are any of this deſcription, would their effect be more beneficial than truth?

CENSURE and praiſe† are the reward or puniſhment that the world poſſeſs to exerciſe at will;
and

* Le premier pas vers la ſageſſe ce'ſt dóſer douter de ſon ſavoir.

† Pour louir dignement il faut meriter foi même beaucoup d'eloges.

and public judgment, if correct, is at once a check, a ſtimulus, and a bleſſing.

The rich, in foreign opinion, may be ſtript by every pelting calumniator or ſneerer: who ſhall rob the being whoſe wealth is in his own well-earn'd opinion?

Characters change; but under reproach, or praiſe, there is only one identity.

Tear off the ſkin of your object rather than diminiſh his ſelf-love: injuſtice is an inſignificant trifle compar'd with want of reſpect. Man is an idol to which his fellow muſt ſacrifice.

Before a reputation is eſtabliſhed, it paſſes through all the gradatory ſhades from black to white.

The quality that the ſage admires is at leaſt a degree above what he poſſeſſes: the fool admires you for ſome inferior quality.

The height and value of reputation ſhould be meaſur'd from the lowneſs of birth, and the obſtacles that have been vanquiſh'd in the ſtruggle to acquire it.

We all have a title to particular confideration, tho' it is feldom publicly acknowledg'd.

The utility * of the adoption, change, or introduction, is its beft recommendation.

What inequality is neceffary in fociety fhould be determin'd by perfonal worth.

Nobility fhould be elective, not hereditary.

Where merit is equal, riches and birth fhould not caufe a preponderation: a preference built on accident is immoral.

Those who enflave the people, are in their turn enflav'd by them.

Sacrifice to reality alone, and for want of appearance you will be ruin'd.

Pleasures wafte the fpirits more than pains; therefore the latter can be endur'd longer, and in greater degrees, than the former.

Liberty

---

* Jófe mettre en doute fi Dracke en apportant les pommes de terre en Europe, ou Anacharfis, en inventant la roue du potier, ne mériterent pas mieux du genre humain que le legiflateur des forces centripetes, & centrifuges. *Major Weifs.*

LIBERTY is our own in spite of tyranny, its dungeons and fetters.

THE unfortunate do not volunteer to become miserable.

MELANCHOLY searches consolation in its weakness; 'tis the relapsive state of resolution.

SUFFERANCE includes experience; and experience is necessary to make us wise, good, or courageous.*

† THE most extended and complicated machinery is put in motion by the simplest means

MEDIOCRITY, if it has any strong passions, chains them down by indolence. *Vivre, ce'st sentir; & qui sont fortement vit plus qu'un autre:* so that enjoyment consists in the exercise of the passions.

VIRGINS continue chaste through vanity, unless they have an agreeable opportunity to become

---

* Tout héros fut premierement un enthusiaste ou un infortuné. *Major Weiss.*

† Etonner la multitude, ce'st la subjuguer à demi.
Major Weiss

come women; then senfuality overpowers sentiment.

The inflection of the lover's voice is the musical expression the enamour'd ear most delights in; words imperfectly unfold what that modulation of sound reveals.

Vulgar amours may be progressively pourtray'd. Who can write the history of exalted attachments? Not even the parties concern'd: their gradations are so finely interwoven; their particulars pass in such rapid succession.

Constancy may be the effect of duty or interest, not of disposition; there is no such fixity of inclination in nature: defire can only stagnate for want of objects.

Love from the first glance does not promise long continuance, it burns too fiercely: what has been kindled with difficulty, retains its heat the longest.

Difficulties only serve to protract whatever hope supports.

'Tis to be deplor'd when private pleasures are opposite to the public good.

Why.

Why may not curiofity be the caufe of gallantry? Curiofity frequently includes the love of novelty.

Love delights not more to conquer, than vanity to make conquefts.

There is no crime in loving, if it entails no fhame or fuffering in its confequences.

Be careful how you deftroy thofe faults you deteft; but never think to conceal your own; fafety, honour, and improvement attends their proclamation.

Custom makes all ftates equal.

Ambition is determin'd by its application and conftancy rather than its object.

When religion is feparated from morality, theology will be divefted of all coercive power.

Envy has an immenfe advantage, in the credit it obtains, and the facility with which it deftroys.

Those who fearch for what is great, expect to find what is agreeable; thofe who are prepar'd to meet the agreeable, are more than ninety-nine times out of a hundred difappointed.

Convince women that they are abus'd at home, and abroad they may be made both abus'd and us'd: Nothing foments infidelity equal to raifing a fpirit of diffatisfaction.

Justly you cannot deal with any being, unlefs you can afcertain what portion of probity he ufes towards you.

Even the filence of the fage fpeaks.

Learn to have, and have to learn: learn to keep, and keep what you learn.

Respect is feldom paid on demand. You will always receive more or lefs than you deferve.

Those who are frugal of their affability are fevere economifts.

Reserve is the effect of deep policy or defign, enormous pride, or exceffive humility. Well has it been announc'd, that " The referv'd man fhould bring a certificate of his honefty before he be admitted into company."

Why

Why should *Virtue charm less than Vice concealed*—and why?—Virtue is so painful that it will be paid either in meal or malt. Austerity is its assumption.

One general sentiment of approbation or disapprobation being established, all the particular qualities of its object become either agreeable or disgusting.

Insipid wine may make good vinegar; so a maukish mistress may be converted into a tolerable wife.

Half our felicity, or infelicity, arises from our sentiment, or obedience to that of others.

Time and circumstance converts the same object—we either abhor or adore it.

Mildness encourages cowards and sinners; it torments the irascible and proud.

Night changes gaiety to sadness, and sadness to gaiety: cheerfulness, like temperance, is less violent, but more durable, than preternatural exaltation.

Polite assemblies are masquerades.

When a man declares he ought to be disappointed, who shall murmur?

When the mind is oppress'd with a consciousness of shame, it needs no additional suffering.

Tho' reproof is couch'd in a mild question, it should not follow the offence too rapidly.

Tho' fancy is the patient's complaint, necessity is oftener the doctor's. When the purse protracts the patient's cure, the medicine should be the physician's reward.

In courtship, plain characters make a poor figure; they must have every thing nuncupative: now the chief puzzle women have, is to explain what they mean.

All who laugh are not mirthful.

'Tis common to hear one opinion repeated in society, whilst 'tis very uncommon to find society of one opinion; tho' their practices are commonly alike.

What excuse does proper behaviour require; what excuse can justify improper conduct?

Girls

Girls who know what a man is fit for, know whether he can fatisfy their wants: hence the preference that is paid to men of gallantry.

The apprehenfion of all evils is greater than the reality; for the arithmetic that calculates for the fufferance, never notices the force provided to bear it.

What is ideal is endlefs. Domeftic centinels therefore find no relief.

Unsuccessful merit has more admirers than are avow'd, more fupporters with good wifhes than with purfes.

Complaisance includes much cowardice and fervility.

Caprice has bitter enmities.

Mildness is often the vizor of weaknefs.

Frequent laughers are fure to be laugh'd at, tho' they are not laugh'd with; loud laughers are fure to incommode.*

---

* The French fay, " Thofe laugh well, who laugh laft."

The amorist lauds her lover as much through pride as ignorance; but more through fondness than either: fondness is the blind of reason.

Praise is not only expensive, but dangerous.

Primarily, favours give more satisfaction to receivers than to givers; ultimately, more dissatisfaction to givers than to receivers. Some favours deserve no return; the manner in which all have been bestowed deserves to be remember'd and return'd.

Favours will not attract the notice, much less the love, of a great man.

Rejoice in the enemies you have, if they are good; curse the friends you may possess, if they are specious.

If mistresses can't make themselves wives, they are unhappy: if wives can't make themselves mistresses as well as wives, they are miserable.

The errors of calculation, and their effects, are the strongest proofs of having acted wrong.

Pictures are often preferable to the original; tho' the poffeffors affect to value the original beyond all the pictures that can be produc'd.

What attention fhould be paid to the tears of women when they are known to proceed from affectation? But let it be credited that affection can produce effects equal to real caufe for fufferance.

Tho' the bread that fupports my life was produc'd by the induftry of many hands, I am not bound in particular gratitude: their convenience, not my hunger, was the object of their labour.

Indolence is the fpell, the opiate, that deftroys our vigour.

* Without an end, and without hope to carry us to it, life is infipid vegetation.

If punifhment follows an improper deed, what fhould follow the omiffion of what is proper to be done? By the Athenian laws the idler was put to death—as a thief that robb'd the ftate.

Economy

---

* L'oifu eté produit l'ennui, qui eft l'abfence de fentimens affez vifs pour intereffen.

Economy appears to be nearly allied to probity.

Economy is the supplement to a small fortune, and the most extensive is not sufficient without it.

Those who are fortunate enough to be moderate, enjoy their pleasures without remorse.

Those who speak with the greatest precision have the fewest ideas; those whose ideas are most numerous, are most confus'd.

Fervent imaginations care least for truth.

'Tis politic to wear good cloaths—more people are capacitated to judge of the garb than of the man.

Intense pleasures cannot come frequently.

* The chamber of the dying mortal is the properest school for those students who would know themselves.

To win much the stake must be large.

Perseverance

* L'etude de l'homme est l'ecole de l'humilité.
Major Weiss.

PERSEVERANCE arrives at the same end as intrepidity; but it travels not so short a road, tho' it has the advantage of being safer.

THOUGHT breaks out in words: the extent of language is the exact proportion of ideas.

THE credit of appearance would be frequently destroy'd, if we cou'd discover the means by which it was obtain'd: for different purposes there are different dresses: in the end they all agree—they are to deceive.

* INSTINCT changes with time.

SOLDIERS are the only carnivorous animals that live in a gregarious state.

To gain respect on earth we appear to respect heaven.

NATIONS, after their establishment, forget to war with beasts—when they have learn'd to war with men.

WERE we under the necessity of first ascertaining the principles of our action, we should be

---

* Qu'est ce que cet instinct? L'arrangement des organes dont le jeu se déploye pas le tems. *Voltaire.*

be at a lofs how to act: 'tis the fame in mechanical inventions.*

'Tis more than probable that the firft idea of perfonal right, or property, originates not in inftinct, but the appropriation we perceive of certain things for our own ufe.

Why through diffidence withdraw from the loftieft of her fex? Do they not generally fall to the lot of fools?

Prudence is the art of giving play to circumftances.

Probable obftacles, and poffible accidents, fhould always be taken into calculation.

Never change your plan until circumftances warrant: difappointment makes us peevifh, and alters our opinion, but it changes not the arrangement of things.

Risk what may be fpar'd, not what is neceffary.

---

* Le payfan le plus ignorant fait partout remuer le plus gros fardeaux pas le fecours du levier, fans fe douter que la puiffance faifant equilibre, eft au poids, comme la diftance du point d'appui à ce poids, eft à la diftance de ce même point d'appui à la puiffance. *Voltaire.*

Pay your respects gracefully; endure the want of ceremony with temper: 'tis but a form, tho' it denotes the state of the mind.

'Tis possible to infuse such candour in your refusal that the disappointed will not murmur.

Every trust should exact responsibility, if it allows the agent to act according to the complexion of circumstances.

* As 'tis impossible to foresee all, 'tis impossible to provide for all.

The credit of your friend, or family, is unjustly suppos'd to be your own, therefore 'tis so minutely defended.

Candour is most safely shewn in trifles.

Divulge what you cannot secrete with the appearance of confidence.

Proclaim aloud what is on the eve of being discover'd.

---

* Opportunity is more or less favourable than has been calculated: a thousand little things occur to advance or destroy a scheme.

Those who appear to be cunning, may be so; but they are not wise.

Awkwardness is a feint of address.

Appear to be a dupe, if you want dupes.

The pen that corrects is to be preferred to that which soothes; instruction is of more value than wealth: the effect of the latter is only temporary, the former gives permanence to felicity.—The test of wisdom is the *happiness* it produces.

When the lover is the counsellor and confessor, 'tis sweet to hear those chidings that root out vice by kindness, and that advice which makes duty a cheerful task.

Neither love or hatred can *be reasoned down*; tho' frequently we find as slight a cause to indulge the passion of love, as that of hatred: nay, the cause exists often without being ascertained.—When a scrutiny into motives is denied,* the inclination generally leads us astray.

To

---

* Duty and inclination are often at variance.

To preserve the power that beauty untouch'd possesses, many of its owners stifle their sensuality; yet consummation, tho' conceal'd, is the immediate or ultimate object of love.

Light sorrows call for the consolatory interference of friendship; and consolation once admitted, lightens the heaviest.

Numerous are those who have made their own prisons; and few who suffer, but are their own destroyers.—Comply with the tyranny of opinion in opposition to the dictates of nature, and you fabricate a scourge for your own punishment.

Judge of the pang of absence by the joy of meeting. Da Corsin,* and Julia Bellamono, two Italian lovers, after a long separation, expir'd with pleasure in each others' arms.

The expectation of the benefits to-morrow may produce, *lessens* our enjoyment of those before us, if it does not absolutely annihilate them.

Run not precipitately into a positive loss to enjoy ideal bliss: ingenuity always improves circumstances,

---

* And the coldness of meeting by the joy of separating.

circumstances, without running the risk of those futurity contains being better.

Reason from the honied lips of elocution, is the golden key that unlocks the secreted mysteries of all hearts.

The greater the admiration of a woman, the less patiently will she hear the cause of it criticized.* What women love or admire, they defend at all hazards, if they are qualities belonging to an individual: divided passion is consequentially—weak.

Infinite are the blessings we do not partake in, yet are within the reach of all whose sentiments are not perverted.

Infamy is no more than the extreme denunciation of opinion; yet it goes further towards producing moral excellence than pain, or even death: yet this infamy is, too frequently, a tyrannical oppression.

Cruelty is always insufficient. Females are call'd cruel when, strictly speaking, they are only capricious, or asserting their right to reject

* Because she does not hold herself amenable to reason for her affections.

reject againſt the more cruel ſolicitations of in-
ſufficient ſuitors.*

MAY the diſappointment, tho' not the fate,
of Tarpeia attend the perfidious: recollect that
perfidy is a breach of confidence, not a rejection of ſlaviſh habits.

ACCEPTANCE, or refuſal, that comes from
caprice, may be capriciouſly chang'd: thoſe who
act without conſulting their reaſon, are neceſſa-
rily unſtable in their amity or inimity.

THOSE who are capable of deceit, are the
moſt dangerous; but thoſe who practiſe it, are
the moſt villainous.

'TIS poſſible to profeſs more than you can
perform; for the ardency of intention frequently
outruns the practicability of performance.†

CHANGING opinion is the graceful act of
judgment when it leads to better: if it involves
the intereſt of perſons in its conſequence, the
fault

---

* The cruelty of perſecution is evident from the diſguſting
perſeverance of ſuitors.

† An honourable teſtimony of what we would perform if
power was within our reach.

fault attaches not to the agent, who only leaves what is indifferent for what is better.

Strange infatuation to covet friends! When they are near to us, they remove us from ourselves; when they are absent, we, ideally, are present with them: anxiety watches each step; apprehension foresees a thousand evils: we deserve from our inquietude, and extract inquietude from their desert.

Pride cannot support a denial; yet pride denies itself many pleasures.*—Murmur not at want of success; the best have been refused: do not refuse to yourself the best that is in your power.

If the end is good, the means of obtaining it cannot be bad: tho', taken abstractedly, they may be vicious.

In how small a space our happiness is encompassed! What an immense circuit, what an immense expenditure, must be made, before this truth is established as a truth!—The smallest tenement—nay, within the arms of a loving and beloved individual, most of the possibilities for felicity may be found.

Disclaim

* Perhaps a pleasure is included in the denial.

Disclaim admiration, and you compliment your difcretion; merit admiration, you may compliment yourfelf, tho' the world fail to pay their tribute to merit.

What has been ordained is frequently incapable of being maintained: nor is the paft a better director for the prefent, than the future will be for the paft.—The paft is an experienced counfellor.*

Opposite doctrine will remove virulent prejudices, if patiently canvaffed, and thoroughly digefted; many are loft in fcepticifm who lack patience or courage to finifh the examination.

Morality and politenefs cannot reach beyond mutal accommodation; love and veneration contain a power of gratifying fuperior to all written precepts, or eftablifhed manners.

Conceal nothing from your paramour, unlefs 'tis refolved that the whole heart fhould be rendered valuelefs. In the dark corner of the apartment the defaulter hides his difgrace; but the light of a friend puts what is difgraceful out of countenance; and thofe who blufh to appear

unworthy,

---

* The prefent may be a future enemy.

unworthy, will be careful to render themselves more perfect.

* LIBERAL of cruelty are those who pamper with promises; promisers destroy while they deceive, and the hope they raise is dearly purchased by the dependence that is sequent to disappointment.

CONVICTION is prevented or destroyed by irritablity; yet there is the consolation of knowing that the malign passions lose much of their power by anger.

GRAVITY contains more impurity than gaiety; reserve is the vizor of hypocrify; but the heart is pure when the countenance wears the air of hilarity: guilt deforms its features.

MANY motives, and as many fears, are united to suppress the genuine sentiments of the female, and many are the causes that adulterate them.

† LOOKS have more signification than words or books; tho' they are not so deeply studied,
they

* A promise is a draft on probability for credit: if tis receiv'd, it raises us as high; as the expectant, by admitting it, shews his abject state.

† Immutability of countenance is a favourer of hypocrify, as fixity of feature would be the destruction of fraud.

they are more attended to, and command more attention.

Forgiveness comes freely after revenge has been gratified, not gracefully; forgivenefs is the condefcenfion of arrogance.

Those who think well of mankind, are at peace with themfelves; thofe who think too well or too ill of them, are either enemies to themfelves or their brethren. Which is attended with moft danger? Which exhibits moft weaknefs?

When you detect an alacrity in fpreading ill news, be affured there exifts a mifchievous difpofition.* Keep all reports to yourfelf that cannot be ferviceable to your neighbour: not only avoid breaking his peace, but endeavour to conferve it.

Modesty that fhrinks at a glance, affeveration that thunders out its facts, and fanctity that is ftrain'd 'till it tortures, are as deteftable as that affected bluntnefs which endeavours to palm off rudenefs for honefty: the polifh that

---

* Or a thirft for novelty, that characterizes the ftagnation of intellect.

the urbane put upon their manners never deſtroys, but lends a grace to their integrity.

Neglect yourſelf, and you will neither be reſpected or reſpectable: value yourſelf at a high rate, and by action prove the correſpondence of your worth.

* Absentees are always in danger of having their characters miſrepreſented: they are either extoll'd or condemn'd for virtues or vices which they are ſtrangers to; and this is done frequently out of contradiction, pride, or envy.

The blood that makes the hero pre-eminent is not viſible when his glory is diſcuſs'd, or we ſhould call him ſlaughterer; and, inſtead of laurels, place a wither'd bramble on his brow.

Love is the pretext that covers many meanneſſes; genuine love is no reſpecter of circumſtances.

Expect reſponſibility,† and you cannot look for impunity: reſponſibility is the key-ſtone of the ſocial fabric.

Art's

---

* The baſe paſſions conſider the departure of merit as a licence for indulgence.

† What ſhould be the mulct when good intention fails of atchievement?

Art's blandishments engage our attention before we perceive their power, but simple nature will have the longest claim to it.

Certain companions will attach you to certain places; but the local is less delightful than the personal attachment, tho' it arises from the same cause. A garment, a bauble, becomes dear, if those who used them were dear: there is an ideal sanctity affixed to those we esteem, that enriches whatsoever object it has touch'd or delighted in.

* Fools cherish what the sage despises: the value of what we love is the amount of our own value.

There is more domal tyranny than parents can justify, or children tolerate; yet those who free themselves, frequently return to implore *forgiveness.*—Children have no appeal but in extreme cases.

When you *must* yield, do it gracefully; when you *must* persist, do it courageously; when you *must*

---

* Some pass through life without evincing partiality of any kind.

muſt reject, respect the feelings of those who suffer, and preserve your own from sufferance.

Persecution appears in many shapes; we have it at home, and abroad: sometimes it addresses us with a voice of mildness, or imperious command; at others it comes from relatives, friends, or suitors.*

When affectation obtrudes without our consciousness, it is the effect of imitation: the guilty, and proudly affected, think that all who look stare.

Those who are good alone should not be left alone; those who are good in company and alone, can alone be vouch'd for.†

Clean vessels hold muddy water, and bad opinions may come from pure hearts: much of what is bad is adventitious. This holds good likewise in the converse proposition; therefore, tho' we highly respect, or bitterly execrate, any sentiment, we must not assimilate to it the character of the utterer, for he is compouded of various principles.

Pride

---

* The most insolent species of persecution is the restless correction of theology.

† Notwithstanding, we are good for very little alone.

Pride begets the admiration we send forth, when our opponents have valour and ingenuity.

Victors praise at the expence of the vanquished, and oftener betray therein meanness than greatness of soul.

Unless the habit leads to happiness, the best habit is to contract none.*

Love, tho' the principal ingredient, requires many accessories to make up a compleat connection. When love springs from liberty, the greatest blessing she has afterwards to bestow, is the liberty of loving.

Deprivations are generally considered as real evils, whereas they are frequently partial blessings. The loss of a fortune we know not how to enjoy, a child we could not manage, a wife constitutionally diseased—are these losses?

What we have we despise—Pride, and the right of possession, cause this. What we have not, we affect to despise or esteem. This envy, or the love of novelty, causes.

That

* Habitual conceit in favour of certain habits will produce happiness.

That creature has great rational powers who suffers them to be controul'd by reason.

The more we require, the less we possess; the less we possess, the more is requir'd of us: the less we acquire, or possess, the more we have.

Affection is the rich gratitude of admiration.

Those who weep the most, often care the least; those who cry the longest, often forget the quickest. Louis the First lov'd Ermengarde, his wife, and, says the historian, Volly, *Il la pleura beaucoup, & l'oublia bien vite.**

Respect once lost is never to be regain'd; for opinion is never renounc'd that confirms inferiority: respect is more easily obtain'd than merited; for the mind frequently imposes on itself: but the best beloved are not always the best respected.

The pourparler will say every thing for himself that he ought not, and nothing for you that he

---

* Those who never wept for a wife till her decease, have had a short sorrow.

he ought; he volunteers, like the adviser, for *his own* interest.

GENEROSITY is much admir'd when it comes from our inferiors, or those we have injur'd.*

THE greatest obligation is to forget all obligation; there are many more ways of obliging than there are services to be render'd.

TIMIDITY opens, and inquietude grows up, with love.

ANGER is often assum'd; there exists a species of satisfaction when the equanimity of those we look down upon is destroy'd. A butt is sure to put his company in good temper if he loses his own: then the supercilious and the presumptuous triumph.

CHILDREN shou'd associate with youth, youth with age, and age with either. Our introduction to the world, as it is call'd, cannot begin too early: now we are immers'd into society like a falling body into water, and the chances are we sink as soon.

A BLOW

* Whatever comes from those above us we think we merit; by the same reasoning, as we expect injuries from those below us, we are surprized at their kind forbearance.

* A BLOW is a reafon for a beaft. Who that forefees the confecutive evils that refult from blows would fpend their paffion in fuch acts?

THE greateft of our cares we care leaft to defend; great in thought, infignificant in deed, are the moft important of mortals.

DEAF people are converfant with effects alone; this, it might be imagined, would make them fuper-eminently happy; but the blind are obferv'd to be the moft cheerful.

COXCOMBS falute themfelves when they notice you.

Who is fhe?—This is a trite, but an extraordinary queftion! The *who* is every thing—the *what* is all.†

As innocence is ridiculed, fo is vice encouraged; but the bad qualities we protect we poffefs.

ADMIRATION is blind; it is often the reflection of grofs flattery.

THOSE

---

* Receive a blow as you do the act of a malicious madman.

† Rank in life determines more than our opinion, it fixes our affections.

Those who know not when to be offended, know not how to be pleas'd.—Be pleas'd with every thing, and you tolerate much impertinence, insignificance, and formality; but you will acquire a train of worthless advocates.

Smart shews sensibility, tho' 'tis a demonstration of feeling, none, except the cruel, wish to call forth. The apathist is all insensibility: pride is its reverse.

* Wisdom is either local or partial knowledge: a small portion, with good animal spirits, and confident activity, will, *within* its circle, push beyond genius or learning. Success must be ravish'd, not wooed.

Coquettry and prudery are neither confin'd to sex or state.

All our distinctions are accidental: beauty and deformity, tho' personal qualities, are neither entitled to praise or censure; yet it so happens that they colour our opinion of those qualities to which mankind have attach'd responsibility.

* If the sages of the various corners of the earth were to meet, and able to speak one language, they would scarcely be tolerable company.

Many volunteer to instruct or correct, who are themselves deaf to their voices; the proud will from the chair of authority cheerfully communicate all they know.*

Hunger deranges the temper: indeed, the senses, in every case, direct the mind. The Roman phrase runs thus, *Venter non habet aures*.†

Vulgar, envious, or impertinent contradiction, is safely responded to by silence—it discourages and expresses contempt at the same instant.

Personal animosity is the brutality of disappointment: ‡ the great no ill treatment can exasperate; no insolence or injury can even make them indifferent; nay, their concern arises with the enormity of the transgression.

'Tis strange to see the revolution that opinion describes in the political sphere: Governors rail at the stupidity of the populace, and the people cry out against the ignorance of their rulers; and

---

* Yet ask for advice, and you are as liable to be insulted as instructed.

† The belly has no ears.

‡ Or powerful envy.

and the strongest party punishes the weakest, without thinking of amendment on either side.

Diffidence is the minority of reason, confidence its maturity. When diffidence lowers into timidity, or confidence swells into presumption, then they have left reason entirely.

* Flattery is the piquant sauce that pamper'd or vitiated understandings require to make life palatable. No creature can obtain credit for not relishing it. 'Tis like salt, the ingredient that savours every viand; no table is complete without it. When offer'd, you cannot refuse it without offending. Acceptance is indirect flattery; so is praising a second person who is favour'd by the first.

Trifle is a word of dangerous consequence as a name.† There is nothing trifling, unless all is trifling: those things that are so denominated, are neglected only because their connection and relative importance is not evident. Trifles often decide our weightiest concerns.

Lysander

---

* 'Tis necessary we should be pleas'd with what we do; and for this satisfaction we depend on foreign opinion.

† A trifler is the most insignificant in the vocabulary of characters.

LYSANDER refus'd the rich garments that Dionysius offer'd to his daughters with this remark: *they are only fit to make unhappy faces more remarkable.* What gaudy attire takes from beauty, it adds to deformity, or homely features: we dress rather after the fashion of what we wish to be, than what we are.

INDOLENCE creates more evils than ambition; they are likewise more durable. The indolent merits a severer punishment than the thief: the latter only does what is wrong; the former does the same, and omits to do every thing that is right.

WHAT we stand in need of, we either dare not, or need not, ask for.* Solicit for relief, and you make out your own indictment; petition for protection, and your weakness will be derided.

IF virtue is its own reward, as the adage pronounces it, who should be surpriz'd at their poverty?

BY not appearing to be the solicitors, women think they are more than half exculpated.

THE

* We cannot ask for: for we know not what we need, tho' we need what we know.

The littleness of the great is to be discover'd within their own walls; his residence is the theatre where the good man shines.

Wisdom often revokes; the opinions of pride and ignorance are irrevocable.

The will of the multitude is despotic, their partiality precarious, their enmity cruel: their idols are seldom chosen, but obtruded; they are generally men of violent passions, and feeble virtues; their abilities shewy rather than profound.

† Suffer nothing to be lost by a refusal or defeat.

Esteem must be merited; things may be purchas'd; love comes gratuitously, and is conserv'd by sincerity and courteous concern: the surrender that is bought is a monument of what we could not conquer.

No amendment in resentment: allow no room for the latter, and open every passage for the former.

Good

---

† Be assur'd likewise of the issue when you ask.

Good friends are safe enemies, and good enemies may become safe friends.

Eloquence, beauty, and good cloaths, are good advocates.

We are the last to acknowledge, but the first to worship, our own picture.

* A requisition is not an offence; neither crouch when you require, or domineer when you are requested.

Independence frightens the slave; and the rude hauteur of assum'd independence is more disgusting than the no opinion of the insipid, or the ever-ready compliance of habitual hypocrisy.

Pecuniary embarrassment is the identical species of adversity that is the touchstone of all dispositions. Beauty and ability, relationship, nay, every connection, shakes when the ensign of poverty is unfurl'd: we must worship wealth, even to idolatry, if the noble disinterestedness of a few individuals was not at all times obtruded to keep us from immerging into the oblivifcence of worth, affection, and merit.

Lovers

---

* Before despotism there can be no greater.

Lovers are prone to prejudicate. An evil opinion, without an exifting caufe, is a punifhment that injures the promulger.

Books are as often condemned for want of conception in the reader, as want of ability in the writer.

What is good cannot be better'd from any circumftance of nativity; nor is it apparent how any particular fociety is honour'd, unlefs it contributed to the expanfion of genius. Supprefs the place of birth, 'twill decreafe, nor will revealing it increafe your value.

* Transitions from virtue to vice are fometimes fo rapid, that the mind is inclin'd to queftion the exiftence of the former.

Man lofes what woman gains by modefty; unlefs the female knows how to appreciate the real character of the male, and diftinguifhes between impertinent importunity and refpectful forbearance.

When

---

* Expedition is always us'd when we are defirous to pafs from what we are indifferent to. Unfortunately in our paffage from error to error, we congratulate ourfelves as much as if we had left folly for truth.

When the tribunal is respected, its verdicts, tho' fallacious, are sure to be thought respectable.

All deceit carries with it a punishment; yet that is the most painful that is in itself venial, namely, the deceit practised on those amiable dispositions whose prejudice, not intention, would make us unhappy.

Our greatest pleasures and virtues, our greatest vices and sorrows, pass under the canopy of secresy.

Luxury is an inhumanity whilst want exists; 'twou'd be useless, if we knew the luxury of simplicity or benevolence.

Certain errors degrade our moral consequence much less than factitious virtues; but when there exists any personal attachment, moral or physical defects are easily overlook'd.

FINIS.

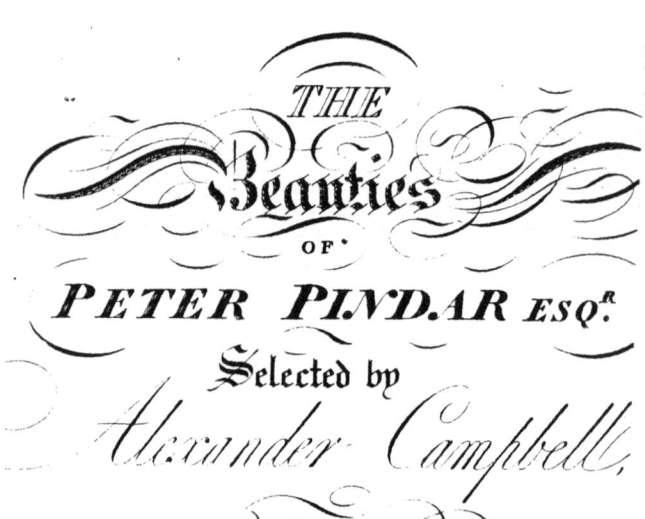

LONDON.
Pub. by The. Tegg,
Sold by Oliver & Co. — Price

THE
BEAUTIES
OF
𝔓𝔦𝔫𝔡𝔞𝔯;

BEING

SELECTIONS FROM THE VARIOUS WORKS

OF THAT

ECCENTRIC AUTHOR;

WITH

A BIOGRAPHICAL MEMOIR

OF HIS

LIFE AND WRITINGS.

"Abundat dulcibus vitiis."
QUINTILLIAN.

SKETCH

OF

THE LIFE AND WRITINGS

OF

JOHN WALCOTT, M.D.

Known by the Name of

PETER PINDAR, ESQ.

Dr. WALCOTT was born at Dodbrook, near Kingsbridge, in that part of Devonshire which has been so justly called, The Garden of England. His education was first conducted by a quaker, in the vicinity of the place where he was born. He was then sent to France, and there his studies were completed.

The uncle of our bard living at Fowey, in Cornwall, as surgeon and apothecary, trained up his nephew to succeed him in business. His medical knowledge of course was at this time acquired. He conducted himself in a manner which did him credit, and cultivated a propensity for drawing, to which he had been addicted.

Sir William Trelawney, a relation and friend of the family, being appointed governor of Jamaica, in the year 1769, Dr. Walcott felt an inclination to accompany him. His uncle was not pleased with the measure, but his remonstrances were not attended with success. He at last complied; and the nephew having received a medical degree, set sail for that distant part of the world. It was, however, a disappointment to the uncle, and therefore his consent was a matter of gratification.

In the prosecution of the voyage, the ship in which he had embarked touched at *Madeira*, a cluster of islands which, in such voyages, are often frequented. The scenery of this sequestered spot has been often celebrated. Here, therefore, he penned some exquisite sonnets, which are admired for their beauty and simplicity.

On his arrival at Jamaica he practised as physician, and was, in length of time, appointed physician general of the island. How long he continued in this situation we cannot precisely say, but from his experience and industry, we are assured that he acquitted himself with ability.

The incumbent of a living in Jamaica dying, the physician officiated for some time in that capacity. He, however, returned to England, and finally settled at Truro, in Cornwall, where he again resumed the medical character, and practised with success. During the present period of his practice in this remote part of England, the Doctor discovered that satirical vein by which he has been since distinguished. It is confidently said, that his natural propensity was the means of occasioning some trouble to him. He ridiculed pomposity, and lashed it with a becoming severity.

At this time it was that Dr. Walcott had it in his power, and embraced the opportunity, of bringing forward Mr. John Opie, who, as a painter, has attained to eminence in his profession. He was only a sign-painter; being actually a parish apprentice to one Wheeler, a house-carpenter!

This celebrated painter received his first instructions from Dr. Walcott; he furnished him with materials, and gave him lessons. Having made a rapid progress, Opie went to Exeter, where, by sketching the likenesses of some of its citizens, he obtained both reputation and money. From this place he removed to London, where he has reached to a distinguished reputation.

We are not sure that Dr. Walcott at this period wrote much; his translation of a Latin epigram, however, was admirable; he produced it in a few minutes—it is as follows:—

> Come, gentle sleep, attend thy vot'ry's prayer,
> And tho' death's image to my couch repair;
> How sweet tho' lifeless, yet with life to lie,
> And without dying, O how sweet to die!

These lines are happy—they express what we all feel—they hold up the sensations which we cannot fail of experiencing every time we resign ourselves to the soothing influence of oblivion.

Our author's first literary production, at least that which attracted public notice, was his *Epistle to the Reviewers*, in the year 1782; this piece was fraught with so much humour, that the public were instantly struck with it; its circulation was great, and some of the sentiments are truly laughable.

In 1785 his *Lyric Ode to the Royal Academicians*, appeared, which, though possessed of considerable merit, was marked by too much severity. Mr. West, the historic painter, is treated most cavalierly; for this we see no good reason; the artist has produced several pieces which will go down with admiration to posterity.

But it was about this time he wrote and published his chief satirical production, called the LOUSIAD, a mock heroic poem.—One of his biographers states the origin of this lively piece in the following words: " His majesty, one afternoon at dinner, actually observed the insect, from which the poem is named, upon his plate among some green peas. This offensive object occasioned a decree to issue forth, that all the cooks, scullions, &c. in the royal kitchen, should have their heads shaved. Great murmurings were excited by this mandate, but the law, like that of the Medes and Persians, was irrevocable. On this incident Peter formed his exquisite production, and it was the *truth* of it alone that exempted him from prosecution." There are several parts, or cantos, in the *Lousiad*, and they were published at different times, so that it was by no means at once completed.

His next publication was an Epistle to James Boswell, Esq. the biographer of Johnson, occasioned by his attending the great Colossus of Modern Literature to the Hebrides, or Western Isles of Scotland. It was followed soon by his very humourous piece, entitled, Bozzi any Piozzi, in which he exposes *tittle-tattle* biographers with an uncommon degree of felicity.

Besides these there were a great many other publications fell from his fruitful pen, particularly his *Majesty's Visit to Whitbread's Brewhouse*, replete with wit and humour; and his *Emperor of Morocco*, addressed to Sir Joseph Banks, a truly laughable story; the zeal of the naturalist in pursuing a butter-fly over the glasses of cucumber-beds, &c. is ridiculed after a manner which possesses a striking originality.

Never did any satirist enjoy more success. Those who reprobated his political sentiments, could not read his effusions with an unruffled gravity. At the same time we must protest against the abuse of such talents; his writings, we are sorry to say, are by no means free, either from profanity or obscenity.

Dr. Walcott, it is said, is at present in easy circumstances, owing to the success of his works, and he even still practises with success in asthmatic complaints. He also has, as we have already related, a taste for painting, in which he indulges himself. In conversation, we are assured, he is not striking, though his productions are characterised with such an extraordinary degree of archness and vivacity.

The Doctor has lately quitted town for his residence in the west of England, nor is it believed that he ever will return to the metropolis. Satisfied with the fame he has already acquired, and few have mounted higher on the Pegasus-crowned hill, he seems to have taken leave of all future productions, in the title of his last performance, ominously designated *Tristia, or the Sorrows of Peter.*—Many ages may elapse, before the Palace will encounter such a severe satirist of *great* littlenesses, folly of every kind be more roughly exposed, or the looser passions meet with a better or more seductive advocate. There, in the bosom of country retirement, and surrounded by the allurements of the pencil, and the benevolent practice of the healing art, the career of his life will terminate with regret to the admirers of genius and utility.

BEAUTIES

OF

PINDAR.

ABSENCE, (1.)

FROM her whom ev'ry heart must love,
　And ev'ry eye with wonder see;
My sad, my lifeless steps remove—
　Ah! were she fair alone for *me!*

In vain to solitudes I fly,
　To bid her form from mem'ry part;
That form still dwells on mem'ry's *eye*,
　And roots it's beauties in my heart.

In ev'ry rose that decks the vales,
　I see her cheek's pure blush appear:
And when the lark the morning hails,
　'Tis Julia's voice salutes my ear.

Thus let me rove the world around,
　Whatever beauty's charm can boast,
Or soothe the soul with sweetest sound,
　Must paint the idol I have lost.

ABSENCE, (2.)

She is dead, who gave life to the groves,
　And covers our valley with gloom!
She who led all the Pleasures and Loves,
　Now joins the pale band of the tomb.

Yet silent was she on the Swain,
  Whose cruelty doom'd her to mourn;
In secret her soul would complain,
  In secret her anguish would burn.

She would sit near yon willow and sigh,
  And pant in the shade of the trees:
" Sweet Zephyr, bring health," she would cry;
  But Health never came with the breeze.

And oft she would drink of the brook,
  But Health never came with the rill;
Then around on the heights she would look,
  But Health never came to the hill.

On her Dog she look'd down with a tear,
  And sigh'd as she patted his head,
" Poor Fidelle! thou wilt suffer, I fear,
  " When thy Mistress, who loves thee, is dead.

" *Thou* hast ever been constant and kind;
  " *My* fondness ne'er met with a *slight*:
" In *thee* a firm friendship I find;
  " How unhappy when out of my sight!

Thus she spoke to her Fav'rite, whose eye
  Was fix'd upon those of the Maid:
Then he lick'd her fond hand at her sigh,
  As if conscious of all she had said!

Sweet Nymph! what a sudden decay!
  Now her limbs she could scarcely sustain;
Now her head would sink feebly away,
  Like the lily press'd down by the rain.

At length on her pillow she fell;
  In silence we watch'd her last breath;
When she bade us for ever farewell,
  How divine, tho' the whisper of Death!

No struggle in dying she knew,
  Life pass'd with such sweetness away!
So calm from the world she withdrew,
  Her last sigh seem'd the zephyr of May.

Beneath a *plain* stone she is laid,
  For needless of *praise* is the tale;
Since the virtues that shone in the Maid,
  May be seen in the tears of the Vale.

ADDRESS OF AN AUTHOR TO HIS BOOK.

Child of my love, go forth, and try thy fate:
  Few are thy friends, and manifold thy foes!
Whether or long or short will be thy date,
  Futurity's dark volume only knows.

By some indeed will Nitre's fuming spirit,
  Be o'er thy form so sweet, so tender, thrown;
Perchance a *Master* hand may try thy merit;
  Perchance an Imp by Folly only know.

Now, now I fancy thee a timid hare,
  Started for beagles, hounds, and curs, to chace!
A mongrel dog may snap thee up unfair;
  For Spite and Hunger boast but little grace.

And now a Lamb!—What devils now-a-days
  The butch'ring Shop of Criticism employs!
Each beardless villain now cuts up, and flays;
  A gang of wanton, brutal, 'prentice boys!

Ah me! how hard to reach the dome of Fame!
  Knock'd down before she gets half way, poor Muse!
For many a Lout that cannot gain a name,
  (Rebus and riddle-maker) now *reviews!*

Poor jealous Eunuchs in the land of Taste,
  Too *weak* to reap a harvest of fair praise;
Malicious, lo! they lay the region waste,
  Fire all they can, and triumph at the blaze!

Too oft, with talents blest, the cruel Few
  Fix on poor Merit's throat, to stop her breath:
How like the beauteous (the Manchineel tree) Fruit
      that turns of Dew
    The life ambrosial, into drops of Death!

ADULATION.

When Flatt'ry sings, Age opes his eyes so clear,
And claps so brisk the trumpet to his ear,
  So *wondrously* inspir'd he lists, and sees!
When Flatt'ry sings, 'pale Colic's pains are off;
Consumption pants not, but forgets his cough ;
  And Asthma's loaded lungs forbear to wheeze.

Sweet on the list'ning ear of stilly Night,
  As warbling dyeth Philomela's song;
So on the ear of man, with rich delight,
  The lulling music flows from Flatt'ry's tongue.

Flatt'ry's a perfect mistress of her art ;
With picklock keys to open ev'ry heart.

What mortal can withstand the fire of Flatt'ry?
No one! 'tis such a most successful batt'ry,
No head, however thick, resists its shot;
Yet each pretends to mock it!—what a sot!

ADULATION, OR SUSAN AND THE SPIDER.

" Come down, you toad," cry'd Susan to a Spider,
High on the gilded cornice a proud rider,
  And wanton, swinging by his silken rope;
" I'll teach thee to spin cobwebs round the room ;
" You're now upon some murder, I presume—
  " I'll *bless* thee—if I don't, say I'm no Pope."

Then Susan brandish'd her long brush,
Determin'd on a fatal push,
To bring the rope-dancer to ground,
And all his schemes of death confound.

The Spider, blest with oratory grace;
Slipp'd down, and, staring Susan in the face,
  " Fie, Susan! lurks there murder in *that* heart,
" O barb'rous, lovely Susan! I'm amaz'd!
" O! can that form, on which so oft I've gaz'd,
  " Possess of cruelty the slightest part?

" Ah! can that swelling bosom of delight,
" On which I've peep'd with wonder many a night,
 " Nay, with these fingers *touch'd* too, let me say,
" Contain a heart of cruelty?—no, no!
" That bosom, which exceeds the new-fall'n snow,
 " All softness, sweetness, one eternal May."

" How!" Susan screech'd, as with disorder'd brain,
" How, Impudence! repeat those words again:
" Come, come, confess with honesty—speak, speak,
 " Say, did you *really* crawl upon my neck?"

" Susan, by all thy heav'nly charms, I did;
 " I saw thee sleeping by the taper's light;
"Thy cheek, so blushful, and thy breast so white:
" I could not stand it, and so down I slid."

" You did, sweet Mr. Spider? so you *saw!*"
" Yes, Susan! Nature is a pow'rful law."

" Arn't you a murd'rer?" gravely Susan cries;
 " Arn't you for ever busy with that claw,
" Killing poor unoffending little flies,
 " Merely to satisfy your nasty maw?"

" But, Susan, don't you feed on gentle *lamb?*
" Don't you on pretty little *pigeons* cram?
 " Don't you on harmless *fishes* often dine?"

" That's very true," quoth Susan, " true indeed;
" Lord! with what eloquence these Spiders plead!
 " This little rascal beats a grave Divine.

" It was no snake, I verily believe,
" But a sly *spider* that seduc'd poor Eve.

" But then you are so *ugly*."—" Ah! sweet Sue,
 " I did not make myself, you know too well:
" Could I have made *myself*, I had been *you*,
 " And kill'd with envy ev'ry beauteous Belle."

" Heav'ns! to this Spider! what a 'witching tongue!
" Well! go about thy bus'ness—go along;

" All animals, indeed, their food must get:
" And hear me, shouldst thou look with longing eyes,
" At any time, on young, fat, luscious flies,
   " I'll drive the little rascals to thy net.
" Lord! then how blind I've been to form and feature!
" I think a Spider, *now*, a comely creature!"

ADULATION IN COURTS.

Behold the manners of a Court:
There (thanks to Education for't)
   Submission cow'ring creeps, with fearful eye,
Unceasing bends the willowy neck to ground,
In rev'rence abject and profound,
   Too humbly modest to behold the sky:

There Adulation, with her silver tongue,
Sweeter than Philomela's sweetest song,
   Says unto Majesty *such things!*
Tells him that Cæsar won not half *his* fame;
That Alexander was a childish name,
   Compar'd to *his*—the King of Kings!

Now smiling, staring huge surprise,
With such a brace of wonder-looking eyes,
   On all the words from Majesty that dart;
As if bright gems, as large as eggs of pullet,
Flow'd from the King's Golconda gullet,
   Enough, indeed, to load a cart:
Her mouth so pleas'd the treasures to devour!
Wide as the port-hole of a Seventy-four!

Such is the picture of a Palace scene,
Drawn by an *amateur*, I ween:
The outline chaste, and easy flowing;
The colouring not a whit too glowing.
Such, such is Adulation, charming maid!
Whose conduct does the servile few degrade.

ADVICE TO YOUNG WOMEN; OR, THE ROSE AND THE STRAWBERRY.

A Rose in all the pride of bloom,
Flinging around her rich perfume,
Her form to public notice pushing,
Amidst the summer's golden glow,
Peep'd on a Strawberry below,
Beneath a leaf, in secret blushing.

" Miss Strawberry," exclaim'd the Rose,
" What's beauty that no mortal knows?
" What is a charm, if never seen?
" You really are a pretty creature:
" Then wherefore hide each blooming feature?
" Come up, and shew your modest mien."

" Miss Rose," the Strawberry replied,
" I never did possess a pride
" That wish'd to *dash* the public eye:
" Indeed I own that I'm *afraid*—
" I think there's safety in the *shade;*
" Ambition causes many a sigh."

" Go, simple child," the Rose rejoin'd,
" See how *I* wanton in the wind:
" I feel no danger's dread alarms:
" And then observe the God of Day,
" How amorous with his golden ray,
" To pay his visits to my charms!"

No sooner said, but with a scream
She started from her fav'rite theme—
A clown had on her fix'd his *pat*,
In vain she screech'd—Hob did but smile;
Rubb'd with her leaves his nose awhile,
Then bluntly stuck her in his hat.

AFFECTION.

Yet for *myself* I wish'd not wealth alone—
For thee, Narcissa, was the wish, in part;

I thought thy beauties once would be my own—
  And sigh'd to give thee *more* than my poor heart.

With *thee* I hop'd to live in rural ease,
  Far from the tumults of the world withdrawn,
Where Health would meet us with her fragrant breeze,
  Lead to the hills, and join us on the lawn.

With thee to tread the dews at early day,
  And meet young Morning on the orient hill;
Pleas'd, as the brooks in murmurs wind away,
  And learn some moral lesson from the rill.

With thee I hop'd, in Summer's golden hour,
  To wander, arm in arm, the glade along!
To touch the lyre of love amid the bow'r—
  And thou the blushing subject of the song.

When Winter ravag'd in his stormy rage,
  With thee I hop'd t'enjoy the cheerful fire;
With thee converse, or read th' instructive page,
  Or mingle with thy sweeter voice the lyre.

And when, at midnight, through the vast of shade,
  The tempest whelm'd the world with wild alarms;
Then to my bosom press a timid Maid,
  And lose its thunder in Narcissa's arms.

Such were my wishes! yet thou still art *fair*;
  And I, tho' lost some blushes of my cheek,
By Time's rude hand, would Fortune grant my pray'r,
With Love's sweet whispers, would thy cottage seek

But grant that beauty were no longer thine—
  Narcissa's converse would the hours *beguile*—
Ev'n in old age would happiness be mine;
  Time leaves a treasure if he leaves thy *smile*.

AFFECTATION, ODE TO.

Nymph of the mincing mouth, and languid eye,
And lisping tongue so soft, and head awry,
  And flutt'ring heart, of leaves of aspin made;

Who were thy parents, blushful Virgin! say—
Perchance Dame Folly gave thee to the day,
　With Gaffer Ignorance's aid.

Great is thy delicacy, dainty Maid;
　At slightest things, thy cheek with crimson glows:
Say, art thou not asham'd, abash'd, afraid,
　When'er thou stealest forth to *pluck a rose?*

'Tis said, when wag-tails thou behold'st, and doves,
And sparrows busy with their feather'd loves;
　Lord! thou hast trembled at their wicked tricks;
And, snatching up thy blush-concealing fan,
As if it were a lady and a man,
　Hast only peep'd upon them through the *sticks.*

And yet so variously thou'rt said to act,
That I have heard it utter'd for a fact,

That often on old Thames's sunny banks,
Where striplings swim, with wanton pranks,
　On bladders some outstretch'd and some on corks;
Thou squinting, most *indiff'rent* girl, art seen,
In contemplation of each youthful skin,
　Admiring God Almighty's handy-works.

Some men have got *strange names,* that raise thy *blush*
　(Pity a *name* should so disturb thy cheek!)
Then dost thou, simpering, beat about the bush,
　When to those men thou art inclin'd to speak.

At length thou biddest Susan (with sweet shame)
　" Go fetch the fellow with the *filthy name.*"

I've heard, that breeches, petticoats, and smock,
Give to thy modest mind a grievous shock;
And that thy brain (so lucky its device)
Christ'neth them *inexpressibles,* so nice!

No novels readest thou, O Nymph, *in sight;*
And yet again I'm told that ev'ry night,
In *secret,* thou art much inclin'd to doat
On rhymes that Rochester so warmly wrote.

Oft dost thou wonder how thy sex, so sweet,
Can fellows, those great two-legg'd monsters, meet
   And swoon not at each Caliban;
And wonder how thy sex can fancy blisses
Contain'd within the black rough-bearded kisses
   Of such a horrid bear-like thing as man.

Inform me, is it so, most dainty maid?
Are thy two lips of kisses thus afraid?

And yet 'tis said, again, O Nymph so bright,
Thou sleep'st with John the coachman ev'ry night—
   Vile tales! invented to destroy thy fame;
For, wert thou, fearful Lass, this instant married,
At night, thy modest cheek would burn with shame,
   Nor wouldst thou go, but to the bed be *carried*.

There, when thy Strephon rush'd, in white array'd,
To clasp with kisses sweet his white-stol'd maid,
   And riot in the luxury of charms;
Flat as a flounder, seeing, hearing gone—
Mute as a fish, and fairly turn'd to stone—
   O Damsel! thou wouldst *die* within his arms.

AFFIRMATION AND NEGATION, A SONG.

When William first woo'd, I said *yes* to the swain,
   And made him as blest as a Lord—
For ye Virgins around, in my speech to be plain,
   That No is a dangerous word!
The girl that will always say *no*, I'm afraid,
Is doom'd by her Planet to die an Old Maid.

The Gentlemen seem one and all to agree,
   That we're made of materials for kissing—
And if so, for I really believe it, good me!
   What joys through one *no* might be missing!
Since the Girl that will always say *no*, I'm afraid,
Is doom'd by her Planet to die an Old Maid.

Say *yes*, and of courtship ye finish the toil—
   Whole mountains at once ye remove—

You brighten the eyes of the Swain by a *smile*,
  For smiles are the sunshine of Love!
Say *yes*, and the world will acquit you of *art*,
Since the *Tongue* will not *then* give the lie to the
    Heart.

AGITATION OF THE HEART.

Thus a large dumpling to its cell confin'd,
(A very apt allusion, to my mind)
Lies snug, until the water waxeth hot,
Then bustles 'midst the tempest of the pot:
In vain!—the lid keeps down the child of dough,
That bouncing, tumbling, sweating, rolls below.

AGITATION OF THE SOUL.

Huge thoughts of diff'rent sizes swell'd his soul;
Now mounting high, now sinking low they roll;
Bustling here, there, up, down, and round about;
So wild the mob, so terrible the rout!
How like a Leg of Mutton in the pot,
With turnips thick surrounded all so hot!
Amid the gulph of broth, sublime, profound,
Tumultuous, jostling, how they rush around!
Now up the turnips mount with skins of snow,
While restless lab'ring Mutton dives below—
Now lofty soaring, climbs the leg of sheep,
While Turnip downward plunges 'mid the deep!

ALARM.

Thus on a bank, upon a summer's day,
  Of some fair stream of East or Western Ind,
When puppies join in wanton play,
  Free from the slightest fear of being skinn'd;

If from that stream, which all so placid flows,
A sly old alligator pokes his nose;
Wishing, *perchance*, to take a slice of cur;
At once the dogs are off upon the spur;

Nor once behind them cast a courtly look,
To compliment the monarch of the brook.

AMBITION, (1.)

What diff'rent roads to Fame Ambition takes!
What hubbub in this under-world she makes!
Ambition, the Queen-passion of the soul—
Ev'n Love, sweet Love, indeed, has less controul.
Ambition makes the *wise* a *fool* at Court;
Ambition drowns an Alderman in port:
Ambition bids the man of ropes, or figs,
Or fish, or brass, or foolscap, peas, or pigs,
Sigh for the golden chain, and coach so fair,
In short, to shine the City's sun—Lord May'r!

AMBITION, (2.)

An Owl, a bachelor of no great soul,
Nor intellect, but very, very proud,
  The tenant of a little dirty hole,
Wish'd from obscurity to clear the cloud:
  Yes, Owl must have his sails unfurl'd,
  And mount majestic on the world.

  Close to his ivy-house liv'd Crow,
  Who on his errands us'd to go.
" Crow," said the Owl, upon a day,
  " I'm sick of solitude and gloom :
  " A bird of my deep sense and plume,
  " Should *mount* amid the blaze of day.
  " In short, dear Crow, I wish to *wed*,
  " And, mind me, take unto my bed
  " A Bird of *birth*, the Eagle's daughter,
    " Miss Eaglet."—" Ah," replied the Crow,
Ready to split his sides with laughter,
    " Indeed! and are things really *so?*
" Right, Sir, to alter your condition—
" O Lord there's nothing like *ambition!*"

" Well, Crow, you'll quickly seek the realms above,
" With my proposals to the Bird of Jove."

Crow takes his leave, ascends the skies,
And to the Eagle's palace flies
The black Ambassador from Owl;
Delivers his credentials to his Grace,
With Auckland's diplomatic face,
Conceiving, like a *penetrating* fowl,
How politics would go *above*;
What answer leave the Bird of Jove.

Thus spake the Royal Bird :—" Sir Crow,
" To my Lord Owl be pleas'd to go,
" And tell him that I like the match :
" I'm much oblig'd to him, indeed,
" For honouring the Eagle breed:
" I've been a good while on the watch
" To throw a *little lustre* round my house :
" Commend me to the Thunderbolt of Mouse.

" Miss Eaglet is at his command—
" Shall join his Lordship in the straw ;
" Who such alliance cannot well withstand ;
" Happy to take him by the *claw*.
" Bid him ascend *sans cérémonie—free*,
" And *pick his mouse* to-day with *me*."

Off flew at once the sable fowl,
And quickly reach'd the house of Owl,
And told him all that he had seen and heard.
Owl instant comb'd, and wash'd his face,
Cut all his claws to *such* a grace,
Trimm'd all his feathers nicely—clipp'd his beard;
Bid to his humble hole good-night,
And rose amid the realms of light.

Mounted a mile or two, behold,
The sun's bright blaze of burnish'd gold
Flash'd on the Owl's poor weak and watering eyes:
Just like a paper-kite, whose string,
Deserting, leaves him on the wing,
To totter, dip, mount, fall agen, and rise ;

So shuffled Owl, lost, reeling blind,
The sport of every gust of wind,
Till down he fell with phiz of woe,
The jest of every bird below.

ANGER, (1.)

Thus water, all so simple, cool, and mild,
So soft, it would not injure e'en a child,
Yet, goaded by the fire, how warm it grows,
Displaying symptoms of disturb'd repose!
Sudden it swells, and, o'er the cauldron's side,
Foams the fierce cataract's tumultuous tide,
And, in a twinkling, see the foolish fire,
Whelm'd by the water, with a whiz expire.

ANGER, (2.)

To bend a piece of iron to your will,
   You always make that iron hot;
For then it asks but little force and skill—
   Its sturdiness is quite forgot:

But, lo! it is quite otherwise with man!
Make *him* red-hot, and bend him as you can:
So widely diff'rent are the metals,
Composing man, or kings indeed, and kettles!

ANTIQUARIES,—RIDICULED.

Rare are the buttons of a Roman's breeches,
In antiquarians eyes surpassing riches:
Rare is each crack'd, black, rotten, earthen dish,
That held of ancient Rome the flesh and fish:
Rare are the talismans that drove the Devil,
And rare the bottles that contain'd old snivel.
Owls' heads, and snoring frogs, preserved in spirits,
Most certainly are not without their merits.

ANXIETY.

Far from my Julia's arms I lonely sigh,
   And wish to clasp' thy beauties, but in vain;

The surly winds my only wish deny,
   Yet would I dare the dangers of the main.

Ye wind and waves, how cruel to combine!
   O let my pray'rs your rude, rude pity prove;
Think of the gloomy moments that are mine!
   Alas! ye know not what it is to *love!*

Oft as I mark the tribes of air, I cry,
   "How with your pinions would I mount the wind!
" Oh! with what rapture lifted, cleave the sky,
   "And, turn'd to Britain, leave my cares behind!"

In wishes thus, I daily waste my breath,
   Chain'd by the tempest to this hated shore;
When shall I leave, alas! this land of death,
   For life and thee, to part, my Love, no more?

ASS PETER, AN ODE TO.

O thou, my solemn friend, of man despis'd,
   But not by *me* despis'd—respected long!
To prove how much thy qualities are priz'd,
   Accept, old fellow-traveller, a song.

Ah, Peter, I remember, oft, when tir'd
And most unpleasantly at times bemir'd,
Bold hast thou said, "I'll budge not one inch further;
"And now, young Master, you may kick or murther."

Then have I cudgell'd thee—a fruitless matter!
For 'twas in vain to kick, or flog, or chatter.
Though, Balaam-like, I curs'd thee with a smack;
Sturdy thou dropp'dst thine ears upon thy back,
And trotting retrograde, with wriggling tail,
In vain did I thy running rump assail:
For, lo, between thy legs thou putt'dst thine head,
And gavest me a puddle for a bed.

O Peter, little didst thou think, I ween,
When I a schoolboy on thy back was seen,
Riding thee oft, in attitude uncouth;
For bridle, an old garter in thy mouth;

Jogging and whistling wild o'er hill and dale,
On sloes, or nuts, or strawb'ries to regale—
I say, O Peter, little didst thou think,
That *I*, thy namesake, in immortal ink
Should dip my pen, and rise a *wond'rous Bard*,
And gain such praise, Sublimity's reward;

But, lo, of *thee* I'll speak, my long-ear'd friend!
　Great were the wonders of thy heels of yore;
Victorious, for lac'd hats didst thou contend;
　And ribbons grac'd thy ears—a gaudy store.

Buff breeches too have crown'd a proud, proud day,
Not *thou*, but which thy *rider* wore away;
Triumphant strutting through the world he strode,
Great soul! deserving an Olympic Ode.

Yet shalt Thou flourish in immortal song,
To *me* if immortality belong;
For stranger things than *this* have come to pass—
　Posterity thine hist'ry shall devour,
　And read with pleasure *how*, when vernal show'r
In gay profusion rais'd the dewy grass,
I led thee forth thine appetite to please,
And 'mid the verdure saw thee up to knees!

How oft I pluck'd the tender blade;
　And, happy, *how* thou cam'st at my command,
And wantoning around, as though afraid,
　With poking neck didst pull it from my hand,
Then scamper, kicking, frolicksome, away,
With such a fascinating bray!

Where oft I paid thee visits, and where thou
　Didst cock with happiness thy kingly ears,
And grin so 'witchingly, I can't tell how,
　And dart at me such friendly leers;

With such a smiling head, and laughing tail;
And when I mov'd, *how* griev'd thou seem'dst to say,
" Dear Master, let your humble Ass prevail;
　" Pray, Master, do not go away"—

And *how* (for what than friendship can be sweeter?)
I gave thee grass again, O pleasant Peter.

And *how*, when Winter bade the herbage die,
And Nature mourn'd beneath the stormy sky;
When waving trees, surcharg'd with chilling rain,
Dropp'd seeming tears upon the harrass'd plain,
I gave thee a good stable, warm as wool,
With oats to grind, and hay to pull:
Thus, whilst *abroad* December rul'd the day,
How plenty shew'd *within*, the blooming May!

And lo, to future times it shall be known,
How, twice a day, to comb and rub thee down,
  And be thy bed-maker at night,
Thy groom attended, both with hay and oat,
By which thy back could boast a handsome coat,
  And laugh at many a fine Court Lord and Knight,
Whose strutting coats belong p'rhaps to the tailor,
And probably their bodies to the jailor!

What though no dimples thou hast got;
Black sparkling eyes (the fashion) are thy lot,
  And oft a 'witching smile and cheerful laugh;
And then thy *cleanliness!*—'tis strange to utter!
Like sin, thy heels avoid a pool, or gutter;
  And then the stream so *daintily* doth quaff!
Unlike a country alderman, who blows,
And in the mug baptizeth mouth and nose!

What though I've heard some voices sweeter;
Yet exquisite thy hearing, gentle Peter!
Some people think thy tones are *rather* coarse;
Ev'n love-sick tones, address'd to Lady Asses—
Octaves indeed of wond'rous force;
And yet thy voice full many a voice surpasses.

Kings did not scorn to press your backs of yore:
  But now, with humbled neck and patient face,
Tied to a thievish miller's dusty door,
  I mark thy fall'n and disregarded race.

B

To chimney-sweepers now a common hack;
Now with a brace of sand-bags on your back!
No gorgeous saddle your's—no iv'ry cribs;
No silken girts surround your ribs;

No Royal hands your cheeks with pleasure pat;
Cheeks by a roguish halter prest—
Your ears and rump, of insolence the jest;
Dragg'd, kick'd, and pummell'd, by a beggar's brat.

Thus, as I've said, your race is much degraded!
And much too is the Poet's glory faded!

ASSIDUITY.

People must mount by slow degrees to glory—
'Tis stairs must lead us to the attic story—
Thus thought my great old Name-sake, Peter Czar;
Who bound himself, in Holland, to a trade;
A very pretty carpenter he made;
And then went home, and built a man of war.

The lad who would a 'pothecary shine,
Should powder claws of crabs, and jalap, fine;
Keep the shop clean, and watch it like a porter;
Learn to boil glysters—nay, to give them too,
If blinking nurses can't the business do;
Write well the labels, and wipe well the mortar.

Before that boys can rise to master-tanners, [ners;
Humble those boys must be, and mind their man-
Despising Pride, whose wish it is to wreck 'em;
And mornings, with a bucket and a stick,
Should never once disdain to bend and pick,
From street to street, rich lumps of *Album Græcum*.

Thus should young limning lads themselves demean;
Learn how to keep their masters's brushes clean,
And learn to squeeze the colours from their bladders;

Furbish up rags; the shining pallet set;
Keep the knives bright, and eke the easel neat—
Such arts, to Fame's high temple are the ladders.

ASSIGNATION.

When dew-clad Evening's modest blushes fade,
And Nature sinks amid the deep'ning shade,
  And Labour pauses on the fainting light;
When beetles hum, and bats in circles skim,
When hills and hamlets, trees and tow'rs, grow dim,
  And Silence steals upon the gloom of night;
    With joy I tread the secret grove,
    To meet the idol of my love.

AT HOME AND ABROAD.

A *Christian* Bard may give a Hoy an Ode,
So oft with valuable people stow'd,
That, thick as rats or maggots, from Wool Quay
Crawl down the ladder to their wat'ry way!
Who, fond of travel, unto Margate roam,
To gain that consequence they want at home.

At Margate how like Quality they strut!
  Nothing is good enough to greet their jaws;
Yet, when at home, are often forc'd, God wot,
  To suck like bears a dinner from their paws—

Forc'd on an old joint stool their tea to take,
  With treacle 'stead of sugar for their gums;
Butt'ring their hungry loaf, or oaten cake,
  Like mighty Charles of Sweden, with their thumbs.

AVARICE (!.)

" Perdition seize the Miser who denies
  " A pittance to the helpless pining poor;
" Who, millions owning, still with watchful eyes,
  " Hawks at *fresh* bags of gold, and screams for more.

" May curates *eat,* and *rear* their infant brood;
" Nay put a little *fat* about their bones;
" Cast from their wounded jaws the curb of blood,
" And dash their *lawn-sleev'd* riders on the stones!

" And may those Lawnmen, born to happier fate,
" Chace not the Curate from their grand abode:
" But gravely *think* of *Heav'n* as well as *prate,*
" And give a *leg of mutton* to their God!"

How base to preach of God's *exhaustless* store;
Of treasures that to mortals will be given;
Yet sooner trust (as though they thought it *poor*)
The Bank of England than the Bank of Heav'n!

How vile to preach of Heav'n *large int'rest,* too,
Seeming to place dependance on its word;
Yet on *sky-credit* look so very blue,
As though 'twere *dang'rous lending* to the Lord!

AVARICE, (2.)

Poor Mistress Levi had a luckless son,
 Who, rushing to obtain the foremost seat,
 In imitation of th' ambitious great,
High from the gall'ry, ere the play begun,
 He fell all plump into the pit,
 Dead in a minute as a nit:
In short, he broke his pretty Hebrew neck;
Indeed and very dreadful was the wreck!
The mother was distracted, raving, wild; [child;
Shriek'd, tore her hair, embrac'd and kiss'd her
 Afflicted ev'ry heart with grief around.

Soon as the show'r of tears was somewhat past,
And moderately calm th' hysteric blast,
 She cast about her eyes in thought profound;
And being with a saving knowledge bless'd,
She thus the playhouse manager address'd;

" Sher, I'm de moder of de poor Chew lad,
" Dat meet misfartin here so bad—
" Sher, I must haf de shilling back, you know,
" Ass Moses haf nat see de show."

AVARICE, (3.)

Forth crawl'd an ancient Dame,
Sharp-nos'd, half-starv'd, and Avarice her name;
With wrinkl'd neck, and parchment-like to view,
That e'en the coarsest 'kerchief seldom knew.
With hawk-like eyes that glisten'd o'er her gold,
And, raptur'd, ev'ry hour her treasure told;
Who of her fingers form'd a comb so fair,
And with a garter filletted her hair;
Who fiercely snatch'd, with wild devouring eyes,
An atom of brown sugar, from the flies;
Made a sad candle from a dab of fat,
And stole a stinking fish-head from a cat;
Sav'd of the mustiest bread the crumbs, and sees
A dinner in the *scrapings* of a cheese:
Whiffing a stump of pipe, a frequent treat,
That gives the stomach smoke, poor thing! for meat:—
Forth hobbled this old Dame, with shaking head,
Like, in her crooked form, the letter *zed*—
The Palace-watch, and guardian most severe
Of drops of dying and of dead small beer:
A Dame who hated idle dogs and cats,
And trembled at a rompus of the rats;
Nay listen'd, jealous scratching of a mouse,
Afraid the imp might swallow the whole house:
The careful province her's to sell old shoes,
Old hats, old coats, and breeches, to the Jews;
And drive, with dog-like fury, from the door,
The plaintive murmurs of the famish'd Poor.—

AVARICE, (4.)

Economy's a very useful broom;
Yet should not ceaseless hunt about the room
  To catch each straggling pin to make a plum.
Too oft Economy's an iron vice,
That squeezes ev'n the little guts of mice,
  That peep with fearful eyes, and ask a crumb.

Proper Economy's a comely thing;
Good in a subject—better in a King;
  Yet, push'd too far, it dulls each finer feeling,
Most easily inclin'd to make folks mean;
Inclines them, too, to villany to lean,
  To over-reaching, perjury, and stealing.

AUTHORS, (1.)

Yes, (as I've said) we Bards are mostly poor,
Can scarcely drive gaunt Famine from the door!
That Helicon's a hellish stream, God knows!
Ah, me! most rarely it *Pactolian* flows:
Though sharp as hawks, and hungry too, and thick,
Few are the golden grains that Poets pick;
And yet each new advent'rer of the Nine
Deems all Parnassus one mere golden mine.

AUTHORS, (2.)

In general, authors are such coward things,
They fear to speak their sentiments of Kings,
  Till those same Kings are dead; and then the crowd,
(Just like a pack of hounds) historian, bard,
With throats of thunder run his mem'ry hard,
  And try to tear him piecemeal from his shroud.

Now, if we wish a Monarch to reclaim,
  In God's name let us speak before he's dead;
Or else 'tis ten to one we miss our aim,
  By staying till the Fates have cut his thread:

After this operation of their knife,
I ne'er knew reformation in my life.

Alas! what is the greatest King when dead,
When dust and worms his eyes and ears o'erspread,
And low he lies beneath the stone?
The man who millions call'd his own,
Howe'er his spectre may be willing,
Cannot give change t'ye for a *shilling!*

BABLERS OF NEWS.—

Reader, didst ever see a water-spout?
 'Tis possible that thou wilt answer, " No."
Well then! he makes a most infernal rout;
 Sucks, like an elephant, the waves below,
With huge proboscis reaching from the sky,
As if he meant to drink the ocean dry:
At length so full he can't hold one drop more—
He bursts—down rush the waters with a roar.

BARN, ODE TO.*

Swift haunt of solitude and rats,
Mice, tuneful owls, and purring cats,
 Who, whilst we mortals sleep, the gloom pervade,
And wish not for the fun's all-seeing eye,
Your mousing mysteries to spy;
 Blest, like philosophers, amidst the shade;

When Persecution, with an iron hand,
Dar'd drive the moral-menders from the land,
 Call'd Players—friendly to the wand'ring crew,
Thine eyes with tears survey'd the mighty wrong,
Thine open arms receiv'd the mournful throng—
 Kings without shirts, and Queens with half a shoe.

Alas! what dangers gloom'd of late around!
Monarchs and Queen's with halters nearly bound—
 Duke, Dukeling, Princess, Prince, consign'd to jail!

* Upon the admission of some persecuted Players to it.

And, what the very soul of Pity shocks,
The poor old Lear was threaten'd with the stocks,
   Cordelia with the cart's unfeeling tail.

Still cherish such rare royalty forlorn—
A Garrick in thy bosom may be born;
   A Siddons too, of future fair renown:
For Love is not a squeamish God, they say;
As pleas'd to see his rites perform'd on hay,
   As on the goose's soft and yielding down.

THE BLIND BEGGAR.

Welcome, thou Man of Sorrows, to my door!
   A willing balm thy wounded heart shall find;
And, lo! thy guiding Dog my cares implore;
   O haste, and shelter from th' unfeeling wind!

Thou bowest for the pity I bestow:
   Bend not to me, because I mourn distress;
I am *thy* debtor—much to *thee* I owe;
   For learn—the greatest blessing is to *bless*.

Thy hoary locks, and wan and pallid cheek,
   And quiv'ring lip, to fancy seem to say,
" A more than *common* Beggar we bespeak;
   " A form that once has known a happier day."

Thy sightless orbs, and venerable beard,
   And press'd, by weight of years, thy palsi'd head,
Though silent, speak with tongues that *must* be heard,
   Nay, must *command*, if Virtue be not dead.

Since Fortune, to my cottage not unkind,
   Strews with *some* flow'rs the road of life for *me*,
Ah! can humanity desert my mind?
   Shall I not soften the rude flint for thee?

Then welcome, Beggar, from the rains and snow,
   And warring elements, to warmth and peace;

Nay, thy companion, too, shall comfort know,
  Who shiv'ring shakes away the icy fleece.

And, lo! he lays him by the fire, elate;
  Now on his Master turns his gladden'd eyes;
Leaps up to greet him on their change of fate,
  Licks his lov'd hand, and then beneath him lies.

A hut is mine, amidst a shelt'ring grove:
  A Hermit there, exalt to Heav'n thy praise;
There shall the village children shew their love,
  And hear from thee the tales of other days.

There shall our feather'd friend, the bird of morn,
  Charm thee with orisons to opening day;
And there the red-breast, on the leafless thorn,
  At eve shall sooth thee with a simple lay.

When Fate shall call thee from a world of woe,
  Thy friends around shall watch thy closing eyes;
With tears, behold thy gentle spirit go,
  And wish to join its passage to the skies.

BASHFULNESS AND BOLDNESS.

O Virgins! tell me how to choose,
  For I'm a novice on it—
Poor Colin at a *distance* woos,
  And sends his soul in *sonnet;*

While Lubin to no forms a slave,
  Won't stay to *write* for blisses;
But prints upon my mouth, the knave,
  His wishes with his kisses.

If Lubin seize a rude embrace,
  And I begin to clatter;
The rogue stares gravely in my face,
  And asks me what's the matter?

Poor Colin turns, if I but frown,
  All white as any fleece is!
Lubin would give me a green gown,
  And rummage me to pieces.

The one, so meek and complaisant,
  All silence, awe, and wonder;
The other, impudence and rant,
  And boist'rous as the thunder.

This begs to press my fingers tip,
  So bashful is my lover;
That savage bounces on my lip,
  And kisses it all over.

O Modesty, thou art so sweet!
  Not wild, and bold, and teasing;
And yet each Sister Nymph I meet
  Thinks boldness *not unpleasing.*

This is a wicked world—O dear!
  And wickedness is in me—
Though Modesty's so sweet, I fear
  That Impudence will *win me.*

BUTTERFLY, ODE TO.

Sweet child of summer, who from flow'r to flow'r,
  To sip each odour, sport'st on silken wing;
I greet thy presence 'mid the golden hour,
  Whilst with the birds the vales of Serdi ring.

I see thee perching on each rose's bloom;
  From fragrance thus to fragrance wont to glide;
Now from the tender vi'let waft perfume;
  Now fix'd upon the lily's snowy pride.

Though blest art thou—my bliss is greater still;
  I kiss the bosom of the brightest Fair!
The charms of Adel all my senses fill;
  And whilst those charms I press, her love I share.

CANDLE, AN ADDRESS TO.

Thou lone companion of the spectr'ed night,
I wake amid thy friendly-watchful light,
  To steal a precious hour from lifeless sleep—
Hark, the wild uproar of the winds! and hark,
Hell's genius roams the regions of the dark,
  And swells the thund'ring horrors of the deep.

From cloud to cloud the pale moon hurrying flies;
Now blacken'd, and now flashing through her skies.

But all is silence here—beneath thy beam,
  I own I labour for the voice of praise—
For who would sink in dull Oblivion's stream?
  Who would not live in songs of distant days?

Thus while I wond'ring pause o'er Shakspeare's page,
I mark, in visions of delight, the Sage,
  High o'er the wrecks of man, who stands sublime;
A Column in the melancholy Waste,
(Its cities humbled, and its glories past)
  Majestic, 'mid the solitude of Time.
Yet now to sadness let me yield the hour—
Yes, let the tears of purest friendship show'r.

I view, alas! what ne'er should die,
A form, that wakes my deepest sigh;
  A form, that feels of Death the leaden sleep—
Descending to the realms of shade,
I view a pale ey'd panting Maid:
  I see the Virtues o'er their fav'rite weep.

Ah! could the Muse's simple pray'r
  Command the envied trump of Fame,
Oblivion should Eliza spare;
  A world should echo with her name.

Art thou departing too, my trembling friend?
Ah! draws thy little lustre to its end?
  Yes, on thy frame Fate too shall fix her seal—
O let me, pensive, watch thy pale decay;
How fast that frame, so tender, wears away!
  How fast thy life the restless minutes steal!

How slender now, alas! thy thread of fire!
Ah! falling, falling, ready to expire!
  In vain thy struggles—all will soon be o'er—

At life thou snatchest with an eager leap:
Now round I see thy flame so feeble creep, [more!
   Faint, less'ning, quiv'ring, glimm'ring—now no

Thus shall the suns of Science sink away,
   And thus of Beauty fade the fairest flow'r—
For where's the Giant who to Time shall say,
   " Destructive tyrant, I arrest thy pow'r?"

CAPTIVATION.

I own I am fickle: to Phillida's ear
   I first told the story of Love: [sincere!
Kiss'd her hand, press'd her lip with what ardour
   And declar'd that I never would rove.

But my sighs were scarce breath'd when Chloe tripp'd by,
   The Nymph was no longer my boast;
From Phillida's beauty away went the sigh,
   And my heart to sweet Chloe was lost.

Could I dream of a change, when Chloe was mine;
   " No, no," I a thousand times swore;
" My heart cannot rove from a girl so divine;
   " No, no, it will wander no more."

But Fate, who delighted to laugh at the Swain,
   Presented a damsel more fair;
My heart! the sad rogue, turn'd inconstant again,
   And sigh'd to Corinna his pray'r.

With Corinna I swore, " Ev'ry hour *must* be blest;
   " These eyes shall no other pursue;"
When agen, to alarm with new tumults my breast,
   Thou, Sylvia, beam'st full on my view.

But, Sylvia, I'm sure thou hast *nothing* to fear,
   That my heart for another can pine;
Since, to make it a traitor, a Girl must appear
   Whose beauty is *equal* to *thine.*

CAPTIVE NEGRO.

Poor Mora eye be wet wid tear,
　And heart like lead sink down wid woe;
She seem her mournful friends to hear,
　And see der eye like fountain flow.

No more she give me song to gay,
But sigh, "Adieu, dear Domahay."

But why do Azid live a slave,
　And see a slave his Mora dear?
Come, let we seek at once de grave—
　No chain, no tyrant den we fear.

Ah, me! I hear a spirit say,
Come, Azid, come to Domahay."

Den gold I find for thee once more,
　For thee to fields for flow'r depart:
To please de idol I adore,
　And give wid gold and flow'r my heart.

Den let we die and haste away,
And live in groves of Domahay.

CELIBACY.

Yet what expect from *thee*, whose icy breast
A stranger to their charm, the Loves detest?—
Thee, o'er whose heart their fascinating pow'r
Ne'er knew the triumph of one soften'd hour?
To give thy flinty soul the tender sigh,
Vain is the radiance of the brightest eye!
In vain, for thee, of beauty blooms the rose:
In vain the swelling bosom spreads its snows—
A *Joseph* thou, against the sex to strive;
Dead to those charms that keep the world alive!

CENSURE.

I own the voice of Censure, very proper;
Greatly resembling a tobacco-stopper;

Confining all the seeds of fire so stout,
And quick in growth, when left to run about:

Thus when an earthquake bids Jamaica tremble;
On Sunday all the folks to church assemble;
　To sooth Jehovah, so devoutly studying—
Prostrate they vow to keep his holy laws:
Returning home, they smite their hungry craws,
　And scarce indulge them with a slice of pudding—
Deeming, in earthquake time, a dainty board,
A sad abomination to the Lord!

Ere Sunday comes again, their hearts recover;
The tempest of their fears blown over,
　Fled ev'ry terror of the burning lake,
They think they have no business now with church;
So, calmly leave th' Almighty in the lurch,
　And sin it—till it gives a *second* shake.

CHICANERY.

Some years ago, I saw a female race;
　The prize a *shift*—a Holland shift I ween:
Ten Damsels, nearly all in *naked grace*,
　Rush'd for the precious prize along the green.

Sylvia, a charming lass (who, if an *air*
　And *face* had been permitted to contend,
Had carried all before her) luckless Fair!
　Was to her Sister Racers forc'd to bend.

When Orson mounted on a goodly Mule,
　Whose love for Sylvia to her cause inclin'd him,
In spite, ye Gods, of ev'ry racing rule,
　Whipp'd up the Damsel on the Beast behind him.

Then off he gallop'd, pass'd each panting Maid,
　Who mark'd the cheat with disappointed eyes;
Soon brought her in, unblushing at his aid,
　And for his Fav'rite boldly claim'd the Prize.

CHLOE, LINES TO.

Dear Chloe, well I know the swain,
Who gladly would embrace thy chain;
   And who, alas! can blame him?
Affect not, Chloe, a surprise;
Look but a moment on *these* eyes,
   Thou'lt ask me not to *name* him.

TO CHLOE, (2.)

Chloe, a thousand charms are thine,
   That give my heart the constant sigh!
Ah! wherefore let thy Poet pine,
   Who canst with ease his wants supply;

Oh, haste, thy charity display;
   With *little* I'll contented be:
The kisses which thou throw'st away
   Upon thy *dog*, will do for *me*.

CHOLER.

A little Welchman, Welchman-like indeed,
   Hot as a Chian, that is to say,
A Batchelor—and therefore ev'ry Need,
   Was, for subsistence, forc'd to *him* to pray:

This Batchelor, to satisfy withall
      His gullet,
Put into a small pot—indeed *too small*,
      A Pullet.

The Pullet's legs were not to be confin'd;
   So out they pok'd themselves, so sleek and white:
The Welchman curs'd her legs with wicked mind,
   And push'd them in again, with monstrous spite.

The Pullet liking not the Pot's embrace,
So *very warm*—indeed a nat'ral case,
   Pok'd forth her shrinking legs *again*, so fair;
With seeming much uneasiness, in troth,
Objecting to her element of broth,
   And wishing much to take a little air.

The Cambro-Briton waxing red and hot,
And highly *foaming* too, just like the pot,
   Ran to the legs, and shov'd them in once more;
But, lo! his oaths and labour all were in vain;
Out pok'd the Pullet's boiling legs again;
   Which put the Welchman's passions in a *roar!*

What will not mortals, urg'd by rage and sin, do?
   Mad at defeat, and with a dev'lish scowl,
   He seizes with ferocity the fowl,
And, full of vengeance, whirls her out at window.

CHURCH BRIEFS.

   Thus reads a parish-clerk in church a brief,
That begs for burnt-out wretches kind relief—
Relief, alas! that very rarely reaches
The poor petitioners, the ruin'd wretches;
But (lost its way) unfortunately steers
To fat churchwardens and fat overseers;
Improves each dish, augments the punch and ale,
And adds new spirits to the smutty tale.

CHURCHWARDEN, THE; OR, THE FEAST ON A CHILD, A TALE.

At Knightsbridge, at a tavern call'd the Swan,
Churchwardens, Overseers, a jolly clan,
   Order'd a dinner for themselves and friends—
A very handsome dinner, of the best:
Lo! to a turn, the diff'rent joints were drest—
   Their lips, wild licking, ev'ry man commends.

As soon as all were cramm'd unto the chin,
And ev'ry one with wine had swell'd his skin,
   In came the Landlord with a cherub smile:
Around to ev'ry one he lowly bow'd,
Was vastly *happy*—*honour'd*—vastly *proud*—
   And then he bow'd again in *such* a style:

"Hop'd *Gemmen* lik'd the dinner, and the wine:
To whom the *Gemmen* answer'd, "Very fine!
   "A glorious dinner, Larder, to be sure."—

To which the Landlord, laden deep with bliss,
Did with his bows so humble almost kiss
        The floor.

Now in an *alter'd* tone—a tone of gravity,
Unto the Landlord full of smiles of suavity,
    Did Mister Guttle the Churchwarden call—
" Come, hither, Larder," said soft Mister Guttle,
With solemn voice and fox-like face so subtle—
    " Larder, a little word or two, that's all."
Forth ran the bowing Landlord with good will,
Thinking most nat'rally upon the bill.

" Landlord," (quoth Guttle, in a small sly sound,
    Not to be heard by any in the room,
Yet which, like claps of thunder, did confound)
    " Do you know any thing of Betty Broom?"

" Sir?" answer'd Larder, stamm'ring—" Sir? what
    " Sir?"   [" Larder;
  " Yes, Sir, yes—yes—she liv'd with Mistress
" But may I never move, nor never stir,
  " If but for *impudence* we discard her!
" No, *Mister* Guttle—Betty was too brassy—
" We never keep a *servant* that is saucy."

" But, Landlord—Betty says she is with child."—
" What's that to *me?*" quoth Larder, starting wild—
  " I never kiss'd the hussy in my life,   [cheek;
" Nor hugg'd her round the waist, nor pinch'd her
" Never once put my hand upon her neck—
  " Lord, Sir, you know that I have got a *wife.*

" Lord! nothing *comely* to the girl belongs—
" I would not touch her with a pair of tongs:
" A little pulling chit, as white as paste;
" Besides! she never suited with *my* taste.

" But then, *suppose*—I only say, *suppose*
    " I *had* been wicked with the girl—alack,
" My wife hath got the cursed'st keenest nose,
    " Why zounds, she would have catch'd me in a
        " crack;

" Then quickly in the fire had been the fat—
" Curse her! she always watch'd me like a cat.

" Then, as I say, Bet did not hit my *taste*,
" It was *impossible* to be unchaste:—
" Therefore it never can be true, you see—
" And Mistress Larder's *full enough* for *me*.

" *I* kiss the maid! why, Lord! the thing I scorn—
" Sir, I'm as innocent's the child unborn."

" Well," answer'd Guttle, " Man, I'll tell ye what;
    " Your wind and eloquence you now are wasting:
" Whether Miss Betty hit your *taste* or not,
" There's good *round* proof enough that you've been
        " *tasting*.

" And, Larder, you've a wife, 'tis very true,
" Perhaps a little somewhat of a shrew;
    " But Betty *was not* a bad piece of stuff."—
" Well, Mister Guttle, may I drop down dead,
" If ever once I crept to Betty's bed!
    " And that, I'm sure, is swearing strong enough."

" But, Larder, all *your* swearing will not *do*,
" If Betty *swears* she is with child by *you*:
    " Now Betty came and said she'd *swear* at once—
" But *you* know best—yet mind, if Betty 'll *swear*,
" And then again! should Mistress Larder *hear*,
    " The Lord have mercy, Larder, on thy *sconce*.

" Why, man, were this affair of Betty told her,
" I really think, not *hell itself* could hold her.

" Then for your modest stiff-rump'd neighbours
        " all!—
" There'd be a pretty kick-up—what a squall!

" Thou couldst not put thy nose into a *shop*.
" There's greasy Mistress Wick, the chandler's
    " wife,
" And Mistress Bull, the butcher's imp of strife,
  " With Mistress Bobbin, Salmon, Muff, and Slop,
" With fifty others of such old *compeers*—
" Zounds, what a hornet's nest about thy ears!"

From cheerful smiles, and looks like Sol so bright,
Poor Larder fell to scowls as black as night;

And now his head he scratch'd, importing guilt—
For people who are innocent *indeed*,
Never look down, so black, and scratch the head;
  But tipp'd with confidence, their noses tilt,
Replying with an unembarrass'd front;
Bold to the charge, and fix'd to stand the brunt.

" Well, Sir,' said Larder, whisp'ring, hemming,
    ha-ing,
Each word so heavy, like a cart-horse drawing—
  " This is a damn'd affair, I can't but say—
" Sir, please t' accept a note of twenty pound;
" Contrive *another* father may be found;
  " And, Sir, here's not a halfpenny to pay."

Thus ended the affair, by prudent treaty; [rather:
  Peace, ev'ry man desires——than war, much
Guttle next morning went and talk'd to Betty,
  When Betty quickly found *another father!*

CLERICAL CONSCIENCE.

A certain Hostler willing to be master,
  And rise in this good world a little faster,
  Left broom and manger at the Old Blue Boar;
Meaning by *pars'ning* to support a table,
Lo, of Divines he kept a liv'ry stable;
  A pretty stud, indeed—about score.

But, lo! to dying persons of nobility,
He sent his parsons of *gentility*,
  To give the necessary pray'r:

To parting people of a mean condition,
Wanting a soul physician,
　　He suited them with blackguards to a hair.

It happen'd on a day when Fate was raging,
Crimp-like, for other regions, troops engaging,
　　When clergymen were busy all as bees,
A poor old dying woman sent
To this same parson-monger, compliment,
　　Begging a clergyman her soul to ease.

Unluckily but *one* was in the stall,
And *he* the very best of all.—
　　　What should be done?
Necessitas non habet legs—
So to the priest he goes, and begs
　　That he would visit the old crone.

" Sir," quoth the parson, " I agreed
" To go to *gentlefolks* in time of need,
　　" But not to ev'ry poor old lousy soul."—
" True," cry'd the patron; " to be sure 'tis true;
" But parson, do oblige me—prithee do—
　　" Let's put her decently into the hole.

" All my black tribe, you know, are now abroad—
" I'd do it, if I could *myself*, by God;
　　" Then what a dickens can I do or say?"
" Go, mumble, man, about a pray'r and half;
" Tell the old b—ch her soul is safe;
　　" Then take your fee, and come away!!!"

COFFEE, ODE TO.

Delicious Berry, but, ah! best
When from the Eastern Ind, not West;
　　Nought richer is, I think, than *thee*:
Into a roaster, with my hand,
I put thee, and then o'er thee stand,
　　And then I catch thy smell with glee.

And now I shake thee round about;
And, when turn'd brown, I take thee out,
   And then I put thee in a mill;
And, when to powder thou art crush'd,
Into a tin pot thou art push'd,
   To feel the boiling smoking rill.

And now from my tin pot's long nose
The fragrant fluid sweetly flows;
   And now I put the lily cream,
And sugar too, the best of brown;
And, happy, now I gulp thee down,
   Keeping my nose upon the steam.

On Hastings now my senses work;
And now on virtuous Edmund Burke,
   Who calmly let Sir Thomas 'scape:
And then unto myself I say,
" Is honour dead? ah, well-a-day!"
   And then my mouth begins to gape.

Now on Sir Joseph Banks I ponder,
And now at his rare merit wonder,
   In flies and tadpoles deep;
And now to many a drowsy head,
I hear the drowsy Blagdon * read,
   And then I fall asleep.

COLDNESS.

The smile of the maid I adore,
   I have sought, but have sought it in vain;
Hope, lull me with flatt'ry no more—
   Fate dooms me to sigh and complain.

O Venus! how cruel thine art,
   That bids us such beauty behold!
In thee, how unkind to impart,
   To such beauty, a heart that is *cold*.

* Sir Joseph's right hand, and secretary to the Royal Society; who has very often read the very respectable meetings of the Royal Society to slumber.

COMMISERATION OF ANIMALS.

How can the eye, in Nature's softness drest,
  So harden'd, see the diff'rent tribes around;
Behold the grazing cattle all so blest,   [sound;
  And lambkins mingling sport, with sweetest
Then glist'ning, in a train of triumph cry,
  " Your throats, young gentlefolks, will soon be cut—
" *You*, sweet Miss Lamb, most speedily shall die—
  " Soon on the spit, you, Master Calf, be put!"

I cannot meet the lambkin's asking eye,
  Pat her soft neck, and fill her mouth with food,
Then say, " Ere evening cometh, thou shalt die,
  " And drench the knives of butchers with thy blood."

I cannot fling with lib'ral hand the grain,
  And tell the feather'd race so blest around,
" For me, ere night, ye feel of death the pain;
  " With broken necks ye flutter on the ground.

" How vile!—Go, creatures of th' Almighty's hand;
  " Enjoy the fruits that bounteous Nature yields;
" Graze at your ease along the sunny land;
  " Skim the free air, and search the fruitful fields:

" Go, and be happy in your mutual loves;
  " No violence shall shake your shelter'd home;
" 'Tis life and liberty shall glad my groves;
  " The cry of murder shall not damn my dome;"

Thus should I say, were mine a house and land—
  And, lo! to me a parent should ye fly,
And run, and lick, and peck with love my hand,
  And crowd around me with a fearless eye.

And you, O wild inhabitants of air,
  To bless, and to be blest, at Peter's call,
Invited by his kindness, should repair;
  Chirp on his roof, and hop amidst his hall.

No schoolboy's hand should dare your nests invade,
  And bear to close captivity your young;
Pleas'd would I see them flutter from the shade,
  And to my window call the sons of song.

And you, O natives of the flood, should play
  Unhurt amid your chrystal realms, and sleep;
No hook should tear you from your loves away;
  No net surrounding from its fatal sweep.

Pleas'd should I gaze upon your gliding throng,
  To sport invited by the summer beam;
Now moving in most solemn march along,
  Now darting, leaping from the dimpled stream.

How far more grateful to the soul the joy,
  Thus daily, like a set of friends, to treat ye,
Than like the bloated epicure, to cry,
  " Zounds! what rare dinners!—God! how I
    could eat ye!"

COMPLIANCE.

Amidst thy walks, should bullies meet thine eye,
Compos'dly let those bullies pass thee by.
To bustling bravoes, for my ease and pride,
I give the wall, and smiling turn aside.
Thus, if a rock or log the stream oppose,
That sweetly lambent from its fountain flows,
No foamy turbulence the rills betray,
But, easy yielding, wind in peace away.

CONCEIT.

Alas! who has not fondness for a name?
Lo, Nature wove it in our infant frame!
  From ear-*delighters*, down to ear-*confounders*,
Each vainly fancies he possesses killing tones;
Ev'n from the Maras and the Billingtons,
  Down to the wide-mouth rascals crying flounders:
Nay, watchmen deem their merits no ways small,
Proud of a loud, clear, melancholy bawl;

Nay, proud too of that instrument the *rattle*,
That draws the hobbling brotherhood to battle.

Yes, yes! much vanity's in human nature—
Like mad dogs, that abhor the water,
   Most people hate to hear their faults display'd;
And though I sing them in the sweetest rhymes,
Such are the reformation-cursing times,
   The foolish fellows wish the Poet dead!

CONFESSION.

When love hath charm'd the virgin's ear,
   She hides the tender thought in vain;
How oft a blush, a sigh, a tear,
   Betrays the sweetly-anxious pain!

Dear youth! a mutual flame I own:
   The sorrows of thy breast are mine;
Thy virtues all my heart have won,
   That boasts a passion pure as thine.

No more shalt thou my coldness mourn—
   I trust the drop that dims thine eye;
I see fair *Truth* thy lips adorn,
   And hear her voice in ev'ry *sigh*.

CONJUGAL FIDELITY.

   Sweet is the song of wedded Love,
   The echo of the turtle-dove;
Then who would turn that song to sounds of woe?
   Bright are the skies, and calm the scene
   Where Hymen holds his halcyon reign;
Then who would bid the howling tempest blow?
   What but a Ruffian would the spot invade,
   To dash the beam of bliss with hellish shade?

CONJUGAL TENDERNESS.

Lo, to the cruel hand of Fate,
My poor dear Grizzle, meek-soul'd mate,
   Resigns her tuneful breath—

Though dropp'd her jaw, her lip though pale,
And blue each harmless finger nail,
    She's beautiful in death.

Death was, indeed, a daring wight,
To take it in his head to smite—
    To lift his dart to hit her;
For as she was so great a woman,
And car'd a single fig for no man,
    I thought he fear'd to meet her.

Whene'er I hear the bagpipe's note,
Shall Fancy fix on Grizzle's throat,
    And loud instructive lungs?
O Death, in her, though only one,
Are lost a thousand charms unknown,
    At least a thousand tongues.

Why do I groan in deep despair,
Since she'll be soon an angel fair?
    Ah! why my bosom smite?
Could grief my Grizzle's life restore!—
But let me give such ravings o'er—
    Whatever is, is right.

Oh, Doctor! you are come too late;
No more of physic's virtues prate,
    That could not save my lamb:
Not one more bolus shall be giv'n—
You shall not ope her mouth, by heav'n,
    And Grizzle's gullet cram.

Enough of boluses, poor heart,
And pills, she took, to load a cart,
    Before she clos'd her eyes;
But now my word is here a law,
Zounds! with a bolus in her jaw,
    She shall not seek the skies,

Good Sir, good Doctor, go away;
To hear my sighs you must not stay,
    For this my poor lost treasure:

I thank you for your pains and skill;
When next you come, pray bring your bill;
  I'll pay it, Sir, with pleasure.

Ye friends who come to mourn her doom,
For God's sake gently tread the room,
  Nor call her from the blest:
In softest silence drop the tear,
In whispers breathe the fervent pray'r
  To bid her spirit rest.

And, carpenter, for my sad sake,
Of stoutest oak her coffin make—
  I'd not be stingy, sure:
Procure of steel the strongest screws;
For who would paltry pence refuse,
  To lodge his wife secure?

CONSTANCY, TO DELIA.

Forlorn I seek the silent scene,
  To keep the image of my fair;
Pale o'er the fountain's brink I lean,
  And view the spectre of despair.

Why should my heart forget its woe?
  The virgin would have mourn'd for *me*—
O nymph, th' eternal tear shall flow;
  The sigh unceasing breathe of *thee*.

Forgetful of the parted maid,
  Too many an unfeeling swain
Forsakes of solitude the shade,
  For Pleasure's gay and wanton train.

Yet, yet of constancy they boast!
  Their easy hearts their tongues belie—
Who loves, reveres the fair-one's ghost,
  And seeks a pleasure in a sigh.

CONSTANCY.

Now, Joan, we are *married*—and now, let me say,
Though both are in youth, yet that youth will decay:
In our journey through life, my dear Joan, I suppose,
We shall oft meet a bramble, and sometimes a rose.

When a cloud on this forehead shall darken my day,
Thy sunshine of sweetness must smile it away;
And when the dull vapour shall dwell upon thine,
To chase it the labour and triumph be mine.

Let us wish not for wealth, to devour and consume;
For luxury's but a short road to the tomb,
Let us sigh not for grandeur, for trust me, my Joan,
The keenest of cares owes its birth to a *throne*.

When finish'd the day, by the fire we'll regale,
And treat our good neighbour at eve with our ale;
For, Joan, who would wish for *self only* to live?
One blessing of life, my dear girl, is to *give*.

E'en the red-breast and wren shall not seek us in vain,
Whilst thou hast a crumb, or thy Corin a grain;
Not only their songs will they pour from the grove,
But yield, by example, sweet lessons of love.

Though thy beauty must fade, yet thy youth I'll remember;
That thy *May* was my own, when thou shewest *December*;
And when Age to my *head* shall his winter impart,
The summer of *Love* shall reside in my *heart*.

CONSCIENCE.

O Conscience! thou straight jacket of the soul,
The madding sallies of the bard controul;
Conscience, thou terrifying little sprite,
That, bat-like, winks by day, and wakes by night;
Who, when the lightnings flash, and thunders crack,
Makes our hair bristle like a hedgehog's back;

Shakes, ague-like, our hearts with wild commotion;
Uplifts our saint-like eyes with dread devotion;
Bids the poor trembling tongue make terms with
    Heav'n,
And promise miracles to be forgiv'n;
Bids spectres rise, not very like the Graces;
With goggling eyes, black beards, and Tyburn faces;
With scenes of fires of glowing brimstone scares,
Spits, forks, and proper culinary wares
For roasting, broiling, frying, fricasseeing
The Soul, that sad offending little *Being*;
That stubborn stuff, of salamander make,
Proof to the fury of the burning lake.

CONTENT, (1.)

Few are the wishes of the constant Pair:
  What tho' no gold their humble cot displays?
Content, their guest, thus cries with careless air,
  " Go, leave us, Wealth, and palaces emblaze."

In *rural* bowers Content delights to dwell;
  To cull the sweets of Nature's simple vale;
To join the *hermit* in the mossy cell,
  And join the *nymphs* and *shepherds* of the dale.

CONTENT, (2.)

What's life, if life has not a bliss to give?
And, if unhappy, who would wish to live?
Content can visit the poor spider'd room;
Pleas'd with the coarse rush mat and birchen broom;
Where parents, children, feast on oaten bread,
With cheeks as round as apples, and as red; [hams,
Where Health with vigour nerves their backs and
Sweet souls, tho' ragged as young colts or rams;

Content, mild maid! delights in *simple* things,
And envies not the state of Queens or Kings;
Can dine on sheep's head, or a dish of broth,
Without a table or a table-cloth:

Nor wishes, with the fashionable group,
To visit Birch's shop for turtle soup;
Can use a bit of packthread for a jack,
And sit upon a chair without a back:
Nay, wanting knives, can with her fingers work,
And use a wooden skewer for a fork. [ing,
Sweet maid! who thinks not shoes of leather shock-
Nor feels the horrors in a worsted stocking;
Her temper mild, no huckaback can shock,
Though for her lovely limbs it forms a smock.
Pleas'd with the nat'ral curls her face that shade,
No graves are robb'd for hair to form a braid:
Her breast of native plumpness ne'er aspires
To swelling *merrythoughts* of gauze and wires.
To look like crops of ducks (with labour borne)
Stretch'd by a superfluity of corn.
With Nature's hips, she sighs not for *cork rumps*,
And scorns the pride of pinching stays or jumps;
But, pleas'd from whalebone prisons to escape,
She trusts to s.mple nature for a shape;
Without a warming-pan can go to bed;
And wrap her petticoat about her head;
Nor sigh for cobweb caps of Mechlin lace,
That shade of Quality the varnish'd face: [nest,
Sweet nymph, like doves, she seeks her straw-built
And in a pair of minutes is undrest;
Whilst all the *fashionable* female clans,
Undressing, seem unloading caravans,
No matter from what source contentment springs;
'Tis just the same in Subjects, as in Kings.

CONTINENCE.

Blest is the simple man by virtue sway'd,
Who wishful burns not for the blooming maid;
   Whose pulses calm as sleeping puppies lie;
Who rusheth not to prey upon her charms,
Full of Love's mad emotions, mad alarms,
   Just like a famish'd spider on a fly,

That in the tyrant's claws resigns its breath,
Unhappy humming till it sleeps in death.

Blest is the man who marks the cherry lip,
And sigheth not the nectar'd sweets to sip,
  Nor press the heaving hills of purest snow;
Who marks the love-alluring waist so taper,
Without one wish, or pulse's single caper,
  And to his hurrying passions cries out, " No!
' Stop, if you please, young imps, your hot career,
' And shun the precipice of fate so near;
' Draw in, or, with the horses of the Sun,
' You drive, like Phaëton, to be undone."

COQUETRY.

Dear Phillis! thou know'st not thy charms;
  That thy cheek boasts the bloom of the rose;
That thine eye, by its lustre, alarms;
  That thy bosom surpasses the snow's.

Not safely a swain can pass by,
  Thou art ready his steps to beguile;
Some lure is thrown out from thine eye,
  Some lure from a song or a smile.

O learn from the Minstrel of night
  A lesson to govern the Maid!
Tho' he fills every ear with delight,
  He sings amid silence and shade.

CORNISH LASSES, A STORY.

Walking one afternoon along the Strand,
My wond'ring eyes did suddenly expand
    Upon a pretty leash of Cornish lasses.—
Heav'ns! my dear beauteous angels, how d'ye do?
" Upon my soul I'm monstrous glad to see ye."
Swinge! Peter, we are glad to meet with you;
" We're just to London come—well, pray how
    be ye?

We're just a going while 'tis light,
" To see St. Paul's before 'tis dark,—

" Lord ! come, for once, be so polite,
  " And condescend to be our spark."

" With all my heart, my cherubs."—On we walk'd
And much of London—much of Cornwall talk'd ;
Now did I hug myself to think
   How much that glorious structure would surprise,
How from its awful grandeur they would shrink
   With open mouths, and marv'ling eyes !

As near to Ludgate-hill we drew,
St. Paul's just opening on our view ;
Behold, my lovely strangers, one and all,
Gave a most diabolic squall,
As if they had been tumbled on the stones,
And some confounded cart had crush'd their bones.

After well fright'ning people with their cries,
And sticking to a ribbon-shop their eyes,
They all rush'd in, and swift to patterns ran,
And, imitating Babel, thus began :—

" Swinge ! here are colours then, to please !
  " Delightful things, I vow to Heav'n !
" Why ! not to see such things as these,
  " We never should have been forgiv'n.—

   " Here, here, are clever things—good Lord !
   " And, sister, here, upon my word—
" Here, here !—look ! here are beauties to delight :
   " Why ! how a body's heels might dance
   " Along from Launceston to Penzance,
" Before that one might meet with such a sight !"

" Come, ladies, 'twill be dark," said I, " I fear :
" Pray let us view St. Paul's, 'tis now so near."—

" Lord ! Peter, (cried the girls) don't mind St.
   Paul !—
" Sure ! you're a most *incurious* soul—
" Why—we can see the church another day ;
" Don't be afraid—St. Paul's can't *run away*."

CREDULITY.

Credulity's a pretty sand
  To blind the people of the land:
O yes, it blinds weak women, and weak men,
  Much like the sand that boys, in fun,
  Fire from an engine called a *gun*,
To knock down a poor humming-bird, or wren.

CURIOSITY. (1.)

──────All Exeter town
Was gapin, rennin up and down,
  Vath, just leek vokes bewitch'd!
Lord! how they lang'd to zee the King;
To hear un zay zom *marv'lous thing!*
  Leek mangy dogs they itch'd;

Leek bullocks sting'd by appledranes,
Currantin it about the lanes,
  Vokes theese way dreav'd and that;
Zom hootin, heavin, soalin, hawlin!
Zom in the mucks, and pellum sprawlin;
  Leek pancakes all zo flat.

Hosses and mares, assnegers, moyles,
Leaping the hedges, ditches, stiles,
  Hundreds comm'd in at least;
Gallopin, trattin, spurrin, vallin,
Halloin, laugin, cryin, squawlin,
  Vour mounted 'pot one beast.

The Ladies vrom the windors all
Pok'd vorth their powls, both gert and small;
  Ecod, there were a power:
Their hair zo white I'd zexpence stake,
That from their powls I'd fairly shake
  A dezen sacks o'vlower.

Vull az an egg was all the Charch,
Vor vokes were mad az hares in March;
  And fath it was dam quare,

To zee ould Dames wey leathern chacks,
Hoisted upon the fellows' backs—
   A penny for a stare.

CURIOSITY, (2.)

Thus have I seen a magpie in the street,
A chatt'ring bird we often meet,
A bird for curiosity well known;
   With head awry,
   And cunning eye,
Peep knowingly into a marrow-bone.

DAISIE,* TO THE.

O modest flower! thou tellest of the Springe!
   Welcome unto this little fielde of myne!
With joy I see thee from the green earth springe,
   And smiling in thy silvery vesture shine!

Ah! nought disturbeth thy fayre tender frame;
   Zephyrus kisseth thee, and tastes thy sweet:
Thou dost not chide the wanton rogue—no blame,
   Nor biddest him sighe lowly at thy feet.

Agayne he whispereth love; and now agayne
   He tasteth of thy honey'd leaves, and sighs!
And though he wantons, thou dost not complayne;
   Thy little snowy bosom nought denies.

O gentle Daisie! speak to her I love
   When she doth come, and casteth looks on thee;
Persuade her my pure passion to approve,
   And not with coldness from her shepheard flee:

But imitate thy ways, and learne thy smyle,
   When I, like Zephyrus, doe press her cheke,
Then may no tempest rude thy form defyle,
   And of thy snowy beauties make a wreck!

* Several pieces have been written by the author in this manner, as innocent deceptions of the style used in the time of Queen Elizabeth.

DANGER OF THE PASSIONS.

The Passions are all prone to sad disorders,
Whose Objects never should approach their *borders!*
   " O lead us not into temptation,"
Is a choice pray'r, and which I much admire—
So *many things* are dangerous to Desire
   So ripe for soul-assassination!

  No harm is in the Passions, to be sure;
   But then they must not gallop wild to door:—
Close keep them, just like hounds that long for hare;
   Or muzzle them, indeed, like ferrets;
   And thus suppress their wanton spirits,
That lawless wish to be as free as air.

The Passions, as I've said, are far from *evil*;
But if not well confin'd, they play the devil.

Learn from *that* Candle—mark its *govern'd* flame,
How in its lustre, gentle, steady, tame,
   So mild, such trembling modesty, so quiet!
But let him touch your curtains, or your bed,
Who on such stuff delighteth to be fed,
   Lo, in a brace of minutes, what a riot!
He pulls, (for nought th' unbridled Rogue reveres)
Like Sampson, an old house about his ears!

DECAY OF BEAUTY.

  O say not with the voice of scorn,
   " The lilies of thy neck are fled,
  " Thine eyes their vanish'd radiance mourn,
   " The roses of thy cheek are dead."

Too cruel Youth, with tears I own,
   The rose and lily's sad decay;
And sorrowing wish for *thee alone,*
   Their transient bloom a longer day.

Yet though thine eyes no longer trace
   The healthful blush of former charms;
Remember that each luckless grace,
   O Colin, faded in *thy arms!*

DECAY OF TASTE, &c.

How is fair Art, and Science, in disgrace!
What Patron meets them with a smiling face?
See, like a shadow, Genius, limping, poor,
In supplication at a Great Man's door!—
And see with insolence his *lacquey* treat him;
And were he *fat enough*, the *Dog* would eat him.

O Taste, O Reason, to our Isle return!
Behold our Great for *littlenesses* burn!

DELIA, LINES TO.

While poets your their happiest lays,
    And call thee ev'ry thing divine;
Not quite so lavish in thy praise,
    To *censure* be the province mine.

Though born with talents to surprise,
    Thou seldom dost those pow'rs display:
Thus seem they trifling in thine eyes!
    Thus heav'n's best gifts are thrown away!

Though rich in charms, thou know'st it not;
    Such is thine ignorance profound:
And then such cruelty thy lot,
    Thy sweetest smile inflicts a *wound*.

DELICACY, A SIMILE.

Thus when the virgin Morn her blushes spreads,
And paints with purest ray the mountain heads;
Behold, those blushes so divine to shroud,
The surly Boreas gathers ev'ry cloud;
Bids the huge phalanx seek the smiling East,
And blot the lustre of her crimson vest;
From pole to pole extends the black'ning band:
Cloud pressing cloud, obeys his rude command:
In tears she moves away, the heav'nly Maid,
And leaves him Monarch of the mighty shade.

DELIGHTS OF THE TOWN.

Sweet Helen! the dews of the morn
  Our steps to the valley invite;
The linnet, the thrush on the thorn,
  Are preparing to yield thee delight.

Then haste from the town and its noise,
  Health is ready to yield thee her treasure;
Then from tumult, repair to our joys,
  To the region of silence and pleasure.

Yet, what folly to think one so fair,
  Would bless with her smile a poor swain,
Be sooth'd, and be won by his pray'r,
  Who can rivet a *world* in her chain!

DEVIL, ODE TO THE.

Prince of the dark abodes! I ween,
Your Highness ne'er till now hath seen
  Yourself in metre shine;
Ne'er hear a song with praise sincere,
Sweet warbled on your smutty ear,
  Before this ode of mine.

Perhaps the reason is too plain,
Thou try'st to starve the tuneful train,
  Of potent verse afraid;
And yet I vow, in all my time,
I've not beheld a single rhyme
  That ever spoil'd thy trade.

What thousands, hourly bent on sin,
With supplication call thee in,
  To aid them to pursue it!
Yet, when detected, with a lie
Ripe at their fingers' ends, they cry,
  " The Devil *made* me do it."

As to thy company, I'm sure,
No man can shun thee on that score;
  The very best is thine:

With Kings, Queens, Ministers of State,
Lords, Ladies, I have seen thee great,
   And many a grave Divine.

I'm sorely griev'd at times to find,
The very instant thou art kind,
   Some people so uncivil;
When aught offends, with face awry,
With base ingratitude I cry,
   " I wish it to the devil."

Should Heav'n their pray'rs so ardent grant,
Thou never company wouldst want
   To make thee downright mad ;
For mind me, in their wishing mood,
They never offer thee what's good,
   But ev'ry thing that's bad.

My honest anger boils to view
A snuffling, long-fac'd, canting crew,
   So much thy humble debtors,
Rushing, on Sundays, one and all,
With desp'rate pray'rs thy head to maul,
   And thus abuse their betters.

Yet when a child—good Lord! I thought
That thou a pair of horns hadst got,
   With eyes like saucers staring!
And then a pair of ears so stout,
A monstrous tail and hairy snout,
   With claws beyond comparing.

Taught to avoid the paths of evil,
By day I us'd to dread the Devil;
   And trembling when 'twas night,
Methought I saw thy horns and ears,
Then sung or whistled to my fears,
   And ran to chase my fright.

A haberdasher's shop is thine,
With sins of all sorts, coarse and fine,
   To suit both man and maid;

Thy wares they buy, with open eyes;
How cruel then, with constant cries,
   To vilify thy trade!

O Satan, whatsoever geer
Thy Proteus form shall choose to wear,
   Black, red, or blue, or yellow;
Whatever hypocrites may say,
They think thee (trust my honest lay)
   A most bewitching fellow.

'Tis order'd (to deaf ears, alas!)
To praise the bridge o'er which we pass;
   Yet often I discover
A numerous band who daily make
An easy bridge of thy poor back,
   And damn it when they're over.

Why art thou then, with cap in hand,
Obsequious to a graceless band,
   Whose souls are scarce worth taking?
O Prince, pursue but my advice,
I'll teach your Highness in a trice
   To set them all a quaking.

Plays, op'ras, masquerades, destroy,
Lock up each charming *fille de joie*;
   Give race-horses the glander—
The dice-box break, and burn each card—
Let virtue be its own reward,
   And gag the mouth of slander:

In one week's time, I'll lay my life,
There's not a man, nor maid, nor wife,
   That will not glad agree,
If thou wilt charm 'em as before,
To show their nose at church no more,
   But quit their God for thee.

'Tis now full time my Ode should end;
And now I tell thee like a friend,
   Howe'er the world may scout thee,

Thy ways are all so wondrous winning,
And folks so very fond of sinning,
  They cannot do without thee.

DIAMOND PIN AND FARTHING CANDLE.

Upon a Lady's toilet, full of lustre,
A Di'mond Pin one night began to bluster:
Highly disgusted at a Farthing Candle,
  Left by the Lady of the *broom*,
  Nam'd Susan, slipp'd into another room,
Something of consequence to handle—

" You nasty tallow thing," exclaim'd Miss Pin,
  " Pray keep your distance—don't stay here, and
      wink;
" I loath ye—you and all your greasy kin—
  " Good heav'ns! how horribly you look and
      stink!"

" Good Lord! Miss Pin," Miss Candle quick re-
" Soften a little that ungrateful pride: [pli'd,
  " You *shine* indeed—to this I must agree:
" Yes, *Miss,* you make a very pretty blaze;
" But let me tell ye, that your wondrous rays
  " Owe all your boasted brilliancy to *me.*"

" How! *Madam* Impudence!" rejoin'd Miss Pin,
First with a frown, and then a scornful grin;
" I should not, sure, have dreamt of *that,*
        " Miss Fat!"

" Susan," Miss Candle bawl'd, " Susan, come here;
" Such saucy language I'll no longer bear:
" Susan, come, satisfy the *Lady's* doubt—
" Take me away, I say, or blow me out."

Susan, who, list'ning, heard the great dispute,
By no means could refuse Miss Candle's suit;
  So into darkness Susan blew her beam;

" *Now*," with a sharp sarcastic sneer,
" *Now*," quoth Miss Candle, *now*, my dear,
 " Where is of radiance *now* your boasted stream?

DINAH, OR MY LADY'S HOUSEKEEPER.

Just forty-five was Mistress Dinah's age,
 My Lady's House-keeper—stiff, dry, and sage,
 Quoting old proverbs oft, with much formality:
A pair of flannel cheeks compos'd her face;
Red were her eyes, her nose of snipe-bill race,
 Which took a deal of snuff of Scottish quality.

Upon her head a small mob-cap she plac'd,
Of lawn so stiff, with large flow'r'd ribbon grac'd,
Yclept a knot and bridle, in a bow
Of scarlet flaming, her long chin below.

A goodly formal handkerchief of lawn,
 Around her scraggy neck, with parchment skin,
Was fair and smooth, with starch precision drawn,
 So that no prying eye might peep within.

Yet *had* it peep'd, it had espied no swell,
 No lovely swell—no more than on a cat:
For, lo! was Dinah's neck (I grieve to tell)
 As any tombstone, or a flounder, flat.
Now on this handkerchief so starch and white,
Was pinn'd a Barcelona, black and tight.

Long, very long, was Mistress Dinah's waist;
The stiff stay high before, for *reasons chaste*.

 A scarlet petticoat she gave to view—
With a broad plaited back she wore a gown,
Of stuff, of yellow oft, and oft of brown,
 And oft a damask, well beflower'd with blue,
Moreover, this same damask gown, or stuff,
Had a large sleeve and a long ruffle cuff.

Black worsted stockings on her legs she wore;
Black leather shoes too, which small buckles bore,

Compos'd of shining silver, also square,
Holding a pretty antiquated air.

Shrill was her voice that whistled through her beard;
And tunes, at times, were most discordant heard;
　　Harsh grating on poor John the Footman's ear:
Harsh grating on the ears of House-maids *too,*
Postillion *eke,* who curs'd her for a shrew,
　　And Kitchen-wench, whom Mis'ry taught to *swear.*

All, all but Jehu, felt her pow'rful tongue,
Whose happier ear was sooth'd by *sweeter* song.

No company but Jehu's did she keep,
In horse-flesh, and a coach, profoundly deep;
　　My Lady's coachman, stout, and young, and ruddy;
Great friends were they!—full oft indeed together
They walk'd, regardless of the wind and weather,
　　So pleas'd each other's happiness to study.

Greatly in sentences did she delight,
So pious! putting people in the right;
　　And often in the pray'r-book would she look—
Where *matrimony* was much thumb'd indeed,
Because she oft'nest here God's word did read,
　　The sweetest page in all the blessed book.

So modest was she, she got turn'd away
Susan the kitchen-wench, for harmless play
　　With Dick the Driver—likewise harmless Dick,
Because he took from Susan's lips a kiss,
Because too, Susan gave him up the bliss,
　　Without a scream, a faint-fit, or a kick.

If e'er she heard of some forsaken Lass,
　　Who lost, by dire mishap, her maiden fame,
At once she call'd her trollop, minx of brass,
　　Strumpet, and every coarse, opprobrious name.

So modest Dinah! if she saw two cats
Ogling and pawing with their pretty pats,
　　Kissing and squinting love, with frisking hops;

Fir'd at the action, what would Dinah do?
Slip down her hand, and slily take her shoe,
 Then launch in thunder at their am'rous chops.

It happen'd on a day, that grievous cries,
By Dinah pour'd, created great surprise—
 Ill, very ill, in bed, alas! she lay:
A dreadful Colic—her good Lady wept,
Gave her rich cordials—to her bedside crept,
 When Dinah begg'd that she would go away.

Down went my Lady to the parlour strait,
Fearful that Dinah soon would yield to fate;
And full of sorrow as my Lady went,
Sighs for her Maid's recov'ry back she sent.

Lo! Doctor Pestle comes to yield relief—
He feels her pulse—is solemn, sage, and brief;
 Prescribeth for the Colic—nought avails;
On Dinah, lo! the dire disorder gains;
Stronger and faster flow the colic pains,
 Fear, trembling, paleness, ev'ry soul assails.

" Poor Dinah!" sighs each mouth around the room,
Join'd to a length'ning face of dread and gloom.

At last, poor Dinah pours a death-like groan—
A ghostly terror seizeth ev'ry one:
 My Lady hears the cry, alas! below—
She sends for Doctor Pestle—Pestle strait
Runs to my Lady—" Doctor, what's her fate?
 " Speak, is it death, dear Doctor, yes, or no?"

 " Not *death*, but *life*, (cries Pestle) forc'd that
  squawl;
 " A little Jehu's come to light, that's all."

DISAPPOINTMENT, (1.)

O summer, thy presence gives warmth to the vale
 The song of the warbler enlivens the groves;
The pipe of the shepherd, too, gladdens the gale:
 Alas! but I hear not the voice of my love.

The lilies appear in their fairest array;
   To the vallies the woodbines a fragrance impart;
The roses the pride of their blushes display;
   Alas! but I meet not the nymph of my heart.

Go, shepherds, and bring the sweet wanderer here,
   The boast of her sex, and delight of the swains;
Go, zephyr, and whisper this truth in her ear,
That the Pleasures with Julia are fled from the plains,

If thus to the maid thou my wishes declare,
   To the cot she has left she will quickly return;
Too soft is her bosom to give us despair,
   That sooner would sigh than *another's* should mourn.

DISAPPOINTMENT, (2.)

Faint as the lustre of a lonely star,
   That sheds through night's abyss his distant fire,
Hope feebly glimmer'd on my heart's despair:
   Behold, behold, at length her lamp expire!

Know, lovely Virgin, thy deluding art
   Hath lodg'd a thousand scorpions in my breast,
Oh, say what happier rival wins thy heart?
   Say, am I there no more a welcome guest?

Nymphs of the vale, for *me* your pity spare;
   Let not my fate, ye Swains, your pity draw:
Alas! for faithless beauty drop the tear,
   And grieve so fair a diamond holds a flaw.

Can Falsehood's stain that dove-like heart defile?
   Ah, see the tear by blushing Honour shed!
Lurks perfidy beneath that heavenly smile?
   See Love with horror mark the guilty maid!

Yet, yet the tyrant of my breast she reigns:
   Restless for *her* it heaves with constant sighs;
My wounded heart of *cruelty* complains,
   Yet softly pleads her pardon while it dies.

DISCONTENT.

Nature at times makes wretched wares;
(Amongst the smiling corn-like tares)
  Men with such miserable souls!
Nought pleases from the moment of their birth;
With horror for a while they blot the earth,
  Then crab-like, crawl into their burying-holes.

How like a dreary dull December Day,
  That shows his muddy discontented head,
Low'rs on the world awhile, then moves away
  In gloom and sullenness to bed!
Have not our Revolution host a few
Of souls of this same Æthiop hue?

DISCONTENT, AN ODE TO.

" Man may be happy if he will:"
I've said it often, and I think so still:
  Doctrines to make the million stare;
Know then, each mortal is an actual Jove;
Can brew what weather he shall most approve,
  Or wind, or calm, or foul, or fair.

Who told him that he must be curs'd on earth?—
  The God of Nature?—No such thing!
Heav'n whisper'd him, the moment of his birth,
  " Don't cry, my lad, but dance and sing;
" Don't be too wise, and be an ape:
" In colours let thy soul be dress'd, not crape.

" Roses shall smooth Life's journey, and adorn;
  " Yet, mind me— if, through want of grace,
  " Thou mean'st to fling the blessing in my face,
" Thou hast full leave to tread upon a thorn."

Yet some there are, of men I think the worst,
Poor imps! unhappy, if they can't be curs'd—
  For ever brooding over Mis'ry's eggs,
As though Life's pleasure were a deadly sin;
    Mousing for ever for a gin
    To catch their happinesses by the legs.

Ev'n at dinner, some will be unbless'd,
However good the viands, and well dress'd:
  They always come to table with a scowl,
Squint with a face of verjuice o'er each dish,
Fault the poor flesh, and quarrel with the fish,
  Curse cook and wife, and loathing, eat and growl.

A cart-load, lo! their stomachs steal,
Yet swear they cannot make a meal.
  I like not the blue-devil-hunting-crew!
I hate to drop the discontented jaw!
  O let me Nature's simple smile pursue,
And pick ev'n pleasure from a straw!

DISCORD.

  Discord, a sleepless hag, who never dies,
With snipe-like nose, and ferret-glowing eyes,
Lean, sallow cheeks, long chin, with beard supply'd,
Poor crackling joints, and wither'd parchment hide,
As if old drums, worn out with martial din,
Had clubb'd their yellow heads to form her skin;
Discord, who, pleas'd a universe to sway,
Is never half so bless'd as in a fray:
Discord, to deeds, indeed, most daring giv'n,
Who bade vile Satan raise a dust in Heav'n;
Stirr'd up the sweetest angels to rebel,
And sunk the fairest forms to darkest Hell.

DOCTORS, THE, A TALE.

  A Fellow troubled with the itch
  (Like Courtier-men) of getting rich,
And learning that a Doctor, (not a *Quack*,)
  By means of a most potent pill,
  Did verily and truly fill
Full many a time with gold his sack—
  Resolv'd, by pill, to make a fortune too,
  So set about it without more ado.
Hoist but the standard, folks will come,
With heads as empty as the *drum.*

The Quack puffs off his pill—none doubt him,
And numbers quickly flock'd about him:
A Bumpkin came among the rest,
And thus the Man of Pill address:
  " *Zur*, hearing what is come to pass,
" That your fine pill hath cur'd the King,
" And able to do every thing,   [Ass?
  " D'ye think, *Zur*, that t'will make me vind my
" I've lost my ass, *Zur*, zo should like to try it:
" If this be your opinion, *Zur*, I'll buy it."
" Undoubtedly!" the Quack replied,
" Yes, Master Hob, it should be tried;"
Then down Hob's gullet, cure or kill,
The grand Impostor push'd the pill.

  Hob paid his fee, and off he went;
And trav'lling on about an hour,
  His bowels sore with pains were rent;
Such was the pill's *surprising* pow'r.

  No longer able to contain,
  Hob, in a hurry, left the lane:
How decent!—what can decency surpass?
  And sought the grove—where Hob's two eyes,
  Wide staring saw with huge surprise
His long-eared servant JACK, his Ass!
  Ye Gods! how happy was the meeting!
  Hob kissing Jack, and Jack, Hob greeting.

  " Adzooks! a lucky pill!" quoth Hob;
  " Yes, yes, the pill hath done the job."
Pill grew the subject of the village tattle:
  At last it gain'd a heap of fame;
  Not only good for *blind* and *lame*,
But good, too, for recovering all *stray'd cattle*.

DUPLICITY, (1.)

A Bishop, not a *British Bishop*,—no—
(Our's are a sweeter set of *Saints*, I trow)
  Was by his Sovereign sent to rule abroad:

Immediately upon the news
Of his arrival, came some Jews
To compliment the mitred Man of God.

" Jews!" bawl'd the Bishop, in the direst passion,
" D'ye think *I'll see* that vile apostate Nation?
" Run, Pierrot—drive them off—run faster, faster;
" Tell them they crucified my Heavenly Master."

" But Sir, but Sir," quoth Pierrot, stepping back,
Devoutly whispering in the Bishop's ear—
" These *Jews* bring presents! Lord! at least a sack."
" Ah! ah!" replied the Bishop—*less austere*—
" These people could know *nothing* of the *sin*—
" Poor creatures! well, well, Pierrot, *let 'em in*."

DUPLICITY, (2.)

Who has not seen a kind old Mother Cat
Deliver a dead bird, or mouse, or rat,
 To her young kitten, Miss Grimalkin?
Miss catches it with raptur'd claws,
Locks it at once within her jaws, [walking,
 Round with *cock'd tail*, and round triumphant
So carefully her treasure holding, watching,
And proudly purring " This is all *my catching*."

DRUNKEN FLY, A SONG.

Poor little reeling, thoughtless soul,
To tumble drunk into the bowl!
 Death to thy thread had clapp'd his knife;
Go, wipe thy nose and wings and thighs,
And brighten up thy maudling eyes,
 And thank thy Saviour for thy life.

In future, get not *quite* so drunk!
Thy girl, perhaps a Lass of *spunk*,
 May wish thy amorous pow'rs to prove;
And shouldest thou, drunk, the wanton chase,
Ebriety may bring *disgrace*;
 And *who* would look a *fool* in Love?

DRUNKENNESS.

How I hate Drunkenness, a nasty pig!
With snuff-stain'd neckcloth, without hat or wig,
  Reeling, and belching wisdom in one's face!
How I hate Bully Uproar from my soul,
Whom nought but whips and prisons can controul,
  Those necessary implements of Grace!

Yet altars rise to Drunkenness and Riot—
How few to mild Sobriety and Quiet!

ECONOMY IN LOVE.

Economy in love is peace to nature,
Much like economy in worldly matter:
We should be prudent, never live too fast,
Profusion will not, cannot always last.

Lovers are really spendthrifts—'tis a shame:
Nothing their thoughtless, wild career can tame,
  Till pea'ry stares them in the face;
And when they find an empty purse,
Grown calmer, wiser, how the fault they curse,
  And, limping, look with such a sneaking grace
Job's war-horse fierce, his neck with thunder hung,
Sunk to a humble hack that carries dung.

Smell to the queen of flowers, the fragrant rose—
Smell twenty times—and then, my dear, thy nose
Will tell thee (not so much for scent athirst)
The twentieth drank less flavour than the *first*.

Love, doubtless, is the sweetest of all fellows;
  Yet often should the little God retire—
Absence, dear Chloe, is a pair of bellows,
  That keeps alive the sacred fire.

EIGHT CATS OF ISRAEL MENDEZ, A JEW, AN ODE TO.

Singers of Israel, O ye singers sweet,
  Who, with your gentle mouths from ear to ear,

Pour forth rich symphonies from street to street,
  And to the sleepless wretch the night endear!
Lo! in my shirt, on you these eyes I fix,
Admiring much the quaintness of your tricks:
  Your friskings, crawlings, squalls, I much ap-
      prove;
Your spittings, pawings, high-rais'd rumps,
Swell'd tails, and merry-andrew jumps,
  With the wild minstrelsy of rapt'rous love.

Singers of Israel, ye no parsons want
  To tie the matrimonial cord;
Ye call the matrimonial service, cant—
  Like our first parents take each other's word:
On no one ceremony pleas'd to fix—
To jump not even o'er two sticks.

You want no furniture, alas!
  Spit, spoon, dish, frying-pan, nor ladle;
No iron, pewter, copper, tin, nor brass;
  No nurses, wet or dry, nor cradle,
(Which custom for our *Christian* babes enjoins)
To rock the staring offspring of your loins.

  No schools ye want for fine behaving;
  No powdering, painting, washing, shaving;
No nightcaps snug—no trouble in undressing
  Before ye seek your strawy nest,
  Pleas'd in each other's arms to rest,   [sing.
To feast on luscious Love, heav'n's greatest bles-

  Good gods! yet sweet love-chanting rams
  How nimble are ye with your hams
To mount a house, to scale a chimney-top;
  And, peeping down that chimney's hole,
  Pour, in a tuneful cry, th' impassion'd soul,
Inviting Miss Grimalkin to come up.

Who, sweet obliging female, far from coy,
Answers your invitation note with joy;
  And scorning 'midst the ashes more to mope,

D

Lo! borne on Love's all-daring wing,
She mounteth with a pickle-herring spring,
　　Without th' assistance of a rope.
Dear mousing tribe, my limbs are waxing cold—
　　Singers of Israel, sweet, adieu, adieu!
I do suppose you need not now be told
　　How much I wish that I was one of *you*.

ELEGY ON THE DEATH OF A MUSICAL FRIEND.

How blest were the Nymphs and the Swains,
　　When Lycidas join'd in the song;
The chief and the pride of the plains,
　　Who led all the Pleasures along!

Of *late*, not a valley was fair,
　　Not a grove gave a musical sound;
The breeze seem'd a sigh of despair,
　　And Pity sat mute on the ground.

But Nature (how sudden the change!)
　　At the presence of Lycidas smil'd—
Health was seen through the valley to range,
　　And an Eden sprung up from the wild!

But the Shepherd for ever is gone—
　　Hark! his knell, how it saddens the gale!
Joy dies, and our pastimes are flown:
　　Fate envies the smiles of our vale.

Now let Mirth from each hamlet retire
　　To the region of silence and gloom:
Sure his death must our sorrow inspire,
　　Since the Virtues will weep at his tomb.

ELEGY TO DELIA.

Lo! the pride of the village is dead!
　　Lo! the bloom of our vale is no more!
Now Sorrow sits dumb in the shade,
　　Where Rapture oft carol'd before.

Like the Morn, she enliven'd the groves;
　　Like the Summer, gave life to the swain;
For her smile was the seat of the Loves,
　　And her voice the sweet song of the plain!

O Delia, divine is thy name!
　　Thy merits we all shall revere;
We shall dwell with delight on thy fame,
　　And think of thy loss with a tear.

Though lodg'd in a Church-yard so drear,
　　Which the yew-tree surrounds with its gloom;
Thy virtue a *sun* shall appear,
　　And thy graces be *flow'rs* on thy tomb.

ELEGY TO JULIA.

Friend of my bosom, all my joys are o'er—
　　Peace, gentle Peace, alas! no longer mine:
Since Julia, once my idol, lives no more,
　　To gloom and solitude I steal to pine.

Thou tellest me that Time a balm will bring,
　　Soothe ev'ry sigh, and calm my keenest woes:
Go, seek in winter's wild the blooms of spring?
　　Go, whisper to the restless surge, repose!

I thought that Grandeur with a liberal hand
　　Could strew my path of life with sweetest flow'rs;
That Wealth omnipotent could Time command,
　　And from his pinions pluck his whitest hours.

What now remains, my horrors to beguile?
　　Away, ye dreams of grandeur, wealth, away!
Who cannot give my cheek one little smile,
　　Nor bribe a single moment to be *gay.*

ELEGY TO MY DYING ASS, PETER.

Friend of my youthful days, for ever past,
　　When whim and harmless folly rul'd the hour;
Ah! art thou stretch'd amid the straw at last!
　　These eyes with tears thy dying looks devour!

Blest, would I soften thy hard bed of death,
  And with new floods the fount of life supply:
Yes, Peter, blest would I prolong thy breath,
  Renew each nerve, and cheer thy beamless eye.

But wherefore wish? Thy lot is that of all! [law—
  Thy friend who mourns, must yield to Nature's
Like thee must sink, and, o'er each dark'ning ball,
  Will Death's cold hand th' eternal curtain draw.

Piteous thou liftest up thy feeble head,
  And mark'st me dimly, with a dumb adieu;
And thus amid thy hopeless looks I read,
  " Faint is thy servant, and his moments few.

" With thee no more the hills and vales I tread!
  " Those times, so happy, are for ever o'er!
" Ah! why should Fate so cruel cut our thread,
  " And part a friendship that must meet no more?

" O, when these languid lids are shut by Fate;
  " O, let in peace these aged limbs be laid
" 'Mid that lov'd field which saw us oft of late,
  " Beneath our fav'rite willow's ample shade!

·And if my Master chance to wander nigh,
  " Beside the spot where Peter's bones repose;
"Let your poor servant claim one little sigh;
  " Grant this—and, blest, these eyes for ever
    close."

Yes, thou poor Spirit, yes—*thy* wish is *mine*—
  Yes, be thy grave beneath the willow's gloom—
There shall the sod, the greenest sod, be thine;
  And there the brightest flow'r of Spring shall
    bloom.

Oft to the field as Health my footstep draws,
  Thy turf shall surely catch thy Master's eye;
There on thy sleep of death shall Friendship pause,
  Dwell on past days, and leave thee with a sigh.

Sweet is remembrance of our youthful hours,
　When Innocence upon our actions smil'd!
What though Ambition scorn'd our humble pow'rs,
　Thou a wild cub, and I a cub as wild?

Pleas'd will I tell how oft we us'd to roam;
　How oft we wander'd at the peep of morn;
Till Night had wrapp'd the world in spectred gloom,
　And Silence listen'd to the beetle's horn.

Thy * victories will I recount with joy;
　The various trophies by thy fleetness won;
And boast that I, thy playfellow, a boy,
　Beheld the feats by namesake Peter done.

Yes, yes, (for grief must yield at times to glee)
　Amidst my friends I oft will give our tale;
When, lo! those friends will rush thy sod to see,
　And call thy peaceful region Peter's Vale!

ELEGY TO EURIPIDES.

O thou, whose deeply-pictur'd scenes of woe
　From Grecian eyes could force the pitying show'r!
Permit a Stranger's sigh unfeign'd to flow—
　Indulge his hand to strew the sweetest flow'r.

Where is thy fame? In Greece no more divine,
　It pours on Albion's isle the radiant day;
There, with a noon-tide lustre may it shine,
　And gild my country with unclouded ray:

Each night retiring, as I whisper peace,
　With each adieu the tear will steal away;
To think that Thou the song of gods shouldst cease,
　And, dying, mingle with the meanest clay.

---

* Peter's racing powers were truly great; and for size and strength he might justly have been called the *Hercules* of Jackasses. It would probably be too ludicrous *here* to affirm, that for a *sostenuto* he might, with equal justice, have been styled not only the *Marchesi*, but the *Apollo*.

Though Greece forgets thee, yet on Fancy's wing
  From distant Albion will I oft return;
Crown thy cold sod with all the blooms of Spring,
  And envy the rich earth that holds thy *urn*.

ELEGIAC VERSES.—QUEEN ANTOINETTE TO HER CHILDREN, BEFORE HER EXECUTION.

From my prison with joy could I go,
  And with smiles meet the savage decree,
Were it only to sleep from my woe,
  Since the grave holds no terrors for *me*.

But from *you*, O my children, to part!
  Oh! a coward I melt at my doom;
Ye draw me to earth, and my heart
  Sighs for life, and shrinks back from the tomb.

In blessings, ah! take my last breath!
  Dear babes of my bosom, adieu!
May the cloud be dispers'd by my death,
  And open a sunshine for *you!*

ENVY.

Oh, for an ointment to destroy the scab
  Call'd Envy, which, alas! too many know!
The heart should be a medlar, not a crab;
  Milk, and not verjuice, from its fount should flow:
But Greatness, sun-like, from the muddy stream
  Draws the foul vapour that obscures its beam!

EPITAPH.

O thou, remov'd from this world's strife,
  Whose relics here below are laid,
May Peace, who watch'd thy harmless life,
  In death protect thy gentle Shade!

Yet not *alone* around thy bier,
  Thy Children's sighs unfeign ascend'd;
The mourner Pity drops a tear,
  And Virtue weeps a vanish'd friend.

EPITAPH ON A FRIEND.

Though here in *death* thy relics lie,
Thy worth shall live in Mem'ry's eye;
Who oft at Night's pale noon shall stray,
To bathe with tears thy lonely clay.

Here Pity too, in weeds forlorn,
Shall, mingling sighs, be heard to mourn;
With Genius drooping o'er thy tomb,
In sorrow for a Brother's doom.

EPITAPH ON A SPANIEL.

Here rests the relics of a friend below,
Blest with more sense than half the folks I know:
Fond of his ease, and to no parties prone,
He damn'd no sect, but calmly knaw'd his bone;
Perform'd his functions well in ev'ry way,—
Blush, Christians, if you can, and copy Tray.

ERROR.

The light of Reason is a little ray,
But still it shows us the right way:
Indeed, the Gentlewoman makes no blaze,
No bonfire tempting a fool's eye to gaze—
A modest dame, remote, and calm, and coy,
And never playeth gambols, to destroy.

But Error, what a meretricious jade,
Amidst her trackless wilds immers'd in shade,
  To tempt the silly and unwary!
Her meteor, lo! she lights here, there,
Up, down, she dances it—now far, now near,
  In mad and riotous vagary.

On the fools wander, in pursuit so stout,
  And love of this same garish light;
All on a sudden goes this meteor out;
  And caught, like badgers, in the sack of night,
Blund'ring, and trying to get back agen,
  They roll about in vain, poor men.

EXAGGERATION OF TRAVELLERS RIDICULED.

Oh, had thy curious eye beheld, like mine,
The Madeira isle, which glads the heart with richest wine!
Beneath its vines, with common clusters crown'd,
At eve my wand'ring steps a passage found,
Where rose the hut, and, neither rich nor poor,
The wife and husband, seated at the door,
Touch'd, when the labours of the day were done,
The wire of music to the setting sun;
Where, blest, a tender offspring, rang'd around,
Join'd their small voices to the silver sound.
But had *thine* eye this simple scene explor'd,
The man at once had sprung a sceptred lord;
Princes and princesses the *bearns* had been;
The hut a palace, and the wife a queen;
Their golden harps had ravish'd thy two ears,
And beggar'd all the music of the spheres.

EXAMPLE.

Thus as the Flocks amid the valley feed,
  Behold! the Bellweather, the Rover,
Like mortals, fickle, takes it in his head
  To taste a neighbouring field of clover!
He *dares* th' opposing hedge, he beats it *Hollow*—
Mounts, leaps, and all the tribes of fleeces follow!

EXPECTATION.

How expectation loads th' important hour!
  Impatience wilder with each moment grows!
Thou loit'ring Fair one, bless th' appointed bow'r,
  And snatch thy lover from a thousand woes.

From vale to vale my eager gaze I strain;
  From glade to glade with wild emotion move;
Now turn and sigh, now move and turn again,
  Devour each sound, and chide my ling'ring love.

Where is my love? alas! my transports die!
  My cheek, that redden'd with despair, turns pale;
With disappointment drops my clouded eye,
  Each pining feature tells a mournful tale.

See, see, the sun descends beneath the deep;
  Behold the melancholy bird of night!—
In vain along the winding gloom I weep,
  And wish in vain to stay the parting light.

EXTREME MODESTY, A TRUE STORY.

A King of France upon a day,
  With a fair Lady of his Court,
Was pleas'd at Battledore to play,—
  A very fashionable sport.

Into the *bosom* of this fair Court Dame, [shame,
Whose whiteness did the snow's pure whiteness
King Louis by an odd mischance did knock
      The Shuttlecock,
Thrice happy rogue, upon the down of Doves,
To nestle with the pretty little Loves!

" Now, Sire, pray take it out"—quoth She,
With an arch smile.—But what did he?
    What? what to charming Modesty belongs!
Obedient to her soft command,
He rais'd it—but not with his *hand!*
  No marv'lling Reader, but the *chimney tongs!*

What a chaste thought in this good King!
      How clever!
When shall we hear agen of such a thing?
      Lord! never.
Now were *our* Princes to be pray'd
To such an act by some fair Maid,
  I'll bet my life *not one* would mind it:
But *handy*, without more ado,
The Youths would search the bosom *thro'*
  Although it took *a day* to find it!

FAME.

Steep is th' ascent, and narrow is the road,
Ah me! that leads to Fame's divine abode:
Yet thick (through lanes, like pilgrimaging rats,
Unaw'd by mortals, and unscar'd by cats)
What crawling hosts attempt her sacred fane,
And dizzy, drunk-like, tumble back again;
Fast as the swains, whose arms the damsels fill,
Embrace of elegance! down Greenwich-Hill.

FASCINATION.

Thus when the wily Snake, beneath a tree,
Darts his red eye upon his feather'd prey;
Poor Bird! no more he swells the song of love,
Waves the wild wing, and glides from grove to
    grove:
With panting heart he tries to shun the foe;
But, looking on the steady fiend below,
In chains of fatal fascination bound,
Captive he hops around him and around;
Till nearer, nearer drawn, with hopeless cries,
He drops upon the poison'd fang, and dies.

FASTS, ETC. SATIRIZED.

——————— 'tis *Gentry* that must Heav'n implore;
God never listens to the ragged Poor.
When Ministers their blundering tricks betray,
'Tis *Gentry* only that must starve and pray.
Yet at their dread petition Heav'n will start,
Nor, cruel, run a Frenchman through the heart,
T' oblige a foolish Briton who shall cry,
I'm fasting, Lord; so let thy vengeance fly:
Indeed, whate'er the Bishops may pretend,
In fast and pray'r we seldom find a friend:
Fasts will not wet French powder; nor will words
Of pious imprecation blunt French swords:

Nor sighs of *Saints* avert the flying ball:
The Pope must run from Rome, and Mantua fall.
How at each solemn phiz the Dev'l must grin!
All sanctity without, and fraud *within!*
Meat must be watch'd, and roasted in its prime;—
Pray'rs for the Lord keep cold for any time.

FEES.

Lo, many a little charming Phillis,
For vending roses sweet, and lilies,
And love-inspiring, luscious, balmy kisses;
  Although the growth of *their own cheek;*
  Although the growth of *their own neck*;
Although the growth of *their own lip,* sweet Misses;
  Are forc'd to Bridewoll's horrid fare,
  For dealing in *unlicens'd* ware—
Spoil'd all their pretty hops, and skips, and
Because the Justice had not got his *fee.*

FLATTERY.

Soft is the voice of Flatt'ry! sweet her song!
  Ah, much too sweet for man, vain man, I fear!
Her oil of fool, too fluent, glides along,
  And winding, drops with *death*, into his ear.

FLY, TO A, TAKEN OUT OF A PUNCH BOWL.

Ah! poor intoxicated little knave,
Now senseless, floating on the fragrant wave;
  Why not content the cakes alone to munch?
Dearly thou pay'st for buzzing round the bowl;
Lost to the world, thou busy sweet-lipp'd soul—
  Thus Death, as well as Pleasure, dwells with Punch.

Now let me take thee out, and moralize.—
Thus 'tis with mortals, as it is with flies,
  For ever hankering after Pleasure's cup:

Though Fate, with all his legions, be had at hand,
The beasts, the draught of Circe can't withstand,
   But in goes every nose—they *must, will* sup.

Mad are the Passions, as a colt untam'd!
   When Prudence mounts their backs to ride them mild,
They fling, they snort, they foam, they rise inflam'd,
   Insisting on their own sole will so wild.

Gadsbud! my buzzing friend, thou art not dead;
The Fates, so kind, have not yet snipp'd thy thread;
By heav'ns, thou mov'st a leg, and now its brother,
And kicking, lo! again thou mov'st another!

And now thy little drunken eyes unclose;
And now thou feelest for thy little nose,
   And, finding it, thou rubbest thy two hands;
Much as to say, "I'm glad I'm here again."
And well mayst thou rejoice—'tis very plain,
   That near wert thou to Death's unsocial lands.

And now thou rollest on thy back about,
Happy to find thyself alive, no doubt—
   Now turnest—on the table making rings;
Now crawling, forming a wet track,
Now shaking the rich liquor from thy back,
   Now flutt'ring nectar from thy silken wings.

Now standing on thy head, thy strength to find,
And poking out thy small, long legs behind;
And now thy pinions dost thou briskly ply;
Preparing now to leave me—farewell, Fly!

Go, join thy brothers on yon sunny board,
And rapture to thy family afford—
   There wilt thou meet a mistress, or a wife,
That saw thee, drunk, drop senseless in the stream;
Who gave, perhaps, the wide-resounding scream,
   And now sits groaning for thy precious life.

Yes, go and carry comfort to thy friends,
And wisely tell them thy imprudence ends.
Let buns and sugar for the future charm;
These will delight, and feed, and work no harm—
  Whilst Punch, the grinning merry imp of sin,
Invites th' unwary wand'rer to a kiss,
Smiles in his face, as though he meant him bliss,
  Then, like an alligator, drags him in.

FOLLY.

Would not one swear that Heav'n lov'd fools,
  There's such a number of them made;
Bum-proof to all the flogging of the schools,
  No ray of knowledge could their skulls pervade?
Yet, gauge the pockets of those fellows breeches,
We stare like congers at their riches.

O Genius! what a wretch art thou,
  Who canst not keep a mare or cow,
With all thy compliment of wit so frisky!
  Whilst Folly, as a mill-horse blind,
  Besides his compter, gold can find,
And Sundays sport a strumpet and a whiskey!

FORGIVENESS.

———— but, *still* good-humour's in his soul;
And now I mark it, stealing forth so sweet—
Stream of forgiveness—what a treat!
  I see his eye, with love rekindling, roll.

Thus, when the Demon of the storm has driv'n,
The Sun, that Youth of splendor, from his heav'n,
  Drown'd ev'ry vale, and blasted ev'ry bloom;
Cast o'er poor Nature's smile a sable shroud,
Each beauty blotted with his inkiest cloud,
  And giv'n a cheerful world to gloom.

Lo! through the giant shade, a lonely ray
  Peeps from the op'ning west with timid air,
(Till forc'd by shouldering clouds away)
  Informing man, "To-morrow will be fair."

FORTUNE—LOVE.

Where Fortune reigns in splendid pride,
   What madding thousands crowd her shrine!
With sweet simplicity their guide,
   O Love, how few resort to *thine!*

Yet when of Fortune's smile possess'd,
   The sigh for *other* days they pour;
Some secret sorrow stings the breast,
   And languor-loaded crawls each hour.

But Love's pure joys unsullied last;
   His vot'ries taste a bliss sublime,
Sigh to regain the moments past,
   And wish to clip the wings of Time.

FORTUNE, A SONG.

Yes, Fortune, I have sought thee long,
Invok'd thee oft, in prose and song;
   Through half Old England woo'd thee;
Through seas of danger, Indian lands,
Through Afric's howling, burning sands:
   But, ah! in vain pursu'd thee!

Now, Fortune, thou wouldst fain be kind!
And now I'll plainly speak my mind—
   I care not straws about thee:
For Delia's hand alone I toil'd;
Unbrib'd by wealth, the Nymph has smil'd;
   And bliss is our's without thee.

FRENCHMEN.

The columns of your Liberty, Death knows,
   Are cannon, swords, and bayonets, and spears;
The *Angels* who this glorious pile compose,
   Hyænas, Tigers, Jackalls, Wolves, and Bears.

What voice to reason can a *Frenchman* bring?
   Go, bid with lullaby the tiger sleep;
Bind with a spider's web the whirlwind's wing;
   And with the wren's small plume keep down the deep.

FRIENDSHIP.

Friendship! where art? in *books* and on the *tongue*;
Who mak'st, like Love, a *very pretty song:*
Too much a stranger to the *heart*, I ween!
Like Angels, *prais'd*, *admir'd*—but seldom *seen!*
Besides *myself*, no Comforter have *I!*
No hopes from parents, and no Friend to die.
Sweet Friendship ev'n for animals I love—
A dog, a cat, a monkey, parrot, dove;
With Alexander's spirit charm'd, of course,
Who built a town in honour of his *horse.*

GENEROSITY.

Ah! Generosity's a tender plant,
Its root is weakly, and its bearings scant!
Self-love, too near it, robs it of each ray,
And thirsty, sucks the rills of life away.
Vile weed! (like docks in coarsest soil they start)
That thriveth in the cold and flinty heart.—
What diff'rent roads to Fame Ambition takes!
What hubbub in this under-world she makes!

GENIUS, (1.)

Dearly I like to see a Genius spring,
Mark his rich plumes, and eye his soaring wing;
  But Death too soon arrests his eagle flight!
Not long upon the meteor can we gaze—
From the dark element, the lightning's blaze,
  That breaks, and sudden shuts in pitchy night.

GENIUS, (2.)

Appear but Genius, Genius soon will find
New matter to improve and charm mankind;
  Teach on the wildest heath the rose to blow:
Genius, the rod of Moses at the rock,
Shall, by a magical and happy stroke,
  Bid the rich stream of wit and wisdom flow.

The brains of men, in general, are a *pool*,
Wrapp'd in death-stillness, comfortably dull;
   Like motionless poor Lethe, void of spirit.
But now and then (like Milton, for example,
Or Shakespeare, each indeed a beauteous sample,)
   Into existence pops a Wight of merit,
An Ocean lo, his brave ideas rise,   [skies!
That mounts, and with its thunders shakes the

GLOW-WORM, ODE TO.

Bright stranger, welcome to my field,
Here feed in safety, here thy radiance yield;
   To me, oh, nightly be thy splendor giv'n!
Oh, could a wish of mine the skies command,
How would I gem thy leaf with lib'ral hand,
   With ev'ry sweetest dew of Heav'n!

Say, dost thou kindly light the Fairy train,
Amidst their gambols on the stilly plain,
   Hanging thy lamp upon the moisten'd blade?
What lamp so fit, so pure as thine,
Amidst the gentle elfin band to shine,
   And chase the horrors of the midnight shade!

Queen of the insect world, what leaves delight?
   Of such these willing hands a bow'r shall form,
To guard thee from the rushing rains of night,
   And hide thee from the wild wing of the storm.
Sweet Child of Stillness, 'midst the awful calm
   Of pausing Nature thou art pleas'd to dwell;
In happy silence to enjoy thy balm,
   And shed through life a lustre round thy cell.

How diff'rent man, the imp of noise and strife,
Who courts the storm that tears and darkens life;
   Blest when the passions wild the soul invade!
How nobler far to bid those whirlwinds cease,
To taste, like thee, the luxury of peace,
   And, silent, shine in solitude and shade!

GOLD.

Blest were the days when gold was yet unknown;
 The man who drew it from the secret earth,
Forc'd from its bosom an eternal groan,
 And, luckless, gave a fatal Demon birth.

I sigh not for a waggon load of gold;
 For wild Ambition never fir'd my wishes;
Some modest little place I hope to hold,
 And taste a morsel of the loaves and fishes.

Who court the glittering gems of Fortune's Mine,
 Court frequent ruin—thus upon the thorn,
The spider spins by night his silken line,
 That catch, and break beneath the drops of morn.

GOOD CHEER, INFLUENCE OF.

I own that nothing like good cheer succeeds—
A man's a *God* whose hogshead freely bleeds:
Champaigne can consecrate the damned'st evil:
A hungry Parasite adores a *Devil*;
In radiant virtues his poor host arrays,
And smooths him with the gossimer of praise;
Stuff'd to the throat till repetition tires,
And Gluttony's huge greasy wish expires;
Apostate then, the knave denies his church,
And leaves his Saint, with laughter, in the *lurch*.

GRATITUDE.

Yes, Gratitude's a sentiment that springs
 'Midst *Gentlefolks,* and *Nobles,* *Queens,* and *Kings!*
Like pine-apples whom soil the richest suits;
 For pine-apples ne'er grow on cold, raw clay,
 But fat manure, amid the solar ray,
That darts its golden influence to their roots.

HEALTH, ODE TO.

eet Nymph, of rosy cheek and sprightly mien,
ho, vagrant, playful, on the hills art seen,
Ere Sol illumines the grey world below;

Now, doe-like, skipping wild from vale to vale,
Enamour'd of the rills and fresh'ning gale, [flow.
  From whose mild wing the streams of fragrance
O! 'midst those hills and vales contented stray—
Thou wilt be ruin'd if thou com'st away—
  Doctors too much like man-traps lie in wait—
They'll tell thee, beauteous Nymph, ten thousand lies,
That they can mend thy bloom, and sparkling eyes—
  Avoid, avoid, my dear, the dangerous bait.

HODGE AND THE RAZOR, A TALE.

A fellow in a market town,
Most musical, cry'd razors up and down,
  And offer'd twelve for eighteen-pence;
Which certainly seem'd wond'rous cheap,
And for the money, quite a heap,
  As ev'ry man would buy, with cash and sense.

A country Bumpkin the great offer heard:
Poor Hodge, who suffer'd by a broad black beard,
  That seem'd a shoe-brush stuck beneath his nose:
With cheerfulness the eighteen-pence he paid,
And proudly to himself, in whispers, said,
  " This rascal stole the razors, I suppose.

" No matter if the fellow *be* a knave,
" Provided that the razors *shave*;
  " It certainly will be a monstrous prize."
So home the clown, with good his fortune went,
Smiling in heart and soul content,
  And quickly soap'd himself to ears and eyes.

Being well lather'd from a dish or tub,
Hodge now began with grinning pain to grub,
  Just like a hedger cutting furze:
'Twas a vile razor!—then the rest he try'd—
All were impostors—" Ah," Hodge sigh'd!
  " I wish my eighteen-pence within my purse."

Hodge sought the fellow—found him—and begun:
" P'rhaps, Master Razor-rogue, to you 'tis fun,
　" That people flay themselves out of their lives:
" You rascal! for an hour have I been grubbing,
" Giving my crying whiskers here a scrubbing,
　" With razors just like oyster-knives.
" Sirrah! I tell you, you're a knave,
" To cry up razors that can't *shave*."

" Friend," quoth the razor-man, " I'm not a knave:
　" As for the razors you have bought,
　" Upon my soul I never thought
　　" That they would *shave*."

" Not think they'd *shave!*" quoth Hodge, with won-
　　d'ring eyes,
And voice not much unlike an Indian yell; [cries.
　" What were they made for then, you dog?" he
　　" Made!" quoth the fellow, with a smile—
　　　" to *sell*."

HOPELESS LOVE.

Night, who to *others* brings the balm of sleep,
And happy dreams to soothe the peaceful breast,
Pours on *my* wakeful eye far diff'rent guests;
The foulest, darkest demons of despair.
Lorn, at the midnight hour, when all is hush'd,
I wander restless; sadly now I sit,
My brimfull eyes for hours both motionless,
Swimming with woe, towards the passing Moon,
Who on me, as she lonely glides along,
Casts a pale beam of melancholy light,
That seems a ray of pity on my fate.

JEALOUSY, ODE TO.

Avaunt, thou squinting Hag, whose listening ear
　Seizes on every *whisper*—whose owl's eye,
When Night's dark mantle wraps the silent sphere,
　Stares watchful of each form that passeth by!

Thou Fiend, what bus'ness hast thou here on earth,
Dissention-breeder from thy very birth?
 How much more of the *serpent* than the *dove!*
I cannot guess thine errand to this world—
By *thee* is Nature *topsy-turvy* hurl'd!
 And nearly ruin'd the soft land of Love!

JEALOUSY, TO CYNTHIA.

O thou! whose love-inspiring air
 Delights, yet gives a thousand woes;
My day declines in dark despair,
 And night has lost her sweet repose.

Nymph of my soul! forgive my sighs:
 Forgive the jealous fires I feel;
Nor blame a trembling wretch, who dies,
 When others to thy beauties kneel.

Lo! theirs is every winning art,
 With Fortune's gifts, unknown to *me!*
I only boast a simple heart,
 In love with Innocence and Thee.

JOHNSON, DR.

While Johnson sought (as Shakespeare says) that
From whence, alas! no travellers return; [bourn,
Parnassus mop'd for days, in business slack,
And, like a hearse, the hill was hung with black;
Minerva, sighing for her fav'rite son,
Pronounc'd, with lengthen'd face, the world un-
Jove wip'd his eyes so red, and told his wife,[done;
He ne'er made Johnson's equal in his life;
And that 'twould be a long, long time, if ever
His art could form a fellow half so clever:
Venus, of all the little Loves the dam,
With all the Graces, sobb'd for brother Sam:
Such were the heav'nly howlings for his death,
As if Dame Nature had resign'd her breath.

ILLIBERAL CRITICISM CONTEMNED.

Rake, if you please, the kennel of your brains,
And pour forth all the loaded head contains;
   I shall not suffer by it, I am sure;—
Nay, my poetic plants will better thrive;
Exalt their heads and smile—be all alive;
   As *mud* is very excellent manure.

Go, take a lesson from the glorious Sun,
Who, when the elements together run
   In wild confusion—earth and wind and water,
Looks on the tumult down without dismay,
Nay, bright and smiling—seeming thus to say,
   " Lord! bustling Gentlefolk, pray what's the matter?"

ILLUSION.

Young Corydon, betroth'd to Delia's charms,
In fancy holds her ever in his arms:
   In mad'ning fancy, cheeks, eyes, lips, devours;
Plays with the ringlets that all flaxen flow
In rich luxuriance o'er a breast of snow,
   And on that breast the soul of rapture pours.

Night too entrances—Slumber brings the dream—
   Gives to his lips his Idol's sweetest kiss;
Bids the wild heart, high panting, swells its stream,
   And deluge every nerve with bliss:
But if his Nymph unfortunately frowns,
Sad, chapfall'n, lo! he hangs himself, or drowns!

IMMODESTY.

   How loose our Ladies in attire,
   To set our peeping Youth on fire;
A hundred instances I soon could pick ye!
   Without a cap we view the Fair,
   The bosom heaving, heaving bare;
The *hips* asham'd, *forsooth*, to wear a dicky;*

* A term used in the *polite* circles for a flannel petticoat.

Quite antique statues—such the dress,
It nothing leaves for Fancy's guess!

Look at our Grannums, good old souls,
With caps and pinners, well mobb'd polls;
With warming dickies, high stiff stays,
To guard the neck from grasp and gaze.
  How diff'rent from our modern Fair,
  Whose ev'ry beauty *takes the air!*

IMPETUOSITY.

Thus the great Æol, when he rushes forth,
With all his winds, East, West, and South, and
   North;
Flutter'd the leaves of trees, with woeful fright,
Shook by his rage, and bullied by his might;
Straws from the lanes dispers'd, and whirl'd in air,
The blustering wonders of his mouth declare.
Heav'd from their deep foundations, with dread
Barns and old houses thunder to the ground,[sound,
And bowing oaks, in ages rooted strong,
Roar through their branches as he sweeps along.

INCONSTANCY, (1.)

Farewell the beam of early day!
 Cold on the eye the valley fades;
The riv'let mourns upon its way,
  And spectres seem to haunt the shades.
  These eyes, alas! no pleasure see,
  Since Colin's love is chang'd from *me.*

Let nought by Daphne be possest—
 The myrtle-wreath that binds my brow;
The knot of love he gave my breast,
  Deep blushing for his broken vow.
   These eyes, &c.

Let all his tokens meet his eye—
 From Daphne all his gifts depart;

And let me send with these a *sigh*,
  To tell him of a broken heart.
    These eyes, &c.

INCONSTANCY, (2.)

Ah! who could from Phillida fly?
  Yet I sought other nymphs of the vale,
Forgot both her blush and her sigh,
  Nay, forgot that I told her my tale.

In sorrow I wish'd to return,
  And the tale of my passion renew;
" False shepherd," she answer'd, with scorn,
  " False shepherd, for ever adieu!

" For thee, no more tears will I shed,
  " To Truth and sweet Friendship I go;
" The Bird by a wound that has bled
  " Is happy to fly from his foe."

INDIFFERENCE, TO VENUS.

O Venus, wherefore is my sigh
  To Delia's beauty breath'd in vain?
Ah! why her cold and clouded eye,
  That sun-like shone upon her swain?

A time there was, when Delia's breast
  At all my griefs with grief would glow,
The Nymph would lull the storm to rest,
  And sooth with ev'ry charm my woe.

Yet Venus, wheresoe'er she flies,
  To Delia all thy blisses give:
In *me* a *single* shepherd dies,
  In *her*, behold, a *thousand live!*

INFLUENCE OF BEAUTY.

Farewell to the fragrance of morn;
  Farewell to the song of the grove—
I go from my Delia forlorn;
  I go from the Daughter of Love!

I was told that I ought not to gaze
  On the Beauty by which I'm undone;
But how could I hide from their rays?
  What mortals can fly from the *Sun?*

INFLUENCE OF LOVE.

Ev'n Age delighteth in an amorous tale;
Love warms his inside like a pot of ale;
  Thaws his cold heart, and makes it beat so cheery!
His eyes, that, owl like, wink'd upon the day,
Bursts open with a keen and twinkling ray,
  And, lo! he hugs and kisses his old deary.

INGRATITUDE.

Sweet Labourer! midst the Summer's golden hour,
  Full oft I trace thy little busy flight—
With pleasure see thee perch from flow'r to flow'r;
  On Violets, Woodbines, Roses, Lillies light.

Yet what to thee is Summer's golden smile?
  And what to thee the flow'r-enamell'd plain?
Will gratitude reward thy daily toil?—
  No! No! thou workest for reward in vain.

Not long the hive of treasure will be thine—
  Rapacity will force thy little door:
Those treasures with thy life must thou resign,
  A breathless victim on the fragrant store.

INNOCENCE, ODE TO.

O Nymph of meek and blushful mien,
Lone wand'rer of the rural scene,
  Who lovest not the city's bustling sound,
But in the still and simple vale
Art pleas'd to hear the turtle's tale,
  'Mid the gay minstrelsy that floats around!

Now on the bank, amid the sunny beam,
I see thee mark the natives of the stream,
  That break the dimpling surface with delight;

Now see thee pitying a poor captive Fly,
Snapp'd from the lov'd companions of his joy,
  And, swallow'd, sink beneath the gulph of *night*.

Now see thee, in the humming golden hour,
Observant of the Bee, from flow'r to flow'r,
  That loads with varied balm his little thighs,
To guard against chill winter's famish'd day,
When rains descend, and clouds obscure the ray,
  And tempests pour their thunder through the skies.

Now see thee playful chase the child of spring,
The winnowing Butterfly with painted wing,
  That busy flickers on from bloom to bloom:
Pursuing wildly now a fav'rite Fair,
Circling amid the golden realm of air,
  And leaving, all for *love*, the pea's perfume.

Now see thee peeping on the secret nest,
Where sits the parent Wren in patient rest;
  While at her side her feather'd partner sings;
Chaunts his short note, to charm her nursing day;
Now for his loves pursues his airy way,
  And now with food returns on cheerful wings.

Pleas'd could I sit with thee, O nymph so sweet,
And hear the happy flocks around thee *bleat*;
  And mark the skipping sports along the land;
Now hear thee to a fav'rite lambkin speak,
Who wanton stretches forth his woolly neck,
  And plucks the fragrant herbage from thy hand.

INNOCENCE, (2.)

Dear Innocence, where'er thou deign'st to dwell,
The Pleasures sport around thy simple cell;
  The song of Nature melts from grove to grove;
Perpetual sunshine sits upon thy vale;
Content, and ruddy Health thy hamlet hail,
  And Echo waits upon the voice of Love.

E

But where—but where is scowling Guilt's abode?
The spectred heath, and Danger's cavern'd road;
  The shuffling monster treads with panting breath—
The cloud-wrapp'd storm insulting roars around,
Fear palls him at the thunder's awful sound,
  He stares with horror on the flash of death.

He calls on Darkness with affright,
And bids her pour her deepest night;
Her clouds impenetrable bring,
And hide him with her raven wing!

Are these the pictures? Then I need not muse,
Nor gape, nor ponder *which* to choose:
O Innocence, this instant I'm thy slave—
What but the greatest *fool* would be a *knave!*

INSECURITY.

Thus, at the solemn, still, and sunless hour,
When to their sports the insect nations pour,
In airy-tumult bless'd, the light-wing'd throng,
  Thoughtless of enemies in ambuscade,
Hums to Night's list'ning ear the choral song,
  And wantons thro' the boundless fields of shade;
When, lo! the mouse-fac'd Demon of the gloom,
Espying, hungry meditates their doom!

Bounce, from his hole so secret bursts the Bat,
  To honour, mercy, moderation, lost!
  Behold him sally on the humming host,
And murd'rous overturn the tribes of Gnat;
Nimbly from right to left, like Tippoo, wheel,
  And snap ten thousand pris'ners at a meal!

INSIGNIFICANT DISCOVERIES.

Thus have these eyes beheld a cock so stately,
(Indeed these lyric eyes beheld one lately)
  Lab'ring upon a dunghill with each knuckle;
When, after many a peck, and scratch, and scrub,
This hunter did unkennel a poor grub,
  On which the fellow did so strut and chuckle!

He peck'd and squinted—peck'd and kenn'd agen,
Hallooing lustily to *Madam Hen*;
To whom, with airs of triumph, he look'd round,
And told what noble treasure he had found.

INSOLENCE.

With feeble voice and deep desponding sighs,
What sallow cheek and pity asking eyes,
A wretch by age and poverty decay'd,
For farthings lately to a Nabob pray'd;
The Nabob, turkey-like, began to swell,
And damn'd the beggar to the pit of hell.
" Oh! Sir," the supplicant was heard to cry,
(The tear of mis'ry trickling from his eye) [poor,
" Though I'm in rags, and wondrous, wondrous
" And *you* with gold and silver cover'd o'er,
" There won't in heav'n such difference, Sir, take
  " place,
" When we before the Lord come face to face."—
" *You* face to face with *me !*" the Nabob cry'd,
" In all the insolence of upstart pride—
" *You* face to face with *me*, you dog, appear!
" I'll kick you back—de, if I catch ye there."

INSOLENCE OF GREATNESS.

Full many a time reluctantly, I own,
I view our mighty Rulers with a groan,
  Who eat the labours of us *vulgar Crew*;
Bask on our shoulders in their lazy state;
And if we dare *look* up for ease, th' ingrate
  Look down, and ask us, " D-m'me, who are you?"

Now such forgetfulness is most unpleasant!
The man who doth receive a hare or pheasant,
Might *somewhat*, certainly, from manners spare,
And say, " I thank ye for the bird or hare."

The lofty Great must have the softest bed
To lay the *soft* luxurious head:
  And from our bosoms we poor *Geese*, so tame,

Must pluck submissively, the tender feather;
Ourselves expos'd to Nature's rudest weather,
  Deny'd the liberty to cry out, "Shame!"
Thus, while *their* heads the pillow's down imprint,
Ours must be only bolster'd by a flint.

INVITATION.

Come, Cynthia, to thy shepherd's vale,
  Though tyrant Winter shade the scene;
The leafless grove has felt his gale,
  And ev'ry warbler mourns his reign.

Yet, what to *me* the howling wind?
  Thy voice the linnet's song supplies.
Or what the cloud to *me*, who find
  Eternal sunshine in thy eyes?

IRONY, ODE TO.

O Thou, with mouth demure and solemn eye,
  Who laughest not, thou Quaker-looking wight,
  But makest others roaring laugh outright,
Thus chasing widow Sorrow, and her sigh—

There was a time, but not like our's so nice,
When thou couldst banish Folly, nay, and Vice—
Leagu'd with thy daughter Humour, damsel quaint,
And Wit, that could have tickled ev'n a Saint.

But times are alter'd! *Certain Greybeards* say,
" Ye vagabonds, you've had indeed your day,
" But never dare to shew your face agen,
" To take vile liberties with lofty men.
" Grin if you please—with joke the world regale—
" Yet mind, a Critic hears you, call'd a Jail."

KISS, TO A.

Soft child of Love—thou balmy bliss,
Inform me, O delicious Kiss,
Why thou so suddenly art gone?
Lost in the moment thou art won?

Yet go—for wherefore should I sigh?
On Delia's lip, with raptur'd eye,
On Delia's blushing lip I see
A thousand full as sweet as *thee.*

KNIGHT, THE, AND THE RATS.

A Knight liv'd in the West not long ago,
Like Knights in general, not *o'er wise,* I trow—
This Knight's great barn was visited by rats,
In spite of poison, gins, and owls, and cats.

Lo! waxing wrath, that neither gins nor cats,
Nor owls, nor poison, could destroy the rats; [he:
" I'll nab them by a scheme, by heav'ns," quoth
So of his neighbourhood he rous'd the mob,
Farmers and farmers' boys, to do this job;

His servants too of high and low degree;
And eke the tribes of Dog, by sound of horn,
To kill the rats that dar'd to taste the corn.

This done, the Knight, resolv'd with god-like ire,
Ran to his kitchen for a stick of fire,
 From whence intrepid to the barn he ran:
Much like the Macedonian and fair Punck,
Who, at Persepolis so very drunk,
 Did with their links the mighty ruin plan.

Now 'midst the dwelling flew the blazing stick:
Soon from the flames rush'd forth the rats so thick;
 Men, dogs, and bats, in furious war unite—
The conquer'd rats lie sprawling on the ground;
The Knight, with eyes triumphant, stares around,
 Surveys the carnage, and enjoys the sight.

Not ev'n Achilles saw, so blest, his blade,
Dismiss whole legions to th' infernal shade!
But, lo! at length by this rat-driving flame, [came:
Burnt was the corn—the walls down thund'ring
 The meaning of it was not far to learn—

When turning up those billiard-balls his eyes,
That held a pretty portion of surprise, [*barn!*"
" Zounds! what a blockhead! I have *burnt the*

LATENT QUALITIES.

" Observe a fat, black, greasy hump of coal;
  " Lo, to that most ungraceful piece of earth,
  " A warm and lively lustre owes its birth ;
" A flame in *this World*, pleasant to the soul!

" To shapeless clouds, that, waggon-like, along
  " Move cumb'rous, scowling on the twilight hea-
" At times, behold, the purest snows belong! [v'n,
  " To such, of rain the lucid drops are giv'n :
" Nay, 'mid the mass so murky and forlorn,
" Behold the lightening's vivid beam is born!"

LAURA, SONG TO.

O my heart! thou so lately wert blest,
  Those days I shall ever adore—
When Pleasure alone was thy guest,
  But to meet thee, ah! meet thee no more.

How dull was the grove and the bow'r,
  If the maid of thy love was not nigh?
She gave bloom, she gave life to each flow'r,
  But with Laura, dear Laura, they die.

Lo! the linnets, enlivening the shade,
  No longer give joy to my ear—
But their carols, how sweet, when the maid,
  The pride of the valley, was near!

To the gloom, near yon fount, let me go,
  Indulging of Fancy, the dream ;
I will listen to murmurs of woe,
  And hear my sad tale in the stream.

LIBERALITY.

Deeply from my soul the man I hate,
  Immers'd in mammon, and by mis'ry got ;

Who, to complete his dinner, licks his plate,
    And wishes to have ev'ry thing for *nought:*
Who, if he gam'd, the dice would meanly cog;
Rob the blind beggar's scrip, and starve his dog:
And that there are such wretches near a throne,
Degraded Nature tells it with a groan.

Perdition catch the money-grasping wretch,
With hook-like fingers ever on the stretch,
Who, fighting, vents on Charity a curse,
That asks, for Want, a penny from his purse!

The heart that lodges in that miser's breast,
    For money, feels the hunger of the shark;
Resembling, too, the rusty iron chest
    That holds his idol—close, and hard, and dark.

LIBERTY.

May Liberty sit *firm* upon her throne;
    And he who dares to shake her, vengeance meet;
No matter what his grandeur—let him groan,[sweat!
    And Hell's best brimstone the black miscreant

LIFE, ODE TO.

Parent of Pleasure, and of many a groan,
I should be loath to part with thee, I own,
I thank thee that thou brought'st me into *being;*
The things of this our world are well *worth seeing,*
No, when it comes that thou and I must part,
Life, I shall leave thee with a sighing heart.

Some wish they never had been born, how odd!
To see the handy works of God,
    In sun, and moon, and starry sky;
Though last, not least, to see sweet Woman's charms,
Nay more, to clasp them in our arms,
    And pour the soul in love's delicious sigh,

Is well worth coming for, I'm sure,
Supposing that thou gav'st us nothing more.

Before us Heav'n hath plac'd the tear and smile;
Each may be won with very trifling toil—
  But if there be in nature such a mule,
Who, willing with misfortune to be curst,
Should, like an ideot, madly choose the first,
  In God's name let him suffer like a fool.

Misfortunes are this lott'ry world's sad blanks;
Presents, in my opinion, not worth thanks:
The Pleasures are the twenty thousand prizes,
Which nothing but a downright ass despises.

LOVE, (1.)

Yes, Love's a cooing, sweet, persuasive pigeon,
Gains all the globe indeed to his religion:
Throughout the world his humble vot'ries pray,
And worship him exactly the same way,
Other religions kill—are torn by strife;
Love *kisses*, and, what's sweeter still, gives *life!*

LOVE, (2.)

Love is a Butterfly that skims about
  From hill to vale, and stops at ev'ry flow'r;
Sucks all the honey with its little snout,
  So pleas'd the rich ambrosia to devour;
Then on wild wing, away it flies again,
The Sultan of the variegated plain.

True Love, my dear, is neither lame nor blind:
  All energy—his life, eternal spring;
Roams the wide world as wanton as the wind,
  And scorns the fetters that would bind his *wing:*
Then, Chloe, learn to prize the varied kiss,
And prove of sweet Inconstancy the bliss.

LOVE, (3.)

Ere 'witching love my heart possest,
  And bade my sighs the nymph pursue;
Calm as the infant's smiling rest,
  No anxious hope nor fear it knew.

But doom'd, ah! doom'd at last to mourn,
    What tumults in that heart arose!
An ocean tumbling wild, and torn
    By tempests from its deep repose.

Yet let me not the virgin blame,
    As though *she* wish'd my heart despair;
How could the maid suspect a flame,
    Who never knew that she was *fair?*

LOVE, (4)

Love is a pretty passion, to be sure;
And long, say I, indeed, may Love endure!
Yet now and then to Prudence should it look—
Yes, take a little leaf from Wisdom's book.

Love, though it deals in *sweets*, has many *sours:*
It does not always furnish happy hours,
    Putting us oft in dismal situations;
The novelty sets people's souls a longing—
What thousands to their ruin thus are thronging!
    Indeed we see the evil in all nations.

I fear Love does at times a deal of harm:
    It keeps the world alive, it is confess'd;
So far, indeed, I like the pleasing charm—
    Yet, through Love, what thousands are distress'd!

LOVE AND WEDLOCK CONTRASTED.

Wedlock's a saucy, sad, familiar state,
Where folks are very apt to scold and hate:
Love keeps a *modest* distance, is divine,
Obliging, and say's ev'ry thing that's fine.

Love wishes, in the vale or on the down,
To give his dear, dear idol a green gown:
Marriage, the brute, so snappish and ill-bred,
Can kick his sighing turtle out of bed;
Turns bluffly from the charms that taste adores,
Then pulls his night-cap o'er his eyes, and snores.

Wedlock's a lock, however, large and thick,
Which ev'ry rascal has a *key* to pick.

O Love! for heav'n's sake, never leave my heart:
No! thou and I will never, never part:
Go, Wedlock, to the men of leaden brains,
Who hate variety, and sigh for chains.

LOW LIFE, A SCENE IN.

Go, with your fellows crack the clumsy joke
'Midst beer and brandy, bread and cheese, and
Descend the ladder to the clouds below, [smoke;
Where *ordinary* men of two-pence go!
Where vagrant knives and forks are bound in chains,
And never tablecloth is spoil'd by stains;
Where, in the board's black hole (superb design!)
Pepper and salt in matrimony join;
And in another hole, with frown and smile,
Much too like marriage, vinegar and oil!—
Where for a towel (economic thought!)
A monstrous mastiff, after dinner brought,
Complacent waits on *Gentlemen*'s commands,
And yields his back of shag to wipe their hands—
Such is the scene where thou shouldst ever sit,
Form'd to thy taste, and suited to thy wit.

LUTE, SONG TO A.

What shade and what stillness around!
   Let us seek the lov'd cot of the Fair;
There soften her sleep with thy sound,
   And banish each phantom of care.

The Virgin may wake to thy strain,
   And be sooth'd, nay, be *pleas'd* with thy song:
Alas! she may *pity* the swain,
   And fancy his sorrows too long.

Could thy voice give a smile to her cheek,
   What a joy, what a rapture were mine!

Then for ever thy fame would I speak—
O my lute, what a triumph were thine!

Ah! whisper kind love in her ear,
And sweetly my wishes impart;
Say, the swain who adores her is near;
Say, thy sounds are the sighs of his heart.

LUXURY.

Chloe, a fav'rite of a rich old Dame,
Was vastly delicate in all her frame;
  Could put down nought at last, but nice *tid bits*:
Nay oft, with much solicitation too,
Her Mistress was oblig'd to kiss and woo,
  For fear poor tender Chloe might have *fits*.

Fat was our Chloe—like a ball of grease;
So round, a foot-ball quite, and fair her fleece.
Oft on the Turkey carpet as she lay,
  And sleep o'er Chloe's eye-lids did prevail;
'Twas very, very difficult to say
  Which was her *head* indeed, and which her *tail*.

At length it came to pass, that Chloe
Did sullenness and sichness show.
The Coachman's call'd—" O Jehu, Chloe's ill;
" Quite lost her appetite—she has no will
  " To move, or say, poor soul, a single thing:
" Jehu, what can the matter be—d'ye know?"
" I think, my Lady, I could *cure* Miss Chlo."
  " Dear Jehu, what delicious news you bring!"

Now to his room the Coachman bore Miss Bitch,
Who, looking back all wistful, felt no itch
To go with Jehu—still he bears her on:—
Arriv'd, kind Jehu offers her a bone.

Miss Chloe in a passion seeks the door:
In vain—'tis shut—she lays her on the floor,
  And whines—gets up, all restless—looks about;

Watches the door so sly, and cocks her ears;
So pleas'd and nimble at each sound she hears,
   In hopes (vain hopes, alas!) of getting out.

Chloe, like lightning, now resolves to pass,
Bounce from her gaoler, through a pane of glass,
   And, by a leap, no more in prison groan:
But, fearing she might spoil her pretty chops,
Nay, break her neck, by chamber-window hops,
   Chloe most wisely lets the leap alone.

Jehu now offer'd her a piece of liver:
   " Chloe, do you love liver?" Jehu said—
" The devil take," she seem'd to say, " the giver:"
   So hurt the dog appear'd—then turn'd her head.

" Well, Chloe, well—heav'n mend your proud di-
   " gestion;
" To-morrow I shall ask you the same question."
   The morrow (ah! a sulky morrow) came:
Chloe scarce slept a single wink all night;
Whining and groaning, longing much to *bite!*
   Calling in vain upon my Lady's name.

Another morning came—a liver meal—
" Chloe, how stands your stomach? how d'ye feel?"
   " Jehu, I will *not* eat."—Jehu goes out—
What does Miss Chloe?—With a nimble pace,
Runs to the liver, without saying grace,
   Gobbling away, with appetite *so stout*;

For now the liver seem'd to meet her wish,
And, not half satisfy'd, she *lick'd the dish!*

Jehu returns, and smiles—Chloe grows good;
   Takes civilly a slice of musty bread;
Rejects from Jehu's hand no kind of food;
   Glad on a *rind of Cheshire* to be fed.

Jehu with Chloe to my Lady goes,
And, triumphing, his little patient shows;
Not once discovering the coarse mode of cure—
Jehu had lost his place then to be sure.

My Lady presses Chloe to her breast,
Half crazy, hugging, kissing her—so blest
　　To see her fav'rite Chloe's chang'd condition:
" Thank ye, good Jehu—Heav'ns, what skill is in
Then into Jehu's hand she slips a guinea, 　[ye !".
　　And Jehu's thought a very fine physician.

MADRIGAL.

When Love and Truth together play'd,
　　So cheerful was the Shepherd's song!
How happy, too, the rural Maid!
　　How light the minutes wing'd along!
But Love has left the sighing vale,
And Truth no longer tells her tale.

Sly stealing, see, from scene to scene,
　　The watchful Jealousy appear;
And pale Distrust with troubl'd mien,
　　The rolling eye, and list'ning ear!
For Love has left the sighing vale,
And Truth no longer tells her tale.

Ah! shall we see no more the hour,
　　That wafted rapture on its wing?
With murmurs shall the riv'let pour,
　　That prattl'd from its crystal spring?
Yes, yes, while Love forsakes the vale,
And Truth no longer tells her tale.

MARGATE.

The Taylor here, the port of Mars assumes;
　　Who cross-legg'd sat in silence on his board—
Forgets his goose and rag besprinkled rooms,
　　And thread and thimble, and now struts a Lord!

Here Crispin too forgets his end, and awl—
　　Here Mistress Cleaver with importance looks!
Forgets the beef, and mutton on her stall,
　　And lights and livers dangling from the hooks.

Here Mistress Tap, from pewter pots withdrawn,
  Walks forth in all the pride and paunch and geer;
Mounts her swoln heels on Dandelion's lawn,
  And at the ball-room heaves her heavy rear.

Chang'd by their travels—mounted high in soul,
  Here Suds forgets whate'er remembrance shocks;
And Mistress Suds forgetteth too the Pole,
  Wigs, bob and pig-tail, basons, razors, blocks!

Here too the most important Dicky Dab
  With puppy-pertness, pretty, pleasant Prig,
Forgets the narrow, fishy house of Crab,
  And drives in Jehu-stile his whirling Gig!

And here 'midst all such consequence am *I*,
  The Poet! *semper idem—just the same—*
Bidding old Satire's hawk at follies fly,
  To fill the shops of Booksellers with *game*.

MARRIAGE.

Now love, now hate; now smile, now tear;
Now sun, now cloud, now mist, now clear;
Now music, now a stunning clap of thunder;
  Now perfect ease, now spiteful strife,
  Resembles matrimonial life!
Pray read the pretty little story under!
      A tale well known:
      'Tis John and Joan.

John married Joan—they frown'd, they smil'd;
Now parted, and now made a child:
  One day they had a desperate quarrel
  About a little small-beer barrel,
Without John's knowledge slily tapp'd by Joan;
  For Joan, t'*oblige* her *old friend* Hodge,
  Thought asking leave of John was fudge;
And so she wisely left the leave alone.

It happ'd that John and Joan had not *two* beds
To rest their angry, frowning brace of heads;

Ergo, there was but *one*
    To rest their gentle jaws upon.
"I'll have a *board* between us," cried the *Man*—
  "With all *my* spirit, John," replied the *wife;*
A *board* was plac'd, according to their plan :
    Thus ended this barrier at once the strife.

On the first night, the husband lay
    Calm as a clock, nor once wink'd over—
Calm as a clock, too let me say,
    Joan never squinted on her lover.

Two, three, four nights, the sulky Pair,
  Like two still mice, devoid of care,
In philosophic silence sought repose;
  On the fifth morn, it chanc'd to please
    John's nose to sneeze—   [nose.
"God bless you, Dear!" quoth Joan at John's loud

At this John gave a sudden start,
And popping o'er the hedge, his head—
  "Joan, did you say it from your *heart?*
"Yes, John, I *did*, indeed, indeed!"
  "You *did?*"—"Yes John, upon my word"—
  "Zounds, Joan, then take away the *Board!*"

MATRIMONY.

There are, for wedded prey, who prowl,
And joy to hear the tempest howl;
O'er Matrimony's smile to cast a cloud,
And put the modest Lady in her shroud!—
Such shall the Muse to infamy consign,
And crush with all the thunders of her line.

MAY-DAY.

The daisies peep from ev'ry field,
And vi'lets sweet their odour yield;
The purple blossom paints the thorn,
And streams reflect the blush of morn.

Then lads and lasses all, be gay,
For this is Nature's holiday.

Let lusty Labour drop his flail,
Nor woodman's hook a tree assail;
The ox shall cease his neck to bow,
And Clodden yield to rest, the plough.

Behold the lark in either float,
While rapture swells the liquid note!
What warbles he, with merry cheer?
" Let Love and Pleasure rule the year."

The insect tribes in myriads pour,
And kiss with Zephyr ev'ry flow'r;
Shall *these* our icy hearts reprove,
And tell us we are foes to Love?

MAY AND SEPTEMBER.

O Nancy! wilt thou go with me,
And all the Poet's treasure see,
  My garden-house, my temple-rooms?
There shall I dwell on those black eyes,
And pour my tuneful soul in sighs,
  And catch thy panting breath's perfumes.

Ah! Nancy, now I hear thee say,
" Lord bless us! I'm the youthful May,
  " And you are Autumn, Sir—September;
" And therefore we by no means suit."
Dear Nancy, that's the time for *fruit*,
  Thou surely oughtest to remember.

Then blest together let us wing—
Love only *blossoms* in the *Spring*.

MARIAN'S COMPLAINT.

Since truth has left the shepherd's tongue,
Adieu the cheerful pipe and song;
Adieu the dance at closing day,
And, ah! the happy morn of May.

How oft he told me I was fair,
And wove the garland for my hair!
How oft for Marian cull'd the bow'r,
And fill'd my lap with ev'ry flow'r!

How oft he vow'd a constant flame,
And carv'd on ev'ry oak my name!
Blush, Colin, that the *wounded tree*
Is all that will remember *me*.

MASCULINITY.

Love! when I marry, give me not an ox—
I hate a woman like a sentry box;
Nor can I deem that dame a charming creature,
Whose hard face holds an *oath* in ev'ry feature.
In woman, angel sweetness let me see:
No galloping horse-godmothers for *me*.

How diff'rent, Cynthia, from thy form so fair,
That triumphs in a love-inspiring air;
Superior beaming ev'n where thousands shine—
Thy form!—where all the tender graces play,
And, blushing, seem in ev'ry smile to say,
" Behold we boast an origin divine!"

MEMORY INFERIOR TO SENSE.

O Genius! thou fair flow'r of rich perfume,
  What stinking weeds have stol'n thy sacred name!
Display'd their tawdry colours, for thy bloom,
  Till blushing Folly's self has cried out " shame!

Possess'd of mem'ry, Nature's gift to fools, [others;
  Thus coxcombs read and learn the thoughts of
And swell'd with Lexicons and grammar rules,
  Scare with Greek-thunder their old aunts and
    mothers.

MERIT.

Mild is the mien of Merit—ah! how meek—
  All diffidence, she looks with downcast eye—

A blush, a crimson blush o'erspreads her cheek—
  And fear of censure gives her soul a sigh.

From tumult, far she loves to wander—far—
  A simple, pensive, silent, thoughtful maid,
All lonely shining, like the evening star
  That sparkles on the solitary shade.

She pants not for the splendor of a name,
  To praise, to flatt'ry, wishing to be deaf;
Trembling, she steals herself away from Fame,—
  A blushing strawb'rry hid beneath a leaf.

Sweet, tho' her song, she hopes not to be heard:
  In groves, the melting softness shuns the light—
In secret warbling, like the tuneful bird
  That, shaded, charms the list'ning ear of night.

MERETRICIOUS EMBRACES.

To false delights the Youths of Britain fly,
  Who court for happiness the Wanton's arms;
Who darts on *all* the fond inflaming eye,
  And *choiceless* yields to *all*, for gold, her charms.

When in the Syren's fond embrace you sigh,
  And on her lips impress the burning kiss,
Doth Friendship mingle with th' unhallow'd joy,
  Or Love's pure spirit swell the surge of bliss?

When droops enjoyment, what is then the Fair?
  A *flow'r* that blooms, but quickly doom'd to fade;
A *sun* that pours a momentary glare,
  And 'mid the tempest sinks o'erwhelm'd in shade.

O swains, to Modesty's fair daughters turn:
  By *mental* beauty let your hearts be led:
Bid by your flight the venal Fair-one mourn,
  And press in tears her solitary bed.

When round your neck her fondling arms she glues,
  And, bent to please, exhausts each winning art;
With false delights she shamefully subdues,
  And leads the Passions captive, not the *heart*.

MENTAL RESTIVENESS.

The mind of man is vastly like a hive;
His thoughts so busy ever—all alive:
  But here the *simile* will go no further!
For bees are making honey, one and all;
Man's thoughts are busy in producing gall,
  Committing, as it were, self-murther.

But let the spirit that surrounds *my* frame
  Sit easy on it, just like an old shoe—
When Disappointment sets my house in flame,
  Let Reason all she can to quench it do:
Reason has engines plentiful and stout,
With water at command to put it out.

I hate to hear men quarrelling through life,
Themselves the fabricators of the strife;
For ever hunting, with a hound-like nose,
That hornet's nest, the tribe of woes:
And when the woes invited greet 'em,
They wonder how the dev'l they meet 'em.

MIRTH.

Care to our coffin adds a nail, no doubt;
And ev'ry grin, so merry, draws one out:
  I own I like to laugh, and hate to sigh;
And think that risibility was giv'n
For human happiness, by gracious Heav'n,
  And that we came not into life to cry:

To wear long faces, just as if our Maker,
The God of Goodness, was an undertaker,
Well pleas'd to wrap the soul's unlucky mien
In sorrow's dismal crape, or bombasin.

Methinks I hear the Lord of Nature say,
" Fools, how ye plague me! go, be wise, be gay;
  " No tortures, penances, your God requires—

"Enjoy, be lively, innocent, adore,
"And know that Heav'n hath not one angel more
   "In consequence of groaning nuns and friars.

"Heav'n never took a pleasure or a pride
"In starving stomachs, or a horsewhipp'd hide.

"Mirth be your motto—merry be your heart:
   "Good laughs are pleasant inoffensive things;
"And if their follies happen to divert,
   "I shall not quarrel at a joke on *Kings*."

MISER, THE WEALTHY.

Griev'd that the Muse attack'd with scorn a Man,
Unlucky form'd on Nature's hungry plan;
Who lord of millions, trembles for his store,
And fears to give a farthing to the poor;
Proclaims that penury will be his fate,
And, scowling, looks on charity with hate;
Whose matchless avarice is meat and drink,
That dreads to spill a single drop of ink;
On each superfluous letter vents a sigh,
And saves the little dot upon an i;
Happy e'en Nature's tenderest ties to flight,
And vilely rob an offspring of his right.

MISER, AND THE DERVISE.

The Miser Sherdi on his sick-bed lying,
Affrighted, groaning, wheezing, praying, sighing,
   Expecting ev'ry hour to lose his breath—
Enter Dervise—"Holy Father, say,
"As life seems parting from this sinful clay,
   "What can preserve me from the jaws of death."

"A sacrifice, dear son—good joints of meat,
   "Of lamb, and mutton, for the Priest and Poor;
"Nay, from the *Koran* shouldst thou lines repeat,
   "*Those lines* may possibly thy health restore,"

" Thank ye, dear Father! you have said *enough*,
 " Your counsel has *already* giv'n me ease;
" Now as my sheep are all a great way off,
 " I'll quote our holy *Koran*, if you please."

MISFORTUNE.

'Tis giv'n as gospel, both in prose and rhymes,
 That people should not be *for ever blest*;
Misfortune therefore must be good at times,
 A salutary, though satiric guest;

That goads to virtuous works the rump of Sloth;
 Like gout, that bites us into health so fair;
Or like the needle, while it wounds the cloth,
 It puts the rag into repair.

MISFORTUNE—TO A CAPTIVE QUEEN.

With radiance rose thy morning sun,
 Fair promise of a happy day;
But, luckless, ere it reach'd its noon,
 The fiend of darkness dimm'd the ray.

What though the brightest gifts are thine,
 And distant nations pour thy praise;
While, raptur'd, on thy form divine
 The eyes of Love and Wonder gaze?

Yet what is life, 'mid Horror's reign,
 Where Murder's triumph cleaves the sky;
Where heaves with death the groaning scene,
 And dungeons loud for vengeance cry?

Yet what is life to spotless fame?
 And *thine* to latest time shall bloom—
The blow that sinks that beauteous frame
 Gives all the Virtues to the tomb.

MODESTY, HYMN TO.

O! Modesty, thou shy and blushful maid,
Don't of a simple shepherd be afraid: [thee;
Wert thou *my* lamb, with sweetest grass I'd treat
I am no wolf so savage that would eat thee:

Then haste with me, O nymph, to dwell,
And give a goddess to my cell.

Thy fragrant breast, like Alpine snows so white,
   Where all the nestling Loves delight to lie;
Thine eyes so soft, that shed the milder light
   Of Night's pale wand'rer o'er her cloudless sky,
Thy luscious lips that heav'nly dreams inspire,
By beauty form'd, and loaded with desire;
With sorrow, and with wonder, lo! I see
(What melting treasures!) *thrown away* on *thee.*
   Then haste with me O nymph, to dwell,
   And give a goddess to my cell.

Thou knowest not that bosom's fair design;
And for those two pouting lips divine,
   Thou think'st them form'd alone for simple chat—
To bill so happy with thy fav'rite dove,
And playful force, with sweetly fondling love,
   Their kisses on a lap-dog or a cat.
     Then haste with me, meek maid, to dwell,
     And give a goddess to my cell.

Oh! fly from Impudence, the brazen rogue,
Whose flippant tongue hath got the Irish brogue:
Whose hands would pluck thee like the fairest
   flow'r;
Thy cheeks, eyes, forehead, lips and neck, devour:
   Shun, shun that Caliban, and with me dwell:
   Then come, and give a goddess to my cell.

The world, O simple maid, is full of art,
Would turn thee pale, and fill with dread thy heart,
Didst thou perceive but half the snares
The Dev'l for charms like thine prepares!
   Then haste, O nymph, with me to dwell,
   And give a goddess to my cell.

MONODY ON A CELEBRATED MUSICIAN.

Adieu to the song of the grove!
　Our Philomel warbles no more!
The loss of his carols of love,
　The shepherds will ever deplore.

And sweet to the Nymphs of the Vale
　Were his lays—what delight on the ear!
Whenever he melted the gale,
　How the Virgins would hasten to hear!

Where is Echo, so fond of his voice,
　So pleas'd on each accent to dwell?
Poor Echo no more will rejoice!
　But silently sleep in his cell.

Though doom'd from the world to depart,
　From remembrance he cannot remove;
While tenderness reigns in the heart,
　For his song was the language of love.

MORALITY.

Morality may wear a ruffle short,
I really think, and not his conscience hurt—
　Morality may also like nice picking;
For since the great All-wise has giv'n us fowls,
Mankind were certainly a set of owls,
　To dare to place damnation in a chicken.

Morality, I ween, may go well-drest;
Keep a good fire, and live upon the *best*;
　Throw by his wheel-barrow, and keep a carriage;
Visit the Op'ra, Masquerade, and Play;
Drink Claret, Burgundy, Champagne, Tokay;
　Get fifty thousand with a girl in marriage.

To eat from splendid plate, or homely manger,
Methinks the soul is just in *equal* danger.

MORNING.

Yes, Modesty, (by very few carest)
Oft condescends to be my guest:

From time to time the maid my rhyme reviews,
And dictates sweet instructions to the Muse;
Yes, frequent deigns my cottage to adorn,
Just like that blushful damsel call'd Miss Morn,
  Who, smiling from the dreary caves of night,
Moves from her east with silent pace and slow
O'er yonder shadowy mount's gigantic brow,
  And to my window steals with dewy light,
Then peeping through the panes with cherub mien,
  Seems to ask liberty to enter in.

NARRATION OF TRAVELLERS SATIRIZED.

Lo! moon-ey'd Wonder opes her lap to thee:
How niggardly, alas! to luckless me!
Where'er through trackless woods thy luckier way,
Marvels, like dew-drops, beam on ev'ry spray.
Blest man! whate'er thou wishest to behold,
Nature as strongly wishes to unfold;
Of all her wardrobe offers ev'ry rag,
Of which thy skill hath form'd a conj'ror's bag.
Thy deeds are giants, covering our's with shame!
Poor wasted pigmies! skeletons of fame!
To thee how kindly hath thy genius giv'n
The massy keys of yonder star-clad heav'n;
With leave, whene'r thou wishest to unlock it,
To put a few eclipses in thy pocket!
Nature, where'er thou treadest, exalts her form;
The whisp'ring zephyr swells a howling storm;
Where pebbles lay, and riv'lets purl'd before,
Huge promontories rise, and oceans roar.
Thrice-envy'd man (if truth each volume sings,)
Thy life how happy! hand and glove with kings!
  'Mid those fair isles, (the Canaries) the happy isles of old,
Plains that the ghosts of kings and chiefs patrol'd,
These eyes have seen; but let me truth confess,
No royal spectre came, these eyes to bless:

Whate'er I saw requir'd no witch's storm—
Slight deeds, that Nature could with ease perform!
Audacious, to purloin my flesh and fish,
No golden eagles hopp'd into my dish;
Nor crocodiles, by love of knowledge led,
To mark my figure, left their oozy bed;
Nor loaded camels, to provoke my stare,
Sublimely whirl'd, like straws, amid the air;
Nor, happy in a stomach form'd of steel,
On roaring lions have I made a meal.
Oh, had thy curious eye beheld, like mine,
The isle (Madeira) which glads the heart with
   richest wine!
Beneath its vines, with common clusters crown'd,
At eve my wand'ring steps a passage found,
Where rose the hut, and, neither rich nor poor,
The wife and husband, seated at the door.
Touch'd, when the labours of the day were done,
The wire of music to the setting sun;
Where, blest, a tender offspring, rang'd around,
Join'd their small voices to the silver sound.
But had *thine* eye this simple scene explor'd,
The man at once had sprung a sceptered lord;
Princes and princesses the *bearns* had been;
The hut a palace, and the wife a queen;
Their golden harps had ravish'd thy two ears,
And beggar'd all the music of the spheres.

NEW-YEAR'S DAY; TO CHARLOTTE.

Behold another year succeed!
But, Charlotte, though hast nought to dread,
 Since Time will ev'ry beauty spare:
Time knows what's *perfect*, and well knows,
'Twould take him *ages* to compose
 Another Damsel *half so fair.*

NIGHTINGALE, SONG TO.

Lone Minstrel of the moonlight hour,
  Who charm'st the silent list'ning plain,
A hapless Pilgrim treads thy bow'r,
  To hear thy solitary strain.

How soothing is the song of woe,
  To *me*, whom Love hath doom'd to pine!
For, 'mid those sounds that plaintive flow,
  I hear *my* sorrows mix with *thine*.

NIGHT.

Now Night, the negro reign'd—" Past one o'clock,"
The drowsy watchman bawl'd—from murky vaults,
The dough-fac'd spectres crowded forth—the eye,
The sunk, the wearied eye of Toil, was clos'd:
Mute, Nature's busied voice, her brawl and hum;
While Horror, creeping on the world of gloom,
Breath'd her dark spirit through the death-like
Now from her silver-fringed east the Moon [hour—
Peep'd on the Vast of shade—up-mounting slow,
In solemn stillness, till her lab'ring orb,
Freed from the caves of Darkness, gain'd its sphere,
And mov'd in splendid solitude along.

NOBLEMAN AND WIDOW.

A Dame near Goodwood own'd a sow, her all,
Which nat'rally did into travail fall,   [ter;
  And brought forth many a comely son and daugh-
On which the widow wond'rously was glad,
Caper'd and sung, as really she were mad—
  But tears oft hang upon the heels of Laughter.

At Goodwood dwelt a duke's great dog, call'd Thunder,
A dog, like courtiers, much inclin'd to plunder;
Bounce! without " by your leave," or least harangue,
Upon this harmless litter, Thunder sprang,
  And murder'd brothers, sisters, quick as thought;

Then sneak'd away, his tail between his *rear*,
Seeming asham'd—unlike great courtiers here,
  Who (Fame reporteth) are asham'd of *nought*.

Now to his Grace, the howling Widow goes,
Wiping her eyes so red, and flowing nose.

" Oh! please your Grace, your Grace's dev'lish
  " Thunder's confounded wicked chops   [dog,
  " Have murder'd all my beauteous hopes—
" I hope your Grace will pay for ev'ry hog."

What answer gave his Grace?—With placid brow,
  " Don't cry," quoth he, " and make so much foul
  " weather—   [sow,
" Go home, Dame; and when Thunder eats the
  " I'll pay for all the *family* together."

NOVELTY.

Lo! Novelty's a barber's strap or hone,
  That keenness to the razor-passions gives:
Use weareth out this barber's strap or stone;
  Thus 'tis by novelty, Enjoyment lives.

In *Love*, a sweet example let us seek:
I have it—Cynthia's soft luxuriant neck— [dwell!
  Fix'd on the charm, how pleas'd the eye can
How sighs the hand within the gauze to creep,
Mouse-like, and on the snowy hills to sleep,
  Rais'd by the most delicious, gentle swell;
Like gulls, those birds that rise, and now subside,
Blest on the bosom of the wavy tide.

But let the breast be *common*—all's undone;
Wishes, and sighs, and longings, all are gone!
Away the hurrying palpitations fly!
Desire lies dead upon the gazeless eye!
Sunk into insipidity is rapture!
Thus finisheth of Love the simple chapter!

Yes, Love's a cooing, sweet, persuasive pigeon,
Gains all the globe indeed to his religion;

Throughout the world his humble vot'ries pray,
And worship him exactly the same way.
Other religions kill—are torn by strife;
Love *kisses*, and, what's sweeter still, gives *life!*

NOVELTY, (2.)

Sweet is the tale, however strange its air,
That bids the public eye *astonish'd* stare!
Sweet is the tale, howe'er uncouth its shape,
That makes the world's wide mouth with wonder [gape!
Behold, our infancies in tales delight,
That bolt like hedge-hog-quills the hair upright.
Of ghosts how pleas'd is ev'ry child to hear!
To such is Jack the Giant-killer dear!
Dread monsters, issuing from the flame or flood,
Charm, tho' with horror cloth'd they chill the blood!
What makes a tale so sleepy, languid, dull?
Things as they happen'd—not of marvel full.
What gives a zest, and keeps alive attention?
A tale that wears the visage of invention:
A tale of lions, spectres, shipwreck, thunder;
A wonder, or first cousin to a wonder.
Mysterious conduct! yet, 'tis Nature's plan
To sow with wonder's seeds the soul of man,
That every where in sweet profusion rise,
And sprout luxuriant through the mouth and eyes!
What makes a girl the shops for novels rove?
The sweet impossibilities of love;
Quixotic deeds to catch the flying fair;
To pant at dangers, and at marvels stare.
What prompteth Chloe, conscious of the charms
That crowd the souls of swains with wild alarms,
To give the swelling bosom's milk-white skin
A veil of gauze so marvellously thin?
What but a kind intention of the fair
To treat the eyes of shepherds with a stare?
Behold! Religion's self, celestial dame,
Founds on the rock of miracles her fame:

A sacred building, that defies decay,
That sin's wild waves can never wash away!

OLD AGE, SONG TO BELLA.

Ah! tell me not that I am old,
   And bid me quit the billing dove;
Though many years have o'er me roll'd,
   My heart is still alive to love.
      Then tell me not that I am old.

When Beauty's blush delights no more,
   And Beauty's smile and sparkling eye;
When these no longer I adore,
   Then Pity yield the Bard *a sigh*.
     I will not quarrel to be told,
     Son of Apollo, thou art old.

OLD OLIVER, OR THE DYING SHEPHERD.

The Shepherd Oliver, grown white with years,
   Like some old oak weigh'd down by winter snows,
Now drew the village sighs, and village tears,
   His eye-lids sinking to their last repose.

Yet ere expir'd Life's trembling flame, and pale,
   Thus to the bleating bands around his door,
That seem'd to mourn his absence from their vale,
   The feeble Shepherd spoke, and spoke no more!

O my Flock! whose kind voices I hear,
   Adieu! ah, for ever adieu!
No more on your hills I appear,
   And together our pleasure pursue:

No more at the peep of the day,
   From valley to valley we rove,
'Mid the stramlets, and verdure of May,
   'Mid the zephyrs, and shade of the grove.

No more to my voice shall ye run,
   And, bleating, your Shepherd surround;
And, while I repose in the sun,
   Like a guard, watch my sleep on the ground.

When Winter, with tempest and cold,
  Dims the eye of pale Nature with woe,
I lead you no more to the fold,
  With your fleeces all cover'd with snow.

Oh, mourn not at Oliver's death!
  Unwept my last sand let it fall:
Ye too must resign your sweet breath,
  For *who* his *past years* can recall?

Oh, take all your Shepherd can give
  Receive my last thanks, and last sigh;
Whose simplicity taught me to *live,*
  And whose innocence teaches to *die!*

OWL AND THE PARROT.

An Owl fell desp'rately in love, poor soul!
Sighing and hooting in his lonely hole—
A Parrot, the dear object of his wishes,
Who in her cage enjoy'd the loaves and fishes,
In short, had all she wanted—meat and drink,
Washing and lodging—full enough, I think.

'Squire Owl most musically tells his tale;
His oaths, his squeezes, kisses, sighs, prevail:
Poll cannot bear, poor heart, to hear him grieve;
So opes her cage, without a " *By your leave;*"
Are married, go to bed with raptur'd faces,
Rich words, and so forth—usual in such cases.

A day or two pass'd amorously sweet;
Love, kissing, cooing, billing, all their meat:
  At length they both felt hungry—" What's for
    " dinner?   [Poll.—
" Pray what have we to eat, my dear?" quoth
" Nothing! by all my wisdom," answer'd Owl;
  " I never thought of that, as I'm a sinner;
" But, Poll, on something I shall put my pats—
" What say'st thou, Deary, to a dish of rats?"

" *Rats,* Mister Owl! d'ye think that I'll eat *rats ?*
" Eat them yourself, or give them to the cats,"

" Whines the poor bride, now bursting into tears.—
" Well, Polly, would you rather dine on *mouse?*
" I'll catch a few, if any in the house;
  " 'Thou shalt not starve, Love, so dispel thy fears."

" I won't eat rats—I won't eat mice—I won't:
" Don't tell me of such dirty vermin—don't:
  " O that within my cage I had but tarried!"
" Polly," quoth Owl, " I'm sorry, I declare,
" So delicate, you relish not our fare— [*married.*"
  " You should have thought of that before you

PAINTERS, ADVICE TO.

Aw'd I approach, ye sov'reigns of the brush,
With Modesty's companion sweet, a blush,
  And hesitation nat'ral to her tongue;
And eye so diffident, with beam so mild,
Like Eve's when Adam on her beauty smil'd,
  And led her blushing, nothing loath, along,
To give the lady a green gown so sweet,
On beds of roses, Love's delicious seat.

Ye landscape painters, may your gold streams
    sleep—
  Sleep, golden skies and bulls, and golden cows,
And golden groves and vales, and golden sheep,
  And golden goats the golden grass that browze,
Which with such golden lustre flame,
  As beat the very golden frame.

PANEGYRIC.

Pray do not fancy what I utter strange—
The love of flatt'ry is the soul's rank mange,
Which, though it gives such tickling joys,
Instead of doing service it destroys:
Just as the mange to lapdogs' skins apply'd,
Though pleasing, spoils the beauty of the hide.

PATIENCE, ODE TO.

Sweet daughter of Religion, modest fair,
  Thy hands upon thy bosom so *tranquille*,

With eyes to Heav'n, with so divine an air,
  So calmly smiling, so resign'd thy will;
Oh, sent to teach us, and our passions cool,
I wish thou hadst a little larger school.

Lo, man, so great his want of grace,
If he but cuts a pimple on his face
      When shaving;
Like man bewitch'd he jumps about,
Kicks up a most infernal rout,
  And seemeth absolutely raving;
And, lo! all this for want of thy tuition:
Thus travel souls of people to perdition!

PERFIDY, TO JULIA.

Much-injur'd Maid, who lies pale below,
  To *thee* a Pilgrim sad I steal away;
In mournful silence steal, o'erpower'd with woe,
  To bathe with floods of penitence thy clay.

Oh! can thy gentle ghost the *wretch* forgive,
  Who seeks thy sod at this lone hour of night—
A wretch, whose greatest hardship is to *live*,
  Who, dead to pleasure, sickens at the light?

Tir'd of the world, my heart no longer prays
  (What others covet) for extended years:
For who would madly court a length of days,
  To count (alas!) the moments by his tears?

PERFIDY, (2.)

To false delights the Youth of Britain fly,
  Who court for happiness the Wanton's arms;
Who darts on *all* the fond inflaming eye,
  And *choiceless* yields to *all*, for gold, her charms.

When in the Syren's fond embrace you sigh,
  And on her lips impress the burning kiss,
Doth Friendship mingle with th' unhallow'd joy,
  Or Love's pure spirit swell the surge of bliss?

When droops enjoyment, what is then the Fair?
  A *flow'r* that blooms, but quickly doom'd to fade

A *sun* that pours a momentary glare,
  And 'mid the tempest sinks o'erwhelm'd in shade.

O swains, to Modesty's fair daughters turn:
  By *mental* beauty let your hearts be led:
Bid by your flight the venal Fair-one mourn,
  And press in tears her solitary bed.

When round your neck her fondling arms she glues,
  And, bent to please, exhausts each winning art;
With false delights she shamefully subdues,
  And leads the Passions captive, not the *heart*.

PERVERSION OF CHARMS, A SONG.

Chloe, a thousand charms are thine,
  That give my heart the constant sigh!
Ah! wherefore let thy Poet pine,
  Who canst with ease his wants supply?

Oh, haste, thy charity display;
  With *little* I'll contented be:
The kisses which thou throw'st away
  Upon thy *dog*, will do for *me*.

PERSEVERANCE.

Thus went a Chambermaid a Flea espies,
How beats her heart! what lightnings fill her eyes!
To seize him, lo! her twinkling fingers spread,
And stop his travels through the realm of bed.

He hops—the eager damsel marks the jump;
Now sudden falls in thunder on his rump—
  She misses—off hops Bloodsucker again:
The nymph with wild alacrity pursues;
Now loses sight of him, and now gets views,
  Whilst all her trembling nerves with ardour strain.

Now fairly tir'd, with melancholy face,
Poor sighing Susan quits th' important chace:—
Once more resolv'd, she brightens up her wits,
And, furious, to her lovely fingers spits—
Thrice happy thought! yet, not to flatter,
'Tis not the cleanliest trick in nature.

Now in the blanket deep she sees him hide,
  Who, winking, fancieth Susan cannot see;
Now Susan drags him forth, with victor pride,
  The culprit crusheth; and thus falls the Flea!

PERSECUTION.

Then Persecution rais'd her Iron crow,
  And saw, with doting eye, her power display'd,
Enjoy'd the flying brains atev'ry blow, [flay'd.
  And bless'd the knives and hooks with which she

Grill'd, roasted, carbonaded, fricaseed
  Men, women, children, for the slightest things!
Burnt, strangled, glorying in the horrid deed;
  Nay, starv'd and flogg'd God's great Vicegerents, Kings!

But things are chang'd—assume a different tone.
  The teeth of Bishops are a *gentle* set;
Content, if nought is near to pick a bone;
  So little pamper'd with delicious meat.

No scorn now frowneth from a bishop's eye,
  No sounds of anger from his lips escape;
Save on a *Curate's* importuning sigh,
  Save on the penury of *ragged crape*.

PETITION OF LOVERS.

Ah! say not " No," unto my pray'r,
  For I have loved thee full long;
To these twin eyes thou art most fayre,
  Surpassing praise of sweetest song.
Then say not " No" unto my prayer,
But be so kynde as thou art fayre.

Why art thou with rare beauty blest?
  Only to bless mankynde, I wiss;
Not for to robbe the harte of rest,
  But fill it with a sea of blisse.
Then say not " No" unto my pray'r,
But be so kynde as thou art fayre.

The sunne was made to warme the harte,
　And plenty make, and kepe off blite;
So should thy beauty's sunne give birthe
　To our soul's harvest of delyte.
Then say not " No" unto my prayer,
But be so kynde as thou art fayre.

PILGRIMS AND THE PEAS, A TALE.

A brace of sinners for no *good*,
　Were order'd to the Virgin Mary's shrine,
Who at Loretto dwelt in wax, stone, wood,
　And, in a curl'd white wig, look'd wond'rous fine.

Fifty long miles had those sad rogues to travel,
With something in their shoes much worse than
In short, their toes, so gentle to amuse, [gravel;
The priest had order'd peas into their shoes:

The knaves set off on the same day,
Peas in their shoes, to go and pray;
　But very diff'rent was their speed, I wot;
One of the sinners gallop'd on,
Light as a bullet from a gun;
　The other limp'd as if he had been shot.

In coming back, however, let me say,
He met his brother rogue about half way; [knees;
Hobbling with out-stretch'd bum and bending
Damning the souls and bodies of the peas:
His eyes in tears, his cheeks and brows in sweat,
Deep sympathizing with his groaning feet.

" How now!" the light-toed, whitewash'd pilgrim
　　　" You lazy lubber!"— [broke;
" Odds curse it!" cried the t'other, " 'tis no *joke*—
" My feet, once hard as any rock,
　" Are now as soft as *blubber*.

" How is't that *you* can like a greyhound *go*,
　" Merry, as if that nought had happen'd, burn
　　　ye!"

"Why," cry'd the other, grinning, "you must know,
  "That just before I ventur'd on my journey,
    "To walk a little more at ease,
    "I took the liberty to boil *my* peas."

PITY.

When bleeding Nature droops to die,
  And begs from Heav'n th' eternal sleep,
Hard is the heart that cannot sigh,
  And curs'd the eye that scorns to weep.

How rich the tear by Pity shed!
  How sweet her sighs for human woes!
They pierce the mansions of the dead,
  And sooth the spectre's pale repose.

PLEASURE.

Blushing, I own, I've been in love with Pleasure,
Look'd on the Nymph's acquaintance as a treasure;
  Never pursued her once with scoff and *kisses*;
But caught the little Hussey in my arms;
Ran o'er the pretty garden of her charms,
  And pluck'd the cherries of her lips—call'd Kisses.

I never cast off Pleasure from me—no:
But hugg'd her, when I met with her—and *so:*
  For lo! a piece of velvet was *my* soul!
Black velvet, mind! which when the God of Day
Doth visit with his all enlivening ray,
  Enjoys the radiance, and *devours* the *whole.*

Velvet, unlike the marble rock indeed,
  Devoid of gratitude and grace;
Who, when the Sun would warm and gild his head,
  Flings back the blessing in his face.

PLYMOUTH CARPENTER AND THE COFFINS.

A carpenter, first cousin to the May'r,
  Hight Master Screw, a man of reputation,
Got leave, through borough int'rest, to prepare
  Good wooden lodgings for the Gallic nation;
I mean, for luckless Frenchmen that were dead:
And very well indeed Screw's contract sped.

For, lo! this man of economic sort
Makes all his coffins much too short:
Yet snugly he accommodates the dead—
Cuts off, with much *sang-froid*, the head;
And then, to keep it safe as well as warm,
He gravely puts it underneath the arm;
Making his dead man quite a Paris beau!
Hugging his jowl *en chapeau bras.*

POETS.

Kings did not scorn to press your backs of yore;
   But now, with humbled neck and patient face,
Tied to a thievish miller's dusty door,
   I mark thy fall'n and diregarded race.

To chimney-sweepers now a common hack;
Now with a brace of sand-bags on your back!
No gorgeous saddles your's—no iv'ry cribs;
No silken girts surround your ribs;

No Royal hands your cheeks with pleasure pat;
   Cheeks by a roguish halter prest—
   Your ears and rump, of insolence the jest;
Dragg'd, kick'd, and pummell'd, by a beggar's brat.

Thus, as I've said, your race is much degraded!
And much too is the Poet's glory faced!

POOR TOM, A BALLAD.

Now the rage of Battle ended,
   And the French for mercy call;
Death no more in smoke and thunder
   Rode upon the vengeful ball.

Yet, what brave and loyal Heroes
   Saw the Sun of morning bright—
Ah! condemn'd by cruel Fortune
   Ne'er to see the Star of Night.

From the main-deck to the quarter,
   Strew'd with limbs and wet with blood,
Poor Tom Halliard, pale and wounded,
   Crawl'd where his brave Captain stood.

"O, my noble Captain! tell me,
  "Ere I'm borne a corpse away,
"Have I done a Seaman's duty
  "On this great and glorious day?

"Tell a dying Sailor truly,
  "For my life is fleeting fast;
"Have I done a Seaman's duty?
  "Can there ought my mem'ry blast?"

"Ah! brave Tom!" the Captain answer'd,
  "Thou a Sailor's part hast done!
"I revere thy wounds with sorrow—
  "Wounds by which our glory's won."

"Thanks, my Captain; life is ebbing
  "Fast from this deep-wounded heart;
"But, O grant one little favour,
  "Ere I from the world depart:

"Bid some kind and trusty Sailor,
  "When I'm number'd with the dead,
"For my dear and constant Catherine
  "Cut a lock from this poor head!

"Bid him to my Catherine give it,
  "Saying, Her's alone I die!
"Kate will keep the mournful present,
  "And embalm it with a sigh.

"Bid him too this letter bear her,
  "Which I've penn'd with panting breath;
"Kate may ponder on the writing,
  "When the hand is cold in death."

"That I will," reply'd the Captain,
  "And be ever Catherine's friend."
"Ah! my good and kind Commander,
  "Now my pains and sorrows end!"

Mute towards his Captain weeping,
  Tom uprais'd a thankful eye—
Grateful then, his foot embracing,
  Sunk, with Kate on his last sigh!

Who, that saw a scene so mournful,
  Could without a tear depart?
He must own a savage nature—
  Pity never warm'd his heart!

Now in his white hammock shrouded,
  By the kind and pensive Crew,
As he dropp'd into the Ocean,
  All burst out—" Poor Tom, adieu!"

POVERTY.

No gunpowder my modest garrets hold,
  Dark-lantherns, blunderbusses, masks, and matches;
Few words my simple furniture unfold;
  A bed, a stool, a rusty coat in patches.

Carpets, nor chandeliers so bright, are mine;
  Nor mirrors, ogling Vanity to please;
Spaniels, nor lap-dogs, with their furs so fine:
  Alas! my little livestock are—my fleas!

POWER, (1.)

Dear as the voice of flatt'ry to the Proud;
Dear as to hackney-coachmen signs of rain,
Who count their shillings in a coming cloud,
  And, pious, pray for Noah's flood again;

So dear to Monarchs is that idol Pow'r!
  So dear is prompt obedience to a King!
Far, of resistance be the trying hour!
  God bless us! what a melancholy thing!

POWER OF GENIUS, (2.)

Thus when a Night of shade involves the pole,
And clouds on clouds in murky masses roll;
Sol through the darkness bids his radiance flow,
And robes with golden light the world below.

POWER, (3.)

Pow'r in the hands of Virtue is heav'n's *dew*,
That fost'ring feeds the flow'r of happiest hue:
  In Vice's grasp, it withers, wounds, and kills;

'Tis *then* the fang so fatal, form'd to make
A passage for the venom of the *snake*,
  That Nature's *life* with *dissolution* fills.

POWER OF TIME, (4.)

Come hither—pry'thee haste, old Time,
  And see what joys amongst us reign;
The bottle, Music, girls, and rhime,
  And Friendship's soul, delight the scene.

  Then hither pr'thee Time, repair,
    And taste the pleasures God should *share*.

The Tuscan juice profusely flows;
  We sing of Love and Delia's charms;
When morning warns us to repose,
  We clasp a fav'rite in our arms.

  Then hither pr'ythee, Time, repair,
    And taste the pleasures God should *share*.

Ah, could our joys *for ever* last!
But, Time, thy minutes fly too fast:
Yet wouldst thou pass *one* evening here,
Thou'dst make each *hour* a *thousand year*.

  Then hither pr'ythee, Time, repair,
    And taste the pleasures God should *share*.

POWER, OR THE KING OF SPAIN AND THE HORSE.

In sev'nteen hundred sev'nty-eight,
  The rich, the proud, the potent King of Spain,
Whose ancestors sent forth their troops to smite
  The peaceful natives of the western main,
With faggots and the blood-delighting sword,
To play the devil, to oblige the Lord!

I say, this King, in sev'nty-eight survey'd,
In tapestry so rich pourtray'd,
  A horse with stirrups, crupper, bridle, saddle:
Within the stirrup, lo! the Monarch try'd
To fix his foot, the palfry to bestride;
  In vain!—he could not o'er the palfry straddle!

Stiff as a Turk the beast of yarn remain'd,
And ev'ry effort of the King disdain'd,
Who 'midst his labours to the ground was tumbled,
And greatly mortified as well as humbled.

Prodigious was the struggle of the day:
The horse attempted not to run away; [grin,
   At which the poor chaf'd Monarch now 'gan
And swore by ev'ry saint and holy martyr,
He would not yield the traitor quarter,
   Until he got possession of his skin.

Not fiercer fam'd La Mancha's knight,
   Hight Quixote, at a puppet show,
Did with more valour stoutly fight,
   And terrify each little squeaking foe,
When bold he pierc'd the lines, immortal fray;
And broke their pasteboard bones, and stabb'd their hearts of hay.

And now a cane, and now a whip he us'd;
And now he kick'd and sore the palfry bruis'd;
Yet, lo! the horse seem'd patient at each kick,
And bore with Christian spirit whip and stick;
And what excessively provok'd this Prince,
The horse so stubborn scorn'd ev'n once to wince.

Now rush'd the Monarch for a bow and arrow,
To shoot the rebel like a sparrow;
And, lo! with shafts well steel'd with all his force,
Just like a pincushion, he stuck the horse!

Now with the fury of the chaf'd wild boar,
With nails and teeth the wounded horse he tore;
   Now to the floor he brought the subborn beast;
Now o'er the vanquish'd horse that dar'd rebel,
Most Indian-like, the Monarch gave a yell,
   Pleas'd on the quadruped his eyes to feast;
Blest as Achilles, when with fatal wound
He brought the mighty Hector to the ground.

Yet more to gratify his godlike ire,
He vengeful flung the palfry in the fire!

Showing his pages round, poor trembling things,
How dang'rous to resist the will of Kings.

PRAISE.

Sweet is the voice of Praise!—from eve to morn,
  From blushing morn to darkling eve again,
My Muse the brows of Merit could adorn,
  And, lark-like, swell the panegyric strain.

Praise, like the balm which evening's dewy star
  Sheds on the dropping herb and fainting flow'r,
Lifts modest, pining Merit from despair,
  And gives her clouded eye a golden hour.

PRAISE AND CENSURE.

Sweet is the voice of Praise!—Oh, soft as silk!
I wish the world's rude veins could run with milk!
Praise is rich sunshine-weather—all enjoy it—
  To catch it, ev'ry one is so alive—
  Blest as the bees, that humming from their hive,
So advantageously employ it.

But Censure is a cloud so cold, that scowls
  And spits—now souses us o'er head and ears,
Spoils our best clothes; and just like poor soak'd [fowls,
  Drooping, so foolish ev'ry man appears.

Praise is a pretty woman's soft white hand,
  That smoothing, tickles to our skin;
Censure, a currycomb we can't withstand,
  Brings blood, and puts us quite upon the grin!

PRAISE AND FLATTERY.

Fair Praise is sterling gold—all should desire it—
  Flatt'ry, base coin—a cheat upon the nation;
And yet, our vanity doth much admire it,
  And really gives it all its circulation.

Flatt'ry's a sly insinuating screw;
  The World—a bottle of Tokay so fine—

The engine always can its cork subdue,
  And make an easy conquest of the wine.

Praise is a modest, unassuming maid,
  As simply as a Quaker beauty drest:
No ostentation her's—no vain parade;
  Sweet nymph! and of few words possest;
Yet, heard with rev'rence when she silence breaks,
And dignifies the man of whom she speaks.

Flatt'ry's a pert French Milliner—a jade
Cover'd with *rouge*, and flauntingly array'd—
Makes saucy love to ev'ry man she meets,
And offers ev'n her favours in the streets.

PRETENSION.

A shabby fellow chanc'd, one day, to meet
The British Roscius in the street,
  Garrick, on whom our nation justly brags;
The fellow hugg'd him with a kind embrace:
" Good Sir, I do not recollect your face,"
  Quote Garrick—" No!" replied the man of rags.

" The boards of Drury you and I have trod
  " Full many a time together, I am sure,"—
" When?" with an oath, cry'd Garrick—" for by
  " I never saw that face of your's before!   [G—
" What characters, I pray,
" Did *you* and *I* together play?
" Lord!" quoth the fellow, " think not that I
    mock:
" When *you* play'd Hamlet, Sir, *I* play'd the
    Cock."*

PRIDE RIDICULED, OR THE OLD MAID.

A winking, hobbling, crabbed, proud Old Maid,
Whose charms had felt a heavy cannonade
From Time's strong batt'ry,—to whose lofty nose
A rotten reputation was a rose,

* In the Ghost Scene.

Liv'd in a country town—there spit her spite,
And dwelt on Scandal's stories with delight.

Proud of her name (though poor) indeed was she;
  In genealogies, and epicure;
Knew, to a hair, each person's pedigree,
  From that of splendour to the most obscure.

Boasting a certain portion of that blood,
Not to be wash'd away by Noah's flood.

This Lady on a certain darksome night,
From cards returning by a lantern's light;
  The lantern by her servant Betty held,
Who walk'd before this Dame, to shew the way;
When thus it happen'd *sadly* let me say,
  Such is th' unhappiness of blinking *Eld*—

As her two eyes so dim could only *stare*,
And therefore wanted cleaning and repair;
Against *some* head, *her* poking head she popp'd—
Dash'd with confusion, suddenly she stopp'd,
Drew back, and bent for *once* her rusty knee—
" I beg your pardon, Sir," said she.

Then follow'd Mistress Betty.—" Bless us, Bet,
" Tell me, who was the Gentleman I met;
  " Whose face I bounc'd so hard against with
Bet could not for her soul the laugh resist—[mine?"
" A *Gentleman!*—a *Jack-ass*, Ma'am, you kiss'd;
  " I hope you found Jack's kisses very fine."

" An *Ass!*" with anger swelling, screech'd the
    Dame—
" An *Ass!*—Lord! Betty, I shall die with *shame!*
" Give me a knife—I'll spoil the rascal's note;
" Give me a knife—I'll run and cut his throat.
" Betty, don't say a word on't—that, alas!
" I curtsied, and ask'd pardon of an *Ass!*"

PROLIFIC WIFE, A TALE.

A Man of some small fortune had a wife,
Sans doute, to be the comfort of his life;
   And pretty well they bore the yoke together:
With little jarring liv'd the pair one year;
Sometimes the matrimonial sky was clear;
   At times 'twas dark, and dull, and hazy weather.

Now came the time when mistress in the straw
   Did, for the world's support, her screams prepare;
And Slop appear'd with fair obstetric paw,
   To introduce his pupil to our air;
Whilst in a neighb'ring room the husband sat,
Musing on this thing now, and now on that;

   Now sighing at the sorrows of his wife;
Praying to Heav'n that he could take the pain;
But recollecting that such pray'rs were vain,
   He made no more an offer of his life.

Alone, as thus he mus'd in solemn study,
Ideas sometimes clear, and sometimes muddy,
   In Betty rush'd with comfortable news:
" Sir, Sir, I wish ye joy, I wish ye joy;
" Madam is brought to bed of a fine boy,
   " As fine as ever stood in shoes."

" I'm glad on't, Betty," cry'd the master:
" I pray there may be no disaster;
   " All's with your mistress, *well,* I hope?"
Quoth she, " All's well as heart can well desire
" With Madam and the fine young 'Squire;
   " So likewise says old Doctor Slop."

Soon happy Betty came again,
Blowing with all her might and main;
   Just like a grampus, or a whale;
In sounds, too, that would Calais reach from Dover:
" Sir, Sir, more happy tidings; 'tis not over—
   " And Madam's brisker than a nightingale:

"A fine young lady to the world is come,
"Squalling away just as I left the room:
"Sir, this is better than a good estate."   [his pate.
"Humph," quoth the happy man, and scratch'd
Now gravely looking up—now looking down;
Not with a smile, but somewhat like a frown—
"Good God!" says he, "why was not I a cock,
"Who never feels of breeding brats the shock;
    "Who, Turk-like, struts amidst his madams pick-
"Whilst to the hen belongs the care   [ing,
"To carry them to eat, or take the air,
    "Or bed beneath her wing the chicken?"

Just as this sweet soliloquy was ended,
He found affairs not greatly mended;
    For in bounc'd Bet, her rump with rapture jigg-
"Another daughter, Sir—a charming child."[ing:
"Another!" cry'd the man, with wonder wild;
    "Zounds! Betty, ask your Mistress if she's *pig-
        ging.*"

PRUDENCE.

Prudence! for man the very best of wives,
Whom Bards have seldom met with in their lives;
Prudence! a sweet, obliging, courtsying lass,
Fit through this hypocritic world to pass!
Who kept at first a little peddling shop,
Swept her own room, twirl'd her own mop,
Wash'd her own smocks, caught her own fleas,
And rose to fame and fortune by degrees;
Who, when she enter'd other people's houses,
Till spoke to was as silent as a mouse is;
And of opinions, though possess'd a store,
She left them, with her pattens, at the door.

PRUDENCE AND PASSION.

Sweet child of summer, who from flow'r to flow'r,
    To sip each odour, sport'st on silken wing;

I greet thy presence 'mid the golden hour,
 Whilst with the birds the vales of Serdi ring.

I see thee perching on each rose's bloom;
 From fragrance thus to fragrance wont to glide;
Now from the tender vi'let waft perfume;
 Now fix'd upon the lily's snowy pride.

Though blest art thou—my bliss is greater still;
 I kiss the bosom of the brightest Fair!
The charms of Adel all my senses fill;
 And whilst those charms I press, her love I share.

PRUDERY, (1.)

Prudery, I hate the hag, whose breath would blight
 The opening buds of gentle May and June;
Blest to spread darkness, like the cloud of night,
 That hangs a dirty malkin, on the moon!

Oh, be the wounded *Prude* who dares *reprove*,
 And furious charge the feeble Maid or Dame,
A Nymph, who, cautious of the Torch of Love,
 Has never *singed her honour* at its flame.

PRUDERY, (2.)

To her grave will I follow the Fair,
 Nor blush her pale corse to sustain;
Whose graces, alas! were her snare,
 Which Prudery beheld with disdain.

So fair and unguarded a form
 Drew the lightnings of danger around;
A victim she fell to the storm,
 And blush'd a sweet wreck on the ground!

I have seen thee when lovers around,
 In hope of thy favour, would stand;
And in sorrow depart, when they found
 Not a smile, nor a kiss from thy hand.

And saw, when no more it inspir'd,
 No longer our hearts to beguile,

From thy bosom, when Rapture retir'd,
  And the loves had withdrawn from thy smile.

And, when conquest, alas! was no more,
  I heard thee in poverty moan,
Asking alms, but in vain, at the door
  Of the mansion that once was thy own.

Unwept shall poor Jessica lie,
  And neglected be scorn'd on the bier?
Tho' hard Virtue refuse her a sigh,
  Yet Pity shall give her a tear.

RE-APPEARANCE OF THE SUN.

Thus oft it happens that the sky
Throws horrid glooms upon the eye;
Breeds clouds like malkins—old, black rags indeed!
  The lands below look dismal drear!
  When suddenly, see Sol appear!
He pushes boldly through the Dark, his head!
At once the shadows to his glories yield,
And cheerful radiance flies from field to field.

REGRET.

Say, lonely maid, with down-cast eye,
  Oh Delia! say, with cheeks so pale,
What gives thy heart the lengthen'd sigh,
  That tells the world a mournful tale?

O tell me, doth some favour'd youth,
  With virtue tir'd, thy beauty slight;
And leave those thrones of love and truth,
  That lip, and bosom of delight?

Perhaps to nymphs of other shades,
  He feigns the soft, impassion'd tear;
With sighs their easy faith invades,
  That treach'rous won *thy* witless ear.

Let not *those* maids thy envy move,
  For whom his heart may seem to pine;
That heart will ne'er be blest by love,
  Whose guilt could force a pang from *thine*.

REITERATION, OR CÆSAR AND THE FOG.

Cæsar, upon a summer's golden day,
Got early from his bed to smell his hay,
  And see if all his fowls were safe and sound;
And likewise see what traps had legs and feet
Belonging unto men who wish'd to treat
  Their chaps with chicken on forbidden ground.

Enter a General (Carpenter) low bowing,
Scraping, and, mandarin-like, nodding, ploughing,
  With nose of rev'rence sweet, the humble grass.
" Hæ, General, hæ? what news, what news in
    " town?"
" None, Sire."—" None, Gen'ral?—Gen'ral, hæ,
    " none, none?"
  " Nothing, indeed, O King, is come to pass."

" Strange! strange!—what, what—see nothing on
    " the way?
  " Hæ, hæ?" cry'd Cæsar, all for news agog.
" Nothing, my Liege—no nothing, I may say,
  " Excepting upon Hounslow, Sir, a *fog*."

" Fog upon Hounslow, Gen'ral? *large* fog, hæ,
  " Or *small* fog, Gen'ral?"—" Large, an't please
    " you, Sire." [fog, pray?
" Strange, vastly strange!—what, *large* fog, *large*
  " Yes, yes, yes—*large* fog, that I much admire."

Cæsar and Carpenter now talk'd of wars,
Of cannon, bullets, swords, and wounds, and scars:
  When, in the middle of the fight, the King
Sudden exclaim'd—" Fog upon Hounslow, hæ?
" Large fog too, Gen'ral?—well, go on, on, pray—
  " Strange! very strange!—extr'ordinary thing!"

Now dwelt the Gen'ral on the battle's rage, [gage,
Where muskets, muskets—guns, great guns, en-
  Redd'ning with blood the field, and stream, and
    ·bog;

G

When, rushing from the murd'rous scene of glory,
The Monarch sudden marr'd the Gen'ral's story—
  "Fog upon Hounslow, Gen'ral—large, large fog?"
"Yes, Sir," said Carpenter unto the King—
"Strange, very strange! extr'ordinary thing!"

At length the Gen'ral *finish'd*—lucky elf;—
  With much politeness, and much sweat and pain.
"Thank God!" the Gen'ral whisper'd to himself—
  "Curse me, if ever I find *fogs* again!"

REVENGE.

Revenge's company for ever shun:
  Too much of danger frequently appears:
A kind of weak and overloaded gun,
  Bursting with horrid crash about our ears.

Ridiculous the triumph will be found,
When, for a penny's worth we lose a pound.

We should not rage for trifling matters,
  And blust'ring kick the world about;
It shews the folly of our natures,
  For a pin's head to make a rout.

Lord! grant a little *fungus* on the *vine*
  And *olive*, yielding oil and juice and gladness;
Who'd root up the whole tree for't? nought but
'Twere idiotism, stupidity, and madness [swine,

REVENGE, OR THE PIG AND MAGPIE, A FABLE.

Cocking his tail, a saucy prig,
A Magpie hopp'd upon a Pig,
  To pull some hair, forsooth, to line his nest;
And with such ease began the hair-attack,
As thinking the fee-simple of the back
  Was by *himself*, and not the *Pig*, possest.

The Boar look'd up, as thunder black, to Mag,
Who, squinting down on him, like an arch wag,
  Inform'd Mynheer some bristles must be torn;

Then busy went to work, not nicely culling;
Got a good handsome beakfull by good pulling,
　And flew, without a " Thank ye," to his thorn.

The Pig set up a dismal yelling;
Follow'd the robber to his dwelling,
　Who, like a fool, had built it 'midst a bramble:
In, manfully, he sallied, full of might,
Determin'd to obtain his right,
　And 'midst the bushes now began to scramble.

He drove the Magpie, tore his nest to rags,
And, happy on the downfall, pour'd his brags:
　But ere he from the brambles came, alack!
His ears and eyes were miserably torn,
His bleeding hide in such a plight forlorn,
　He could not count ten hairs upon his back.

REJECTION.

Sore troubled by the tooth-ach, Lubin ran
To get the murd'rer of his quiet *drawn;*
　An Artist in an instant whips it out—
" Well, Master Snag—hæ? what *has* to pay?"—
" A shilling"—" Younds; a shilling do ye zay?"
　With a long staring face, replies the Lout.

" Lord! why Ize did not *veel it*—'twas *nort in it*;
" You *knows* ye wern't about it half a minute:
　" To gee *zo much* Ize cursedly unwilling—
" Lord! vor a tooth, but yesterday old Slop
" Did drag me by the head about his shop
　" *Three times,* poor man, and *only ax'd a shilling.*"

RELAPSE.

Thus when an earthquake bids Jamaica tremble;
On Sunday all the folks to church assemble;
　To soothe Jehovah, so devoutly studying—
Prostrate they vow to keep his holy laws:
Returning home, they smite their hungry craws,
　And scarce indulge them with a slice of pudding.

Deeming, in earthquake-time, a dainty board,
A sad abomination to the Lord!

Ere Sunday comes again, their hearts recover;
The tempest of their fears blown over.
  Fled ev'ry terror of the burning lake,
They think they have no business now with church;
So, calmly leave th' Almighty in the lurch;
  And sin it—till it gives a *second* shake.

RIGOUR, PARENTAL.

A cat is with her kittens much delighted;
  She licks so lovingly their mouths and chins:
At ev'ry danger, lord! how puss is frighted!
  She curls her back, and swells her tail, and grins,
Rolls her wild eyes, and claws the backs of curs
Who smell too curious to her children's furs.

No more she sports and pats them, frisks and purs:
Plays with their twinkling tails, and licks their furs:
But when they beg her blessing and embraces,
Spits, like a dirty vixen, in their faces.

Nay, after making the poor lambkins fly,
She watches the dear babes with squinting eye;
And if she spies them with a bit of meat,
Springs on their property, and steals their treat.

ROBIN-REDBREASTS, ODE TO SOME IN A CATHEDRAL.

Sweet Minstrels of the sounding choir,
Your ditties soothe, delight, inspire;
That wake the echoes from their deep repose;
  Soft echoes dying through the Dome,
  (As though from Spirits of the tomb)
Soon as your voices sink in plaintive close!

Again, O! lull me with your lay,
And let it never die away.
How welcome rise your hymns to Heav'n,
In gratitude so simply giv'n!

Sweet Race, to you I turn again!
Now all the ear-distracting Train
   Has left the dome, the cherub Peace restor'd.—
How different *your* delighting throats!
How different all *your* liquidnotes!
   How different too *your* merits with the Lord!

Yes! all is hush'd the vault along;
Resume, resume the choral song,
   And make atonement for the horrid cry.
Lo! in her shroud, near yonder tomb,
A gentle Spectre breaks the gloom!
   She listens! lo! she listens with a sigh!
Ah! bid your airs divinely flow,
And, soothing steal a tear from woe.

The deep'ning shades of Night prevail,
They wrap the hollow-sounding aisle,
   And steal each column from the eye:
What solemn solitude around!
Here Nature's true Sublime is found,
   Hence Thought should travel to the sky!

Mild tenants of the Fane, farewell!
At early dawn I quit my cell,
   And haste, a Pilgrim, to these shrines again:
Simplicity will join my way,
And listen to your mingled lay,
   And, list'ning, learn a lesson from *your strain.*

ROMISH PRIEST, A TALE.

A Parson in the neighbourhood of Rome,
   Some years ago—how many, I don't say—
Handled so well his heav'nly broom,
   He brush'd, like cobwebs, sins away.

With shoulders, arms, and hands, this Priest devout,
   So well his evolutions did perform;
His pray'rs, those holy small-shot, flew about
   So thick!—it seem'd like taking Heav'n by *storm!*

Well then! this Parson was so much admir'd,
  So sought, so courted, so desir'd,
Thousands with putrid souls, like putrid meat,
  Came for his holy pickle, to be sweet.

Such vast impressions did his sermons make,
He always kept his flock *awake*—
In *summer* too—hear, parsons, this strange news,
Ye who so often preach to nodding pews!

A neighb'ring town, into whose people's souls,
  Sin, like a rat, had eat large holes,
Begg'd him to be their tinker—their hole-stopper—
  For, gentle reader, sin of such a sort is,
  It souls corrodeth just as *aqua fortis*
    Corrodeth iron, brass, or copper.

They told him they would give him better pay,
  If he'd agree to change his quarters;
Protesting when his soul should leave its clay, [tyrs.
  To rank his bones with those of Saints and Mar-

This was a handsome bribe, all Papists know!
But stop—his parish would not let him go:
Then surly did the *other* parish look,
And swore to have the man by *hook* or *crook*.

  Now in the fire was all the fat:
    Just as two bulldogs pull a cat,
Both parishes with furious zeal contended—
  So heartily the holy man was hugg'd,
  So much from place to place his limbs were lugg'd,
That very fatally the battle ended!
  In short, by hugging, lugging, and kind squeezes,
  The man of God was pull'd in fifty pieces!

SAPPHO, SONG TO.

At length, O fairest Nymph, farewell!
Let sighs alone my passion tell;
  With tears I quit thy arms:

Adieu each eve of pure delight;
Adieu each morn with rapture bright;
   Adieu thy *brighter* charms!

Where'er by Fate condemn'd to stray,
Where Phœbus pours the golden day,
   Or sleeps beneath the wave,
Thine image will my path pursue,
And ever present on my view,
   Detain me still a slave.

In vain I roam—I strive in vain
To break, O beauteous Maid, thy chain!
   Yet why my fetters part?
Ev'n now thy sighs, my sighs approve;
Ev'n now thy love, returns my love,
   And yields me heart for heart!

SATIRISTS.

Upon me what a host I've got!
Who by their black abuses boil their pot.
Ay, that's the reason—wide-mouth'd Hunger calls;
And from the hollows of each stomach bawls!

Thus the poor silk-worms, born to bless mankind,
   Whilst for the shiv'ring world the robe they spin,
In ev'ry ring a thousand insects find,
   Gnawing voraciously their harmless skin.

And thus the lambs, whose useful fleeces treat
   With coats and blankets people of all stations,
By preying maggots are beset,
   Harb'ring whole stinking nations;
Which, from their backs, the crows so kindly pick,
Enough to make a Christian sick.

Oh, would some critic crow but eat the pack
Now nestling in my lyric back,
That daily in their hosts increase,
And try to spoil the finest fleece!

SECURITY.

Thus, when a breach is made in some fair town,
The Volunteers, agog to gain renown,
Beg hard to enter first, to fall with glory,
And give Posterity a *beauteous story*;
While *wiser some*, averse to *making mould*,
Would rather *tell* the tale, than have it *told*.

SEDUCTION.

Lo, poor deserted Julia! once how fair;
With cheek so wan and pale, and scatter'd hair;
  Her gentle heart by Love's mad tempest torn!
She runs, she stops, and wildly stares around!
Now nails the eye of thought into the ground!
  Now, drown'd in tears, she lifts its beam forlorn;

Pale as the moon, amidst the midnight storm!
When rains and driving clouds her face deform!

She grasps the earth—the sod her fingers tear—
  Now wearied, disappointed, to the skies
  She lifts her lids of woe and plaintive sighs,
(Soul-piercing sound!) " Alas, he is not here!"
Rich pearls of sorrow from their fountains stray,
And drop (too precious for the ground!) away.

" How could he, cruel, give my heart a blow?"
  She moans—now sits upon the bank and sings;
Oft breaks her dirge with lengthen'd sighs of woe,
  And, pausing, mutters incoherent things.

Now plucking lilies from the sod, she cries,
  " Sweet flow'rs, I once was innocent like *you*;
" The tear, alas! a stranger to these eyes-[knew."
  " Nor blush my cheek, nor wound my bosom

Now with a smile, and now with melting wail,
She whisp'ring tells of Colin's Love the tale.
Again her mind is on the wing! she starts!
Hope to her eyes her eagle beam imparts!

Sudden she springs from earth—" He's there, he's
" I see him pass the flood—dear Colin, dear![there;
" Thy Julia calls thee—'tis thy Julia, stay—
" Thy Julia calls thee—wherefore haste away?
" Thy Julia loves thee—do not, cruel, fly?
" Stay, or thy Julia's heart with grief will *die*—
" If danger urge, that danger let *me* share;
" Thou must not live unwatch'd by Julia's care."

Sweet wretch! in vain her feet the phantom chace!
  Wildly she plunges 'mid the torrent's roar—
She shrieks! her arms her fancied Love embrace,
  She grasps the gulph—ah! soon to grasp no more.

Lost Maid! in vain the shepherds try to *save!*
Breath'd is her spirit in the whelming wave!
No longer doom'd Life's bitter cup to taste,
Behold her hours of woe for ever past!

Deaf to the song of Flatt'ry, now, her ear!
Deaf to a *Demon's* whispers once so dear!
  Cold too the bosom of the once warm maid!
The heart that swell'd with Love's delicious sighs,
Still, in its silent cell of darkness lies,
  And dim her eyes in Death's eternal shade.
Those orbs that sparkling bade a world adore,
Ah, doom'd to sparkle, and to *stream* no more!

Lo! on the bank her pale limbs stretch'd along,
Amidst the sorrows of a rural throng!
A sight to strike the voice of Rapture mute,
And wake the *tenderest* string of Pity's lute!

Thee, thee, her murd'rer, Vengeance soon shall find,
Sure blood-hound, trace thee in the weeping wind;
Pursue thee where the Desert grins with death:
  For not to *man* again shalt thou return—
  A shrinking world thy Cain-like form shall spurn,
And kneeling curse thee with its keenest breath.

Smote and unburied, shall thy carcase lie:
Afar, affrighted shall the vultures fly;
  Of fiends like thee, a *breathless* fiend, afraid;

And, lo! the frowning Genius of the gloom
Shall shun the Solitude that hails thy doom,
   And bid each savage seek a *distant* shade.

SELFISHNESS.

Thus saw I once a Cuckoo in a cage,
And Thrush, a very *Purser* of the age!
Boil'd beef, and cabbage, had the Pair for dinner;
When, lo, the Thrush (a knowing *Purser-sinner,*)
Soon as he met a bit of beef, the elf
Sans ceremonie gobbled it *himself:*
But when a *stump of cabbage!*—chang'd his note,
He ramm'd it down the gaping *Cuckoo's* throat.

SERVILITY, (1.)

Thus when a little fearful puppy meets
A noble Newfoundland dog in the streets,
   He creeps, and whines, and licks the lofty brute;
Curls round him, falls upon his back, and then
Springs up and gambols—frisks it back agen,
   And crawls in dread submission to his foot;
Looks up, and hugs his neck, and seems t'intreat
With ev'ry mark of terror, not to eat him. [him,

The Newfoundland dog, conscious of his might,
   Cocks high his tail and ears, his state to show;
Then lifts his leg (a little unpolite)
   And almost drowns the supplicant below.

SERVILITY, (2.)

How pleasant 'tis the Courtier clan to see!
So prompt to drop to richer men the knee;
To start, to run, to leap, to fly;
And gambol in their better's eye!
And, if expectant of some high employ,
How kicks the heart against the ribs, for joy!

How rich the incense to the titled nose!
How liquidly the oil of Flatt'ry flows!
But should the Nabob turn from sweet to sour,
Which cometh oft to pass in half an hour,

How alter'd instantly the Courtier clan!
How faint! how pale! how woe-begone, and wan!

SHAME.

Shame putt'st me of the Morning much in mind,
Who seems afraid to peep upon mankind;
So slow her motions! all so very slow!
And then her cheeks so deep with crimson glow:

But safe deliver'd of her boy, the Sun,
The lusty lad, so proud his race to run,
   Mounts high, exulting in his birth;
Dries up her tears, her blushes puts to flight,
Tow'rs in bold triumph o'er the cloud of night,
   And pours a flood of radiance o'er the earth.

SHEPHERD'S (THE) OLD DOG.

The old Shepherd's Dog, like his master, was grey;
  His teeth all departed, and feeble his tongue;
Yet where'er Corin went, he was follow'd by *Tray*;
  Thus happy through life did they hobble along.

When Winter was heard on the hill and the plain,
  And torrents descended, and cold was the wind,
If Corin went forth 'midst the tempests and rain,
  Tray scorn'd to be left in the chimney behind.

At length in the straw *Tray* made his last bed;
  For vain, against death, is the stoutest endeavour;
To lick Corin's hand he rear'd up his weak head,
  Then fell back, clos'd his eyes, and, ah! clos'd
     them for ever.

Not long after *Tray* did the Shepherd remain,
  Who oft o'er his grave with true sorrow would
    bend;
And, when dying, thus feebly was heard the poor
    swain,
    " O bury me, neighbours, beside my old Friend!"

SHEPHERD'S PIPE, A PASTORAL.

Lo! the Pipe of poor Colin, mute, mute, how it lies!
No more to be swell'd by his hopes, or his sighs!
" Go, leave me!" said he, " since unpriz'd by the Fair,"
Then he wistfully flung it away in despair. [Fair,"

Who, like Colin, could give it of rapture the sound,
Which the echoes with raptures repeated around?
Or give it, like Colin, a soul to complain?
And who like the Shepherd e'er gave it in vain?

'Twas here, at the peep of the morn, that he stray'd
To soothe with its music the ear of the maid!
'Twas here that he wak'd its sweet voice, to delight
(Not Philomel's sweeter!) her slumber at night.

But vain were his vows, and the voice of his reed;
The heart of poor Colin was fated to bleed! [laid,
See his grave! near yon tree his pale relick's are
'Mid the bow'r that he planted, of silence and shade.

Ah! blame not the Nymph who was deaf to his tale,
Since her heart was betroth'd to a Youth of the Vale,
Come, Virgins, we'll gather the flow'rs of the grove,
And strew on the victim of Sorrow and Love.

Thus as the Flocks amid the valley feed,
  Behold! the Bellweather, the Rover,
Like mortals, fickle, takes it in his head
  To taste a neighbouring field of clover!
He *dares* th' opposing hedge, he beats it *Hollow*—
Mounts, leaps, and all the tribes of fleeces follow!

SIGHS.

O cruel Maid, adieu! adieu!
  Thy loss I ever shall deplore;
A thousand griefs my path pursue,
  And joy shall gild thy path no more.

Lost to the world—of hope bereft—
  I view my fate with streaming eyes—
By Love forgot, by Friendship left,
  By all deserted but my sighs.

SILENCE, (1.)

Now Silence in the country stalk'd the dews,
As if she wore a flannel pair of shoes,
Lone list'ning, as the Poets well remark,
To falling mill-streams, and the mastiff's bark;
To loves of wide-mouth'd cats, most mournful tales;
To hoot of owls amid the dusky vales,
To hum of beetles, and the bull-frog's snore,
The spectre's shriek, and ocean's drowzy roar.

SILENCE, (2.)

O Silence! to our earth by Wisdom giv'n,
Yet from the *fashionable* circles driv'n;
To breathing Zephyrs, and the limpid stream,
Whose murmurs sweetly sooth the shepherd's dream,
For thee I often sigh, but sigh in vain,
When Folly stuns me with her noisy train.

SILENCE, TO AN OWL.

" Thou solemn Bird on yonder ivy'd tow'r,
  " Wilt thou exchange thy nature, Owl, with me?
" Happy to take possession of thy bow'r,
  " I here protest I would exchange with *thee*.

" When to his western bed the Sun retires,
" Obeys the curfew, and puts out his fires;
  " And Evening, blushful harbinger of Night,
" Gems with the dews of health the drooping flow'r;
" With cooling zephyr fans the sober hour,
  " And wakes the * songstress to the fading light;

" Forth, 'mid the deep'ning gloom I pass,
" And tread the moist reviving grass,

* The nightingale.

" To meet the tribes by Nature made
" To crawl and wing the world of shade !
" Ye harmless nations, with averted eyes,
" The sons of men your silent world despise,
  " Because their eyes no punch-houses behold ;
" Because no mobs, nor fires, nor thieves appear ;
" Because no riots with their yells they hear ;
  " No brothels, scenes of sallow fate unfold.

SLEEP.

Now Morpheus (in compassion to mankind,
Made, by his magic, deaf, and dumb, and blind)
Amus'd with dreams man's ambulating soul,
To recompense him for the time he stole ;
Bade the beau dance, his Delia melt away,
Who box'd his ears so cruel through the day ;
Of ancient damsels eas'd the lovesick pains,
Brought back lost charms, and fill'd their laps with
Gave placid cuckoldom a constant dame ;   [swains ;
To brainless authors, bread and cheese and fame ;
Made driv'ling rulers schemes of wisdom plan,
And Nature's rankest coward kill his man.

SLIGHTED LOVE.

When Night spreads her shadows around,
  I will watch with delight on thy rest ;
I will soften thy bed on the ground,
  And thy cheek shall recline on my breast.

Love heeds not the storm, and the rain ;
  On *me*, let their fury descend ;
This bosom shall scorn to complain,
  While it shelters the life of a friend.

What tempts thee to wander away ?
  To *another*, ah ! dost thou depart ?
Believe me, in time thou wilt say,
  None e'er lov'd thee like Phillida's heart.

Though resolv'd from a Mourner to fly;
  To mem'ry thou still shalt be dear:
The winds shall oft waft thee a sigh,
  And the ocean convey thee a tear.

SOLDIER AND VIRGIN MARY, A TALE.

A Soldier at Loretto's wond'rous chapel,
  To parry from his soul the wrath divine,
That follow'd mother Eve's unlucky apple,
  Did visit oft the Virgin Mary's shrine;
Who ev'ry day is gorgeously deck'd out,
  In silks, or velvets, jewels, great and small,
Just like a fine young lady for a rout,
  A concert, opera, wedding, or a ball.

At first the Soldier at a distance kept,
  Begging her vote and interest in heav'n:
With seeming bitterness the sinner wept,
  Wrung his two hands, and hop'd to be forgiv'n;
Dinn'd her two years with Ave-Mary flummery;
  Declar'd what miracles the dame could do,
Ev'n with her garter, stocking, or her shoe,
  And such like wonder-working mummery.

What answer Mary gave the wheedling sinner,
Who nearly, and more nearly mov'd to win her,
The musty mouth of Hist'ry doth not mention;
And therefore I can't tell but by invention.

One day as he was making love and praying,
And pious Aves, thick as herrings, saying,
  And damned sins so manifold confessing,
He drew, as if to whisper, very near,
And twitch'd a pretty diamond from her ear,
  Instead of taking the good lady's blessing.

Then off he set with nimble shanks,
Nor once turn'd back to give her thanks:
A hue and cry the thief pursu'd,
Who, to his cost, soon understood
That he was not arriv'd beyond the paw
Of that same long-legg'd tiger, christen'd Law.

With horror did his Judges quake:
　As for the tender-conscienc'd Jury,
They doom'd him quickly to the stake,
　Such was their dev'lish pious fury.

However, after calling him hard names,
　They ask'd if ought he had in vindication,
To save his wretched body from the flames,
　And sinful soul from terrible damnation?

The Soldier answer'd them with much *sang-froid*,
Which seem'd to show, of sin, a conscience void,
　That if they meant to kill him, they might kill:
As for the di'mond which they found about him,
He hop'd their Worships would by no means doubt him,
　That Madam *gave* it him from pure good will.

The answer turn'd both Judge and Jury pale:
　The punishment was for a time deferr'd,
Until his Holiness should hear the tale,
　And his infallibility be heard.

The Pope to all his Counsellors made known
　This strange affair—to Cardinals and Friars,
Good pious gentlemen, who ne'er were known
　To act like hypocrites, and thieves, and liars.
The question now was banded to and fro,
If Mary had the pow'r to *give* or *no?*

That Mary *could not* give it, was to say,
　The wonder-working Lady wanted pow'r—
This was a stumbling block that stopp'd the way—
　This made Pope, Cardinals, and Friars low'r.

To save the Virgin's credit, lo!
　And keep secure the di'monds that were left;
They said, she *might,* indeed, the gem bestow,
　And consequently it might be no theft:

But then they pass'd immediately an Act,
That ev'ry one discover'd in the fact
Of taking presents from the Virgin's hand,
Or from the Saints of any land,

Should know no mercy, but be led to slaughter,
Flay'd here, and fry'd eternally hereafter.

Ladies, I deem the moral much too clear
　　To need poetical assistance;
Which bids you not let men approach too near,
　　But keep the saucy fellows at a distance;
Since men you find, so bold, are apt to seize
Jewels from ladies, ev'n upon their *knees!*

SOLITUDE.

Thou art my Goddess, Solitude—to thee,
Parent of dove-ey'd Peace, I bend the knee!
O with what joy I roam thy calm retreat,
Whence soars the lark amid the radiant hour,
Where many a varied chaste and fragrant flow'r
　　Turns coyly from Rogue Zephyr's whisper sweet!
Blest Imp! who wantons o'er thy wide domain,
And kisses all the Beauties of the plain:

Where Health so wild and gay, with bosom bare,
And rosy cheek, keen eye, and flowing hair,
Trips with a smile the breezy scenes along,
And pours the spirit of content in song!

Thus tastes are various, as I've said before—
These damn most cordially what *those adore.*

SOLOMON AND THE MOUSE-TRAP.

A mighty man, *hight* Solomon, one day,
In quest of novelty pursu'd his way;
Like great Columbus, that fam'd navigator,
Who found the world we've lost, across the water.
But rather on a somewhat narrower scale,
Lo! on dry land the Gentleman set sail:

　　That day it chanc'd to be his will,
　　To make discoveries at Salt-hill:
Where bounce he hopp'd into a widow's house,
Whose hands were both employ'd so clever,
Doing their very best endeavour
　　To catch that vile free-booter, Monsieur Mouse;

Whose death she oft did most devoutly pray for,
Because he eat the meat he could not pay for:
Eager did Solomon so curious clap
His rare round optics on the widow's trap
  That did the duty of a cat;
And always fond of useful information,
Thus wisely spoke he with vociferation, [that?"
 " What's that!—What, what? hæ, hæ? what's
To whom repli'd the mistress of the house,
" A trap, an't please you, Sir, to catch a mouse."

" Mouse!—catch a mouse!" said Solomon with
   glee—
" Let's see—let's see—'tis comical—let's see—
" Mouse!—mouse;"—then pleas'd his eyes began
   to roll—   [cry'd—
" Where, where doth he go in?" he marvelling
" There," pointing to the hole, the dame reply'd.
" What! here?" cry'd Solomon; " this hole? this
  " hole?"

Then in he push'd his finger 'midst the wire,
That with such pains that finger did inspire,
 He wish'd it out again with all his soul:
However, by a little squall and shaking,
He freed his finger from its piteous taking—
 That is to say, he got it from the hole.

" What makes the mouse, pray, go into the trap?
 " Something," he cry'd, " that must their palates
  " please."
" Yes," answer'd the fair woman, " Sir, a scrap
 " Of rusty bacon, or of toasted cheese."

" Oh! oh! said Solomon, oh! oh! oh! oh!
" Yes, yes, I see the meaning of it now:
" The mouse goes in, a rogue, to steal the meat,
" Thinking to give his gums a pretty treat."
Then laugh'd he loudly, stretch'd his mouth a mile,
Which made the muscles of the widow smile.

"Let's see, let's see," cry'd Solomon—"let's see—
"Let me, let me, let me, let me, let me, let me."
Then took he up some bacon, and did clap
A little slice so clever in the trap:
Thus did he, by his own sole, sage advice,
Induce himself to bait a trap for mice!

Next day the Man of Wisdom came,
All glorious, to the house of this fair dame,
  To know if Master Mouse had smelt to bacon;
When, lo! to fill with joy his eager eyes,
And load those staring optics with surprise,
  A real mouse was absolutely taken!

Around the room the captive mouse he bore,
Insulting the poor pris'ner o'er and o'er;
Laughing, and peeping through the wire,
As if his eyes and mouth would never tire!

Six days the Man of Wisdom went
Triumphant to Salt-hill, with big intent
  To catch the bacon-stealing-mouse;
Six mice successively proclaim'd his art,
With which, safe pocketed, he did depart,
  And show'd to all his much astonish'd house.

But pleasures will not last for aye;
Witness the sequel of my lay;
The widow's vanity, her sex's flaw,
  Much like the vanity of other people—
A vapour, like the blast that lifts a straw,
  As high, or higher, than Saint Martin's steeple—

For, lo! by this same vanity impell'd,
  And to a middle-siz'd balloon,
With *gas* of consequence sublimely swell'd,
  She bursted with th' important secret soon.

Loud laugh'd the tickled people of Salt-hill;
  Loud laugh'd the merry Windsor folks around:

This was to Solomon an ugly pill!
  Her fatal error soon the widow found;
For Solomon relinquish'd mouse-campaign,
  Nor deign'd to bait the widow's trap again!

SORROWS OF THE POOR SOLDIER.

War is a wholesome blister for the back;
  Draining away the humours all so *gross*;
Else would the Empire be of guts a sack—
  A Falstaff—woolsack—an unwieldly Joss.

War yieldeth such rare spirits to a nation!
Giving the blood so brisk a circulation!
A kingdom, and a poet, and a cat,
Should never, never, never be *too fat*.

SORROW, (1.)

Farewell, O farewell to the day,
  That smiling with happiness flew!
Ye verdure and blushes of May,
  Ye songs of the linnet, adieu!

In tears from the vale I depart;
  In anguish I move from the Fair:
For what are those scenes to the heart
  Which Fortune has doom'd to despair?

With envy I wander forlorn,
  At the breeze which her beauty has fann'd;
And I envy the bird on the thorn,
  Who sits watching the crumbs from her hand.

I envy the lark o'er her cot,
  Who calls her from slumber, so blest;
Nay, I envy the nightingale's note,
  The Syren who sings her to rest.

On her hamlet *once more* let me dwell—
  One look! (the *last* comfort!) be mine—
O Pleasure, and Delia, farewell!
  Now, Sorrow, I ever am *thine*.

SORROW, (2.)

Folks cannot be for ever sniv'ling—no!
With fountain noses that for ever flow—
　The world would quickly be undone;
Widows, and lovelorn girls, poor souls, would die;
And for his rich old father, sob and sigh,
　And hang himself, *perchance* a *hopeful* son;

And, for their cats that happ'd to slip their breath,
Old maids, so sweet, might mourn themselves to
Sorrow may therefore have her decent day, [death;
And smiling Pleasure come again in play.

No! folks can't brood for ever upon Grief:
　Pleasure must steal into her place at last;
Thus then the heart from horror finds relief,
　Snatch'd from the cloud by which it is o'ercast.

SPECTRE, THE, OR JENNY'S COMPLAINT.

The night was still and full of fear,
　And all the world seem'd dead;
When pond'ring on poor Robin Gray,
　I went with sighs to bed.

There, while my heart did heave with grief,
　The moon, that wand'rer pale,
In at my window peep'd and shin'd
　So faint against the wall.

I clos'd my eye in vain to sleep,
　And sigh'd, " Ah! well-a-day!"
For then I dwelt on my dear love,
　My buried Robin Gray.

As on my arm I lean'd my head,
　All dreary and forlorn,
My hair did drink the briny tears
　That down my cheek did mourn.

Sudden a cloud, like ink so black,
　The moon's pale face o'ercast;

The window shook, and horror howl'd,
  Amid the hollow blast.

But my poor bleeding heart forlorn
  Did sink with no dismay,
Since often it had wish'd to *die*
  For dear auld Robin Gray.

Now did a spectre form appear,
  All aged, pale, and wan;
And, by his visage, I could spy
  He was my last auld Man.

Now on my bed-side did he sit,
  As harmless as a dove;
And though he had two hollow eyes,
  They look'd with tend'rest love.

Forth from their sockets then did rush
  Full many a drop of woe;
So from the cave or rugged rock
  The pearly waters flow.

"Jesu!" I cry'd, and stretch'd my arms
  To clasp him round the waist;
But nought of his poor spectre drear
  My longing arms embrac'd.

"Oh! Jenny (then he said) in vain
  "Thy arms would clasp me in;
"For Spirits, such as thou behold'st,
  "Have neither bones nor skin."

Full on his visage did I gaze,
  All hurried with surprise;
And, eager to devour each look,
  My soul rush'd through my eyes.

Now did I strive to catch his hand,
  That press'd so often mine;
But 'twas in vain—'twas nought but air,
  Which made my heart to pine.

"And art thou happy, then," I cry'd,
  "In this thy present state?"

He smil'd like Angels then, and said,
  " God well hath chang'd my fate.

" Let Innocence, O Jane, be thine,
  " And peace shall dwell with thee;
" And when just Heav'n shall call thee hence,
  " With Robin thou shalt be."

With that he look'd a sweet farewell,
  And rais'd each wetted eye;
Then glided off, and, as he went,
  I heard the kindest sigh.

Auld Robin's kindnesses to me,
  Whilst we in love did live,
Deserve more *streams* from these sad eyes,
  Than they have *drops* to give.

The evening that he sought his grave
  Did wear a dismal gloom:
And all who did the burying see,
  With eyes so red went home.

The honest tribute of their tears,
  I thought was sweetest fame;
And when I die, God grant my bier
  Be sprinkled with the same!

The harmless children, too, in bands,
  Did pour their little sighs,
And on the coffin near the grave
  They strain'd their wat'ry eyes.

And when into the earth below
  His corpse at length was giv'n,
They look'd towards each other's eyes,
  And sigh'd, " He's gone to Heaven.'

Then on his grave they sat them down,
  And lisp'd his name with praise,
Till all the little wights did wish
  To be auld Robin Gray's.

STUTTERING.

The broken language such a mouth affords
Are heads and tails, and legs and wings of words,
That give imagination's laughing eye
A lively picture of a giblet pye.—

SULTAN AND HIS DOG.

A mighty Sultan of the East,
  On every dainty us'd to feast;
(How different from the beggar and his bone!)
  Who drank, too, Burgundy, I ween:
  For every thing *in style* was seen,
Becoming one who sat upon a *throne*.

  It chanc'd that War, all powerful war,
  So apt the wisest schemes to mar,
And change the master to the humble *slave*,
  Fix'd on the Sultan his steel claws,
  Clapp'd an embargo on his jaws,
And *words, hard words,* instead of victuals, gave.

  The King was *beat*—to prison sent, in short—
  Coarse was his fare, the coarsest sort:
A jug of milk was sent to him for dinner:
  Enter a dog, who, while the King
  Was musing on some *lofty thing*,
Stole slily to the milk, the thievish sinner;
Forc'd in his head, and lapp'd *each drop*, no doubt,
But could not get his head felonious *out*.

  So off, with his jugg'd jowl, the rascal ran,
The Monarch, smiling, mark'd the theft,
And of his dinner though bereft,
  With much good-humour thus began:

  " Fortune's a *fickle* Dame: but *yesterday*
  " An hundred Camels scarce could bear
  " My *quantitics* of kitchen-ware,
    " And now a *Cur* can carry it away!

SUN, ODE TO THE.

O thou, bright Ruler of the day,
To whom unnumber'd millions pray,
   And, kneeling, deem thee all divine;
Eternal foe of inky Night,
Who puttest all her imps to flight,
   Receive the Poet's grateful line.

I own I love thy early beam,
That gilds the hill, and vale, and stream,
   And trees, and cots, and rural spires;
And, happy, 'mid the vallies' song,
   I listen to the minstrel throng,
   And, thankful, hail thy genial fires.

Yet, lo! the Lords of this huge place (London)
Care not three straws for thy bright face.
   Nay, thy rich lamp with curses load,
When thou gett'st up, they go to bed;
And when the nightcap's on *thy* head,
   They stare, and flit like owls abroad.

The Footmen too, with winking eyes,
Abuse thy journey up the skies;
   Messieurs Postillions, *Mesdames* Cooks—
Content to lie a-bed all day,
They hate, alas! thy rising ray,
   And curse thy all-observing looks.

Vex'd to their houses to be driv'n,
The Great retire from routs, their heav'n,
   And break up in a horrid passion,
And cry, " In *times of old*, indeed,
" The *tasteless world* a sun might need,
   " But now the fool is out of fashion.

" About his business let him go,
" And light on *other* systems throw,
   " *Vulgars!* that never wax-lights handle!
" Nay, while a *mutton* light remains,
" A *sun* with us no credit gains,
   " But yields to ev'ry *farthing candle.*"

H

SUN, HYMN TO THE, (2.)

O sacred fount of life to All!
Before thy glorious beam we fall,
   And strike with raptur'd hand the lyre;
To thee we lift our wond'ring eyes;
To thee the hymn of morn shall rise,
   And bless thy mounting orb of fire.

Hail to that Orb, from whose rich fountain flow
Beams that illume and glad the world below.
Unseen by thee had Nature mourn'd;
No smile her Æthiop cheek adorn'd;
Pale Night had spread her spectr'd reign,
And death-like Horror rul'd the scene.

All hail the beams that Night destroy,
And wake an op'ning world to joy!
Bright spreading o'er the vast of gloom,
That chase the spectres to their tomb.

SUN AND PEACOCK.

A Peacock, mounted on a barn one day,
   Blest with a *quantum sufficit* of pride,
All consequence amid the solar ray,
   Spread with a strut his circling plumage wide.

"Good morrow, (quoth the Coxcomb,) Master Sun;
   "Your brassy face has greatly been admir'd—
"Now pray, Sol, answer me—I'm not in fun—
   "What is there in it to be so desir'd?
     "If I have any eyes to see,
     "And, that I have, is clear to *me*,
"My *tail* possesses far more splendid grace,
"By far more beauty than your Worship's *face*."

The Sun look'd down with smiles upon the fowl,
Supposing it at first an owl:
   And thus with gravity reply'd, "Sir, know,
"That though unluckily my *Worship's face*
"Seems far beneath your *tail* in splendid grace,
   "Still to *my face that* glitt'ring *tail* you owe."

"Poh! (quoth the Peacock) Master Sun,
"Your *Highness* loves a bit of *fun*."
 "I beg your pardon," answer'd Sol again—
"And, if you please, I'll condescend to show
"How much to *me* you ev'ry moment owe
 "The boasted beauties of your waving train."

"Agreed, with all my soul!" the Bird reply'd,
In all the full blown insolence of pride;
 "To credit such a tale I'm not the noddy:
"Prove that the glorious plumage I display
"Owes all its happy colours to thy ray,
 "D-m'me I'll tear my feathers from my body."

The challeng'd Sun in clouds withdrew
His flaming beams from ev'ry view,
 And o'er the world a depth of darkness spread:
The bats their churches left, to wing the air;
The cocks, and hens, and cows, began to stare,
 And sulky went all supperless to bed;
For not an almanack had op'd its lips
About so very wondrous an eclipse.

The Peacock too, amongst the rest
Of marv'lling fowl and staring beast,
Turn'd to his feathers with some doubt,
Amaz'd to find his hundred eyes put out;
Indeed all nature appear'd as black
As if old Sol had popp'd into a sack.

Pleas'd with his triumph, from a cloud,
The Sun, still hiding, call'd aloud,
 "Well! can ye merit to *my face* allow? [eyes?
"What's now your colour? where your hundred
"The mingled radiance of a thousand dies? [now?"
 "Speak, Master Peacock, what's your colour

"What colour!" quoth the Bird, as much asham'd
As courtiers high by loss of office tam'd—
"To own the truth, much-injur'd Phœbus, know,
"I'm not one atom better than a *crow*.

"I see my folly--pity my poor train;
"And let thy goodness bid it shine again."
Tyrants of *eastern* realms, whose subjects' noses,
Like a smith's vice, your iron pow'r incloses;
Who treat your people just like dogs or swine;
The meaning of my tale, can ye divine?
If *not*, go try to *find* it, I beseech ye,
And do not let your angry subjects *teach* ye.

SAINTS.

Yet, 'tis not strange, that *Kings* should lose repute,
   Consid'ring man's so *nat'rally* a brute.
  Ev'n Saints themselves have lost their reputation:
Rome formerly had thirty thousand gods;
And now, I warrant ye, 'tis odds,   [tion.
  They own scarce *one* through all the Romish na-
Alas! who now believes in sticks and stones,
Old rags, and hair, and nails, and marrow bones?

Saint Agnes, that sweet lady, void of sin,
Was stripp'd, poor gentlewoman, to her skin,
   And, for religion, carried to the stews;
When, as the lady was so bare,
God gave her such a quantity of hair,
   As reached unto her very shoes.

When to the bawdy-house arriv'd the Dame,
An angel from above commission'd came,
And spread around her such a heav'nly light,
   As dazzled every body's sight.

However a young officer, a buck,
Wishing prodigiously to have a *look*,
   Dash'd forth, to pierce the middle of the light,
Meaning to violate the Dame so good;
Which meaning, when the Devil understood,
   He choak'd the wanton Rogue out-right.

Such is the tale! true ev'ry crumb;
Now, no more heeded than Tom Thumb.

SATIRE ON ROYAL FAVOUR, (1.)

To have Kings lean familiar on one's shoulder,
Becoming thus the royal arm-upholder,
 A heart of very stone must glad!
Oh! would some King so far himself demean,
As on *my* shoulder but for *once* to lean,
 Th' excess of joy would nearly make me mad!
How on the honour'd garment I should dote,
And think a glory blaz'd around the coat!

Blest, I should make this coat my coat of arms,
In fancy glitt'ring with a thousand charms;
 And show my children's children o'er and o'er:
" Here, Babies," I should say, " with awe behold
" This coat—worth fifty times its weight in gold:
 " This very very coat your grandsire wore!
" Here," pointing to the shoulder, I should say,
" Here Majesty's *own* hand so sacred lay :" [utter;
 Then p'rhaps repeat some speech the King might
As—" Peter, how go the sheep a score? what?
 what?
" What's cheapest meat to make a bullock fat?
 " Hæ? hæ? what, what's the price of country
 " butter?"

Then should I, strutting, give myself an air,
 And deem my house adorn'd with immortality:
Thus should I make my children, calf-like, stare,
 And fancy grandfather a man of quality:
And yet, not stopping here, with cheerful note,
The Muse should sing an *ode* upon the coat.

SATIRE ON CYNTHIA, (2.)

Cynthia, the Dryads are in tears,
 Because thou visit'st not their groves;
The Graces grieve, and Cupid swears,
 And very sullen look the Loves.

The Naiads through the vales declare,
 No rill of theirs shall purl away;

The Lark too scorns to mount in air,
  And vows to keep his nest all day.

The Sun resolves to hide his head,
  And blot his lustre from the skies;
Yet that were little loss indeed,
  While we possess'd that pair of eyes.

Well then, to *pique* thee, from each lay,
  From all my lines I'll blot thy *name*.
" Aye, do," I hear thee smiling say,
  " And blot what only gives them *fame*."

SECLUSION, TO DELIA.

Ah, foolish Delia! since you hate
  That people of your charms should prate;
Give *me* that face, that air divine,
  And in exchange accept of *mine*.

Thus shall I gain my heart's desire,
  And set a raptur'd world on fire—
You'll too be pleas'd, (no longer doubt ye)
  As folks won't say one word about ye.

SELF-IMPORTANCE.

Do, Hoy, inform me—who is she on board,
That seems the Lady of a first-rate Lord,
With stomach high push'd forth as if in scorn,
Like craws of ducks and geese o'ercharg'd with corn:
Dress'd in a gorgeous damask gown,
Which roses, like the leaves of cabbage, crown;
With also a bright petticoat of pink,
To make the eye from such a lustre shrink?

Yes, who is she, the Patagonian dame,
  As bulky as of Heidelberg the tun;
Her face, as if by brandy taught to flame,
  In blaze superior to the noonday sun—

With fingers just like sausages, fat things;
And loaded much like curtain rods with rings?

Yes, who is she that with a squinting eye
Surveys poor passengers who sick'ning sigh;
Sad, pale-nos'd, gaping, puling, mournful faces;
Deserted by the blooming, smiling Graces;
That, reaching o'er thy side, so doleful throw
The stomach's treasure to the fish below?
'Tis Madam Bacon, proud of wordly goods,
   Whose first spouse shav'd and bled—drew teeth, made wigs;
Who having by her tongue destroy'd poor Suds,
   Married a wight that educated pigs!

But, hark! she speaks! extremely like a man!
Raising a furious tempest with her fan—
" Why, Captain, what a beastly ship! good God!
" Why, Captain, this indeed is very odd!
" Why, what a grunting dirty pack of doings!
" For heav'n's sake, Captain, stop the creatures' sp-w-gs."

Now, hark! the Captain answers—" Mistress Ba-
" I own I can't be with *such matters* taken. [cou,
  " I likes not vomitings no more than *you*;
" But if so be that gentlefolks be sick,
" A woman hath the bowels of *Old Nick*, [Jew."
" Poor souls, to bung their mouths—'twere like a

Majestic Mistress Bacon speaks agen!
" *Folks* have no bus'ness to make others sick:
" I don't know, Mister Captain, what you mean
  " About your Jews, and bowels of *Old Nick*:
" If all your cattle will such hubbub keep,
" I know that I shall leave your stinking ship.

" Some folks have dev'lish dainty guts, good Lord!
" What bus'ness have such cattle here aboard?
" *Such gang indeed* to foreign places roam!
" 'Tis more becoming them to sp-w at home."

But, hark! the Captain *properly* replies—
" Why, what a breeze is here, G-d d-mn my eyes!

"God bless us, Mistress Bacon! who are *you?*
"Zounds, *Ma'am,* I say *my* passengers *shall sp-w.*"

SELIMA, MIRZA'S COMPLAINT TO.

Where is the Nymph of Sardi's green domain,
　The Nymph whom every Bard of Persia sings?
To find the wand'rer out, and sooth my pain,
　Sweet bird of morn, to Mirza lend thy wings.

But wherefore seek the Nymph of Sardi's vale,
　Who sullen flies where Horar's waters roll;
Scorns all my plaints, that mourn along the gale,
　And scorns the surge of grief, that sinks my soul?

Ah! can that cheek, where Beauty's summer dwells,
　Retain a smile, whilst Mirza's sorrows flow?
Ah! can that heart, that every softness swells,
　Forbear to heave on Mirza's songs of woe?

Come, like the morn, pure virgin of delight,
　And, blushing, chase the cloud of Mirza's fears;
Come, like the sun upon the dews of night,
　And, with thy radiance, smile away my tears.

SERVILITY TO KINGS.

Lo! when from Windsor mighty Kings arrive,
Like London mack'rel, all alive!
Terrenes of flatt'ry are prepar'd so hot
By courtiers—a delicious pepper-pot;
Which, to be sure, the royal maw devours,
Kings boasting very strong digestive pow'rs.

A Pointer thus, lock'd up a week,
Half starv'd, and longing for a steak;
Behold him now turn'd loose so wild to eat—
Gods! how he gobbles down the broth and meat!
Yes, flatt'ry-soups are all prepar'd so hot,
As I have hinted, a fine pepper-pot:

Side-dishes too, of curtsies, bows, and scrapes,
With stare and wonder in all sorts of shapes;
Attentions darting from the full stretch'd eye,
That not a royal glance may pass unheeded by.

SIGNIOR SQUALINI AND LORD ———.

A Lord, most musically mad,
Yet with a taste superlatively bad,
  Ask'd a squeal eunuch to his house one day;
A poor old *semivir*, whose throat
Had lost its love-resounding note,
  Which Art had giv'n, and Time had stol'n away.

" Signor Squalini," with a solemn air,
The Lord began, grave rising from his chair,
  Taking Squalini kindly by the hand—
" Signor Squalini, much I fear
" I've got a most unlucky ear,
  " And that 'tis known to all the music band.

" Fond of abuse each fiddling coxcomb carps;
" And, true it is, I don't know flats from sharps:
  " Indeed, Signior Squalini, 'tis no hum;
" So ill doth music with my organs suit,
" I scarcely know a fiddle from a flute,
  " The hautbois from the double drum.

" Now, though with Lords, a number, of this nation,
" I go to Op'ras, more through fashion
  " Than for the love of music, I could wish
" The world might think I had some little taste,
" That those two ears were tolerably chaste;
  " But, Sir, I am as stupid as a fish.

" Get me the credit of a *Cognoscente*,
" Gold sha'n't be wanting to content ye."

" *Bravissimo!* my Lor," replied Squalini,
  With acquiescent bow, and smile of suavity;
" De nobleman muss never look de ninny."—
  " True," grunts the noble Lord, with German gravity.

" My Lor, ven men vant money in der purse,
  " Dey do no vant de vorld to tink them *poor*;
" Because, my Lor, dat be von shabby curse;
  " Dis all same ting wid ignorance, my Lor."

"Right," cried his Lordship in a grumbling tone,
Much like a mastiff jealous of his bone.

"But first I want some technicals, Signor."—
Bowing, the Eunuch answer'd—"Iss, my Lor;
"I teash your Lordship queekly, queekly all—
"Dere vat be call de *sostenuto* note,
"Dat be ven singer oppen vide de troat, [squawl];
"And den for long time make de squawl, squawl,
"Mush long, long note, dat do continue while
"A man, my Lor, can valk a mile.

"My Lor, der likewise be de *cromatique*,
"As if de singer vas in greef, or sick,
"And had de colick—dat be ver, ver fine:
"De high, oh, dat musician call *soprano*;
"De low voice, *basso*; de soff note, *piano*—
"*Bravoura*, queek, bold—here Marchesi shine.
"Dis Mara, too, and Billington, do know—
"*Allegro*, quick; *Adagio*, be de slow;
"*Pomposo*, dat be manner make de roar:
"*Maestoso*, dat be slow, grand, nobel ting,
"Mush like de voice of Emperor, or de King;
       "Or *you*, my Lor,
"When in de House you make de grand oration,
"For save, my Lor, de noble Englis nation.
"*Da Capo*, dat's, my Lor, begin again,
"And end, my Lor, wid de first strain."

"Signor Squalini," cried the happy Lord,
"The Op'ra is begun, upon my word—
"*Allons*, Signor, and hear me—mind,
"As soon as ever you shall find
"A singer's voice above or under pitch,
"Just touch my toe, or give my arm a twitch."

"Iss, iss, my Lor, (the Eunuch strait reply'd,)
"My Lor, I sheet close by your Lordship side;
"And den, accordin to your Lordship wish,
"I give your Lordship elbow littel twish."

Now to the Op'ra, music's sounds to hear,
The old Castrato and the noble Peer
   Proceeded—Near the orchestra they sat,
Before the portals of the singers' throats!
The critic couple mousing for bad notes
   With all the keenness of a hungry cat.

Now came an *out-of-tunish* note—
The Eunuch twitch'd his Lordship's coat: ["Psha!"
   Full-mouth'd at once his Lordship roar'd out
Sudden the orchestra, amaz'd, turn round,
To find from whence arose the critic sound,
   When, lo! they heard the Lord, and saw!

The Eunuch kept most slily twitching;
   His frowning Lordship all the while,
     (Not in the cream of courtly style)
Be-*dogging* this poor singer, that be-*bitching*;
Uniting, too, a host of damning *pshas*,
Reap'd a most plenteous harvest of applause;
Grew from that hour a Lord of tuneful skill,
And, though the Eunuch's dead, remains so still.

SIMPLICITY, OR THE CURATE.

How difficult, alas! to please mankind!
   One or the other ev'ry moment *mutters*:
This wants an eastern, that a western wind;
   A third, petition for a southern, utters.

Some pray for rain, and some for frost and snow:
How can Heav'n suit *all* palates?—I don't know.

Good Lamb, the Curate, much approv'd,
Indeed by all his flock *belov'd*,
   Was one dry summer begg'd to pray for rain:
The Parson most devoutly pray'd—
The pow'rs of pray'r were soon display'd;
   Immediately a *torrent* drench'd the plain.

It chanc'd that the Churchwarden, Robin Jay,
Had of his meadow not yet *sav'd* the hay:
   Thus was his hay to *health* quite past restoring.

It happen'd too that Robin was from home;
But when he heard the story, in a foam
   He sought the Parson, like a lion roaring.

" Zounds! Parson Lamb, why, what have you been doing?
" A pretty storm indeed ye have been brewing!
  " What! pray for *rain* before I *sav'd* my hay!
" Oh! you're a cruel and ungrateful man!
" *I* that for ever help you all I can;
  " Ask you to dine with me and Mistress Jay,
" Whenever we have something on the spit,
" Or in the pot a nice and dainty bit;

" Send you a goose, a pair of chicken,
" Whose bones you are so fond of picking;
  " And often too a cag of brandy!
" *You* that were welcome to a treat,
" To smoke and chat, and drink and eat;
  " Making my house so very handy!

" *You*, Parson, serve one such a scurvy trick!
" Zounds! you must have the bowels of Old Nick.
" What! bring the flood of Noah from the skies,
" With *my* fine field of hay before your eyes!
" A numscull, that I wer'n't of this aware!—
" Curse me but I had stopp'd your pretty pray'r!"

" Dear Mister Jay! (quoth Lamb) alas! alas!
" I never thought upon your field of grass "

" Lord! Parson, you're a fool, one might suppose—
" Was not the field just underneath your *nose?*
" This is a very pretty losing job!"—
" Sir," quoth the Curate, " know that Harry Cobb
  " Your Brother Warden join'd, to have the pray'r."—
" Cobb! Cobb! why this for Cobb was only *sport:*
" What doth Cobb own that any rain can *hurt?*"
  Roar'd furious Jay as broad as he could stare.

" The fellow owns, as far as I can *larn*,
" A few old houses only, and a barn; [*him?*
" As that's the case, zounds ! what are show'rs to
" Not Noah's flood could make *his* trump'ry *swim*.

" Besides—why could you not for *drizzle* pray ?
" Why force it down in *buckets* on the hay ?
" Would I have play'd with *your* hay such a freak ?
" No ! I'd have stopp'd the weather for a week."

" Dear Mister Jay, I do protest
" I acted solely for the best;
　" I do affirm it, Mister Jay, indeed.
" Your anger for this *once* restrain,
" I'll never bring a drop again
　" Till you and all the Parish are *agreed*."

SIMPLICITY.—TO DELIA.

Delia, thou really dost not know thy worth—
　Nature has made a very idle blunder,
To give thee roses, lilies, and so forth,
　Eyes, dimples, merely to excite our *wonder*.

See *other* girls, of far inferior charms !
Behold them spreading through the world alarms,
　With not one quarter of thy ammunition ;
Dark'ning the dang'rous air with dreadful darts ;
Transfixing Lovers' livers, heads, and hearts,
　Putting the beaux into a sad condition ;

Whilst thou, so idle, mak'st not *Man* thy game,
As though the *creature* were not worth thy aim,
But, Delia, come—on *me* thy prowess try ;
Let loose the lightnings of thy coal-black eye ;
　Attack, pursue—I like the dang'rous strife—
Sweet Nymph, 'tis ten to one thou lay'st me low ;
Yet do not *kill* me, my dear gen'rous foe,
　But make me *pris'ner to thy arms for life.*

SIR J. BANKS AND THE FLEAS.

One morning, at his house in Soho-Square,
As, with a solemn, awe-inspiring air,
　Amidst some royal sycophants he sat;
Most manfully their masticators using,
Most pleasantly their greasy mouths amusing
With coffee, butter'd toast, and birds-nest chat;
In Jonas Dryander, the fav'rite, came,
Who manufactures all Sir Joseph's fame— [say?"
　" What luck?" Sir Joseph bawl'd—" say, Jonas,
" I've boil'd just fifteen hundred," Jonas whin'd;
" The dev'l a one chang'd colour could I find."
　Intelligence creating dire dismay!

Then Jonas curs'd, with many a wicked wish,
Then show'd the stubborn fleas within the dish.
" How!" roar'd the President, and backward fell—
" There goes, then, my hypothesis to hell!"—
　And now his head in deep despair he shook;
Now clos'd his eyes; and now upon his breast,
He, mutt'ring, dropp'd his sable beard unblest;
　Now twirl'd his thumbs, and groan'd with piteous
　　　look.

Now gaining speech, the parasitic crowd
Leap'd up, and roar'd in unison aloud:

" Heav'ns! what's the matter! dear Sir Joseph,
　　　pray?"
　Dumb to their questions the Great Man remain'd:
The Knight, deep pond'ring, nought vouchsaf'd to
　Again the *Gentlemen* their voices strain'd: [say,
Sudden the President of Flies, so sad,
Strides round the room, with disappointment mad,
　Whilst ev'ry eye enlarg'd with wonder rolls;
And now his head against the wainscot leaning,
" Since you *must* know, *must* know (he sigh'd) the
　　　meaning,
　" Fleas are not lobsters, d-mn their souls!"

SKITTLE-PLAYING, OR GOOD FRIDAY, A TALE.

Sir Harry, a high priest, and deep divine,
Ambitious much 'mid *modern* Saints to shine,
  On a Good Friday ev'ning took an airing:—
Not far had he proceeded, ere a sound
Did the two ears of this *good* priest *astound*;
  Such as loud laughs, commix'd with some small swearing.

Now in an orchard peep'd the Knight so sly,
With such a staring, rolling, frenzied eye;
  Where, lo! a band of rural swains were blest:—
Too proud to *join* the *crew*, he wav'd his hand,
Beck'ning to this unholy playful band—
  Forth came a *boy*, obedient to the Priest.

" What wicked things are ye all doing here,
" On this most solemn day of all the year?"
" Playing *to* skittles," said the simple lad.
" Playing at skittles!—Devils, are ye mad?
" For *what?*"—" A Jack-ass, Sir," the boy replies—
" A *Jack-ass!*" roars the Priest, with wolf-like eyes:
" Run, run, and tell them Heav'n will not be sham-
    m'd—
" Tell them this instant, that they'll all be *damn'd!*"

" I *wull*, Sir Harry—*iss*, I *wull*, Sir Harry"—
Then off he set th' important news to carry,
  To warn them what dread torments would ensue:
But suddenly the scamp'ring lad turn'd round,
And thus, with much simplicity of sound,
  " Sir Harry, must the *Jack-ass* be *damn'd* too?"

SMILING BAR-MAID, ODE TO A.

Sweet Nymph, with teeth of pearl, and dimpled [chin,
And roses that would tempt a saint to sin,
  Daily to thee so constant I return;

Whose smile improves the coffee's ev'ry drop,
Gives tenderness to ev'ry steak and chop,
   And bids our pockets at expences spurn.

What Youth, well powder'd, of pomatum smelling,
Shall on thy lovely bosom fix his dwelling?
   Perhaps the Waiter, of himself so full!
With *thee* he means the coffee-house to quit;
Open a tavern, and become a *cit*,
   And proudly keep the head of the *Black Bull*.

Nymph of the roguish smile, which thousands seek,
Give me another, and *another* steak;
   A *kingdom* for another steak, but giv'n
By *thy* fair hand, that shames the snow of heav'n.

Give me a glass of punch, O smiling lass,
And let thy luscious lip embalm the glass—
   Touch it, and spread a charm around the brim:
Health to thy beauties, Nancy, and may Time
Ne'er meddle with thy present healthful prime,
   Thy ringlets spoil, and eyes of di'monds dim.

Lo, from each box thy lute-ton'd voice to hear,
Youth nimbly turns him round, with wanton leer:
   Nay, wrinkled Age himself, with locks so white,
Findeth *within* a kind of bastard fire,
Whose mouth, poor cripple, wav'ring with desire,
   Opes toothless on thy beauties in delight.
Now for thy lamb-like flesh he seems to hunger!
He feels himself a pair of ages younger!

Tell me again, O Nymph, *whose* happy arms
Are doom'd, for life, to circle those bright charms,
   And to that bosom give brave girls and boys?
That lucky lot, alas! will ne'er be *mine*—
A gaze, a squeeze, perchance a kiss divine,
   Must form the bounds, O Nancy, of my joys.

Yet if rich favours, far beyond a smile,
So kind, thy Poet's moments to beguile,

Thou wishest to bestow!—in Love's name *give* 'em;
And, thankful, on my *knees* will I *receive* 'em.

SMOKING, OR THE KING AND BRICKMAKER.

A King, near Pimlico, with nose and state,
Did very much a neighb'ring brick-kiln hate,
Because the kiln did vomit nasty smoke;
  Which smoke—I can't say very nicely bred—
  Did very often take it in its head
To blacken the Great House, and try the K—— to [choke.

His sacred Majesty would, sputt'ring, say,
    Upon a windy day,
" I'll make the rascal and his brick-kiln hop—
  " P–x take the smoke—the sulphur!—zounds!—
  " It forces down my throat by pounds;
" My belly is a downright blacksmith's shop."

One day, he was so pester'd by a cloud—
He could not bear it, and thus bawl'd aloud:
" Go," roar'd his M——y unto a Page,
Work'd, like a lion, to a dev'lish rage,
  " Go, tell the rascal who the brick-kiln owns,
  " That, if he dares to burn another brick,
  " Black all my house like hell, and make me sick,
    " I'll tear his kiln to rags, and break his bones."

  Off Billy Ramus set, his errand told:
  On which the Brickmaker, a little bold,
Exclaim'd, " *He* break my bones, good Master Page,
  " *He* say my kiln shan't burn another brick,
  " Because it blacks his house, and makes him
" Billy, go, give my love to Master's rage, [sick!
  " And say, more bricks I am resolv'd to burn;
  " And if the smoke his Worship's stomach turn,
" Tell him to stop his mouth and snout:
  " Nay more, good Page; his M——y shall find
  " I'll always take th' advantage of the wind,
" And, dam'me, try to smoke him *out*."

SONGS.

TO CYNTHIA.

The Youth by Love and Hope betray'd,
  Who breathes his ardent vows in vain,
Learns to forget the scornful Maid,
  And bravely breaks her galling chain.

" Farewell (he cries) a fruitless flame;
  " A Nymph less cruel let me find;
" The world holds many a blooming Dame;
  " An *equal* Chloe may be kind."

But, ah! how hard the Lover's fate,
  Who feels the triumph of *thine* eye!
What Virgin shall *his* fires abate,
  And sooth *his* bosom's hopeless sigh?

For, lo! the Loves, to make thee fair,
  Agreed with ev'ry charm to part;
And all the Virtues too declare,
  They robb'd *their own* to grace *thy* heart.

TO NEPTUNE, FROM SUSAN.

Good Lord! when I think of the storm,
  And, old Neptune, thy horrible spleen,
That endeavour'd to make of this form
  A feast for the fish at nineteen!

It had giv'n my poor heart some alarms,
  As well as some grief to my spark,
To have found, that, instead of *his* arms,
  I had fill'd up the mouth of a *shark*.

Dear Neptune, a Sweetheart is mine—
  Not a handsomer England possesses:
Shouldst thou bury these limbs in thy brine,
  They will lose a whole world of caresses.

Oh! afford me one glance of my lover—
  Oh! grant but one kiss from my swain;
Thou shalt drown me a thousand times over,
  If ever I trust thee again.

TO PHILLIDA.

Dear Phillida, do not my passion despise;
Ah! wherefore disdain all my vows and my sighs?
   Can cruelty dwell with the dove?
O Phillida! think not I mean to deceive,
Whatever I tell thee, with safety believe;
   For Truth is the daughter of Love.

Of beauty and grace thou hast got such a store;
The eye that beholds thee at once must *adore*,
   Nor wish from thine altar to rove:
Distrust not, I beg thee, the pow'r of thy smile;
The swain who now woos thee is void of all guile;
   And Truth is the daughter of Love.

Yet, Phillida, let me confess in thine ear,
I would fly from thy charms, which so much I re-
   But their magic forbids me to move: [vere,
And yet, as *inconstancy* governs the Fair,
Perhaps thou mayst *smile*, and thus end my despair;
   Hope too is the daughter of Love.

ANACREONTIC.

Who dares talk of hours? Seize the bell of that
   Seize his hammer, and cut off his hands: [clock;
To the bottle, dear bottle, I'll stick like a rock,
   And obey only Pleasure's commands.

Let him strike the short hours, and hint at a bed—
   Waiter, bring us more wine—what a whim!
Say that Time, his old master, for *Topers* was made,
   And not jolly Topers for *him*.

ANACREONTIC.

O far from me those lightnings dart!
   On others bid thy beauty shine:
Beyond the hopes of this sad heart,
   I view that peerless form, to pine.

Whilst ev'ry shepherd sings her praise,
  'Tis mine of Sylvia to *complain*;
Made a poor pris'ner while I gaze,
  I feel in ev'ry smile a chain.

ANACREONTIC.

What danger lurks in those bright eyes!
Lo! by their fire thy Poet dies:
  Yet bravely let me meet my doom—
And since to *thee* I owe my death,
I beg thee, with my parting breath,
  To let thy bosom be my tomb.

ANACREONTIC.

Ah! wherefore did I daring gaze
  Upon the radiance of thy charms?
And, vent'ring nearer to their rays,
  How dar'd I clasp thee in my arms!

That kiss will give my heart a pain,
  Which thy sweet pity will deplore:
Then, Cynthia, take the kiss again,
  Or let me take ten thousand more.

SONNET TO KISSING.

When we dwell on the lips of the lass we adore,
  Not a pleasure in nature is missing;
May his soul be in Heav'n, he deserv'd it, I'm sure,
  Who was the first inventor of kissing.

Master Adam, I verily think, was the man,
  Whose discov'ry will ne'er be surpast;
Well, since the sweet game with *creation* began,
  To the *end of the world* may it last!

SPEECH *of the Louse to the King, when found on his Plate.*

" Know, mighty Monarch, I was born and bred
" Deep in the burrows of a Page's head;

"There took I sweet Lousilla unto wife,
"My soul's delight—the comfort of my life:
"But, on a day, your Page, Sir, dar'd invade
"Cowslip's sweet lips, your faithful dairy maid;
"Great was the struggle for the short-'liv'd bliss;
"At length he won the long-contested kiss!—
"Lo! mid the struggle, thus it came to pass;
"Down dropp'd my wife and I upon the lass;
"From whence we crawl'd (and who's without ambition?
"Who does not wish to better his condition?)
"To *You*, dread Sir, where, lo! we lov'd, and fed,
"Charm'd with the fortune of a royal head;
"Where, safe from nail and comb, and blustring wind,
"We nestled in your little lock behind;
"Where many a beauteous baby plainly proves,
"Heav'n, like a King's, can bless a Louse's loves;
"Where many a time, at court, I've join'd your
 "Grace,
"And with you gallop'd in the glorious chace;
"Lousilla, too, my children, and my nits,
"Just frighten'd, sometimes, out of all their wits.
"It happen'd, Sir, ah! luckless, luckless day!
"I foolish took it in my head to stray—
"How many a father, mother, daughter, son,
"Are oft by curiosity undone!
"Dire wish! for 'midst my travels, urg'd by Fate,
"From you, O King, I fell upon your plate!
"Sad was the precipice!—and now I'm here,
"Far from Lousilla and my children dear!
"Who now, poor souls! in deepest mourning all,
"Groan for my presence, and lament my fall.
"Such is the history of your loyal Louse,
"Whose presence breeds such tumult in the house."

SPLENDOR, FALLACIOUS.

O nymph! of Fortune's smiles beware,
  Nor heed the Syren's flatt'ring tongue;

She lures thee to the haunts of Care,
　　Where Sorrow pours a ceaseless song.

Ah! what are all her piles of gold?
　　Can those the hosts of Care control?
The splendor which thine eyes behold
　　Is not the sunshine of the soul.

To Love alone thy homage pay,
　　The Queen of ev'ry true delight;
Her smiles with joy shall gild thy day,
　　And bless the visions of the night.

SPORT, JUVENILE, OR THE FROGS.

A thousand frogs, upon a summer's day,
　　Were sporting 'midst the sunny ray,
In a large pool, reflecting ev'ry face;—
　　They show'd their gold-lac'd clothes with pride,
　　In harmless sallies frequent vied,
And gambol'd through the water with a grace.

It happen'd that a band of boys,
　　Observant of their harmless joys,
Thoughtless, resolv'd to spoil their happy sport:
　　One frenzy seiz'd both great and small;
　　On the poor frogs the rogues began to fall,
Meaning to splash them, not to do them hurt.

Lo, as old authors sing, ' the stones 'gan pour,'
　　Indeed an Otaheite show'r!
The consequence was dreadful, let me tell ye;
　　One's eye was beat out of his head,
　　This limp'd away, that lay for dead;
Here mourn'd a broken back, and there a belly.

Amongst the smitten, it was found
　　Their beauteous Queen receiv'd a wound;
　　The blow gave ev'ry heart a sigh,
　　And drew a tear from ev'ry eye:
At length King Croak got up, and thus begun:
" My lads, you think this very pretty fun!

"Your pebbles round us fly as thick as hops;
"Have warmly complimented all our chops:
"To *you* I guess that these are pleasant stones!
  "And so they might be to us frogs,
  "You damn'd young good-for-nothing dogs,
"But that they are so hard they break our bones."

STABILITY IN LOVE, (1.)

Ah! tell me no more, my dear girl, with a sigh,
  That a coldness will creep o'er my heart;
That a sullen indiff'rence will dwell on my eye,
  When thy beauty begins to depart.

Shall thy graces, O Cynthia, that gladden my day,
  And brighten the gloom of the night,
Till life be extinguish'd, from memory stray,
  Which it ought to review with delight?

Upbraiding, shall Gratitude say with a tear,
  "That no longer I think of those charms
"Which gave to my bosom such rapture sincere,
  "And faded at length in my arms?"

Why yes! it may happen, thou Damsel divine:
  To be honest—I freely declare,
That e'en *now* to thy *converse* so much I incline,
  I *already forget* thou art *fair*.

STABILITY IN LOVE, (2).

How happy was my morn of love,
  When first thy beauty won my heart:
How guiltless of a wish to rove!
  I deem'd it more than death to part!

Whene'er from *thee* I chanc'd to stray,
  How fancy dwelt upon thy mien,
That spread with flow'rs my distant way,
  And show'r'd delight on ev'ry scene!

But Fortune, envious of my joys,
  Hath robb'd a lover of thy charms;

From me thy sweetest smile decoys,
　And gives thee to another's arms.

Yet, though *my* tears are doom'd to flow,
　May tears be never Laura's lot!
Let Love protect *thy* heart from woe;
　His wound to *mine* shall be forgot.

STANZAS.

TO BELLA.

Ah! tell me not that I am old,
　And bid me quit the billing dove;
Tho' many years have o'er me roll'd,
　My heart is still alive to love.
　　Then tell me not that I am old.

When Beauty's blush delights no more,
　And Beauty's smile and sparkling eye;
When these no longer I adore,
　Then Pity yield the Bard a *sigh*.
　　I will not quarrel to be told,
　　Son of Apollo, thou art old.

TO CHLOE, (1.)

Chloe, a thousand charms are thine,
　That give my heart the constant sigh!
Ah! wherefore let thy Poet pine,
　Who canst with ease his wants supply?

Oh, haste, thy charity display;
　With *little* I'll contented be;
The kisses which thou throw'st away
　Upon thy *dog*, will do for *me*.

TO CHLOE, (2.)

Ah! tell me not that I grow old,
　That love but ill becomes my tongue;
Chloe, by me, thou ne'er wert told,
　Sweet damsel! that thou wert *too young*.

TO CHLOE, (3.)

Chloe, no more must we be billing—
There goes my last, my poor last shilling:
   Vile Fortune bids us part!
Yet, Chloe, this my bosom charms,
That, when thou'rt in another's arms,
   I still possess thy *heart*.

Fortune's a whimsical old Dame,
And possibly may blush with shame
   At this her freak with *me:*
But should she smile *again*, and offer,
Well fill'd with gold, an ample coffer,
   I'll send the key to *Thee*.

TO DELIA.

While poets pour their happiest lays,
   And call thee ev'ry thing divine;
Not quite so lavish in thy praise,
   To *censure* be the province mine.

Though born with talents to surprise,
   Thou seldom dost those pow'rs display:
Thus seem they trifling in thine eyes!
   Thus heav'n's best gifts are thrown away!

Though rich in charms, thou know'st it not;
   Such is thine ignorance profound:
And then such cruelty thy lot,
   Thy sweetest smile inflicts a *wound*.

TO LADY E. ON THE DEATH OF HER PIG CUPID.

O dry that tear, so round and big;
   Nor waste in sighs your precious wind!
Death only tastes a single Pig—
   Your Lord and Son are still behind.

TO MISS H. OF BATH.

" Alas, alas, I've lost a day!"
Good Titus once was heard to say,
   And sorely, sorely to repent it—
What was it made the Emp'ror groan?
I'd give a good round sum, I own,
   To be inform'd how 'twas he spent it.

Dear Titus, quickly leave thy tomb;
Enter of Harrington the room,
   Whom Music and each Grace reveres—
I'll answer for't thou wilt not say,
" Alas, alas, I've lost a *day*;"
   But, " Gods! I've found *five hundred years!*"

TO THE NIGHTINGALE.

Lone Minstrel of the moonlight hour,
   Who charm'st the silent list'ning plain,
A hapless Pilgrim treads thy bow'r,
   To hear thy solitary strain.

How soothing is the song of woe,
   To *me*, whom Love hath doom'd to pine!
For, 'mid those sounds that plaintive flow,
   I hear *my* sorrows mix with *thine*.

FROM ANACREON TO HIMSELF.

On fragrant myrtles let me lie,
And Love, my slave, the wine supply.
   Too soon we seek the Stygian gloom:
Time flies; and, since to dust we go,
Why idly bid the incense flow,
   And spill the juice upon the tomb?

Ah! rather let me quaff the *wine*,
And bid the rose my brows entwine,
   While youth, while health, the bosom warms—
Then pr'ythee, Love, delight my heart,
Ere Death dispatch his certain dart,
   And bring a Chloe to my arms.

STERILITY.—TO CELIA.

Envy must own that thou art passing fair
Love in thy smiles, and Juno in thy air:
  Yet, Celia, if with Gods I may be free,
I think that Jove commits a sort of sin,
By stripping all the Graces to the skin,
    Merely to make a *nonpareille* of *thee*.

When Nature sent thee blooming from above,
She meant thee to support the cause of Love—
  To keep alive a beautiful creation:
Thy graces hoarded, girl, thou must be told,
Are really like the sordid Miser's gold,
    Worthless, for want of circulation.

Behold! a guinea, by a proper use,
Another pretty guinea will produce;
  And thus, O peerless girl, thy beauty
May bring the *cent. per cent.* within the year;
That is, another beauty may appear,
    If properly it minds its duty.

Of wonder, lo! thou puttest on the stare—
It seems a dark and intricate affair;
  Thou wantest a good, able, sound, adviser:
Well, then, my dear, at once agree,
As *chamber*-counsel to take *me*;
    I know none better qualified, nor wiser.

STORM DESCRIBED.

Thus in Western India, Jove ordains
At times an aspect wild of hurricanes:
Dark grows the sky, with gleams of threat'ning red:
All nature dumb, the smallest zephyr dead—
Bird, beast, and mortal, trembling, pausing, still,
Expectant of the tempest's mighty will.
Tremendous pause! when, lo! by small degrees,
Light melts the mass; with life returns the breeze;

And Danger, on his cloud, who scowl'd dismay,
Moves sullen with his congregated glooms away.

ST. THOMAS'S THUMB.

In France, some years ago—some twenty-three,
   At a fam'd church, where hundreds daily jostle,
I wisely paid a priest six sols to see
   The thumb of Thomas the Apostle.

Gaping upon Tom's thumb, with *me* in wonder,
The rabble rais'd its eyes, like ducks in thunder;
Because in virtues it was vastly rich,
Had cur'd possess'd of devils, and the itch;
Work'd various wonders on a scabby pate;
Made little sucking children strait
   Though crook'd like rams horns by the rickets;
Made people see, though blind as moles;
And made your sad hysteric souls
   As gay as grasshoppers and crickets.
Lo! had the Priest *permitted*, with their kisses,
The mob had smack'd this holy thumb to pieces.

Though, Reader, 'twas not the Apostle's thumb—
       But, mum!——
It play'd as well of miracles the trick,
Although a painted piece of rotten stick!

SWEETS OF AMBITION.

Lo, thus the Lad, in base Saint Giles's born,
   Blest with a barrow, first begins to bawl;
Where Plenty, ah! exalteth not her horn—
   Potatoes the poor barrow's *little all*.

At length, succeeding by a *lucky cry*,
And Fortune's fav'ring smile, the Lad can buy
   A basket!—nay, *two* baskets for his barrow;
To which he hangs the baskets with much pride,
With endive, celery, and greens beside— [row—
   Yes with *much* pride, that warms his inmost mar-

With all the gaping energy of song,
Proudly he rolls his whole estate along!

Ambition still inspires his panting heart;
And now sublime he rises to a *cart*,
But not without a Jackass, let me say:
A Jack is harness'd—on the cart he mounts—
Looks round—elate, his cabbages he counts,
  And triumphs in his Partner's Brudenell-bray.

He stops not here—Ambition goads his soul
To bid his orb in loftier regions roll.
  In Covent Garden, lo! a shop he gains;
Pines, nect'rines, plums, and apricots, and peaches,
Behold! his laudable ambition reaches;
  And now the *Jackass* and the *cart* disdains.

An Ass's *ditty* wounds his *nicer* ear,
Bringing to mind his late and humble sphere:
  Archbishop-like, he *tow'rs* within his stall—
Looks on the barrow, cart, and basket crew,
With all the consequence of man, askew,
  And, for a pack of beggars, damns them *all*.

SYLVIA.—ANACREONTIC.

How canst thou smile at my despair,
  And bid me *other* nymphs adore?
Shew me a girl but *half* so fair,
  And I will trouble thee no more.

Hide then that neck, and lip, and eye,
  Since thus resolv'd to seek pursuit;
For Love will follow, like the fly,
  That always seeks the *fairest* fruit.

SYMPTOMS OF LOVE.

Dear girl, I'm up to ears in love;
The fact, a thousand follies prove;
  Yes, yes, I feel the dart!
Well! now I'm wounded, give the cure;
Thou'rt not a cruel girl, I'm sure,
  So try to ease the smart.

"Lord bless us! it is all a lie,"
I hear thee with emotion cry,
  "I'm sure there's nothing in't:"
Indeed there is, I'm sore afraid,
Nay, take the symptoms, sceptic Maid,
  That make it plain as print.

From those dear lips, delicious bliss,
If saucy coxcombs steal a kiss,
  My eyes so jealous roll:
Aside, I call the puppies names,
My heart is Ætna-like in flames,
  Consuming to a coal.

I cannot bear to be *alone*;
I yawn, I sigh, I gape, I groan,
  And writhe as if with pain:
Now on a sudden seize a book,
Just half a minute in it look,
  Then fling it down again.

Now ruminating wild, I walk;
Nod to myself, and smile, and talk;
  Now hunt for something lost;
Now sit, jump up—now stare, now wink
On some deep problem seem to think—
  Now vacant as a post.

Now full resolv'd to visit thee,
To take a social cup of tea,
  And give my heart a plaster;
I draw my watch, not over cool,
Call him a little limping fool,
  And bid him travel faster.

Now bustling round the room, here, there,
I try to find my hat, and swear,
  And wish him damn'd, and dead;
Now raging from my inmost soul,
I roar, "What thief my hat hath stole?"
  Then find it on my head.

Nay, nay, I'd *marry* thee, my dear—
Love's symptoms now *too plain* appear;
  There's no-body can miss it:
Yet if these symptoms are not love,
And *this* the passion fail to prove,
  Why, what the devil is it?

TASTE, DIFFERENCE OF.

How varied are our tastes! Dame Nature's plan,
All for *wise* reasons, since the world began:
  Yes, yes, the good old Lady acted right:
Had things been *otherwise*, like wolves and bears,
We all had fall'n together by the ears—
  One object had produc'd an endless fight.

*Nettle*s had strew'd Life's path instead of *roses*;
  And multitudes of mortal faces,
Printed with histories of bloody noses,
  Had taken leave of absence of the Graces.

Now interrupting not each other's line,
You ride *your* hobby-horse, and *I* ride *mine*—
You press the blue-ey'd Chloe to your arms,
And *I* the black-ey'd Sappho's browner charms;
Thus situated in our different blisses,
We squint not envious on each other's kisses.

Thus tastes are various, as I've said before—
These damn most cordially what *those adore*.

TEMPERAMENT.

My passions are the children (easy creatures)
Of Moderation! boast the Mother's features,
  And Mother's chaste simplicity, the dove;
Can sleep upon the humble sod, and swill,
With great good glee, the valley's lucid rill,
  And batten on the berries of the grove.

Look at yon groupe of sucking pigs—how blest!
What makes them so?—clean straw to form a nest!
  So *slight* a thing their happiness composes!

What dialogue! how arch they squint *about!*
Now bury their sweet heads—now pull them *out*,
   And toss the wisps so white upon their noses.

These pigs are just my passions, that can draw
Mirth and contentment from a simple straw.

TEMPTATION, ODE TO.

O nymph with all the luxury of skin,
Pea-bloom breath, and dimpled chin;
   Rose cheek, and eyes that beat the blackest sloe;
With flaxen ringlets thy soft bosom shading,
So white, so plump, so lusciously-persuading;
   And lips that none but mouths of cherubs know!

Oh, leering, lure me not to Charlotte-street,
That too, too fair seducing form to meet;
Then shall I trembling fall, for want of grace,
And die, yes, die perhaps upon my face!

Ah! cease to turn, and look, and leer, and smile,
My too imprudent senses to beguile!
   Ah! keep that taper leg so tempting from me;
Ah! form'd to foil a Phidias's art,
So much unlike that leg in ev'ry part;
   By me abhorr'd indeed, and christen'd *gummy*.

In vain I turn around to run away:
Thine eyes, those basilisks, command my stay:
   Whilst through its gauze thy snowy bosom peep-
Seems to that rogue interpreter, my eye,   [ing,
To heave a soft, desponding, tender, sigh—
   Like gossamer, my thoughts of goodness sweeping.

Abound, I say, abound in grace, my feet;
And do not follow her to Charlotte-street.

Alas! alas! you have no grace, I see,
But wish to carry off poor struggling *me*:
   Yes, the wild bed of Beauty wish to seek;
Yet, if ye do—to make your two hearts ake,
A sweet, a sweet revenge I mean to take;
   For, curse me, if you shall not stay a week.

Yet let me not thus pond'ring, gaping, stand;
But, lo! I am not at my own command:
Bed, bosom, kiss, embraces, storm my brains,
And, lawless tyrants, bind my will in chains.
O lovely Lass! too pow'rful are thy charms,
And fascination dwells within thy arms.

TENDENCY OF FAT.

Painters and poets never should be fat—
 Sons of Apollo! listen well to that:
Fat is foul weather, dims the fancy's sight:
 In poverty, the wits more nimbly muster:
Thus stars, when pinch'd by frost, cast keener lustre
On the black blanket of Old Mother Night.

 Your heavy fat, I will maintain,
 Is perfect birdlime of the brain;
 And, as to goldfinches the birdlime clings,
 Fat holds ideas by the legs and wings.

Fat flattens the most brilliant thoughts,
 Like the buff-stop on harpsichords or spinnets—
Muffling their pretty tuneful throats,
 That would have chirp'd away like linnets.

Not only fat is hurtful to the Arts,
But love, at fat—ev'n Love Almighty starts:
Love hates large, lubberly, fat, clumsy, fellows,
Panting and blowing like a blacksmith's bellows.

TENDERNESS OF CONSCIENCE.

At Rome, each hour, are horrid actions done!
 By *thee* approv'd, thou dar'st not Pope, deny:
Yes, yes, the lawless places are well known,
 Where youth for venal pleasures madly fly,
Bargain for beauteous charm, and pick, and cull it,
As at a poult'rer's *Betty* turns a pullet.

I like examples of a wicked act—
Take, therefore, Reader, from the Bard a fact.

An old *Procuress* groaning, sighing, dying,
A rake-hell enters the old Beldame's room—
" Hæ, mother! thinking on the day of doom?
  " Hæ—dam'me, slabb'ring, whining, praying,
    crying?
" Well, mother! what young filly hast thou got
" To give a gentleman a little trot?"

" O Captain, pray, your idle nonsense cease,
" And let a poor old soul depart in peace!
" What wicked things the dev'l puts in your head!
" Where can you hope to go when you are dead?"

" How now, old Beldame?—shamming Heav'n with
    praying!   [ing;
" Come, come, to bus'ness—don't keep such a bray-
" Let's see your stuff—come, Beldame, show your
    ware;
" Some little Phillis, fresh from country air?"

" O Captain, how *unpiously* you prate!
" Well, well, I see there's no resisting fate;
  " Go, go to the next room, and there's a bed—
" And such a charming creature in't—such grace!
" Such sweet simplicity! and *such* a face!—
  " Captain, you are a devil—you are, indeed.

" I thank my stars that nought *my* conscience twits;
  " Which to my parting soul doth joy afford.
" O Captain! Captain! what, for nice young *Tits*,
  " What will you do, when I am with the Lord?"

TEN FOR ONE—ANACREONTIC.

Fie, Sylvia! why so gravely look,
Because a kiss or two I took?
Those luscious lips might thousands grant—
Rich rogues that never feel the want.
So little in the kiss I see,
A hundred thou may'st take from *me*.

But, since, like misers o'er their store,
Thou hat'st to give, though running o'er,

I scorn to cause the slightest pain,
So pr'ythee take them back again ;
Nay, with good int'rest be it done—
Thou'rt welcome to take *ten for one.*

THRIFT AT ST. JAMES'S.

Sill was the Palace, save where some poor fly,
With thirst just ready to drop down and die,
Buzz'd faint petitions to his Maker's ear,
To show him one small drop of dead small beer ;
Save where the cat, for mice, so hungry watching,
Swore the lean animals were scarce worth catching ;
Save where the dog so gaunt, in grumbling tone,
By dreams deluded, mouth'd a mutton bone ;
Save where, with throats to sounds of horror strain'd,
Crickets of coughs and rheumatisms complain'd,
Lamenting sore, amid a Royal hold,
" How hard that crickets should be kill'd by cold!"

TIME, (1.)

When once a woman's handsome, smart, and clever,
In God's name let her bloom for ever! [hand,
Ah! could I snatch Time's ploughshare from his
Who, with that ease a farmer skirts his land,
   Furrows so cruelly o'er the fairest face !
     Relentless as a Mohawk, on he goes,
      Cuts up the lily and the rose, [grace—
Roots up each wavy curl, and bends the neck of
Ah! could I simply do but this,
The sweetest lips would give me many a kiss.
By raising, then destroying, like a Turk,
It seems as though Time did not like his work ;
As though he wanted something *better* still,
Than e'er was manufactur'd at his mill.

TIME, PETITION TO, (2.)

Too long, O Time, in *Bienséance*'s school,
Have I been bred, to *call* thee an old fool ;
Yet take I liberty to let thee know,
That I have always *thought* thee so :

Full old art thou, indeed, to have more sense:
Then, with an idle custom, Time, dispense.

Thou really actest now like little misses,
  Who, when a pretty doll they make,
  Their curious fingers itch to take
The pretty image all to pieces:
Thus, after thou hast form'd a charming Fair,
  Thou canst not quit the Syren for thy soul,
Till, meddling, thou hast spoil'd the bloom and air,
  And dimm'd her eye, with radiance taught to roll.

But now forbear such doings, I desire;
Hurt not the form that all admire:
  Oh, never with white hairs her temple sprinkle!
Oh, sacred be her cheek, her lip, her bloom!
And do not, in a lovely dimple's room,
  Place a hard mortifying wrinkle.

TIME, TO CYNTHIA, (3.)

O Time, 'tis childish, let me say,
To give, then take a grace away;
The Damsel from her charms to sever,
So pleas'd to keep them all *for ever*.

When Cynthia *tires* with conq'ring hearts,
And says, " O Time, *receive* my darts;"
Her beauties are a lawful prize—
Then take the lightnings of her eyes.

Pluck all the roses from her cheek,
And root the lilies from her neck;
Her dimples seize, her smile, her air,
And with them make a thousand *fair*.

TIME, TO CYNTHIA, (4.)

Ah, what an envious rogue is Time,
Who means one day to crop thy prime
  This were a barb'rous deed, I vow:
If thus the Tyrant can behave,
Lord, let us disappoint the knave,
And let me take those beauties *now*.

TINKER AND MILLER'S DAUGHTER.

Upon a day, a poor and trav'lling Tinker,
On Fortune's various tricks a constant thinker,
   Pass'd in some village near a Miller's door;
Where, lo! his eye did most astonish'd catch
The Miller's daughter peeping o'er the hatch,
   Deform'd, and monstrous ugly, to be sure.

Struck with th' uncommon form, the Tinker *started,*
Just like a frighten'd horse, or murd'rer carted,
   Up gazing at the gibbet and the rope:
Turning his brain about in a brown study,
(For, as I've said, his brain was not so muddy)
     " 'Sbud! (quoth the Tinker) I have now some hope;
" Fortune, the jade, is not far off, perchance !"—
And then began to rub his hands and dance.

Now all so full of love, o'erjoy'd he ran,
Embrac'd and squeez'd Miss Grist, and thus began:
   " My dear, my soul, my angel, sweet Miss Grist;
" Now may I never mend a kettle more,
" If ever I saw one like *you* before !"   [kiss'd.
   Then, " nothing loth," like Eve, the nymph he

Now, very sensibly indeed, Miss Grist
Thought opportunity should not be miss'd;
Knowing that prudery oft lets slip of joy:
Thus was Miss Grist too *prudent* to be *coy.*
For really 'tis with girls a dangerous farce
To flout a swain, when offers are but scarce.

Soon won, the Nymph agreed to join his bed,
And, when the Tinker chose, to church he led.
Now to the Father the brisk Lover hied,
Who at his noisy mill so busy plied.

" Ho! Master Miller !" did the Tinker say—
   Forth from the cloud of flour the Miller came:
" Nice weather, Master Miller !—charming day—
   " God's very kind :"—the Miller said the *same.*

" Now, Miller, possibly you may not guess
    " At this same business I am come about:
" 'Tis this then—know, I love your daughter Bess:—
    " There, Master Miller!—now the riddle's *out*.

" I'm not for mincing matters, Lord! d'ye see—
" I *likes* your daughter Bess, and she likes *me*."
" Poh!" quoth the Miller, grinning at the Tinker,
    " Thou dost not mean to marriage to persuade her;
" Ugly as is the Dev'l I needs must think her, [her.
    " Though, to be sure, 'tis said, 'twas *me* that *made*

" No, no, though she's my daughter, I'm not *blind*:
" But, Tinker, what hath now possess'd thy mind?
" Thou'rt the first offer she has met, by *Gad*—
" But tell me, Tinker, art thou drunk, or mad?"

" No—I'm not drunk, nor mad," the Tinker cried,
" But Bet's the maid I wish to make my bride;
    " No girl in these two eyes doth Bet excel."
" Why, fool, (the Miller said) Bet hath a *hump!*
" And then her *nose!*—the nose of my old pump."
    " I know it, (quoth the Tinker,) know it well."

" Her *face* (quoth Grist) is freckled, wrinkled, flat;
" Her mouth as wide as that of my Tom Cat;
    " And then she squints a thousand ways at once—
" Her waist, a corkscrew; and her hair, how red!
" A downright bunch of carrots on her head—
    " Why what the dev'l is got into thy sconce?"
" No dev'l is in *my* sconce," rejoin'd the Tinker;
" But, Lord! what's that to *you*, if *fine I* think her?"

" Why, man, (quoth Grist) she's fit to make a Show,
    " And therefore sure I am that thou must banter!"
" Miller, (replied the Tinker) right! for know,
    " 'Tis for that *very thing*, a Show, I want her."

THOMAS, SONG TO, FROM DOLLY THE COOK.

Dear Thomas, I pity thy love;
    But, Thomas, thou wilt not *expire:*
Like a ladle of dripping 'twill prove
    That I frequently fling on the fire.

It makes a most wonderful blaze,
  And frightens the chimney no doubt;
Sets the family all in amaze;
  But, Thomas, it quickly goes out.

Before we were married a year,
  Mighty Love, he would lose all his forces;
And the musical tongue of thy *Dear*
  Would yield to the neigh of thy horses.

I believe that thou thinkest sincere,
  This *sweet passion* would last all thy life;
But too many can tell with a tear,
  They have thought the same thing of a *wife*.

Too often we find, to our cost,
  That the Passions are easily cloy'd;
That the object which pleases us *mo st*
  Is the *object* that ne'er was *enjoy'd*.

Love-matches may do very well,
  In worlds where folks never want meat;
But in this, 'tis with sorrow I tell
  We are looking for somewhat *to eat*.

Dear Thomas, then let me alone
  To my roasting, and boiling, and carving;
I don't like to live on a *bone*—
  Lord! nothing's more dismal than *starving*.

To thy stable then stick all thy life;
  That will bring thee thy meat ev'ry day:
A houseful of brats and a wife—
  What would they?—*why take it away*.

THRALE AND THE DRAYMAN.

" Conscience has nought to say to Trade,"
Says Slander—happy to degrade.
I'll prove it otherwise, by good old Thrale,
Great in the annals of good beer;
An ocean too, the Brewer's sphere,
  Himself the master—the important whale.
I own that consciences are ninnies,
Dupes unto fascinating guineas;

Indeed, so 'witching are their splendid faces!
Shillings, and pence too, let me say,
Can lead *some* consciences astray,
    For *these* are not without their *winning* graces.

Now for my tale—The Drayman Mat,
Wishing to peep into the vat,
    And view the sea of boiling foaming wort;
When lo! (a very serious matter)
His star—of most malignant nature—   [for't;
    Sous'd him plump in; who did not *thank* him

For loud the Drayman roar'd, and vainly toil'd;
And, like a chicken, soon the *man* was boil'd!
I say, indeed, extremely like a chicken;
As tender quite—but not so pleasant picking.

Lord! what was done? Attend—you'll hear:
Compassionating the poor beer,
    The Brewer scorn'd to give it a *bad name:*
Not to a single soul he told it,
But, like the former, calmly sold it;
    When, strange to tell, it won immortal fame.

A customer, call'd Peter Pot,
Whose lucky, very lucky lot
    Was to be favour'd with this christian beer,
Proceeds to Thrale's—proclaims its praise:
" Ne'er drank such beer in my *born* days!
    " A glorious, glorious brew! liked *ev'ry where*—

" So pleas'd were folks—Sir, hundreds I can name;
" So let me always have the *very same.*
" Your name is up, Sir; you may lie abed—
" You've hit the nail at last upon the head."

" Well, Master Pot," quoth Master Thrale,
" I'm glad the beer had such a sale—
" Depend on't, it shall be my constant plan
" To make the next as *near* it as I can."

    What could be fairer? Yet, God wot,
    This answer pleas'd not Peter Pot.

"As *near* it as you *can!*" cried Pot—
"Why not the *very same?*—why *not?*
"Put in the same materials, and 'twill *do.*"
"Damme," quoth Thrale, enrag'd, "dost think
"I'll make my conscience always *wink,*
"And boil a Drayman *ev'ry time* I *brew?*"

TOPER AND THE FLIES.

A Groupe of Topers at a table sat,
  With punch that much regales the thirsty soul:
Flies soon the party join'd, and join'd the chat,
  Humming, and pitching round the mantling bowl.

At length those flies got drunk, and, for their sin,
Some hundreds lost their legs, and tumbled in;
And sprawling 'midst the gulph profound,
Like Pharaoh and his daring host, were drown'd!

Wanting to drink—one of the men
  Dipp'd from the bowl the drunken host,
  And drank—then taking care that none were lost,
He put in ev'ry mother's son agen.

Up jump'd the bacchanalian crew on this,
  Taking it very much amiss—
Swearing, and in the attitude to *smite:*
  "Lord!" cried the man, with gravely-lifted eyes,
  "Though I don't like to swallow flies,
"I did not know but *others might.*"

TRAVELLER AND JUPITER.

A certain Traveller, in ancient days,
  When gods and goddesses were thick as hops,
Wishing, as he was beating the highways,
  For something dainty to amuse his chops,

Knelt down to Jupiter, and thus began:
"O Jupiter, as I'm an honest man,
  "I'll keep my word, if thou wilt grant my pray'r;
"Amidst my travels, let me *something* find—
"Little or much, good, bad, of any kind,
  "I vow to thee, thy godship *half* shall share."

He had not walk'd a mile, before he found
A handsome bag of filberts on the ground;
At sight of which, his lips with rapture smacking,
Plump down he squats, and falls at once to cracking.

To cut my story short, he crack'd and eat
From ev'ry nut, each atom of the meat;
  When, gravely gathering up the shells, he cries,
" Jove, sacred have I kept my word—for see,
" The *better* half indeed I leave to *thee*,
  " The *shells*, O mighty Ruler of the skies!

" There are they all, great Jove—survey 'em:
" Shouldst thou suspect my honour—*weigh 'em!*"

TREACHERY.

Thus when grimalkin in its cage espies
  A linnet or canary-bird, so sweet;
The scoundrel lifts, so sanctified, his eyes,
  Contriving how the warbler's back to greet:

He squints, and licks his lips, stalks round and round,
  Twinkling with mischief fraught his tiger tail;
Now on his rump he sits, in thought profound,
  Looks up with hungry wishes to assail;
When sudden enters master with a roar,
And kicks the scheming murd'rer to the door.

TRISTIA, OR THE SORROWS OF PETER PINDAR.

No Nymph of quality on Peter calls;
  No Lesbia fond of sparrows and the dove;
And bid me make them melting madrigals,
  And say, " sweet Peter sing us songs of love!"

The man who carries Punch about the streets,
  His scolding wife, the baker, and the devil,
With fair rewards from all spectators meet,
  And to his poverty each purse is civil.

The man who leads his camel up and down,
  Where sports a grinning monkey on his hump,
Dines princely, such the favour of the town,
  And never mourns like me in doleful dump.

The man who leads about a dancing bear,
   Or dancing dogs, *good living* never lack,
While *I*, who lead the Muses, (fate severe!),
   Can neither treat my belly or my back.

The clowns of thirty pounds a year (no more)
   Laugh at the sons of song, and scornful pass us;
" One little *rood* of dirty land," they roar,
   " Is worth a *thousand acres* of Parnassus."

TRUTH, (1.)

Oh! what an inexperienc'd thing is youth!
How very little knowest thou of Truth!
Truth for a very dang'rous Dame believe:
Too oft, alas! the fairest forms deceive:
Mid Winter's shiv'ring *scene* the simple hare
Finds in the purest snow a fatal snare:
Forth as she scuds, to feed at early day,
The treach'rous *softness* tells her winding way:
Where'er it feels her feet, the fair Betrayer
Informs the treach'rous Poacher where to slay her.
The Muse that tells plain truth with edge-tools
    sports:—
Go, deal in fiction, Man, and flatter Courts.

TRUTH, (2.)

Fair Truth! to towns and courts a stranger grown,
And now to rural swains almost unknown,
Whose company was once their prudent choice;
Who once, delighted, listen'd to her voice;
When in their hearts the *gentler* passion strove,
And Constancy went hand in hand with Love!
Sweet Truth, who steals through lonely shades
And mingles with the turtle's note her song; [along,
Whilst Falsehood, rais'd by sycophantic tricks,
Unblushing, flaunts it in a coach and six.

TRUTH, (3.)

Truth is a tow'ring Dame—divine her air;
   In native bloom she walks the world with *state:*
But Falsehood is a meretricious Fair,
   Painted and mean, and shuffling in her gait;

Dares not look up with Resolution's mien,
But sneaking hides, and hopes not to be seen;
For ever haunted by the Ghost of Doubt!
Trembling for fear the world will find her out.

TRUTH IN LOVE—TO CHLOE.

Chloe, I live, and live for *thee alone*;
   'Trust me, there's nought worth living for beside:
Nought for thine absence, Chloe, can atone, [pride.
   Though Phœbus shines, and Nature pours her

Lo! full of innocence the lambkins bleat;
   The brooks in sweetest murmurs purl along;
The lark's, the linnet's voices too, are sweet—
   But what are these to Chloe's tuneful tongue?

With ev'ry balm, the breath of Zephyr blows;
   But thine can yield a thousand times more blisses:
I own the fragrance of the blushing rose,
   But, ah! how faint to balm of Chloe's kisses!

Ye Gods! I mark thy frown, and scornful eye,
   And now the bridling chin of scorn I see:
And now I hear thee, so contemptuous, cry,
   " What are my kisses, saucy Swain, to thee?"

True, dearest Chloe—yet each kiss divine,
   Which dwelleth on thy lips so very teazing,
Would quickly change its nature were it *mine*,
   And *rapt'rous* prove—*superlatively pleasing!*

Love is a *gen'rous* God, and 'tis his pleasure
   To see the *gold* he gives in *circulation*—
Then cease to *hoard* such *quantities* of treasure,
   And be afraid to put him in a *passion*.

Thy beauties should the angry God *divide*,
   And throw amongst thy sex, 'twould be alarming;
And not a little mortify thy pride,
   To meet, dear Chloe, ev'ry woman *charming*.

TRUTH AND FLATTERY.

Flatt'ry's the turnpike-road to Fortune's door—
   Truth is a narrow lane, all full of quags,
     Leading to broken heads, abuse, and rags.

And workhouses—sad refuge for the poor!
Flattery's a mountebank so spruce—gets riches:
  Truth, a plain Simon Pure, a Quaker Preacher,
  A moral member, a disgusting teacher,
That never got a sixpence by her speeches!

TWO MICE IN A TRAP, ODE TO.

So, Sir and Madam, you at length are taken,
After your dances over cheese and bacon,
  And tasting ev'ry dainty in your way;
Now to my question answer, if you please—
Speak, did ye *make* the bacon or the cheese?
  What sort of a defence d'ye set up, pray?

I see ye are two lovers by your eyes;
I hear ye are two lovers by your sighs:
  But what avail your looks, or what avail
Your sighs so soft, or what indeed your tears,
Or what your parting agonies and fears,
  Since Death must pay a visit to your jail?

Ay, you may kiss and pant, and pant and kiss,
  And put your pretty noses through the wire;
Ay, peep away, sweet Sir and gentle Miss;
  No more the moon shall mark your am'rous fire,
Around the loaded pantry pour the ray,
And guide your gambols with her silver day.

Your prison-door now, culprits, let me ope—
Now, now! you're off! it is a *lucky* hop.

TYRANNY.

Now let my soul enjoy the hour!
See Night her grisly spectres pour!
  The clock proclaims her at her highest noon;
Lone Silence shall my work befriend;
Her shoes of cygnet down shall lend;
  The cloud's black mantle muffle the pale moon.

Oh! would kind Night extend th' *eternal* shade,
  And help in Murder's cause my panting breath!
For, lo! to Murder with his reeking blade,
  The beam of Morning seems the gloom of death.

Lo, where the Innocents repose,
Our longing hands shall scatter woes,
  And Fear shall whiten ev'ry haggard face.
Sly to the pillow will we creep,
Dash with rude arm the bonds of Sleep,
  And drag a *husband* from a *wife's* embrace.

In vain shall Terror lift her suppliant cries—
My heart, a rugged rock, the sound defies.

TYRANTS, AN ODE TO.

Who, and *what* are ye, sceptred bullies?—speak,
That millions to *your* will must bow the neck,
  And, ox-like, meanly take the galling yoke?
Philosophers your ignorance despise;
E'en Folly, laughing, lifts her maudlin eyes,
  And freely on your *wisdoms* cracks her joke.

How dare ye on the men of labour tread,
Whose honest toils supply your mouths with bread;
Who, groaning, sweating, like so many hacks,
Work you the very clothes upon your backs?
    Clothes of *calamity*, I fear,
    That hold in ev'ry stitch a tear.

Tyrants with all your wonderful dominion,
Ye ar'n't a whit like God, in my opinion;
  Though *you* think otherwise, I do presume:
Hot to the marrow with the *ruling* lust,
Fancying your crouching subjects so much *dust*,
  Your *lofty selves* the mighty sweeping *broom*.

Are *these* the *Beings* to bestride a world?
To *such* sad beasts has God his creatures hurl'd?

Men want not *Tyrants*—overbearing knaves;
Despots that rule a realm of *slaves*;
  Proud to be gaz'd at by a *reptile* race:
Charm'd with the music of their clanking chains,
Pleas'd with the fog of State that clouds their brains,
  Who cry with all the impudence of face,

"Behold your Gods!—down, rascals, on your knees;
  "Your money, miscreants—quick, no words, no
      "strife; [fleas;
  "Your lands too, scoundrels, vermin, lice, bugs,
  "And thank our mercy that allows you *life!*"

Who would not laugh to see a Tailor bow
Submissive to a pair of satin breeches?
Saying, " O breeches, all men must allow
  " There's something in your aspect that bewitches!
" Let me admire you, Breeches, crown'd with glory !
" And though *I made* you, let me still *adore* ye :
" Though a Rump's humble servant, form'd for need,
  " To keep it warm, yet, Lord ! you are so fine,
" I cannot think you are my work indeed—
" Though merely mortal, lo! ye seem divine!"

See! Crispin makes a pair of handsome shoes,
Silk and bespangled, such as ladies use—
  Suppose the shoes so proud, upon each heel,
Perk it in Crispin's face, with saucy pride,
And all the meanness of his trade deride,
  And all the state of self-importance feel:

Tell him the distance between *them* and *him*,
Crispin would quickly cry, " A pretty whim!
  " Confound your little bodies, though so fine,
" Is not the silk and spangles that ye boast
" Put on you at *my* proper cost?
  " Whatever's on ye, is it not all *mine?*
" Did not I put you *thus* together, pray?"
What could the simple shoes in answer say?

There too are *some* (thank Heav'n they do not *swarm*)
Who deem it *foul* to stay a Tyrant's arm,
  That falls with fate upon their humble skulls:
Some for a Despot's rod have heav'd the sigh!—
Let *such* on wiser Æsop cast an eye,
  And read the fable of the *Frogs*, the fools.

THE FROGS AND JUPITER.

The Frogs, so happy, 'midst their peaceful pond,
Of *Emp'rors* grew at once extremely fond ;
  Yes, yes, an *Emp'ror* was a *glorious thing*:
Each really took it in his addle pate
'Twould be so *charming* to exchange their state!
  An *Emp'ror* would *such* heaps of blisses bring!

Sudden out hopp'd the Nation on the grass,
Frog-man and yellow wife, and youth and lass,
  A numerous tribe, to knuckle down to Jove,
And pray the gods to send an *Emp'ror* down,
'Twas such a pretty thing, th' Imperial Crown!
  So form'd their pleasures, honours, to improve.

Forth from his old blue *weather-box*, the skies,
Jove briskly stepp'd, with two wide-wond'ring eyes:
  " Mynheers," quoth Jove, " if ye are wise, be quiet;
" Know when you're happy"—but he preach'd
They made the most abominable riot;   [in vain;
  " An Emp'ror, Emp'ror, yes, we *must* obtain."

" Well, *take* one," cried the God, and down he swopp'd
A monstrous piece of wood, from whence he chopp'd
  Kings for the gentlefolks of ancient days :
Stunn'd at the sound, the frogs all shook with dread ;
Like dabchicks, under water push'd each head,
  Afraid a single nose so pale to raise.

At length *one* stole a peep, and then a *second*,
Who, slily winking to a *third* frog, beckon'd ;
  And so on, till they all obtain'd a peep;
Now nearer, nearer edging on they drew,
And finding nothing terrible, nor new,
  Bold on his Majesty began to *leap*:

Such hopping this way, that way, off and on!
Such croaking, laughing, ridiculing fun!
In short, so very shameless were they grown,
  So much of grace and manners did they lack,

One little villain saucily squats down,
    And, with a grin, defil'd the Royal Back.

Now unto Jove, they, kneeling, pray'd again,
    " O Jupiter, this is so sad a beast,
" So *dull* a Monarch—so devoid of brain!
    " Give us a king of *spirit*, Jove, *at least*."

The god complied, and sent them Emp'ror Stork,
Who with his loving subjects went to work;
Chas'd the poor sprawling imps from pool to pool,
Resolv'd to get a handsome belly full.

Now gasping, wedg'd within his iron beak,
Did griggling scores most lamentably squeak:
Bold push'd the Emp'ror on, with stride *so* noble,
Bolting * his subjects with majestic gobble.

Again the croaking Tribe began to pray,
'Midst hoppings, scramblings, murder, and dismay.

" O save us, Jove, from this inhuman Turk!
    " O save us from this Imp of Hell!"   [Stork—
" Mynheers," quoth Jove, " pray keep thy *Emp'ror*
    " Fools never know when they are *well*."

UGLINESS, ODE TO.

Daughter of Hecate, thou'rt undone!
    Joy to my soul, thine empire falls:
No more, thou hobbling envious *Crone*,
    Thy pow'r the female world appalls.

With smiles the Queen of Love appears,
    No longer trembling for the Graces:
No more thy rude attack she fears,
    On faultless forms and fairest faces.

Beauty will never lose her prime,
    Nor mourn her losses, as of *yore!*

---

* A term to be found in the Hampshire Dictionary, implying a *rapid* deglutition of bacon, without the *sober ceremony* of mastication. It is, moreover, to be observed, that Hampshire servants, who are bacon-*bolters*, have always less wages than bacon-*chewers.*

Defeated, too, thy brother Time,
  The God of wrinkles, wounds no more.

See Age display her iv'ry rows!
  Her lip preserves its purple bloom!
Her bosom heaves with Alpine snows,
  And kisses breathe the rich perfume!

The furrow'd cheek, and hoary head,
  No longer now, as usual, greet;
And, what our Grandmother's all dread,
  The nose and chin no longer meet.

Time's pow'r the good old Grannies *brave*,
  And, ogling, dart their am'rous fire;
Decline with graces to the grave,
  And with the blush of health *expire!*

UNWORTHINESS.

But *souls* in *common* are a dreary waste,
By brambles, thistles, barb'rous docks, disgrac'd;
  That need the ploughshare, harrow, and the fire—
Some souls are caves of filth and spectred gloom,
That want a window and a broom
  To yield them light, and clear the mire.

When honours lift th' unworthy fool on high,
  On Fortune how with fierce contempt I scowl!
She hangs a dirty cloud upon the sky,
  And with an eagle's pinion imps an owl.

Yet knaves and fools enjoy their *lucky hours*,
  And ribbons, 'stead of ropes, their backs adorn—
Thus crawls the Toad amid the fairest flow'rs,
  And with the Lily drinks the dews of morn.

VANITY.

Sweet Girl, the man's a downright fool,
  That asks for constancy in love—
Variety's a charming school:
  How nat'ral for the heart to rove!

A form like thine can never cloy—
  And, lo! thy graces, what a plenty!
Then tell me, why should *one* enjoy
  The beauties that suffice for *twenty?*

VANITY OF GREATNESS.

Ah me! *sic transit gloria mundi*—
Such things will *be* till moon and sun die,
And Earth our ashes, our pale embers cover:
  And really when we sum up *all*,
  What's life?—A blast—a little squawl.—
Death's calm must come at last, and all *is over*—
  All in our tombs in peace—not *one*
  To read " *Hic jacet*" on the *stone*.

VARIETY, AVIDITY FOR.

You've seen a flock of starlings, to be sure,
A hundred thousand in a mess, or more,
Who fortunately having found
A lump of horse-litter upon the ground,
  Down drops the chattering cloud upon the dung;
Then, Lord, what doings! Heav'ns, what admiration!
What joy, what transport 'midst the speckled nation!
  How busy ev'ry beak, and ev'ry tongue!
All talking, gabbling, but none list'ning,
Just like a group of gossips at a christ'ning:
Let but a *cowdab* show its grass-green face,
They're *up*, without so much as saying grace;
And lo! the busy flock around it pitches;
  Just as upon the lump before,
  They gabble, wonder, and adore!
And equal *brother* Martyn's* speeches. [priety
These starlings show the world, with great pro-
Mad as March hares or curlews for variety.

* A *much-admired* speaker in the House of Commons, who, *nem. con.* was baptized the *Starling* Martyn.

K 2

VERSATILITY.

O Versatility, I hold thee dear!
　The Proteus pow'r be mine to take each shape;
Skip like a Will-o'-wisp—be here, be there—
　Now the grave moralist, and now an ape.

Now roar the savage of the Lybian shade,
　Where horror listens to the shrieking ghost;
Now Pompey in Belinda's bosom laid,
　Or whining, pawing, for a piece of toast.

Now roll the Monarch of the stormy deep,
　The flound'ring terror of the finny race;
Now the slim eel, of ponds so lucid, creep;
　Now leap a salmon, and now glide a plaice.

Thrice happy change of soul-delighting song!
　This were my talent, blest would Peter be!
But who, alas! is thus divinely strong?
　Shakespeare, that envied pow'r I mark in thee.

VERSATILITY OF FORTUNE.

Sad loit'ring Fortune, thou art come too late:
　Ah! wherefore give me not thy smiles before,
　When all my youthful passions in a roar,
Rare hunters, fearless leap'd each five-bar gate?

Unknown by thee, how often did I meet
The loveliest forms of nature in the street,
　The fair, the black, and lasting brown!
And, while their charms enraptur'd I survey'd,
This pretty legend on their lips I read—
　" Kisses, O gentle shepherd, for a crown."

How oft I look'd, and sigh'd, and look'd again,
　Upon the smiling Loves of ev'ry Phillis!
How wish'd myself a cock, and her a hen,
　To crop at once her roses and her lilies!
Not only *gratis*, but with perfect ease—
Without so much as, " Madam, if you please."

"At Otaheité," I have said with tears,
"No gentleman a jail so horrid fears
"For taking loving liberties with lasses:
"Soon as they heard how Love in England far'd,
"The glorious Otaheitans all were scar'd,
"And call'd us Englishmen a pack of asses.

"But they, indeed, are heathens—have no souls,
"But such as must be fried on burning coals.

"But I'm a *Christian*, and abhor a rape:
"Yet, if a lass would *sell* her lean and fat,
"I'm not so great an enemy to *that*—
"Though *that* might whelp a little kind of scrape;
"Since 'tis believ'd e'en *simple fornication*
"May step between a man and his salvation."

Damn'd Fortune! thus to make the poet groan;
To offer *now*, forsooth, thy shining pieces;
For *now* my passions nearly all are flown,
Departed to my nephews and my nieces.

VILLAGE COURTSHIP.

Joanny, my dear, wut ha poor Hob?
Vor I'm upon a coortin job—
Gadswunds! Iss leek thee, Joan;
I'd fert vor thee—Iss, that Iss wud;
Iss love thee well, as pigs love mud,
Or dogs to gna a bone.

What thoff Iss ban't so hugeous smart,
Forsooth leek voaks that go to curt,
Voakes zay I'm perty vitty:
Lord, Joan, a man may be *alive*,
Ha a long puss, and kep a wive,
That ne'er zeed Lundun zitty.

A man may ha the best o'hearts,
Although no chitterlins to's sharts,
And lace that gentry uze;
Theed'st vend me honest—Iss, rert down,
Altho' thee hadsn't got a gown,
Nor stockings vath ner shooze.

Now, Joanny, pr'ythee dant now blish;
Vor zich, Iss wudd'n gee a rish;
　　Dant copy voakes o' town:
No, Joan, don't gee thy zel an air,
An ren and squat, just leek a hare,
　　And think I'll hunt thee down.

No, that's dam voalish, let me zay;
No—dant ren off, and heed away,
　　Leek paltriges in stubble:
No, no, the easiest means be best;
Iss can't turmoil, an looze one's rest;
　　Iss can't avoard the trouble.

Now, Joan, beleek, thee waantst to know,
About my houze-keppin and zo,
　　Bevore thee tak'st the nooze—
Why vlesh an dumplin ev'ry day;
But az vor *Zunday*, let me zay,
　　We'll ha a gud vat gooze.

Now break thy meend, zay " dun an dun ;"
I'll make thee a good husband, mun;
　　And, Joan, I'll love thee dearly;
Iss waant do leek our neighbour Flail,
That huffih his wive, and kickth her tail,
　　And drashth her just leek barley.

Joanny, Iss now have broke *my* meend;
Zo speak, and let the bisness eend,
　　And dant stand shilly shally;
But if thee wutt'n—Lord, lay't alone;
Go hang thy zel vor me, mun, Joan;
　　I'll curt thy zester *Mally*.

VIRTUE AND MERIT.

Some start in youth, some sin at bald fourscore;
But known—the voice of Fame is heard no more.
Virtue's pure Robe with dirt I scorn to load,
Or offer incense to embalm a *Toad*.
Let talents, virtues, meet my happy eyes;
I ask not, truly, from *what soil* they rise.

If 'mid the lorn cold vale of Want they spring,
The Muse shall hen-like spread her fost'ring wing;
Or Grandeur's sun-clad mountain, to their glory,
My verse (though scarce-believ'd) shall tell the [story:
Give me the riches, and I'll find the soul
To lead poor pining Merit from her hole.
Friend to the Arts, were George's millions mine,
What heav'nly Maid in poverty should pine?
For lab'ring Genius, palaces should rise;
Not for Court-sycophants, the carrion flies:
These would I flay—and change at once the scene;
To taste the attic Nymph, restore her reign;
With Raphaels, Titians, the glad world renew,
And lead a second Angelo to view;
Bid, for our Board of Works, Palladios spring,
And cast a ray of glory round a King.

VIRTUES, ODE TO THE.

Ah, Virtues, ye are pretty-looking creatures;
But then so meek and feeble in your natures!—
   Thou charming Chastity now, *par exemple*,
Who guard'st the luscious lip and snowy breast,
And all that maketh wishing shepherds blest,
   Forbidding thieves on sacred ground to trample.

Appear but Love, the savage, all is lost;
Faint, trembling, blushing, thou giv'st up the ghost:
   Lo, there's an end of all thy mincing care!
The field so guarded, in the Tyrant's pow'r;
Each fence torn down, despoil'd each mossy bow'r,
   All, all is rudely plunder'd, and laid bare.

Virtues, ye *blunder'd* on the world, I fear—
Design'd, I ween, for some more *gentle* sphere.

I know your parentage and education—
Born in the skies—a lofty habitation;
But for a *perfect* system were intended,
Where people never needed to be *mended*.
How could *ye* think the Passions to withstand,
Those roaring Blades, so out of all command,

Whose slightest *touch* would pull ye all to pieces?
They are Goliahs—you but *little* Misses!
Then pray go home again, each *pretty* Dear—
Ye but *disgrace* yourselves by coming *here*.

VIRTUOSO, HIS PRAYER.

O thou, whose wisdom plann'd the skies,
And form'd the wings of butterflies,
  Attend my humble pray'r!
Like Egypt, as in days of yore,
Let earth with flies be cover'd o'er,
  And darken'd all the air.

This, Lord, would be the best of news:
Then might thy servant pick and choose
  For such a glorious heap:
Forth to the world I'd boldly rush,
Put all Musæums to the blush,
  And hold them all dog cheap.

Pharaoh had not one grain of taste;
The flies on *him* were thrown to waste,
  Nay, met with strong objection:
But had thy servant, Lord, been there,
I should have made, or much I err,
  A wonderful collection!

Since monsters are my great delight,
With monsters charm thy servant's sight,
  Turn feathers into hair:
Make legs where legs were never seen,
And eyes, no bigger than a pin,
  As broad as saucers stare.

The reptiles that are born with claws,
Oh! let thy pow'r supply with paws,
  Adorn'd with human nails;
In value more to make them rise,
Transplant, from all their heads, their eyes,
  And place them in their tails.

And if thou wisely wouldst contrive
To make me butterflies alive,

To fly without a head;
To skim the hedges and the fields,
Nay, eat the meat thy bounty yields;
Such wonders were indeed!

VULGARITY.

Build not, alas! your popularity
On that beast's back yclep'd *Vulgarity*;
A beast that many a booby takes a pride in;
A beast beneath the noble Peter's riding.

How should the man with appetite unchaste,
   Stuffing on carrion dead his hound-like paunch,
Judge of an ortolan's delicious taste,
   Or feel the flavour of a dainty haunch?

Or, wont with bitter purl to wet his clay,
How should *he* judge of Claret or Tokay?

WAGGONER AND JUPITER.

A luckless waggon roll'd into a slough— [brow;
Clod scratch'd his head, and growl'd, and knit his
   But what avail'd it?—Fast the waggon lay.
Now Clod imagin'd, like an idle lout,
A pray'r or two might help the pris'ner out;
   Then unto Jupiter he howl'd away.

" How now! you lazy lubber!" cried the god—
" Clap to the wheel your shoulder, master Clod;
   " And (mind me) let your horses be well flogg'd."
Clod took th' advice, exerted all his strength:
The waggon mov'd, and mov'd; and, lo! at length,
   Forc'd from the quagmire, on again it jogg'd.

WAR, (1.)

Say, didst thou * fear that Britain was too blest,
Of Peace thou most delicious pest?
How shameful that this pin's-head of an Isle,
While half the Globe's in grief, should wear a smile!

* Thomas Paine.

How dares the Wren amidst his hedges sing,
While Eagles droop the beak, and flag the wing?

Oh, must the scythe of Desolation sleep,
So keen for carnage, stay its mighty sweep,
   And Havock on his hunter drop his lash;
Spurr'd, arm'd, and ripe to storm with groans the
To chase an empire, and enjoy the cry,   [sky,
   The cry of millions—what a glorious crash!

What pity thy combustibles were bad!
How Death had grinn'd delight, and Hell been glad,
   To see our liberties o'erturning;
And War, whose expectation tiptoe stood,
Ready for hills of slain, and seas of blood,
   Who drops his death's-head flag, and puts on
      mourning!

WAR, (2.)

Ah! Peace, thy triumph now is o'er!
Thy cheek so cheerful smiles no more;
   Thine eye with disappointment glooms!
Our Music shall be Nature's cry;
Our ears shall feast on Pity's sigh—
   Lo, haggard Death prepares his tombs!

Hot with the fascinating grape, we reel;
The full proud spirit of Rebellion feel!
   Son of Sedition, daring Paine,
While speech endues thy treason tongue,
Bid the roof ring with damned song,
   And Erebus shall echo back the strain.

WAR SATIRIZED.

War is a wholesome blister for the back,
   Draining away the humours all so *gross*;
Else would the Empire be of guts a sack—
   A Falstaff—woolsack—an unwieldly Joss.

War yieldeth such rare spirits to a nation!
Giving the blood so brisk a circulation!

A kingdom, and a poet, and a cat,
Should never, never, never be *too fat!*

WATER, HOLY.

Thus when a host of grasshoppers and rats,
By men undaunted, unabash'd by cats,
In hopping and in running legions pours,
Affrights the Papists, and their grass devours;

Lo, arm'd with pray'rs to thunder in their ears,
A Bishop boldly meets the buccaneers;
Sprinkles his holy water on the sod,
And drives and damns them in the name of God!

WEDLOCK AND CELIBACY.

The world was never wickeder than now—
   Wedlock abus'd—her bond pronounc'd a jail;
A wife call'd vilely ' ev'ry body's cow,
   ' A canister, or bone to a dog's tail!'
What dare not knaves of this degen'rate day
Of marriage, decent hallow'd marriage, say?
  " Wedlock's a heavy piece of beef, the rump!
" Returns to table hash'd, and stew'd, and fried,
" And in the stomach much to lead allied,
   " A hard, unpleasant, undigested, lump.

  " But fornication ev'ry man enjoys—
  " A smart anchovy sandwich—that ne'er cloys—
  " A *bonne bouche* men are ready to *devour*—
  " Swallowing a neat half dozen in an hour.
  " Wedlock," they cry, " is a hard pinching boot,
   " But fornication is an easy shoe—
     " The first wont suit;
      " It will not do.

  " A girl of pleasure's a light fowling-piece—
  " With this you follow up your game with ease:
   " That heavy lump, a *wife*, (confound her!)
     " Makes the bones crack,
  " And seems, upon the sportsman's breaking back,
   " A lumb'ring eighteen-pounder.

" *One* is a summer-house, so neat and trim,
" To visit afternoons for Pleasure's whim;
  " So airy, like a butterfly so light:
" The *other*, an old castle with huge walls—
" Where Melancholy mopes amid the halls,
  " Wrapp'd in the doleful dusky veil of Night."

WHITE SATIN PETTICOAT, *Verses to one spoiled by a Cup of Coffee spilt by* P. P.

O fair protectress of the fairest Maid,
  How shall the Poet for this crime atone?
So lately blest as thou, I'm sore afraid
  I have no recompence to offer!—*none!*

But Molly parts with thee with pitying eye!
  Then from this moment do not *dare complain:*
Nay, more—-the Nymph surveys thee with a *sigh!*
  Then *boast!*—the *envy* thou of ev'ry swain.

WIDOW OF EPHESUS.

Balm are the sighs for breathless Husbands shed!
And *Pearl* the eye-drops that adorn the Dead!
At Ephesus (a handsome town of Greece)
There liv'd a Lady—a most lovely Piece!

  In short, the charming *toast* of all the town:
In Wedlock's *velvet* bonds had liv'd the Dame—
Yes! brightly did the torch of Hymen flame,
  When Death, too cruel, knock'd her husband down.

This was indeed a lamentable stroke!
Prudentia's gentle heart was nearly broke!
  Tears pea-like trickle, shrieks her face deform—
Sighs, sighs succeeding, leave her snowy breast—
Winds, call'd hysterical, expand her chest,
  As tho' she really had devour'd a *storm.*

Now, fainting, calls she on her poor dead Love,
How like the wailings of the widow'd Dove!

All Ephesus upon the wonder gaz'd!
Men, women, children, really were amaz'd.
'Tis true, a few old *Maids* abus'd the pother—
" Heav'ns! if one husband dies, why take another!"
    Said they—contemptuous cocking up their nose:
" Ridiculous enough! and what about?
" To make for a *dead husband* such a rout!
    " There are as fine as *he*, one might suppose.

" A body would presume, by grief so mad,
" Another husband was not to be *had*;
" But men are not so very scarce indeed—
" More than are *good* there are, God mend the
        breed!"

Such was the conversation of old Maids,
Upon this husband's visits to the shades.
At length her Spouse was carried to the *tomb*,
And poor Prudentia mop'd amid the gloom.
One little lamp, with solitary beam,
    Shew'd the dark coffin that contain'd her Dear,
    And gave a beauteous sparkle to each tear,
That rill-like dropp'd—or rather like a *stream*.

Resolv'd was she amid this tomb to sigh;
To weep, and wail, and groan, and starve, and die—
    No comfort! no! no comfort would she take:
Her Friends beheld her anguish with great pain,
Begg'd her to try amusement, but in vain—
    " No! she would perish, perish for his sake!"

Her flaxen tresses all dishevell'd flow'd—
Her vestments loose—her tucker all abroad,
    Revealing *such* fair swelling orbs of woe!
Her lids, in swimming grief, now look'd on high,
Now downward droop'd, and now she pour'd a sigh,
    How *tuneful*, on her dear pale Spouse below.

Who would not covet death for such sweet sighs,
And be bewail'd by *such* a pair of eyes?
It happen'd that a Rogue, condemn'd to death,
Resign'd (to please the Law) his roguish breath,

And near the vault did this same felon swing:
For fear the Rogue's relations, or a friend,
Might steal him from the rope's disgraceful end,
    A smart young Soldier watch'd the thief and
        string.

This Son of Mars, upon his silent station,
Hearing, at night, a dismal lamentation,
    Stole to the place of woe—that is, the tomb—
And, peeping in, beheld a beauteous face,
That look'd with such a charming tragic grace,
    Displaying sorrow for a husband's doom.

The Youth most nat'rally express'd surprise,
And scarcely could he credit his two eyes:
    " Good God, Ma'am!—pray, Ma'am, what's the
        matter here?
" Sweet Ma'am be comforted—you *must*, you *shall*
" At times misfortunes e'en the *best* befall—
    " Pray stop your grief, Ma'am, *save* that precious
        tear."

" Go, Soldier, leave me!" sigh'd the Fair again,
In *such* a melting melancholy strain,
    Casting her eyes of woe upon the Youth—
" I *cannot*, *will* not live without my love!"
And then she threw her glist'ning eyes above,
    That swam in tears of constancy and truth.

" Madam!" rejoin'd the Youth, and press'd her
" Indeed you shall not my advice withstand; [hand,
    " For heav'n's sake don't stay here to weep and
" Pray take refreshment!" Off at once he set,[howl!
And quickly brought the Mourner drink and meat;
    A bottle of Madeira, and a fowl;
        And bread and beer,
        Her heart to cheer.

" Ah! gentle Youth, you bid me eat in vain!
" Leave me! oh, leave me, Soldier, to complain!
    " Yes, sympathising Youth, withdraw your wine!

" My *sighs* and *tears* shall be *my* only food—
" Thou knowest not my Husband kind and good,
  " For whom this heart shall ever, ever pine !"

" What ! howl for ever for a breathless clod !
" Ma'am, you *shall* eat a leg of fowl, by G—!"
With that he clapp'd wine, fowl, bread, beer, and all,
Without more ceremony, on the pall.

  " Well, Soldier, if you *do* insist," quoth she,
All in a saint-like, sweet, complying, tone,
" I'll *try* if Grief will let me pick a *bone!*
  " Your health, Sir,"—" Thank you kindly, Ma'am," quoth he.

And now, whate'er philosophers may think,
Sorrow is much oblig'd to *meat* and *drink*.

Prudentia found it so: a *gentler* sigh
  Stole from her lovely breast—a *smaller* tear,
  Containing *less* of anguish, did appear
Within the pretty corner of her eye;
  Her eye's dark cloud dispersing too apace,
  (Just like a cloud that oft conceals the Moon,)
  Let out a brighter lustre o'er her face,
Seeming to indicate *dry weather* soon.

Now Mars's Son a minute left the Dame,
  To see if all went well with Rogue and rope;
But, ere he to the fatal gibbet came,
  The Knave had deem'd it proper to *elope*.

In short, attendance on the Lady's grief
Had lost him his companion, the hang'd Thief,
  Whose Friends had kindly filch'd him from the string:
Quick to the Lady did the Soldier run:
" Madam, I shall be hang'd, as sure's a gun !
  " O Lord ! the Thief's gone off, and *I* shall swing !
" Madam, it was the royal declaration,
  " That, if the Rogue was carried off,
  " Whether by *soft* means or by *rough*—
" *No matter*—*I* should take his situation.

"Cheer up, my gallant Friend," replied the Dame,
  "Squeezing his hand and smoothing down his
    face—
"No, no, you shan't be hang'd, nor come to shame;
  "My husband here shall take the Fellow's place—
"Nought but a lump of clay can he be counted!
"Then let *him* mount!"—and lo! the Corpse was
    mounted.
Made a good thief—nay, so complete,
The people never smelt the cheat.

Now from the Gibbet to the Tomb again,
  Haste, arm-in-arm, the Soldier and the Fair;
T'exchange for kisses, and the Turtle's strain,
  Sad hymns of *Death*, and ditties of *Despair*.

WIFE, THE, OR THE HECTIC.

Lo! midst the hollow-sounding vault of Night,
Deep coughing by the taper's lonely light,
  The hopeless Hectic rolls his eye-balls, sighing;
"Sleep on," he cries, and drops the tend'rest tear;
Then kisses his wife's cherub cheek so dear: [ing:
  "Blest be thy slumbers, Love! though I am dy-
  'Ah! whilst *thou* sleepest with the sweetest breath,
"*I* pump, for life, the putrid well of death!
"*I* feel of Fate's hard hand th' oppressive pow'r;
"*I* count the iron tongue of ev'ry hour,
"That seems in Fancy's startled ear to say—
"Soon must thou wander from thy wife away."

"Dread sound! too solemn for the soul to bear,
"Murm'ring deep melancholy on my ear:
"And sullen—ling'ring, as if loth to part,
"And ease the terrors of my fainting heart.
"Yet, though *I* pant for life, sleep *thou*, my dove,
"For well thy constancy deserves my love."

And, lo! all young and beauteous, by his side,
His soft, fresh-blooming, incense-breathing, bride,
  Whose cheek the dream of rapt'rous kisses warms,

Anticipates her spouse's wish so good;
Feels Love's wild ardours tingling thro' her blood,
 And pants amidst a *second* husband's arms;
Now opes her eyes, and turning round her head,
" Wonders the filthy fellow is not dead!"

Wig *of Judge Buller and Mrs. Robinson's Handkerchief.*

A Handkerchief, that long had press'd
The snows of Laura's swelling breast,
 O'er which fair scene full many a longing lover,
With panting heart, and frequent sighs,
And pretty modest leering eyes,
 Had very often been observ'd to hover—

This Handkerchief, to Kitty giv'n,
Was forc'd at length to leave its heav'n,
 For a Jew clothes-man's most unchristian bag:
O what a sad reverse, poor soul!
To sweat in such a horrid hole,
 Cramm'd in with ev'ry sort of dirty rag!

" Pray, who are *you?*" the plaintive 'Kerchief
Perceiving a rough neighbour at her side: [cried,
 " You smell as though your master was a *pig*—
" What are ye? tell me, stinking creature."——
  " Ma'am,"
The hairy neighbour grave replied, I am
 " That *worthy* man's, the mild Judge Buller's
So sweetly tender! that, when'er he dies, [Wig."
Mercy will weep to blindness both her eyes.

" Indeed, Sir!" quoth the 'Kerchief—" Strange
  " our fate!
" Alas! how diff"rent were we both of late!
  " Now stuff'd in this abominable place!
" What will become of us at last? O dear!
" Something more terrible than this, I fear;
  " Something that carries horrible disgrace."

"Madam," rejoin'd the Wig, "don't cry;
"No cause have you indeed to sigh;
  "So trust for once a Wig's prophetic words—
"*My* fate is to be just the same, I find;
"Still for a Scarecrow's head design'd,
  "To frighten thieves—I mean the birds.

"But, luckier, *you* so chang'd will rise,
"A fav'rite of ten thousand eyes;
  "Not burnt (as you suppose perhaps) to tinder;
"Chang'd to the whitest paper—happy leaves,
"For *him*, the Bard who like a god conceives,
  "The great, th' immortal Peter Pindar."

"La, Sir, then what a piece of news!
"God bless, I say, God bless the Jews—
  "I wish my dear dear Mistress did but know it:
"Her hands then I shall happy touch again;
"For Madam always did maintain
  "That Mister Pindar was a *charming* Poet."

WILLIAM PENN, NATHAN, AND THE BAILIFF.

As well as I can recollect,
  It is a story of fam'd William Penn,
By bailiffs oft beset, without effect,
  Like numbers of our Lords and Gentlemen—

William had got a private hole to spy
  The folks who came with writs, or "How d'ye [do?"
Possessing, too, a penetrating eye,
  Friends from his foes the Quaker quickly knew.

A bailiff in disguise one day,
  Though not disguis'd to our friend Will,
Came, to Will's shoulder compliments to pay,
  Conceal'd, the catchpole thought, with wond'rous skill.

Boldly he knock'd at William's door,
  Drest like a gentleman from top to toe,
Expecting quick admittance, to be sure—
          But no!

Will's servant Nathan, with a strait-hair'd head,
  Unto the window gravely stalk'd, not *ran*—
" Master at home ?" the Bailiff, sweetly said—
  " Thou canst not speak to him," replied the man.
" What," quoth the Bailiff, "won't he see me then ?"
  " Nay," snuffled Nathan, " let it not thus strike
" Know, verily, that William Penn   [thee;
  " *Hath seen* thee, but he doth not *like* thee."

WINDSOR GARDENERS, *or the progress of Admiration.*

When first their Majesties to Windsor went,
Lo! almost ev'ry curious mouth was rent—
  With what ?—with gaping on the Royal Pair:
Indeed from East and West and North and South,
Arriv'd large cargoes both of eye and mouth,
  To feast on Majesty their gape and stare.

Amongst the thousands full of admiration,
Appear'd fair Windsor's Gard'ning Nation,
  Blazing with Loyalty's bright torches:
They humbly came their Majesties to greet,
Begging their Majesties to come and treat,
  On ev'ry sort of fruit, their grand Allforches.
The Couple smil'd assent, and ask'd grand questions,
Resolv'd to gratify their grand digestions.

Forth went his Majesty, so condescending—
Forth went our gracious Queen, the fruits com-
  Munching away at a majestic rate: [mending—
The Gardeners saw themselves bespread with glory;
Told unto all the ale-houses the story;
  Which houses did again the tale relate.
Yes, they were all so pleas'd that their *poor things*
Should find such favour in the mouths of Kings—
So happy at the sudden turn of fate,
As though they all had found a fine estate.

With awe deep stricken were the Gard'ners mute—
So sharp they ey'd them as they ate their fruit—
  Marv'ling to find that such as wear a crown

Had actions very much like *theirs* in eating;
And that they mov'd, when pines and nect'rines
      greeting,
   Their jaws, like other people, *up* and *down*;
And that, like many *folks*, they ate a *deal*—
Making (that is to say) a ploughman's meal.

And now the Gard'ners, all so glorious, wanted
To send to Majesty rare things—'twas granted.
   Both horse and foot so labour'd to embark it!
So much indeed unto their Graces came,
In consequence of this most loyal flame,
   The palace look'd like Covent-Garden Market.

And, lo! their Majesties went forth each day,
Their compliments to dainty fruits to pay:
   The Gardeners met them with best looks and
And then the royal reputation rais'd—   [bows;
The vegetable wisdom highly prais'd
   Of George the glorious, and his glorious Spouse.

Reader, prepare to drop thy jaw with wonder!
Prepare thee now to hear a sound like thunder!
The Gardeners, lo! with Majesty grew *tir'd!*
No more their gracious visitors *desir'd!*
In short, when Monarchs did themselves display,
The Gardeners, *bonâ fide*, ran away.

WISDOM FROM THE DOVE.—TO CHLOE.

Let Sorrow seek her native night,
   For why should mortals court the tear?
Joy, Joy, should wing each moment's flight,.
   And Echo nought but rapture hear.

I'll gather wisdom from the dove,
And make my life a life of love.

While Youth sits sparkling in thine eyes,
   And lips are rich with many a kiss;
Aloud the voice of Nature cries,
   "I form'd those charms alone for bliss:
" Go, Nymph, learn wisdom from my dove,
   " And by thy life a life of love."

WOMAN, (1.)

Dame Nature, from her store so kind,
To bulls the guardian horns assign'd,
  And arm'd with hoofs the bounding steed;
Teeth to the lion's jaws she gave;
Fins to the tenant of the wave;
  And cloth'd the little hare with speed.

But what should Nature grant the Fair?
Grant!—Beauty's fascinating air:
With this the Charmer takes the field,
And bids the world to Woman yield.

WOMAN, MASCULINE, (2.)

  The masculine I like not in a wife,
  Such heroines, in a matrimonial strife,
Might hammer from one's *tender* head *hard* notes:
  I own my delicacy is so great,
  I cannot in dispute, with rapture, meet
Women who look like men in petticoats.

  Oft in a learn'd dispute upon a cap,
  By way of *answer* one might have a *slap*—
P'rhaps on a simple petticoat or gown—
  Nay! possibly on Madam's being *kiss'd!*
And really I would rather be knock'd down
  By weight of argument, than weight of fist.

  I like not dames whose conversation runs
  On battles, sieges, mortars, and great guns:
The *milder* Beauties win *my* soften'd soul,
  Who look for fashions with desiring eyes:
Pleas'd when on *têtes* the conversations roll, [sighs.
  Cork rumps, and merry-thoughts, and lovers'

WORLD.

This world's a charming world, I do declare—
  The man who *understands* it, I suppose,
May, with a *modicum* of sense and care,
  Convert with ease each *thorn* into a *rose*.

But folks *become* such *idiots*, or are *born*,
They change life's fragrant rose into a thorn;
On ev'ry smile of sunshine fling a cloud,
And then on *cruel* Fortune cry aloud.

WYNTER—BALLAD ON.

Loud blowe the wynds with blustering breath,
And snows fall cold upon the heath,
   And hill and vale looke drear;
The torrents foam with headlong roar,
And trees their chilly loads deplore,
   And droppe the icy tear.

The little birdes, with wishfull eye,
For almes unto my cottage flye,
   Sith they can boaste no hoarde:
Sharpe in myne house the pilgrims peep,
But Robin will not distance keepe,
   So percheth on my boarde.

Now on the cradle doth he hye,
And kenneth down, with connying eye,
   Upon my babe below;
And finding comfort in my cote,
He tweedles forth a simple note,
   And shakes his wings of snow.

Come in, ye little minstrels sweete,
And from your feathers shake the sleete,
   And warme your freezing bloode:
No cat shall touch a single plume;
Come in, sweete choir—nay, fill my room,
   And take of grain a treat.

Then flicker gay about my beams,
And hoppe and doe what pleasant seems,
   And be a joyfull throng,
Till Spring cloath the naked grove;
Then go and build your nests and love,
   And thank me with a song.

YOUNG CUCKOO, NURSED BY A HEDGE-SPARROW, ODE TO.

Ah, whining, anxious, restless bird!
Thou art a fool, upon my word:
   Now on the bush, and now upon the ground;
Now hov'ring o'er my head, and saying
Such bitter things—now begging, praying;
   Poor wretch, surveying me so sharp all round.

Imploring me to leave the nest,
Where all thy dearest wishes rest.
How busy thou in catching grub and fly,
As soon as dewy morning paints the sky;
Now twitt'ring near the nest such strains of joy,
Proclaiming to the world a hopeful boy!

Great is thy triumph in thy fancied child!
Immense thy pride—thy ecstacy how wild!
   Yet not one trait of thee doth he display:
Indeed thou never didst *beget* the youth;
And more—to tell thee an unpleasant truth,
   His *father* will be here the First of May.

Nor *singular* art thou—for, lo!
A little gamesome Knight *we* know,
   Who fosters children—loves them to distraction;
Shews them about from morn to night,
Drinking such draughts of rich delight
   From ev'ry feature—so much satisfaction!

Sees his *own* eyes, *own* mouth, *own* lip, *own* ear,
Own nose, *own* dimple, in each pretty Dear!—
But who's the *real* parent?—Am'rous John,
Good-natur'd fellow, made them *ev'ry one*.

YOUTH IN AGE, (1.)

Ah! tell me not that I am old,
   And bid me quit the billing dove;
Though many years have o'er me roll'd,
   My heart is still alive to love.
      Then tell me not that I am old.

When Beauty's blush delights no more,
   And Beauty's smile and sparkling eye;
When these no longer I adore,
    Then Pity yield the Bard *a sigh*.
       I will not quarrel to be told,
       Son of Apollo, thou art old.

YOUTH IN AGE, (2.)

Ah! say not that the Bard grows old—
   For what to me are passing years?
I feel not Age's palsied cold—
   To-day like yesterday appears.

When Beauty beams, the world is gay!
   What mortal is not *then* alive?
Thus kindling at its magic ray,
   Fourscore leaps back to *twenty-five*.

THE END.

www.ingramcontent.com/pod-product-compliance
Lightning Source LLC
Chambersburg PA
CBHW052042290426
44111CB00011B/1585